Java
Crash Course

*Implementing core Java features, including data
types, operators, and flow control mechanisms*

Dr. Edward Lavieri Jr.

bpb

www.bpbonline.com

First Edition 2026

Copyright © BPB Publications, India

ISBN: 978-93-65896-237

To View Complete
BPB Publications Catalogue
Scan the QR Code:

Dedicated to

Java, not the language, but our late Tri-Color Pembroke Welsh Corgi. She was named Java for my fondness of the language and my wife's love of quality organic coffee. She was on my mind throughout the process of writing this book.

About the Author

Dr. Edward Lavieri Jr. is a software engineer and academic. He has developed software for nearly four decades. His projects include distributed, full-stack applications, mobile, desktop, and component apps. While a software engineer at his core, he also serves as a university dean at a university system which includes a college of computer science, a school of information technology, and a coding bootcamp, where he serves as the chief academic officer. He enjoys solving real-world business problems with technology.

Edward earned his doctorate in computer science from Colorado Technical University in 2014, holds three master's degrees and multiple postgraduate certificates, and is a senior member of the *Institute of Electrical and Electronics Engineers (IEEE)*. He has published over a dozen technical books.

About the Reviewers

❖ **Dimakatso** is a software developer with a BSc degree in computer science with over 8 years of experience in software development. He specializes in using cutting-edge technologies, such as Spring/Quarkus for high-performance backends, Angular/React for intuitive user interfaces, and React Native for mobile development. His expertise extends across the full development lifecycle, from system design to deployment, ensuring seamless integration and user satisfaction.

❖ **Serhad** is a Java developer with 17 years of experience. He works extensively with Spring and the broader Java ecosystem, building scalable and maintainable software solutions. His professional background includes deep involvement in enterprise application development and system integration. Outside of work, he enjoys reading about history and exploring programming languages; always curious about the ideas that shape both technology and human progress.

Acknowledgement

I am very grateful to everyone who has contributed to the existence of this book.

I would like to thank my wife who was critical to my ability to maintain a work-authorship-life balance.

I am also very grateful to BPB Publications for trusting me with this book. Thank you for your guidance and support in every step of writing this book.

I would also like to acknowledge the reviewers, technical experts and editors who helped shape the book into its final form. Your insights and expertise have undoubtedly enhanced the quality of this book.

Preface

Java is one of the most prevalent programming languages today, powering everything from enterprise applications to mobile platforms. Whether you are just starting your programming journey or transitioning to Java from another language, Java Crash Course is your essential guide to mastering this powerful language.

This book takes you step-by-step from the basics of Java syntax, data types, and control structures, through core **object-oriented programming** (**OOP**) concepts, to advanced topics like concurrency, streams, and **graphical user interfaces** (**GUIs**). Along the way, you will learn how to handle exceptions, work with collections, connect to databases, and gain experience with modern Java features such as lambdas and functional programming. Hands-on exercises, real-world projects, and clear examples can reinforce your understanding and provide practical skills you can apply immediately.

By the end of this book, you should not only have a deep understanding of Java, but also the confidence to build scalable, efficient applications and tackle real-world coding challenges with ease. Whether you are a student, developer, or IT professional, this crash course can equip you with the skills to succeed in your career.

Chapter 1: Introduction to Java Programming- This chapter introduces the Java programming language and its ecosystem. The chapter begins with a brief history of Java, how it has evolved, and how it has maintained relevance in the modern software development industry. The benefits of learning Java have never been greater, especially in today's world of enterprise applications, cloud computing, and mobile development. This chapter also walks you through setting up your development environment, including installing the **Java Development Kit** (**JDK**) and configuring an **integrated development environment** (**IDE**). Finally, you will have the opportunity to write and run your first Java program, giving you hands-on experience with the language from the very start.

Chapter 2: Core Java Concepts- This chapter explores the foundational concepts that every Java programmer must master. Starting with data types and variables, the chapter covers how Java handles information, followed by a look at operators and control structures that form the basis of decision-making and logic in programs. The chapter explores how to write methods, understanding parameters, return types, and scope, which are essential for building reusable code. By the end of this chapter, you should have a solid grasp of core Java syntax and functionality and be ready to tackle more complex problems.

Chapter 3: Object-oriented Programming Basics- This chapter introduces OOP, one of the key paradigms that make Java a versatile and powerful language. Coverage includes the fundamental OOP principles of encapsulation, inheritance, polymorphism, and abstraction. The chapter also covers how to define and use classes and objects, manage constructors and overloading, and explore the super keyword to enhance code reusability and maintainability. Through examples and hands-on practice, this chapter shows you how to apply these principles to design robust, scalable software applications.

Chapter 4: Advanced OOP Concepts- Building on the basics of OOP, this chapter explores advanced topics like interfaces and abstract classes, which provide flexibility and extensibility in Java design. The chapter demonstrates how to implement multiple inheritance using interfaces and explores functional interfaces and default methods, which are powerful modern Java tools. The chapter also covers lambdas and method references, which simplify functional programming in Java, making your code cleaner and more concise. By the end of this chapter, you should have a deeper understanding of how to structure large, complex applications with an object-oriented approach.

Chapter 5: Handling Errors and Exceptions- Effective error handling is crucial for creating robust Java applications, and this chapter introduces you to Java's sophisticated exception handling system. The chapter explores the difference between checked and unchecked exceptions, how to use try-catch-finally blocks, and how to throw and handle exceptions in your code. Additionally, you can learn how to create custom exceptions and implement best practices for handling errors. The aim of this chapter is to help ensure you can handle unexpected issues gracefully and build applications that fail safely and informatively.

Chapter 6: Data Structures and Collections- This chapter explores data structures, beginning with arrays and array lists, and extending into the **Java Collections Framework (JCF)**. Coverage includes how to work with lists, sets, maps, and queues, helping you to understand when to use each. The chapter also covers sorting and searching collections and the role of iterators and enhanced for loops. You can learn how to compare objects using Comparable and Comparator interfaces and leverage Java's utility classes to simplify collection management. Mastering these structures can help enable you to write efficient, scalable code for handling large datasets.

Chapter 7: Concurrency and Multithreading- Concurrency is a vital aspect of modern software, and this chapter introduces you to multithreading in Java. The chapter starts by explaining how to create and manage threads using the Thread class and the Runnable interface. From there, the chapter explores synchronization, locks, and the Executor framework, which simplify concurrent programming. The chapter also covers Java's concurrency utilities like

CountDownLatch and CyclicBarrier, giving you tools to manage complex thread interactions. Best practices for writing thread-safe code are emphasized to help you avoid common pitfalls in concurrent programming.

Chapter 8: Streams and Functional Programming- This chapter focuses on functional programming in Java, particularly the Streams API introduced in Java 8. This chapter explains how to work with streams, performing operations like filtering, mapping, and reducing data in a functional style. The chapter also explores functional interfaces such as Predicate, Consumer, and Supplier, which power much of modern Java's functional capabilities. Hands-on opportunities are provided for working with lambdas and parallel streams to handle large datasets efficiently. By mastering these techniques, you can be better prepared to write cleaner, more efficient code.

Chapter 9: Input/Output- File handling is essential for many Java applications, and this chapter introduces you to Java's I/O systems. The chapter explains how to read and write files using the java.nio package and explores streams for handling both character and byte data. The chapter also covers serialization and deserialization for storing and retrieving objects from files. Buffered and data streams are introduced for optimizing performance, giving you the skills to manage files efficiently and securely in your applications.

Chapter 10: Database Connectivity- This chapter covers connecting Java applications to databases using **Java Database Connectivity (JDBC)**. The chapter shows how to setup JDBC in your projects, establish connections to databases, and execute SQL queries. The chapter also explains how to use prepared statements and callable statements for interacting with databases securely and efficiently. Additionally, the chapter explores how to handle database transactions in Java, ensuring consistency and reliability in your applications. Best practices for database operations are emphasized to ensure optimal performance.

Chapter 11: GUI Programming- GUIs allow users to interact with applications visually, and this chapter introduces you to JavaFX, Java's modern GUI framework. The chapter explains how to setup JavaFX in your environment and work with the scene graph to create visually appealing layouts. The chapter also covers handling user events, creating controls like buttons and text fields, and binding properties to enhance your application's interactivity. By the end of this chapter, you should be able to build simple, functional GUI applications in Java.

Chapter 12: Modern Java Features- Java has evolved significantly over the years, and this chapter explores the most important recent Java features. You will have the opportunity to work with streams and lambdas, explore Project Jigsaw's modules, and dive into features from the latest Java releases like JEP 477 (implicitly declared classes and instance main methods).

This chapter also includes best practices for modern Java development, covering the latest tools and techniques for writing efficient, maintainable code.

Chapter 13: Debugging, Testing, and Deployment- Once our Java code is written, we must be able to debug, test, deploy, and support our applications. This chapter shows you how to debug Java programs using IDE tools and logging. You can learn how to write unit tests using JUnit and apply **test-driven development (TDD)** principles to ensure your code is reliable. Finally, the chapter covers packaging and deploying Java applications using build tools like Maven and Gradle, helping to prepare you to release production-ready software.

Chapter 14: Real-world Java Projects- This chapter provides you the opportunity to apply the skills you learned in earlier chapters to real-world Java projects. This starts by building a simple command-line application, then progressing to a database application using JDBC and a JavaFX-based GUI application. You will have the opportunity to tackle a multithreaded data processor and write a functional program using streams and lambdas. These projects are designed to help reinforce your understanding of key Java concepts while giving you practical experience that can be applied in real-world development scenarios.

Chapter 15: Conclusion and Next Steps- The final chapter recaps the key concepts covered in the book and provides guidance on how to continue learning Java beyond this book. The chapter includes advice on preparing for industry certifications, along with resources to further deepen your knowledge. The chapter also looks ahead to trends in Java development, helping to ensure you stay current in this fast-evolving field.

Code Bundle and Coloured Images

Please follow the link to download the
Code Bundle and the *Coloured Images* of the book:

https://rebrand.ly/5ab372

The code bundle for the book is also hosted on GitHub at
https://github.com/bpbpublications/Java-Crash-Course.
In case there's an update to the code, it will be updated on the existing GitHub repository.

We have code bundles from our rich catalogue of books and videos available at
https://github.com/bpbpublications. Check them out!

Errata

We take immense pride in our work at BPB Publications and follow best practices to ensure the accuracy of our content to provide an indulging reading experience to our subscribers. Our readers are our mirrors, and we use their inputs to reflect and improve upon human errors, if any, that may have occurred during the publishing processes involved. To let us maintain the quality and help us reach out to any readers who might be having difficulties due to any unforeseen errors, please write to us at: errata@bpbonline.com

Your support, suggestions and feedback are highly appreciated by the BPB Publications' Family.

At www.bpbonline.com, you can also read a collection of free technical articles, sign up for a range of free newsletters, and receive exclusive discounts and offers on BPB books and eBooks. You can check our social media handles below:

Instagram	*Facebook*	*Linkedin*	*YouTube*

Get in touch with us at: business@bpbonline.com for more details.

Piracy

If you come across any illegal copies of our works in any form on the internet, we would be grateful if you would provide us with the location address or website name. Please contact us at business@bpbonline.com with a link to the material.

If you are interested in becoming an author

If there is a topic that you have expertise in, and you are interested in either writing or contributing to a book, please visit www.bpbonline.com. We have worked with thousands of developers and tech professionals, just like you, to help them share their insights with the global tech community. You can make a general application, apply for a specific hot topic that we are recruiting an author for, or submit your own idea.

Reviews

Please leave a review. Once you have read and used this book, why not leave a review on the site that you purchased it from? Potential readers can then see and use your unbiased opinion to make purchase decisions. We at BPB can understand what you think about our products, and our authors can see your feedback on their book. Thank you!

For more information about BPB, please visit www.bpbonline.com.

Join our Discord space

Join our Discord workspace for latest updates, offers, tech happenings around the world, new releases, and sessions with the authors:

https://discord.bpbonline.com

Table of Contents

1. Introduction to Java Programming 1

Introduction 1

Structure 1

Objectives 2

Overview of Java 2

Key features 2

Java architecture 3

Java platforms 4

History and evolution of Java 4

Rapid adoption 4

Oracle years 5

Ready for the future 5

Importance of Java 5

Java's relevance to modern software development 6

New paradigms 6

Security 6

Setting up the development environment 7

Downloading and installing the JDK 7

Setting up environment variables 8

Verify your installation 9

Choosing and configuring an IDE 9

Downloading and installing VS Code 10

Installing the Java extension pack 10

Writing and running your first Java program 12

Writing a Java program 12

Running a Java program 12

Conclusion 13

Points to remember 13

Case studies 13

Multiple choice questions 15

    Answers 16

Questions 16

Challenges 16

Self-assessment 18

    Answers 18

2. Core Java Concepts 21

Introduction 21

Structure 21

Objectives 22

Data types and variables 22

    Variables 22

        Variable naming conventions 22

        Constants 23

    Data types 23

        Primitive data types 24

        Reference data types 24

    Declaring variables 24

    Variable scope 25

        Local variables 25

        Instance variables 25

        Class variables 26

    Typecasting and conversion 26

        Implicit casting 26

        Explicit casting 27

        Converting between integers and strings 27

    Arithmetic operators 28

    Assignment operators 29

    Bitwise operators 30

    Logical operators 30

    Relational operators 31

Ternary operator 34

Unary operators 34

Control structures...36

Conditional statements..36

If...36

If-else...37

Else-if..37

Switch..37

Looping..38

For...38

While..38

Do-while 39

Branching...39

Break..39

Continue 39

Return..40

Methods 40

More on parameters...41

Scope...42

Detailed example 42

Best practices...46

Conclusion...46

Points to remember 47

Case studies...49

Multiple choice questions 51

Answers..52

Questions...52

Challenges 53

Self-assessment 55

Answers..55

3. Object-oriented Programming Basics 57

    Introduction.. 57

    Structure... 57

    Objectives 58

    Introduction to OOP principles... 58

        Encapsulation... 58

        Inheritance.. 59

        Polymorphism 60

        Abstraction... 60

    Defining and using classes and objects... 60

        Defining a class 61

        Creating an object.. 62

        Initializing an object 62

        Manipulating attributes... 64

    Constructors and overloading.. 65

        Constructor overloading use case... 66

        Calling constructors... 69

        Benefits 70

    Inheritance and the super keyword.. 70

        Implementing inheritance 70

        Full inheritance demonstration.. 73

        Benefits 74

        Polymorphism and method overriding... 74

        Method overriding.. 74

        Dynamic method dispatch.. 75

        Full implementation... 76

        Benefits 77

    Access modifiers and encapsulation 78

        Private 78

        Protected... 80

        Full implementation 80

    Conclusion.. 82

Points to remember 82

Case studies 83

Multiple choice questions 85

    Answers 86

Questions 86

Challenges 87

Self-assessment 90

    Answers 90

4. **Advanced OOP Concepts** 93

Introduction 93

Structure 94

Objectives 94

Introduction to interfaces 94

    Syntax and implementation 95

    Multiple inheritance 97

    Polymorphism 98

    Default and static methods 99

Working with abstract classes 100

    Abstract class implementation 100

    Wrapping up abstract classes 102

    Multiple inheritance in Java via interfaces 102

    Advantages and use cases 103

    Practical application 103

Functional interfaces and default methods 105

    Default methods 105

Lambdas and method references 106

    Lambdas 107

    Method references 108

    Use cases 108

    Object lifecycle 109

    Object creation 110

Object use *110*

Object destruction *111*

Best practices *112*

Minimize object creation *112*

    Manage object references *112*

    Explicitly close resources *113*

Example *113*

Conclusion 114

Points to remember 115

Case studies 116

Multiple choice questions 118

    Answers *119*

Questions 119

Challenges 120

Self-assessment 122

    Answers *122*

5. Handling Errors and Exceptions 125

Introduction 125

Structure 126

Objectives 126

Understanding Java exception hierarchy 126

    Throwable class *126*

    Errors vs. exceptions *127*

    Throwable methods *129*

    Best practices *129*

Checked vs. unchecked exceptions 130

    Checked exceptions *130*

    Unchecked exceptions *131*

Try-catch-finally blocks 132

    Structure of try-catch-finally block *132*

        Try block *132*

Catch block...133

Finally block 133

Multiple catch blocks..134

Best practices and pitfalls..135

Throwing exceptions and exception propagation..135

Throwing exceptions 136

Exception propagation...136

Closer look at the throws keyword..137

Best practices 138

Creating custom exceptions..139

Designing custom exceptions...139

Using a custom checked exception 140

Custom unchecked exceptions 141

Best practices 142

Testing exception handling 142

Testing checked exceptions 143

Testing unchecked exceptions..144

Testing custom exceptions 145

Exception properties validation..146

Best practices 147

Conclusion..147

Points to remember 148

Case studies..149

Multiple choice questions 151

Answers...152

Questions..152

Challenges 153

Self-assessment 155

Answers...156

6. Data Structures and Collections...159

Introduction..159

Structure...159

Objectives 160

Introduction to arrays and ArrayLists.. 160

    Implementing arrays 161

    Implementing ArrayLists... 161

Java Collection Framework.. 163

    Collection operations 164

Working with iterators and enhanced for loops 164

    Iterators 164

    Enhanced for loops 165

Sorting and searching collections... 166

    Sorting collections... 166

    Searching collections 168

Comparable vs. Comparator 171

    Comparable... 171

    Comparator... 173

    Combined use 174

Using Java's utility classes 176

    Primary utility classes 176

    Dae... 177

    Calendar 177

    Random 178

    Scanner 179

Conclusion.. 179

Points to remember 179

Case studies.. 181

Multiple choice questions 182

    Answers... 183

Questions.. 183

Challenges 184

Self-assessment 186

    Answers... 186

7. Concurrency and Multithreading 189

    Introduction 189

    Structure 189

    Objectives 190

    Introduction to Java multithreading 190

    Thread class and Runnable interface 192

        Video game use case 192

            Thread class in a video game 192

            Runnable interface in a video game 193

        Enterprise banking use case 194

            Thread class in enterprise banking 194

            Runnable interface in enterprise banking 195

    Synchronization and locks 196

        Using synchronization 197

            Synchronization example 197

        Using locks 199

            Locks example 199

        Avoiding deadlocks with tryLock 201

            Example without blocking 201

            Example of time out 202

    Executor framework 204

        Executor example for a video game 205

        Executor example for a banking application 206

        ScheduledExecutorService example 206

    Concurrency utilities 207

        CountDownLatch 208

        CyclicBarrier 210

        Semaphore 212

    Best practices for writing concurrent code 213

    Conclusion 215

    Points to remember 215

    Case studies 217

Multiple choice questions 219

    Answers 220

Questions 220

Challenges 221

Self-assessment 224

    Answers 224

8. **Streams and Functional Programming** 227

Introduction 227

Structure 228

Objectives 228

Introduction to Streams API 228

    Streams API advantages 229

    Examples 229

Intermediate and terminal operations 230

    Intermediate operations 230

    Terminal operations 231

    Final thoughts on terminal operators 232

Functional interfaces 233

    Functional interface examples 234

Using lambdas with streams 235

    Lambada examples 235

    Final thoughts on lambdas 236

Parallel streams 239

    Considerations 239

    Implementation 239

    Parallel streams examples 240

Optional class and handling nulls 241

    Implementing the Optional class 241

    Optional class examples 241

    Final thoughts on the Optional class 242

Conclusion 245

Points to remember 245

Case studies.. 246

Multiple choice questions 248

    Answers.. 249

Questions... 249

Challenges 250

Self-assessment 252

    Answers.. 252

9. Input/Output.. 255

Introduction.. 255

Structure... 255

Objectives 256

Introduction to Java I/O... 256

    Overview of I/O streams 256

        Introduction to character streams 257

        Introduction to byte streams 257

    Importance of I/O in programming.. 258

        Handling user input... 258

        Managing file storage 259

        Buffered streams 259

        Object persistence... 259

        Network communication 260

Using the Scanner class for input... 260

    Overview of the Scanner class... 260

    Reading input from the console... 262

    Reading and parsing data from files... 263

    Common pitfalls and best practices... 265

        Best practices 267

File handling with java.nio 268

    Basics of working with files in Java.. 268

    Reading and writing text files using java.nio 269

Working with serialization and deserialization...272

    Storing and retrieving objects from files 272

        Serialization...273

        Deserialization...274

    Serialization and deserialization examples...................................275

        Appending serialized data without overwriting 275

        Handling class version changes 277

        Improving performance with buffered streams.........................278

Buffered streams and data streams..279

    Using buffered streams for efficiency 280

    Overview of DataInputStream and DataOutputStream 281

        DataOutputStream 282

        DataInputStream...282

Handling character and byte streams...283

    Difference between character and byte streams.............................283

        Character streams..284

        Byte streams 284

    Use cases for each type of stream..285

        Usage of character streams 285

        Usage of byte streams 286

Conclusion..286

Points to remember 287

Case studies..288

Multiple choice questions 290

    Answers..291

Questions...291

Challenges 292

Self-assessment 294

    Answers..295

10. Database Connectivity 297

Introduction 297

Structure...298

Objectives 298

Introduction to databases for Java applications.......................................298

Overview of relational databases...298

Storing and managing structured data...300

Data consistency..300

Managing relationships..301

Storing and managing data...301

Optimizing data storage...302

mportance of databases in Java applications 303

Persistent data storage 303

Efficient searches...303

Data consistency and integrity 304

Multi-user access...304

Scalability 305

Security 305

Working with databases in Java 305

Basic SQL operations 306

Retrieving data..306

Adding data 306

Updating data..306

Deleting data 307

Executing SQL queries 307

Using SQLite 308

Creating the Bougie Books database...310

Using JDBC for database connectivity 311

Transaction management 312

Database operations best practices 314

Preventing SQL injection 314

Optimizing query performance 315

Managing database connections 316

Handling query results 316

Handle errors and exceptions 317

Conclusion 318

Points to remember 318

Case studies 320

Multiple choice questions 322

Answers 323

Questions 323

Challenges 324

Self-assessment 326

Answers 327

11. **GUI Programming** 329

Introduction 329

Structure 330

Objectives 330

Basics of JavaFX 330

Architecture 331

PFT planning 332

Setting up a JavaFX environment 332

Prerequisites 332

Java Development Kit 333

JavaFX SDK 333

VS Code and extensions 333

Creating a JavaFX project 334

Next steps and PFT 336

Understanding the scene graph 336

Core components 337

Setting up the PFT stage and scene 338

Layouts, controls, and event handling 340

Layouts 340

Input controls 344

Handling events 345

Binding properties and observables 348

Implementing binding properties 349

Implementing observables 353

Completing the PFT application 353

Window size 354

UI styling 354

Transaction table 354

Adding timestamps 355

Store time stamps and enable deletion.. 355

Data persistence 357

Final review 359

Conclusion... 368

Points to remember 368

Case studies... 369

Multiple choice questions 371

Answers... 372

Questions... 372

Challenges 373

Self-assessment 375

Answers... 375

12. Modern Java Features... 379

Introduction.. 379

Structure.. 379

Objectives 380

Overview of modern Java 380

Release cycle 380

Modern Java themes 381

Project Jigsaw 382

Module system 383

Implementation benefits 384

Using modules... 384

Recent Java enhancements 386

   Pattern matching..386

      Pattern matching with instanceof...386

      Pattern matching with switch..387

      Records 388

   Sealed classes..388

   Virtual threads...389

Java 24, including JEP 477 390

   JEP 477..390

   Additional enhancements..391

Best practices..392

   Use records 392

   Use pattern matching 393

   Implement virtual threads...394

   Implement modular design...394

   Additional considerations 394

Conclusion...395

Points to remember 396

Case studies...397

Multiple choice questions 398

   Answers..399

Questions...400

Challenges 400

Self-assessment 403

   Answers..403

13. Debugging, Testing, and Deployment...405

Introduction..405

Structure..406

Objectives 406

Debugging in Java..406

   IDE debugging tools...407

Breakpoints 408

Call stack inspection 408

Console logging 409

Step execution 410

Debugging strategies 411

Unit testing with JUnit 411

JUnit setup 412

Writing testable code 413

Avoid hardcoded dependencies 413

Implement interfaces 414

Return values 415

Avoid static methods 416

Avoid global variables 416

Testable methods 417

Testing code in VS Code 418

Test-driven development 418

Applying TDD 419

Packaging and deploying Java applications 420

Compile 421

Create JAR files 421

Make a runnable JAR 422

Include external dependencies 423

Deploy 423

Local deployment 423

Server deployment 423

Introduction to build tools 424

Conclusion 424

Points to remember 425

Case studies 426

Multiple choice questions 428

Answers 429

Questions 429

Challenges 430

Self-assessment 432

    Answers 432

14. Real-world Java Projects 435

Introduction 435

Structure 435

Objectives 436

Building a simple command-line application 436

    Design 436

    Implementation 438

    Testing 439

    Extending the project 440

Developing a basic database application 440

    Design 441

    Implementation 442

        Database initialization 442

        Menu system 444

        Adding functionality 446

    Testing 446

    Extending the project 447

Building a multithreaded data processor 447

    Design 448

    Implementation 449

    Testing 452

    Extending the project 452

Writing a functional program using streams and lambdas 452

    Design 453

    Implementation 454

    Testing 455

    Extending the project 455

Conclusion 455

Points to remember 456

Case studies 457

Multiple choice questions 458

    Answers 459

Questions 459

Challenges 460

Self-assessment 462

    Answers 462

15. Conclusion and Next Steps 465

Introduction 465

Structure 465

Objectives 466

Trends in Java development 466

Continuing your Java learning 466

    Recommended resources 467

    Preparing for industry certifications 468

    Certifications matter 468

    Certification options 468

        Oracle 468

        BlueCert 469

        University certificates 469

        Preparation strategies 470

Final thoughts 470

Conclusion 471

Points to remember 471

Case studies 472

Multiple choice questions 473

    Answers 474

Questions 474

Challenges 475

Self-assessment 478

    Answers 478

Index 481-489

CHAPTER 1
Introduction to Java Programming

Introduction

In this chapter, we will be introduced to Java and its family of tools, libraries, frameworks, and other resources. We will briefly look at Java's creation and then document its evolution over the years. We will also understand why Java remains relevant today as a powerful application development suite for enterprise applications, distributed systems, cloud-based systems, mobile applications, embedded systems, and more.

This chapter will highlight why understanding Java can benefit modern software developers and engineers. We will mainly cover setting up a Java development environment and providing a guide to help you write and run your first Java application.

Structure

This chapter covers the following topics:

- Overview of Java

- History and evolution of Java

- Importance of Java

- Java's relevance to modern software development

- Setting up the development environment
- Writing and running your first Java program

Objectives

By the end of this chapter, we will cover Java's history and evolution and describe the significance of learning Java. We will also setup a development environment for programming with Java, write and execute a simple Java program, and understand Java syntax.

Overview of Java

Java is a high-level programming language introduced in 1995 and continues to be one of the most popular languages today. This popularity is due to a myriad of reasons, including its readability, object-oriented nature, available libraries and tools, scalability, and more. It is characterized as a high-level language because humans and computers can read Java code. Another reason for Java's wide use is that it is a cross-platform language. This means you can write Java code on your computer (regardless of whether it is a Mac, PC, or Linux machine), and your compiled code can be run on any device that has a **Java Virtual Machine (JVM)** installed. This represents a tremendous advantage for developers.

In the following sections, we will discuss Java's key features, architecture, and platforms in detail.

Key features

Java is the programming language of choice because of its plethora of features. Let us look at some of these features as follows:

- **Platform independence**: When we program in Java, we create text files with the .java extension. Once we complete our application, we compile our code into **bytecode**, which can be executed on any device with a JVM installed. This is perhaps the most revered feature of the Java programming language, as we do not need to be concerned about the executing computer's **operating system (OS)** or environment. Java allows us to focus on coding our application and not worry about troublesome porting operations to multiple systems.

- **Object-oriented programming (OOP)**: Java is an object-oriented language, which means that objects represent both behavior and our application's data. This programming approach helps us create modular, scalable, and maintainable applications. As covered in *Chapter 3, Object-oriented Programming Basics*, the primary OOP principles are abstraction, encapsulation, inheritance, and polymorphism. Java's implementation of OOP makes it easy for developers and is, therefore, one of Java's key features.

- **Garbage collection (GC)**: Java includes an automatic memory management system called GC that automatically deallocates memory occupied by application data that is no longer required. Having this automated for us is a tremendous time saver. We will cover GC in *Chapter 4, Advanced OOP Concepts*, when we talk about the object lifecycle. The automated and efficient manner of GC makes this a key feature worth studying.

- **Security focus**: Java is referred to as a secure language due to its secure runtime environment. The JVM does a wonderful job of verifying our bytecode (remember, that is the intermediate file between our code and the JVM) to ensure it does not include malicious code. Java has additional security-related features, including a security **application programming interface (API)** that enables us to use encryption, authentication, and more. The security focus of Java makes it an attractive choice when selecting programming languages.

- **Standard library**: Java has an extensive standard library, which gives us a robust set of utilities that we can include in our programs without having to code them. This includes mathematical functions, **graphical user interfaces (GUIs)**, file handling, networking, database connectivity, and so much more. This impressive library is a key reason why Java is so popular. We will use several utilities from the standard library throughout this book.

- **Multithread support**: In *Chapter 7, Concurrency and Multithreading*, we will have the opportunity to explore Java's native multithreading support. This allows us to program our applications to run multiple operations simultaneously (concurrently). This lets us take advantage of modern systems with multiple cores. As you will see, Java includes an Executor framework that we can use to control our thread pools, resulting in greater efficiency and smarter resource management.

A review of these six features provides insight into the robustness of the Java programming language.

Java architecture

The three core components of Java's architecture are the **Java Development Kit (JDK)**, JVM, and the **Java Runtime Environment (JRE)**. The definitions for each of these components are as follows:

- **JDK**: We use the JDK to develop Java applications; it is a requirement. The JDK includes the JRE (explained in the subsequent points) and the tool that compiles our Java code into bytecode.

- **JVM**: The JVM executes this bytecode (compiled Java code). As we mentioned earlier, the JVM is responsible for making Java a platform-independent language. It achieves this by acting as an intermediary between the host computer's OS and the Java application. The JVM's intermediary role involves abstracting away any hardware and OS specifics and translating the bytecode (platform-independent) into machine code.

- **JRE**: The JRE is the third core component of the Java programming language. It contains the JVM and libraries that allow us to execute our Java programs.

Java platforms

Java offers four platforms; each designed for unique development purposes. The first edition is the **Java Standard Edition (Java SE)**. This version offers core libraries and APIs that are foundational to all Java programs. This standard edition is extremely powerful and is used for coding examples throughout this book.

The **Java Enterprise Edition (Java EE)** platform can be considered the next step up from Java SE. Java EE includes libraries that support enterprise-level application development, including large-scale systems, multi-tiered applications, and secure and scalable network applications.

The **Java Micro Edition (Java ME)** platform is a subset of Java SE, as it is designed to run on devices that lack computing, memory, and storage resources evident in larger systems. The JVM contained in this edition has a small footprint. Typical deployments include embedded systems and **Internet of Things (IoT)** devices.

The fourth platform is **JavaFX**, which is used for creating dynamic internet applications. One benefit of using JavaFX is that the resultant applications use hardware acceleration to support graphic rendering. We will cover JavaFX in *Chapter 11, GUI Programming*.

History and evolution of Java

Java celebrated its 30th birthday on May 23, 2025. Introduced by *Sun Microsystems* in 1995, Java aimed to achieve platform independence by writing software once and running it on a wide range of different hardware platforms. Originally called **Oak**, Java was transformed from a predominantly embedded systems language into a cross-platform language ready to support the growth of internet technology.

Rapid adoption

Software developers quickly adopted the Java platform to create web-based applications, and as Java improved, it started being used for enterprise and large-scale systems. Java 2 was introduced in the late 1990s and introduced the Java SE, Java EE, and Java ME described in the previous section. This made the language applicable to all developers regardless of whether they were developing desktop computers, creating large-scale enterprise systems, creating applications for mobile devices, or coding embedded systems. Java catapulted to the most frequently used programming language for new applications.

Oracle years

Approximately 15 years after Java was introduced, it was acquired by *Oracle* in October 2010. Oracle has been a great steward of Java, as we have seen it continue to evolve and keep pace with contemporary development needs. They implemented a six-month release schema, resulting in new features being continually released. This helps keep Java relevant for developers who have choices. There are several hundred programming languages in use today. Java has been in the top five of most lists since its initial release.

Ready for the future

Today, Java continues to be one of the most popular programming environments used in multiple industries, including academia, business, communications, finance, healthcare, and more. It continues to evolve and has an extremely active developers' community. Java's ongoing evolution will keep pace with our modern development needs.

Importance of Java

Java is one of the most widely used programming languages for applications of all types, including embedded systems, mobile applications, desktop solutions, large-scale enterprise systems, distributed systems, and more. This popularity is different from why you should learn Java; what makes Java so popular is why learning to program with Java is worth your time.

Here are some reasons why Java could be a good choice for your development needs:

- You can develop with Java using a system running Windows, macOS, or Linux.
- Java is platform-independent, so you can develop once on your computer and deploy your app everywhere.
- Java is object-oriented, which makes it easy for us to implement abstraction, encapsulation, inheritance, and polymorphism. More on those concepts in *Chapter 3, Object-oriented Programming Basics.*
- Java supports modern concepts such as modularity, multithreading, streams, and more.
- Java includes automatic memory deallocation with its garbage collector. This saves us tremendous time from having to program memory deallocation into our apps.
- The number of tools, libraries, and extensions to the Java language is tremendous, as is the developer community.

In the subsequent sections, you will see that getting started with Java is easy. We can download Java SE and the JDK at no cost and use them inside a free **integrated development environment (IDE)**, so the startup cost is nonexistent.

Beyond learning Java to solve current programming requirements, Java developers are in great demand. Search any job board, and you will see multiple listings for Java developers and software engineers with Java knowledge.

Java's relevance to modern software development

Java is highly relevant to modern software development and is the language of choice for countless developers who create and maintain applications across industries. Developers are typically required to develop systems that can be deployed on multiple devices. Java's platform independence makes this easy, saving developers and product teams time and frustration.

One of the reasons Java is so relevant for modern software development is its robust ecosystem, which includes tools, libraries, and frameworks that streamline and shorten development time. This ecosystem lets us easily create systems that are scalable, modular, and maintainable.

New paradigms

As new paradigms and requirements are introduced, Java continues to answer the call. For example, the need to support functional programming was implemented in Java with the use of lambda expressions and the Stream API. As you will see in *Chapter 8, Streams and Functional Programming*, this is an essential advancement for dealing with large-scale systems, big data, and cloud computing. Java makes it easy to develop modular systems and implement a microservice architecture; both are key to modern software development.

Security

Security is paramount to virtually all software development projects when privacy and data protection are important, such as in finance, government, and healthcare applications. Java is a type-safe language, which means that it only permits operations to be performed on specified data types.

Paramount to the security of our applications at runtime is how data in memory is managed. As you will read about in *Chapter 4, Advanced OOP Concepts*, Java has automated processes to free up data in memory when it is no longer needed by the application. This process, GC, is not only a security feature but also contributes to overall system performance.

Java has APIs for cryptography, **public key infrastructure** (**PKI**), authentication, and secure communications. Furthermore, several modules of the JDK contain security APIs. As you will see in *Chapter 3, Object-oriented Programming Basics*, Java's object-oriented approach allows us to abstract and encapsulate data, intensifying the secure nature of Java applications.

Setting up the development environment

To setup your computer for Java development, the following steps are involved:

1. Download and install the JDK

2. Setup environment variables

3. Choosing and configuring an IDE

Let us get started with the first step.

Downloading and installing the JDK

Oracle maintains an OpenJDK website at **https://jdk.java.net**. This site will list the available JDK versions. You can click on the latest JDK version listed in the **Ready for use** area. As shown in *Figure 1.1*, that version, at the time of this writing, is **JDK 23**:

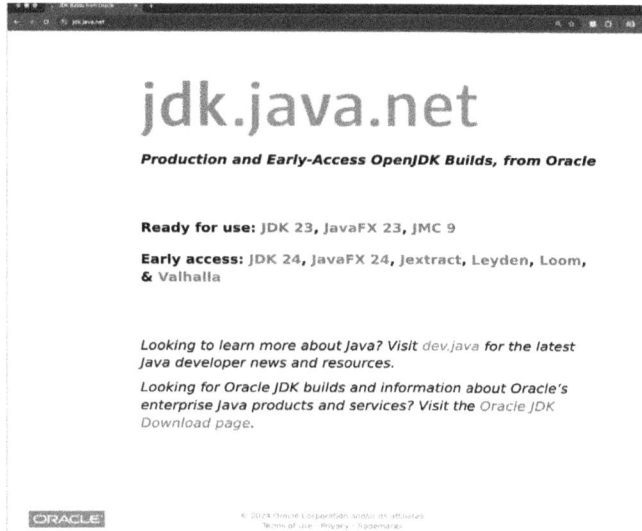

Figure 1.1: OpenJDK page showing JDK 23 as the latest version

> Note: **You can also visit Oracle's JDK download page to download the latest JDK: https://www.oracle.com/java/technologies/downloads/**

The OpenJDK page provides a concise list of available versions and a link to Oracle's official download page, shown in *Figure 1.2*. You can see the available JDKs on that page, starting with JDK 23 as the latest. That is the one we will download and install. At the bottom of *Figure 1.2*, you can see tabs for **Linux**, **macOS**, and **Windows**. Select the tab for your computer's OS. With JDK 23 and your OS tab selected, you will see download options. Select the one that is specific to your computer, as shown in the following figure:

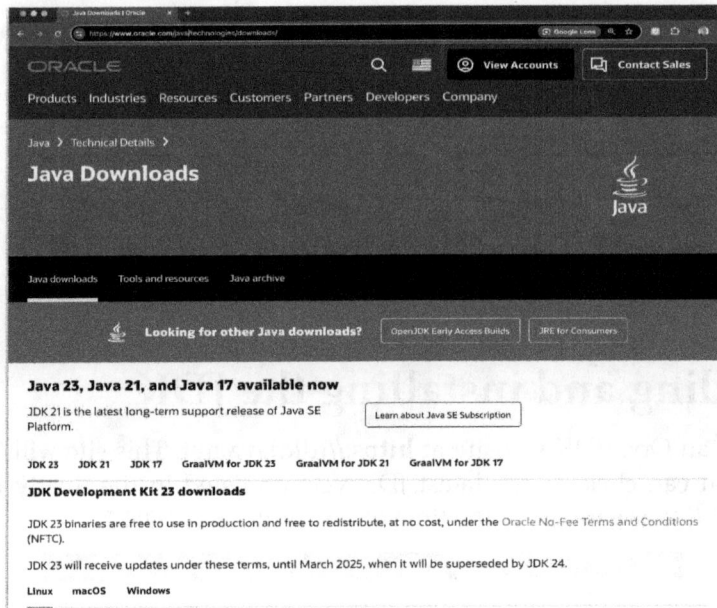

Figure 1.2: Oracle's official JDK download page

Follow the on-screen instructions to complete the JDK installation process.

Note: **You installed it on your computer, as you will need that information in the next section.**

Setting up environment variables

Environment variables are user-defined values that we can employ to ensure our system recognizes our Java installation. The following are the instructions specific to your OS:

1. **In Windows**:

    a. Open the **System Properties**.

    b. Select the **Advanced** tab.

    c. Click on **Environmental Variables**.

    d. Add a new system variable named `JAVA_HOME` and set the value to the JDK installation path.

    e. Go to the *Verify your installation* section below.

2. **In MacOS or Linux**:

    a. Open a Terminal window.

b. Enter the following in the Terminal window: **export JAVA_HOME=/actual-path/**.

Note: **replace /actual-path/ with the file path to your JDK 23 bin folder. For example: export JAVA_HOME=/Library/Java/JavaVirtualMachines/jdk-23. jdk/Contents/Home/bin.**

c. Enter the following in the Terminal window: **export PATH=$JAVA_HOME/ bin:$PATH**.

d. Go to the *Verify Your Installation* section below.

Verify your installation

You are now ready to verify your installation. Open a terminal window (macOS or Linux) or a command prompt (Windows) and enter the **java -version** to ensure your system recognizes JDK 23.

The output will be as follows:

```
java version "23" 2024-09-17
Java(TM) SE Runtime Environment (build 23+37-2369)
Java HotSpot(TM) 64-Bit Server VM (build 23+37-2369, mixed mode, sharing)
```

Next, we will verify that our system recognizes the Java compiler. Enter **javac -version**. Your output should reflect the following:

```
javac 23
```

Now that we have installed JDK 23, created our environmental variable, and verified our installation, we are ready to select, download, and configure an IDE.

Choosing and configuring an IDE

Now that we have successfully installed Java on our machine, we must choose an IDE. IDEs are software applications that we use to develop software. They provide rich source code editing, code completion, debugging tools, and more. There are several IDEs available to us. The following are the major ones:

- Eclipse
- IntelliJ IDEA
- NetBeans
- **Visual Studio Code (VS Code)**

Your IDE is up to you and will not impact your final Java application. Much like driving to a store, it does not matter if you take your car, minivan, or truck; they all get you to your destination. So, IDE selection is up to the developer. Of course, the IDE might be mandated if you are working on a team or in a company. This book uses VS Code because it is easy to use.

Downloading and installing VS Code

VS Code's download page is at **https://code.visualstudio.com/Download**. Visit that page and select the version specific to your OS. As shown in *Figure 1.3*, there are **Windows**, **Linux**, and **macOS** versions:

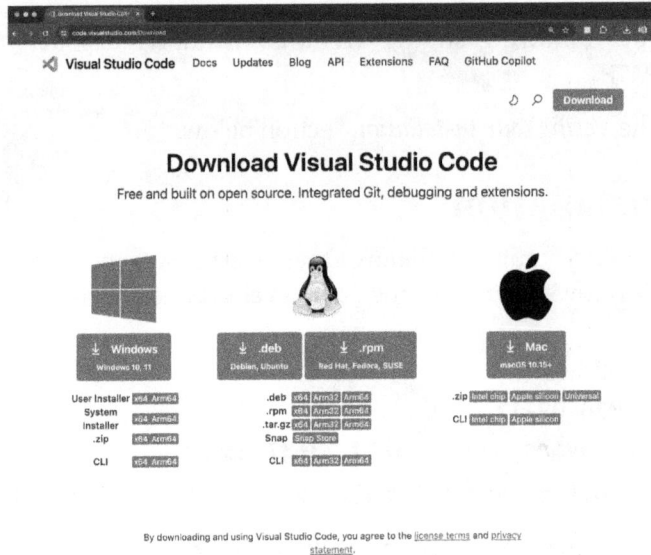

Figure 1.3: *VS Code download page*

Once your download is complete, follow the installation instructions.

Installing the Java extension pack

Our next step is to install the Java extension pack in VS Code. VS Code is not just for Java. The base installation of VS Code supports CSS, HTML, JavaScript, TypeScript, and more without needing extensions. With extensions, VS Code can support C, C++, C#, Python, Java, and more.

Open VS Code and click the *extensions* icon at the bottom of the left navigation panel in *Figure 1.4*. Using the search bar, locate the **Extension Pack for Java** by *Microsoft*, as follows:

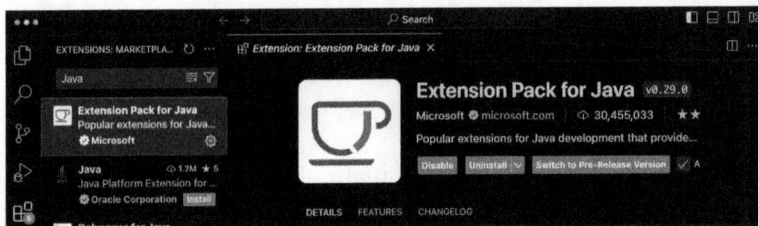

Figure 1.4: *Top section of VS Code extensions area with Extension Pack for Java selected*

Click the installation button and follow any on-screen instructions.

Configure VS Code for Java

In the VS Code interface, the *manage* icon (a cog wheel) is at the bottom of the main interface's left panel. Click that icon and select **Settings**. This opens a **Settings** tab. Here, search for `java.configuration.runtimes` (refer to *Figure 1.5*) as follows:

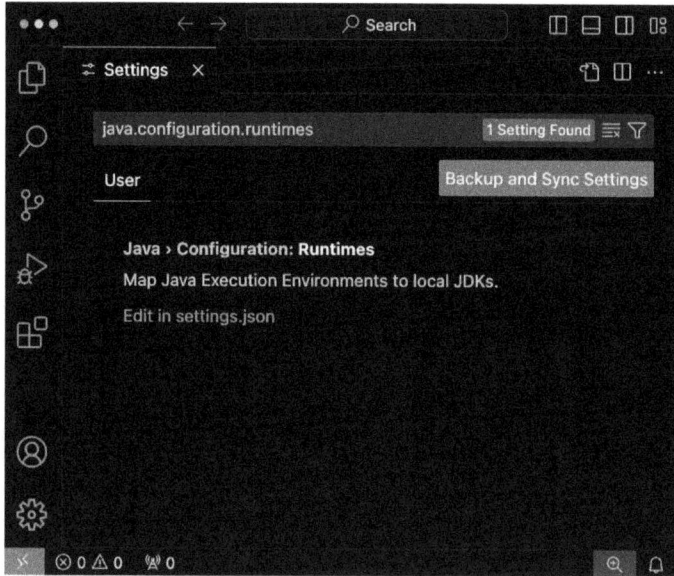

Figure 1.5: java.configuration.runtimes setting

Click the **Edit in settings.json** link. Add (or edit) the entry so your version of the JDK and its path are accurate. The following is an example:

```
{
    "window.zoomLevel": 1,
    "java.configuration.runtimes": [
        {
            "name": "JavaSE-23",
            "path": "/Library/Java/JavaVirtualMachines/jdk-23.jdk"
        }
    ]
}
```

In the next section, we will test our VS Code installation and configuration with our first Java program.

Writing and running your first Java program

Now that our development environment is properly configured, we are primed to start writing and running Java programs. In this section, we will start with a simple program that prints a message to the screen. Welcome programs are the typical starting point for learning new programming languages. As you will soon learn, the process of writing and running Java programs using VS Code is relatively simple.

Writing a Java program

Follow these steps to write your first Java program:

1. Create a folder on your computer where you want your code saved.

2. Open VS Code.

3. In the VS Code menu system, select **File** and then **Open Folder**. Use the file explorer window to select the folder you created in *step 1*.

4. In the VS Code **Explorer** window, click the **New File** window and enter **Welcome.java**. Note: **Java uses the .java file extension for Java source files. These are plain text files.**

5. Enter the code provided in the **Welcome.java** file, as follows:

```
public class Welcome {
    public static void main(String[] args) {
        System.out.println("Welcome to Java Programming!");
    }
}
```

6. Save your work.

In the next section, we will run this application.

Running a Java program

To run the application, we merely need to select the run Java icon, which is in the top-right of the VS Code interface. It is a right-facing triangle like a *play* button. Click that button and look in the console output window. You should see the following:

Welcome to Java Programming!

That is all there is to it for simple programs.

Conclusion

In this chapter, we explored the fundamentals of Java and the Java ecosystem. This included Java's history, its key features, how it has evolved over the years, and why Java remains relevant for modern software development. We also walked through the steps necessary to setup our development environment, which included installing JDK 23 and VS Code. Additionally, we tested our development environment by writing and running our first Java program.

In the next chapter, we will examine core Java concepts, including syntax, data types, variables, operators, control structures, and methods.

Points to remember

- GC automates memory management by deallocating memory that is no longer in use.

- Java architecture includes JVM, JRE, and JDK, each serving a unique role in developing and executing Java programs.

- Java's object-oriented approach helps create modular, reusable, and scalable code.

- Java provides extensive platform independence through bytecode executed by the JVM.

- Java's rich standard library includes utilities for data structures, networking, file handling, and more.

- Java supports multithreading, allowing applications to execute multiple operations concurrently.

- Platform independence allows Java programs to run on any device with a JVM, regardless of the underlying OS.

- Security features of Java, including the secure runtime environment and encryption APIs, help us build secure applications.

Case studies

The following case studies are designed to help you understand the relevance of Java's core features to real-world challenges. As you review these case studies, consider the benefits and potential disadvantages to help solidify your understanding of Java:

- **Cross-platform application development**: *Zorgon Enterprises*, a fictitious company specializing in industrial automation, is tasked with developing a monitoring application that needs to run on Windows, Linux, and macOS. Their development team decides to use Java because of its platform independence. They understand that Java compiles source code to bytecode, which can then be executed by any device equipped with a JVM. The Zorgon Enterprise team uses Java SE for the core functionality and JavaFX to create a GUI that adapts seamlessly to the different OSs.

- o **For your consideration**: How does Java's **Write Once, Run Anywhere (WORA)** capability simplify the development process for Zorgon Enterprises? What challenges might arise with platform-specific features?

- **Utilizing Java's multithreading for performance**: *Vulcanix Technologies* operates an e-commerce platform that has been experiencing heavy traffic, especially during holiday sales. They wanted their system to handle multiple user requests simultaneously without affecting response time. The development team selected Java because of its robust multithreading support.

  - o **For your consideration**: How does Java's multithreading support benefit Vulcanix Technologies in handling concurrent tasks? What potential issues should they be aware of regarding resource management?

- **Leveraging Java EE for scalability**: *Andorian Data Services*, a fictitious company providing data analytics solutions, needs to build a scalable backend for its clients. The company decides to use Java EE to implement web services and manage distributed data processing. Using Java EE allows them to take advantage of enterprise-level features like transaction management, security, and more.

  - o **For your consideration**: How do the Java EE features help Andorian Data Services build a scalable and secure enterprise solution? What are the specific advantages of Java EE over other approaches for large-scale projects?

- **Securing for financial software development**: *T'Khasi,* a fictitious **financial technology (fintech)** startup, is building a new mobile banking application. In view of the sensitive nature of user data, security is a critical concern. The company opts to develop its application using Java due to its strong security model. This includes JVM security checks and APIs for encryption and secure communication. The application leverages Java's cryptography package to ensure transactions are secure with data encryption. They are also excited about the JVM's secure execution environment to reduce the risks of unauthorized code execution.

  - o **For your consideration**: How do Java's built-in security features benefit T'Khasi systems in ensuring user data protection? What additional practices can they implement to enhance security further?

- **Java ME for IoT devices**: *Betazoid Embedded Solutions*, a fictitious firm in the IoT industry, wants to develop software for a line of smart home devices, including thermostats, ceiling fans, and light switches. Due to the limited hardware resources of these devices, Betazoid chooses Java ME because it is specifically designed for resource-constrained environments. Java ME allows them to build efficient applications that can run with low memory and processing power, while still using familiar Java syntax and features.

- o **For your consideration**: What challenges do the developers at Betazoid Embedded Solutions face when working with Java ME compared to Java SE? How does Java ME help address the specific needs of embedded systems?

Multiple choice questions

1. **What is the primary goal of Java's WORA philosophy?**
   a. To make Java code run faster than other programming languages.
   b. To make Java code reusable across different platforms without modification.
   c. To ensure Java programs are only executed on Unix systems.
   d. To reduce the cost of software development.

2. **Which Java component is responsible for executing Java bytecode?**
   a. JDK
   b. JRE
   c. JVM
   d. Java compiler

3. **Which feature of Java helps manage memory automatically?**
   a. Multithreading
   b. GC
   c. **Just-In-Time (JIT)** Compiler
   d. Bytecode

4. **Which Java edition is best suited for enterprise-level applications?**
   a. Java SE
   b. Java EE
   c. Java ME
   d. JavaFX

5. **Which Java edition is best suited for IoT applications?**
   a. Java SE
   b. Java EE
   c. Java ME
   d. JavaFX

Answers

1.	b.
2.	c.
3.	b.
4.	b.
5.	c.

Questions

1. Java is known for its platform independence. What are the advantages and challenges of writing platform-independent code compared to platform-specific code?

2. Explain how the JVM plays a role in Java's WORA philosophy.

3. Java is an OOP language. What are the main advantages of OOP?

4. How does Java's GC system contribute to memory management, and how does it impact performance?

5. Java provides strong support for multithreading. Discuss a scenario where multithreading would be beneficial.

6. Java offers various editions, such as Java SE, Java EE, and Java ME. How do these different editions cater to the needs of different types of development?

7. How does the Java Standard Library help developers in building applications more efficiently?

8. What security features does Java provide at both the language and runtime levels?

9. In the context of modern software development, why is Java still a popular choice despite the rise of newer programming languages?

10. Setting up the development environment is a crucial first step in writing Java code. What are the key components that need to be installed and configured?

Challenges

- **Plan a simple multithreaded application**:
    - **Objective**: Gain hands-on experience with Java's multithreading features.
    - **Activity**: Plan a simple Java program that uses multiple threads to perform different tasks concurrently. For instance, you might design a program that

simulates downloading files by having each thread print a message representing the progress of each download.

- o **Real-world applicability**: Understanding multithreading is crucial for building responsive applications that simultaneously handle multiple operations, such as downloading files while processing user input.

- **Implementing object-oriented principles (advanced)**:

  - o **Objective**: Practice applying OOP concepts in Java.

  - o **Activity**: Design a small system that models a simple inventory management application. Based on your current understanding, use the object-oriented principle of inheritance to create classes representing different items, categories, and operations, such as adding and removing items from the inventory.

  - o **Real-world applicability**: OOP is widely used in software design. This paradigm allows us to create modular and maintainable applications, which is crucial in enterprise software development.

- **Understanding the Java architecture**:

  - o **Objective**: Deepen your understanding of JVM, JRE, and JDK.

  - o **Activity**: Write a report explaining the relationships between the JVM, JRE, and JDK. Provide examples of when you would need each and describe how they work together to allow Java applications to be developed and run. Include a diagram that visually represents these relationships.

  - o **Real-world applicability**: Understanding the components of Java's architecture is fundamental to troubleshooting issues in Java applications and configuring development environments effectively.

- **Design a platform-independent application**:

  - o **Objective**: Contemplate the benefits of Java's platform independence.

  - o **Activity**: Design a Java application that reads input from the user and performs simple calculations (e.g., calculating the square footage of different rooms). Consider how your application will work on different OSs (e.g., Windows and Linux). Reflect on any anticipated challenges.

  - o **Real-world applicability**: Developing platform-independent applications allows software to be deployed in diverse environments without custom programming or modification. This is crucial for enterprises supporting multiple OSs.

- **Update your welcome application**:

  - o **Objective**: Understand Java's basic syntax.

- o **Activity**: Modify the Welcome.java application you wrote earlier to print multiple lines of text.
- o **Real-world applicability**: Understanding Java's syntax is core to being able to write Java applications.

Self-assessment

The following questions are provided to self-assess your knowledge of the chapter's content and apply critical thinking to key concepts:

1. What is the role of the JVM in executing Java programs? Why is it an essential part of Java's platform independence?

2. Describe how Java's GC system supports memory management. What are the benefits, and are there any potential issues that developers should be aware of?

3. Explain how multithreading in Java can enhance an application's performance. Provide an example of a scenario where multithreading would be particularly beneficial.

4. Provide an example of how the concept of platform independence can be applied in a real-world scenario.

5. What are some of the key differences between Java SE, Java EE, and Java ME? When would you choose one over the others?

Answers

1. The JVM executes Java bytecode, which is compiled from Java source code. This allows Java programs to be platform-independent by translating the bytecode into machine-specific instructions at runtime.

2. Java's GC system automatically deallocates memory that is no longer used by an application. This helps prevent memory leaks and reduces the burden on developers as they do not have to write code that manages memory. The benefit is a reduction in memory-related errors, making applications more stable. However, relying solely on GC can sometimes lead to performance issues.

3. Multithreading allows Java programs to perform multiple tasks simultaneously. This can significantly enhance performance by making better use of CPU resources. For example, in a server handling multiple client requests, each request can be handled in a separate thread, allowing the server to respond to multiple clients at the same time without delays. This simultaneous execution improves efficiency and overall application responsiveness.

4. Platform independence allows businesses with diverse IT environments to run the same Java application across all their platforms without requiring modifications. This

reduces development and maintenance costs, as there is no need to write and support separate application versions for each platform.

5.   Java SE is the core Java platform for developing general-purpose applications. Java EE builds on Java SE and includes additional APIs for large-scale, distributed, and web-based applications, making it suitable for enterprise environments. Java ME is designed for resource-constrained devices like mobile phones and embedded systems. At a high-level, you would choose Java SE for standalone desktop applications, Java EE for enterprise-level business applications, and Java ME for mobile and IoT devices.

Join our Discord space

Join our Discord workspace for latest updates, offers, tech happenings around the world, new releases, and sessions with the authors:

https://discord.bpbonline.com

CHAPTER 2
Core Java Concepts

Introduction

In this chapter, we will explore the foundational concepts that every Java programmer must master. We will start with a look at data types and variables that we need to store and manipulate data in our programs. Next, we will cover operators so we can implement logic and perform calculations in our programs. Control structures are used to implement repetitive logic and logic decisions, so we will explore them to ensure you are well-versed in their implementation. The chapter concludes with a section on methods, which are a critical element for organizing our code, implementing modularity, and creating readable, reusable, and maintainable code. This chapter serves as a prerequisite to the next two chapters that cover **object-oriented programming (OOP)** in depth.

Structure

This chapter covers the following topics:

- Data types and variables
- Operators
- Control structures
- Methods

Objectives

By the end of this chapter, we will understand the differences and uses of data types in Java. We will also define and use variables in a Java program and perform calculations and logical operations using Java operators. Moreover, we will use control structures to implement repetitive logic, as well as control structures for flow control. Additionally, we will write reusable methods with appropriate parameters, return types, and scope.

Data types and variables

Every Java program uses some data from simple on-screen text labels to large databases. Regardless of the size of your program, you need to fully understand data types (the different types of data) and variables. This section is designed to help you understand and be comfortable implementing data types in your variables. We will start with a look at variables and then explore data types. This section also covers the scope of variables.

Variables

Variables are named memory locations that we use to store data. Instead of needing to know where in memory something is stored, we use variables as **references**. For example, we can create a variable named **quantity** to store the number of items in an e-commerce system. The value of the variable can change. To create this variable, we simply need to identify its data type and name:

```
int quantity;
```

In the preceding line of code, **int** refers to **integer**, a whole number, and **quantity** is the variable name. Before we dive into data types, let us explore how to name our variables using a combination of Java's rules, industry norms, and best practices.

Variable naming conventions

How we name our variables matters. Here are a couple of rules that Java enforces regarding variable names:

- It cannot start with a number; it must start with a letter, a $, or the _ character.
- It cannot contain spaces.
- It cannot be a Java keyword (i.e., **int**, **else**, etc.).

Note: Letter case matters! For example, `Beehive`, `BeeHive`, and `beehive` are three distinctly different variable names.

The previous contains the rules that Java will not let you violate. The following list contains guidelines based on industry norms and best practices. These norms and best practices are in place to help make your code readable and maintainable.

- Variable names should be self-descriptive, such as **gradePointAverage** or **cartPreTaxTotal**.

- Do not use $ in your variable names.

- Do not start your variable name with an underscore character.

- Avoid using a single-letter variable name except for temporary throwaway names, as are typically used in loops and other areas.

- You might create your own variable naming schema. Whatever you do, be consistent throughout your entire application.

- Use camelCase, where the first word starts with a lowercase letter, and the second and subsequent words start with an uppercase letter. For example, **itemQuantity** and **myAccountBalance** correctly implement camelCase.

Note: **camelCase is used for variables, and PascalCase is used for class names. This makes it easy to identify classes and variables.**

Constants

Constants are a special kind of variable, the value of which cannot be changed after it is assigned. We use the final keyword to designate a variable as a constant as follows:

```
final double TN_SALES_TAX = 0.975;
```

By convention, constants should be self-descriptive, all uppercase, and have an underscore between each word. This is not enforced by Java, but following naming conventions will help make your code more readable and maintainable. This also makes troubleshooting much easier.

Data types

There are a lot of data types, and we will cover the most commonly used types in this section. Data types are grouped into two categories: primitive data types and reference data types. Primitive data types are the most common and are built into the Java language. As you will see, these types include characters and several number formats. Reference data types are more complex, and they will be explained in this section. Additional data types will be covered in *Chapter 6, Data Structures and Collections*.

Primitive data types

Data types named primitive are those that hold simple values and are not objects. These are the easiest to implement and work with. *Table 2.1* lists the primitive data types along with examples:

Data type	Description	Example
Byte	8-bit integer	100
short	16-bit integer	1000
Int	32-bit integer	5000
Long	64-bit integer	100000L
float	Single-precision decimal	31.9
double	Double-precision decimal	24.99
char	Single character	'E'
boolean	true or false	true

Table 2.1: Primitive data types

The most common primitive data types are **int** for whole numbers, **float** for numbers with a decimal, **char** for a single letter or character, and **boolean**.

Reference data types

Reference data types are those that refer to objects. These objects can include strings, classes, interfaces, and arrays. Objects can contain more than one value. For example, an array of numbers might include a sequence of numbers, and a string might contain a password, name, phrase, or even an entire book.

Declaring variables

For our applications to work with our variables, we must declare them first. This consists of identifying the data type and providing a name for the variable. In the following example, we identified **room** as an **int** variable:

```
int room;
```

We can also assign a value as part of the variable declaration process. The following line of code combines the declaration and assignment:

```
int room = 319;
```

Here are two more examples of variable declaration and value assignment:

```
String name = "Neo Anderson"'
int roomNumber = 319;
```

We can assign new values to variables during program execution. For example, we create an **int** variable and assign the initial value of **8**, then change it to **24**, as shown in the following code:

```
int jerseyNumber = 8;
jerseyNumber =24;
```

As you can see, after the variable is declared, we no longer need to supply the data type; Java remembers.

Variable scope

Variable scope refers to where within the program a variable is accessible from. For data security, code readability, and performance efficiency, we need to declare our variables with the proper type of scope purposefully. In Java, variables can be local, instance, or static. Let us look at each of those.

Local variables

The use of local variables is restricted to the method or code block where they are defined.

Let us look at two examples. For example, the following **dogBreed** variable is a **String** and is only accessible within the **main()** method, where it is defined as:

```
public class Local {
    public static void main(String[] args) {
        String dogBreed = "Corgi";
        System.out.println(dogBreed);
    }
}
```

Instance variables

Instance variables are those that are declared within a class but outside a method. This makes them accessible throughout the class. This is where we typically would define the properties of an object. As shown in the following code, we declare the **dogBreed** instance variable within the **Instance** class and outside any method:

```
public class Instance {
    String dogBreed = "Corgi";
    public void corgiType() {
        System.out.println(dogBreed);
```

```
    }
    public void main(String[] args) {
        corgiType();
    }
}
```

This example allows us to use the **dogBreed** variable anywhere in the class.

Class variables

A third type of variable is a **class variable**, also referred to as a **static variable**. These variables are defined with Java's **static** keyword. This ensures that the variable is shared among all instances (copies) of a class. Here is an example:

```
public class ClassVariable {
    static String dogBreed = "Corgi";
    public static void corgiType() {
        System.out.println(dogBreed);
    }
    public static void main(String[] args) {
        corgiType();
    }
}
```

We will explore class instances in *Chapter 3, Object-oriented Programming Basics*.

Typecasting and conversion

While each variable can only be of one data type, Java allows us to convert from one data type to another. This is referred to as **typecasting**. We can cast from narrow to wide (**implicit casting**) or from wide to narrow (**explicit casting**).

Let us look at examples of both.

Implicit casting

The implicit nature of implicit casting is that it occurs automatically when we convert a smaller data type to a larger one. This type of casting is considered safe because the larger data type can always accommodate the value of the smaller data type. This means there is no risk of losing data.

In the following example, we cast an **int** variable to a **double** variable and then cast that **double** variable to a **float**:

```
int num = 33;
double convertedPrice = num;
float convertedDoublePrice = num;
```

Let us next look at explicit casting.

Explicit casting

Unlike implicit casting, explicit casting requires us to explicitly cast from a larger data type to a smaller type. Java forces us to be explicit about this type of conversion due to the potential data loss with the narrowing operation.

In the following example, we convert a **double** variable to an **int**. Since integers are whole numbers, any decimal value is lost.

```
double price = 31.99;

int newPrice = (int) price;
```

As you can see above, we had to add (**int**) in our statement, which differs from what you saw with implicit casting.

> Note: **When explicit casting involves a decimal value in the source variable that is cast to an integer, the decimal value is truncated. It is not rounded.**

Let us next look at explicit casting.

Converting between integers and strings

Converting between integers and strings represents an interesting set of opportunities. Java gives us several ways to convert from an integer to a string and from a string to an integer. Let us look at some examples.

This first example uses the **String.valueOf()** method to convert an **int** to a **String**:

```
int jerseyNumber = 24;
String strJerseyNbr = String.valueof(jerseyNumber);
System.output.println("The jersey number is: " + strJerseyNbr);
```

The following example uses the **Integer.toString()** method to convert from an **int** to a **String**:

```
int jerseyNumber = 24;
String strJerseyNbr = Integer.toString(jerseyNumber);
System.output.println("The jersey number is: " + strJerseyNbr);
```

The next example is another way to convert an **int** to a **String**. We simply concatenate with an empty **String**. As you can see, we do this using a pair of double quotation marks with no space between them as follows:

```
int jerseyNumber = 24;
String strJerseyNbr = jerseyNumber + "";
System.output.println("The jersey number is: " + strJerseyNbr);
```

Note: **It is common to convert an int to a String, such as when we need to display numbers as part of a graphical user interface or concatenate an output message.**

Next, we will see how to convert a **String** to an **int**. In the following example, use the **Integer.parseInt()** method:

```
String strPhoneNumber = "3125550690";
int phoneNumber = Integer.parseInt(strPhoneNumber);
```

In our final example, we use the **Integer.valueOf()** method to convert a **String** to an **int**:

```
String strPhoneNumber = "3125550690";
int phoneNumber = Integer.valueOf(strPhoneNumber);
```

Note: **Converting strings to integers is a common practice when converting user input. We might take user input as a String, perform validations on it, and then store it as an int.**

Operators

Java includes special symbols that we can use to perform operations on variables, changing their values. These symbols are called operators and are common across nearly all modern programming languages. This section covers the seven types of operators. For each operator, we will cover what they are, why we would use them, and review a code example.

Arithmetic operators

Arithmetic operators are used for mathematical operations and are limited to addition, subtraction, multiplication, and division. More advanced mathematical operators require the use of Java's **Math** class.

Table 2.2 lists the arithmetic operators. They are likely familiar to you, as they replicate basic math symbols used in and outside of programming:

Operator	Description
+	Addition
-	Subtraction
*	Multiplication
/	Division
%	Modulus (the remainder of division)

Table 2.2: Arithmetic operators

Let us use each of these operators in the code:

```
int nbrA = 3;
int nbrB = 19;
int sum = nbrA + nbrB; // result is 22
int difference = nbrB - nbrA; // result is 16
int product = nbrA * nbrB; // result is 57
int quotient = nbrB / nbrA; // result is 6
int remainder = nbrB / nbrA; // result is 1
```

Note: **When dividing two integers, the result will always be an integer. If you want more precision in your results, one of the values used in the equation should be a double or a float.**

Assignment operators

Assignment operators are used to assign a value to a variable. The most common assignment operator is =, which we can translate to mean set the value to. For example, `int age = 24` could be read as set the value of integer **age** to **24**. Any subsequent use of an assignment operator with that variable would result in the new value overwriting the previous value.

Java also includes compound operators; those are the ones with two symbols, as shown in *Table 2.3*:

Operator	Description
=	Simple assign value
+=	Add and assign value
-=	Subtract and assign value
*=	Multiply and assign value
/=	Divide and assign value
%=	Modulus and assign a value

Table 2.3: Assignment operators

The following example shows how compound operators work. They are essentially shortcuts, which result in more concise and readable code:

```
int nbr = 24;
int nbr += 8;
```

The example first uses the assignment operator to assign the value of **24** to the variable **nbr**. Then, we use the += compound operator, which, in this case, is equivalent to **nbr = nbr + 8**.

Bitwise operators

Bitwise operators are less common but important to understand. They are used to perform operations on individual bits of integer data. This gives us finite control over our data. One of the most common uses of bitwise operators is when we need our software to interact with system hardware.

The listing and description of bitwise operators are provided in *Table 2.4*:

Operator	Description
&	Bitwise AND
|	Bitwise OR
^	Bitwise XOR
~	Bitwise complement (NOT)
<<	Left shift
>>	Right shift
>>>	Unsigned right shift

Table 2.4 Bitwise operators

For example, if we compare **5** and **3** using **5 & 3**, the result is 1. This is because **0101 & 0011 = 0001**.

Note: **The use of bitwise operators can be confusing. We will not use them again in this book as they are less common than other operators.**

Logical operators

Logical operators allow us to combine Boolean expressions, empowering us to perform complex logical tests. As you can see in *Table 2.5*, there are logical operators for **AND, OR**, and **NOT**:

Operator	Description
&&	Logical AND
|	Logical OR
!	Logical NOT

Table 2.5: Logical operators

The following example program shows the power of logical operators:

```java
public class LogicalOperatorExample {
    public static void main(String[] args) {
        boolean isRainy = true;
        boolean isWeekend = false;
        boolean isHoliday = true;
        // Logical AND (&&) - Both conditions must be true
        if (isRainy && isWeekend) {
            System.out.println("It is a rainny weekend!");
        } else {
            System.out.println("It is not both rainy and a weekend.");
        }
        // Logical OR (||) - At least one condition must be true
        if (isWeekend || isHoliday) {
            System.out.println("Relaxation time, it is either a weekend or
holiday.");
        } else {
            System.out.println("It is neither a weekend nor a holiday.");
        }
        // Logical NOT (!) - Negates the condition
        if (!isRainy) {
            System.out.println("It is not rainy today.");
        } else {
            System.out.println("It is rainy today.");
        }
    }
}
```

In the preceding code, we see that the logical AND (**&&**) checks if both **isRainy** and **isWeekend** are true. The logical OR (**||**) checked to see if at least one of the following is true: **isWeekend** or **isHoliday**. Finally, the logical NOT (**!**) negates the value of **isRainy** to check if it is not rainy.

Relational operators

Relational operators are used to compare two values. The result is either **true** or **false**. *Table 2.6* shows the six relational operators:

Operator	Description
==	Equal
!=	Not equal
>	Greater than
<	Less than
>=	Greater than or equal
<=	Less than or equal

Table 2.6: Relational operators

The following code illustrates how each relational operator can be implemented:

```java
public class RelationalOperatorExample {
    public static void main(String[] args) {
        int nbrA = 24;
        int nbrB = 319;
        // Equal to (==)
        if (nbrA == nbrB) {
            System.out.println("A is equal to B.");
        } else {
            System.out.println("A is not equal to B.");
        }

        // Not equal to (!=)
        if (nbrA != nbrB) {
            System.out.println("A is not equal to B.");
        } else {
            System.out.println("A is equal to B.");
        }
        // Greater than (>)
        if (nbrA > nbrB) {
            System.out.println("A is greater than B.");
        } else {
            System.out.println("A is not greater than B.");
        }
        // Less than (<)
        if (nbrA < nbrB) {
            System.out.println("A is less than B.");
        } else {
```

```java
        System.out.println("A is not less than B.");
    }
    // Greater than or equal to (>=)
    if (nbrA >= nbrB) {
        System.out.println("A is greater than or equal to B.");
    } else {
        System.out.println("A is not greater than or equal to B.");
    }

    // Less than or equal to (<=)
    if (nbrA <= nbrB) {
        System.out.println("A is less than or equal to B.");
    } else {
        System.out.println("A is not less than or equal to B.");
    }
    }
}
```

You can review the preceding code and refer the following output to help solidify your understanding:

A is not equal to B.

A is not equal to B.

A is not greater than B.

A is less than B.

A is not greater than or equal to B.

A is less than or equal to B.

We can also use more than one relational operator together to form more complex condition checking. Consider the code as follows:

```java
public class MultipleRelationals {
    public static void main(String[] args) {
        int nbrA = 15;
        int nbrB = 10;
        int nbrC = 20;

        // Using multiple relational operators in a single line
        if (nbrA > nbrB && nbrA < nbrC) {
            System.out.println("A is greater than B AND less than C.");
        } else {
            System.out.println("A does not satisfy both conditions.");
```

```
        }
    }
}
```

The preceding example uses two relational operators and the logical AND (**&&**) operator to check if **nbrA** is greater than **nbrB** and if **nbrA** is less than **nbrC**.

Ternary operator

Java also has a ternary operator that we can use to concisely evaluate a condition and return one or two values based on the **true**/**false** result of the condition checked. Here is the syntax:

```
result = condition ? value_if_true : value_if_false;
```

The condition is the expression we are evaluating. The only requirement is that it results in **true** or **false**. The following is an example in code that uses the ternary operator to find the larger of two numbers:

```
public class Ternary {
    public static void main(String[] args) {
        int nbrA = 8;
        int nbrB = 24;

        // Ternary operator to find the larger of two numbers
        int largest = (nbrA > nbrB) ? nbrA : nbrB;

        System.out.println("The largest value is: " + largest);
    }
}
```

The following is another example. Here, we use the ternary operator to determine if a number is **odd** or **even**.

```
        String result = (nbrA % 2 == 0) ? "Even" : "Odd";
        System.out.println("nbrA is: " + result);
```

Note: **The ternary operator is essentially a shortcut for the if-else statement, which is covered in the Control structures section later in this chapter.**

Unary operators

Unary operators are used to perform an operation on a single number. Unary means involving a single component. As you can see in *Table 2.7*, there are five unary operators:

Operator	Description
+	Unary plus
-	Unary minus
++	Increment
--	Decrement
!	Logical complement (NOT)

Table 2.7: *Unary operators*

Let us use each of these operators in the code:

```java
public class UnaryExample {
    public static void main(String[] args) {
        int nbrA = 5;
        int nbrB = -10;
        boolean boolC = true;

        // Unary plus (+)
        int positiveA = +nbrA;   // No change in value
        System.out.println("Unary plus of nbrA: " + positiveA);   // Output: 5

        // Unary minus (-)
        int negativeB = -nbrB;   // Negates the value of nbrB
        System.out.println("Unary minus of nbrB: " + negativeB);   // Output:
10

        // Increment operator (++)
        nbrA++;   // nbrA = nbrA + 1
        System.out.println("After incrementing, nbrA: " + nbrA);   // Output: 6

        // Decrement operator (--)
        nbrB--;   // nbrB = nbrB - 1
        System.out.println("After decrementing, nbrB: " + nbrB);   // Output:
-11

        // Logical complement (!)
        boolean notC = !boolC;   // Negates the boolean value of boolC
        System.out.println("Logical complement of boolC: " + notC);   //
Output: false
```

```
    }
}
```

The output of the preceding code is provided as follows:

```
Unary plus of nbrA: 5
Unary minus of nbrB: 10
After incrementing, nbrA: 6
After decrementing, nbrB: -11
Logical complement of boolC: false
```

Control structures

Java includes a series of structures that allow us to control the flow of our programs. We do this by evaluating conditions and executing specific code based on the results. There are three primary types of control structures in Java: conditional statements, looping constructs, and branching statements.

Conditional statements

Conditional statements allow us to direct the flow of our program's execution by deciding which block of code to execute based on conditions we program. Think of a non-programming example where if a person's age is at least a minimum age, they will be allowed entry to ride a carnival ride. That same type of logic can be implemented in Java using conditional statements.

In this section, we will cover four conditional statements: **if**, **if-else**, **else-if**, and **switch**.

If

The **if** statement is the most common and simplest conditional control structure. We can use it to evaluate a specific condition and then, if the condition is true, execute a block of code. Here is an example:

```
int age = 21
if (age > 17) {
    System.out.println("You can ride the Ferris Wheel!");
}
```

In the preceding example, we only print the message in the code block if our condition (**age > 17**) evaluates as true.

If-else

The **if-else** statement allows us to execute two blocks of code: one if the condition is true and another if it is false. Here is an example:

```
int age = 21
if (age > 17) {
    System.out.println("You can ride the Ferris Wheel!");
} else {
    System.out.println("Sorry, you are too young to ride the Ferris Wheel.");
}
```

In the aforementioned example, we have different code blocks for each condition result (**true** or **false**).

Else-if

The **else-if** statement allows us to implement several conditions in one block. Here is an example:

```
int age = 21
if (age < 18) {
    System.out.println("Sorry, you are too young to ride the Ferris Wheel ");
} else if (age >= 65) {
    System.out.println("Sorry, you are too old to ride the Ferris Wheel.");
} else {
    System.out.println("You can ride the Ferris Wheel!");
}
```

In the preceding example, a specific output is provided based on our conditional statements.

Switch

The **switch** statement is a simplified version of a series of **else-if** statements. This can increase the readability of your code. The following is an example:

```
int weekDay = 3;
switch (weekDay) {
    case 1:
        System.out.println("Monday");
        break;
    case 2:
        System.out.println("Tuesday");
        break;
```

```
case 3:
    System.out.println("Wednesday");
    break;
case 4:
    System.out.println("Thursday");
    break;
case 5:
    System.out.println("Friday");
    break;
default:
    System.out.println("Invalid day detected.");
}
```

The preceding program snippet would output **Wednesday** based on the value of **weekDay**.

Looping

Looping allows us to repeat the execution of code blocks. This section looks at three types of looping: **for, while**, and **do-while**.

For

The **for** loop is commonly used when we know how often we want a block of code repeated. There are three parts to the **for** statement: initialization, condition, and increment. Let us look at an example in code and use it as a reference to explore these parts further:

```
for (int i = 0; i < 6; i++) {
    System.out.println(i);
}
```

The preceding example prints numbers **0** through **5**. The initialization part is **int i =0;** the condition is **i < 6**, and the increment is **i++**. After each pass through the loop, the variable **i** is incremented. When the condition **i < 6** is no longer true, the loop ends.

Note: **It is common to use throwaway variables in loops, such as i, j, and k. Their scope is within the loop, so we are less concerned about making their names descriptive.**

While

The **while** loop is used to run a block of code while a specific condition is **true**. An example follows:

```
int i = 0;
while (i < 6) {
    System.out.println(i);
```

```
        i++;
}
```

The aforementioned example prints numbers **0** through **5**.

Do-while

The **do-while** loop is used when we want the block of code to run at least once. It is implemented in a manner where the condition check occurs at the end of each loop iteration, unlike the other types that check the condition first. The following is an example:

```
int i = 0;
do {
        System.out.println(i);
        i++;
} while (i < 6);
```

The preceding example prints numbers **0** through **5**. As you can see, the condition is located after the code block.

Branching

Branching allows us to disrupt the normal flow of other control structures. In this section, we will look at three Java keywords that can be used for branching: **break**, **continue**, and **return**.

Break

The **break** keyword is used to exit a loop abruptly before it has run its full course.

The following is an example:

```
for (int i = 0; i < 24; i++) {
        if (i == 8) {
                break;
        }
        System.out.println(i);
}
```

The preceding code exits when **i == 8** evaluates to true.

Continue

The **continue** keyword is used to skip the current loop iteration and move on to the next.

The following is an example:

```
for (int i = 0; i < 25; i++) {
    if (i == 8) {
        continue;
    }
    System.out.println(i);
}
```

The preceding example will not print **8**.

Return

The **return** keyword is used to exit a method. Depending on how we write our method (more on that in the next section), we can optionally return a value when we exit.

Here is an example:

```
for (int i = 0; i < 24; i++) {
    if (i == 8) {
        System.out.println("Exiting the loop because i = " + i);
        return;
    }
    System.out.println(i);
}
```

The preceding example exits the loop and terminates the current execution after the condition **i == 8** evaluates as true.

Methods

Methods are blocks of code that are written to perform a specific task. They can accept inputs (**parameters**) and return results. Methods can be reused and are a core part of Java's modularity. Using methods in our applications helps us avoid duplicate code, makes our code easier to read, and is more maintainable.

The syntax for a method follows:

```
returnType methodName (parameters) {
    // method body goes here
}
```

The return type identifies the data type the method returns. If it returns nothing, we use the **void** keyword instead of a specific data type. The method name should be self-descriptive and use camelCase. Parameters are optional, and if the method does not accept a parameter, then we simply use a set of open and closed parentheses with nothing in between them. The method body is enclosed in a set of curly brackets.

The following is an example method that does not accept any parameters and does not return a value. It simply prints a message to the screen as follows:

```
public void welcome() {
    System.out.println("Welcome to my world!");
}
```

We can call this method with a simple line of code as follows:

```
welcome();
```

Let us look at the following example method that accepts parameters and returns a value:

```
public int add(int nbrA, int nbrB) {
    return nbrA + nbrB;
}
```

The **add()** method shown in the following code accepts two values, both of which must be integers. The return statement returns the sum of the two variables. The way we would call this in a program could be in one of the following forms:

```
// example 1
myTotal = add(8, 24);
// example 2
int a = 8;
int b = 24;
myTotal = add(a, b);
```

More on parameters

As we previously covered, methods can optionally accept parameters. These parameters are inputs to the method. If we write a method and identify that it accepts parameters, they must be provided. Our **add(int nbrA, int nbrB)** example required two parameters, both of which must be integers. If they are not, our code will not compile, and our IDE will remind us of our error.

Here are a few rules to keep in mind regarding method parameters:

- If a method requires parameters, they must be passed.

- The parameters passed must match what is defined in the method name.

- Java passes by value, so a copy of the argument's (parameter) value is passed to the method, not the actual variable.

- If a method does not specify **void** as the return type, it must contain a **return** statement.

Scope

We previously covered scope and defined it as a reference to where a variable is accessible in a program. Variables defined within a method are local variables and are only accessible inside the method. Using the method shown as a reference, the **jerseyNumber** variable is local and is destroyed after the method execution ends:

```java
public void displayJerseyNumber() {
    int jerseyNumber = 24;  // Local variable
    System.out.println(jerseyNumber);
}
```

The **jerseyNumber** variable is not accessible outside of the **displayJerseyNumber()** method.

Detailed example

Let us take a closer look at method implementation with part of an e-commerce system that allows users to select a type of plate (dinner, salad, or dessert), choose prints, colors, and other customization options like material type or engraving. We will review this code one section at a time.

The first section sets up our **CustomPlate** class, imports necessary Java packages, establishes the variables we need, and includes the constructor. All these aspects will be covered in *Chapter 3, Object-oriented Programming Basics*. They are presented here for code clarity and completeness as follows:

```java
import java.util.ArrayList;
import java.util.List;
public class CustomPlate {
    // Variables for plate configuration
    private String plateType;        // Type of plate (e.g., Dinner, Salad,
Dessert)
    private String print;            // Print pattern (e.g., Floral,
Geometric)
    private String color;            // Color of the plate
    private String material;         // Material (e.g., Porcelain, Glass,
Plastic)
    private String engraving;        // Custom engraving text (optional)
    private List<String> additionalOptions; // Any extra customizations (e.g.,
gold trim, matte finish)
    private double basePrice;
    // Constructor
    public CustomPlate() {
        this.additionalOptions = new ArrayList<>();
```

```
        this.basePrice = 0.0;
    }
```

The next section of the code includes a **setPlateType()** that sets the type of plate and assigns the appropriate base price:

```
    // Method to set the plate type
    public void setPlateType(String plateType) {
        this.plateType = plateType;
        // Set base price based on the plate type
        switch (plateType.toLowerCase()) {
            case "dinner":
                this.basePrice = 75.00;
                break;
            case "salad":
                this.basePrice = 55.00;
                break;
            case "dessert":
                this.basePrice = 35.00;
                break;
            default:
                System.out.println("Invalid plate type. Please choose
'dinner', 'salad', or 'dessert'.");
                break;
        }
    }
```

The next section of code includes the **setPrint()**, **setColor()**, **setMaterial()**, and **setEngraving()** methods. Since we followed best practice, our method names are self-describing.

```
    // Method to set the print pattern
    public void setPrint(String print) {
        this.print = print;
    }
    // Method to set the color of the plate
    public void setColor(String color) {
        this.color = color;
    }

    // Method to set the material of the plate
    public void setMaterial(String material) {
```

```
            if (material.equalsIgnoreCase("porcelain") || material.
equalsIgnoreCase("glass") || material.equalsIgnoreCase("plastic")) {
            this.material = material;
        } else {
            System.out.println("Invalid material type. Please choose
'Porcelain', 'Glass', or 'Plastic'.");
        }
    }


    // Method to add custom engraving (optional)
    public void setEngraving(String engraving) {
        if (engraving.length() <= 30) {  // Limit engraving text to 30
characters
            this.engraving = engraving;
        } else {
            System.out.println("Engraving text too long. Please keep it under
30 characters.");
        }
    }
```

The next section contains the **addAdditionalOption()** and **calculateCost()** methods:

```
    // Method to add additional customizations (like gold trim, matte finish,
etc.)
    public void addAdditionalOption(String option) {
        this.additionalOptions.add(option);
    }
    // Method to calculate the total cost of the custom plate
    public double calculateCost() {
        double totalCost = this.basePrice;
        // Additional costs based on customizations
        if (this.engraving != null && !this.engraving.isEmpty()) {
            totalCost += 5.00;   // Engraving costs $5.00
        }
        // Add $3.00 for each additional option
        totalCost += this.additionalOptions.size() * 3.00;
        return totalCost;
    }
```

The next section contains the method to display the plate details:

```
// Method to display the plate details
    public void displayPlateDetails() {
```

```java
        if (this.plateType == null || this.print == null || this.color == null
|| this.material == null) {
            System.out.println("Please complete the plate configuration.");
            return;
        }
        System.out.println("Plate Type: " + this.plateType);
        System.out.println("Print: " + this.print);
        System.out.println("Color: " + this.color);
        System.out.println("Material: " + this.material);

        if (this.engraving != null && !this.engraving.isEmpty()) {
            System.out.println("Engraving: " + this.engraving);
        } else {
            System.out.println("No engraving.");
        }

        if (this.additionalOptions.isEmpty()) {
            System.out.println("No additional customizations.");
        } else {
            System.out.println("Additional Customizations: " + String.join(",
", this.additionalOptions));
        }
        System.out.printf("Total Cost: $%.2f%n", calculateCost());
    }
```

Our program ends with the **main()** method, from which the other methods are called:

```java
    // Main method to test the CustomPlate class
    public static void main(String[] args) {
        // Create a new CustomPlate instance
        CustomPlate customPlate = new CustomPlate();
        // Set plate configuration
        customPlate.setPlateType("Dinner");
        customPlate.setPrint("Floral");
        customPlate.setColor("Blue");
        customPlate.setMaterial("Porcelain");
        customPlate.setEngraving("Happy Birthday");
        customPlate.addAdditionalOption("Gold Trim");
        customPlate.addAdditionalOption("Matte Finish");
        // Display the plate details
```

```
        customPlate.displayPlateDetails();
    }
}
```

The output of our program is displayed as follows:

Plate Type: Dinner
Print: Floral
Color: Blue
Material: Porcelain
Engraving: Happy Birthday
Additional Customizations: Gold Trim, Matte Finish
Total Cost: $86.00

This detailed example demonstrated the modular approach to programming and data validation. This type of programming approach makes it more efficient for us to write, read, and maintain code.

Best practices

Let us review best practices with regard to methods as follows:

- **Avoid data corruption**: Our methods should not modify data unexpectedly. It is preferable to return new values rather than modifying arguments directly.

- **Be concise**: Methods should have a singular focus. When a method starts to grow too large, consider breaking it into smaller, more specific methods.

- **Document methods**: Use in code comments to explain what the method does, the parameters it takes, and what it returns.

- **Follow naming conventions**: Choose descriptive names that make it clear what the method does. For example, **calculateSalesTax()** is better than **calculate()** or **tax()**.

- **Use parameters and return values**: Avoid relying on global variables. Instead, data can be passed via parameters and returned.

Note: **Always check if the passed values are correct. Handling errors on your own is a better approach than receiving errors at runtime. More on that in Chapter 5, Handling Errors and Exceptions.**

Conclusion

By the end of this chapter, we explored the core concepts of the Java programming language. We discussed data types and variables, highlighting their use in storing and manipulating data. Our coverage included the differences between primitive and reference data types.

We also covered operators and focused on their use in performing a variety of logical operations and calculation comparisons of variables. During the chapter's coverage of control structures, we explored how to use conditional statements, loops, and branching to control the flow of our programs. Our examples showed how these structures allow us to execute specific code blocks based on conditions. We also reviewed how looping can be used to repeat code multiple times. The chapter concluded with a section on methods that are fundamental to programming for modular, reusable, and maintainable code.

In the next chapter, we will explore OOP, starting with the OOP principles of encapsulation, inheritance, polymorphism, and abstraction. We will also cover classes, objects, constructors, overloading, access modifiers, etc.

Points to remember

- Arithmetic operators perform basic mathematical operations like addition, subtraction, multiplication, and division.

- Assignment operators, including compound operators, allow values to be assigned to variables and updated concisely.

- Bitwise operators manipulate individual bits within an integer, offering finite control for system-level programming tasks, though they are less commonly used in everyday applications.

- Break is used to exit loops or switch statements early based on a specified condition.

- camelCase is used for naming variables and methods, while PascalCase is reserved for naming classes.

- Class variables (static variables) are shared across all instances of a class and are declared with the static keyword.

- Compound operators, such as += and -=, are shortcuts for performing an operation and assigning the result in one step.

- Conditional statements like if, if-else, and switch allow our programs to make decisions and execute code based on certain conditions.

- Constants are variables declared with the final keyword and cannot be modified after their initial assignment.

- Control structures include conditionals, loops, and branching, and they are essential for controlling the flow of a program.

- Data types in Java are categorized into primitive and reference types.

- Do-while loops execute code at least once before checking the loop condition at the end of the iteration.

- Loops are commonly used for iterations where the number of iterations is known beforehand and consists of initialization, condition, and increment.

- Increment and decrement operators (++ and --) are unary operators used to increase or decrease a variable's value by one.

- Logical operators (&&, | |, !) combine or negate Boolean expressions, enabling more complex condition checking.

- Local variables are declared inside methods and are only accessible within that method.

- Methods encapsulate a set of instructions that perform a specific task, making code reusable and modular.

- Operators in Java are divided into categories such as arithmetic, relational, logical, bitwise, and assignment, each serving a distinct purpose in manipulating data.

- Primitive data types hold simple values like numbers and characters, while reference data types refer to objects and complex structures.

- Relational operators compare two values and return a boolean result (true or false).

- Return exits a method and optionally returns a value if the method is not void.

- Scope defines the visibility of variables within different parts of a program, including local, instance, and class-level scope.

- Strings are reference data types used to store sequences of characters, and methods such as String.valueOf() or Integer.toString() are used for conversion between strings and numbers.

- Switch statements provide a cleaner alternative to multiple else-if conditions when checking a variable against different values.

- Ternary operators are a compact way to return one of two values based on the result of a Boolean expression.

- Unary operators operate on a single operand, with examples including increment (++) and logical NOT (!).

- Variables are memory locations used to store data, and proper naming conventions improve code readability and maintenance.

- Variable scope determines where a variable can be accessed, including local, instance, and class-level scopes.

- While loops continue executing as long as a specified condition remains true, offering flexibility when the number of iterations is not predetermined.

Case studies

The following case studies are designed to help you understand the relevance of Java's core features to real-world challenges. As you review these case studies, consider the benefits and potential disadvantages to help solidify your understanding of Java:

- **Optimizing inventory management with variables and control structures**: *LambdaTech* is a fictitious technology retailer that sells products ranging from laptops to gaming accessories. They have an inventory management system that needs optimization. Currently, they have a single quantity variable to track stock for each product, but as their inventory grows, they need a more flexible approach to handle complex conditions, such as handling low stock notifications, automatically reordering when stock reaches a threshold, and generating reports for out-of-stock products. You are tasked with improving the system by implementing more efficient data storage using arrays and enhancing its logic through control structures like if-else statements and loops. You also need to ensure that variables are appropriately scoped to avoid conflicts between different sections of the inventory management code.

  - **For your consideration**: How could you refactor the code to use an array for storing stock quantities of multiple products? How would you implement a control structure to alert the system when stock for any product is low (e.g., less than 10 units)? How would you add a loop to automatically reorder products when stock reaches zero and log the reorder events? Finally, discuss how scope plays a role in avoiding variable conflicts in this system, and suggest best practices for managing variables in different parts of the inventory management system.

- **Designing a custom print selection system**: *NovaCore* is a fictitious e-commerce company specializing in custom print plates for science-fiction-themed events. Their online platform allows customers to select the type of plate (dinner, dessert, etc.), choose a print (e.g., starship, alien landscapes), and customize colors and materials. However, their system is experiencing performance issues, as each selection triggers unnecessary recalculations and database queries. You are brought in to optimize the custom plate selection system by improving the use of variables, methods, and control structures. One issue you notice is the lack of efficient use of methods to handle repetitive tasks, such as applying discounts or calculating total costs. The current system uses global variables excessively, which is causing unexpected behavior during order processing.

  - **For your consideration**: How could you refactor the system to use methods for calculating the cost of the custom plate based on user selected options? As part of your solution, ensure the methods are modular, reusable, and follow best practices for parameter passing and return values. How would you improve control structures to ensure that database queries are only triggered when necessary, reducing redundant checks and improving system performance?

Propose a method to calculate bulk discounts based on the quantity of plates ordered and include this logic in the refactored code. Finally, discuss how variable scope improvements might reduce bugs and unexpected behavior in the system.

- **Implementing logic for employee scheduling**: *Omega Dynamics* is a fictitious engineering firm with a global workforce. They need a scheduling system that can handle the complexity of employee work shifts across different time zones. Employees are assigned shifts based on project needs, and certain conditions must be met, such as ensuring that no employee works more than 40 hours a week and that shifts do not overlap. You are tasked with developing a new scheduling system using control structures and methods to enforce work hour limits, manage shift overlap, and automate scheduling. The current system uses hardcoded values and lacks flexibility, resulting in frequent errors and scheduling conflicts.

  o **For your consideration**: Explain your approach to writing a method that checks if an employee has reached their weekly hour limit and returns whether they can be scheduled for additional shifts. How would you implement a control structure that checks for overlapping shifts and reassigns employees to new shifts if a conflict is detected? How could you make use of relational operators to compare the start and end times of shifts and ensure that no two shifts overlap? Finally, discuss how modular methods can improve the overall maintainability of the scheduling system and how different types of control structures can be leveraged to solve complex scheduling problems.

- **Automating financial calculations with operators**: *Stellar Solutions* is a fictitious financial consultancy that provides automated financial reporting for its clients. They recently expanded their services to include profit margin analysis and require an update to their existing software to perform calculations based on client-specific data. The challenge is to use arithmetic and relational operators effectively to generate financial reports. You are tasked with developing a module that automatically calculates profit margins based on revenue and expenses data provided by clients. You need to use operators to ensure the system calculates correct profit margins and flags any negative profit values for further review.

  o **For your consideration**: How would you write a method that accepts two parameters, revenue and expenses, and returns the profit margin as a percentage? Explain how you would use relational operators to detect negative profit margins and generate a warning message for the client. How would you implement a ternary operator to return different messages based on whether the profit margin is positive or negative? Finally, discuss how using operators and control structures can automate the financial calculations and reduce the risk of human error in the reporting process.

- **Optimizing production with loops and branching**: *Aegis Forge* is a fictitious manufacturer of high-tech armor for intergalactic exploration. They use an automated production line to create parts for their armor, but their current production control system lacks the flexibility to handle different production speeds and interruptions due to machine malfunctions. You are tasked with optimizing the production control system by implementing loops and branching structures. The goal is to allow the system to dynamically adjust production speed and handle errors in real-time.

  o **For your consideration**: How would you use a while loop to simulate the production of armor parts, with a condition that stops the loop when the required number of parts is produced? How would you add a break statement to exit the loop early if a machine malfunction is detected? Explain how you would implement a continue statement that skips the production of a part if a minor error occurs, but allows the system to continue with the next part. Finally, discuss how branching structures like break and continue can improve production efficiency and error handling in a real-world manufacturing system.

Multiple choice questions

1. **What is the purpose of using a control structure in a Java program?**
   a. To store data
   b. To manipulate memory addresses
   c. To control the execution flow
   d. To define a new class

2. **Which of the following is a valid variable name in Java?**
   a. 1variable
   b. $totalCount
   c. total#count
   d. break

3. **What is the value of x after the following code is executed?**
   ```
   int x = 10;
   x += 5;
   ```
   a. 5
   b. 10
   c. 15
   d. 50

4. **Which of the following statements about Java methods is true?**

   a. A method can have multiple return types.

   b. A method can be called without being defined.

   c. A method cannot accept parameters in Java.

   d. A method with a void return type does not return any value.

5. **What will the following if-else statement print?**

```java
int age = 25;
if (age < 18) {
    System.out.println("You are a minor.");
} else if (age >= 18 && age <= 65) {
    System.out.println("You are an adult.");
} else {
    System.out.println("You are a senior.");
}
```

   a. You are a minor.

   b. You are an adult.

   c. You are a senior.

   d. None of the above.

Answers

1.	c.
2.	b.
3.	c.
4.	d.
5.	b.

Questions

1. How does variable scope impact the design and maintainability of a Java program?

2. Consider the differences between local, instance, and class variables. In what scenarios might each type of variable be most appropriate, and how can poor management of scope lead to issues in large applications?

3. Discuss the advantages and disadvantages of using compound operators in Java.

4. In what scenarios would you choose to use a switch statement over a series of if-else statements?

5. Provide an example of when a switch might be more efficient or easier to understand, and discuss any perceived limitations.

6. What are the key differences between a for loop, a while loop, and a do-while loop?

7. How do you decide which looping structure to use for a given task?

8. How can logical operators (e.g., &&, | |, !) help simplify complex condition checks?

9. Think about parameters, return types, and how you handle input validation. How can methods be written to maximize their usefulness across different parts of a program or even in future projects?

10. How does the use of constants improve code readability and maintainability?

Challenges

- **Create an inventory stock checker**:

    ○ **Objective**: Implement control structures to manage inventory status.

    ○ **Activity**: Write a Java program that simulates inventory tracking for a small online store. Create an array to store the stock quantity of 10 different items. The program should loop through the inventory and alert when stock levels drop below five units. Add logic to automatically reorder when any item's stock reaches 0, updating the inventory with 20 additional units for that item.

    ○ **Real-world applicability**: Inventory management is crucial in e-commerce systems. Automating reordering and stock tracking ensures that businesses run efficiently and avoid stockouts.

- **Create a custom product configuration system**:

    ○ **Objective**: Use methods and control structures to create a customizable product configuration schema.

    ○ **Activity**: Develop a Java program that allows users to configure a custom product (e.g., a custom t-shirt). The program should offer options for the type of product (t-shirt, hoodie, jacket), color, and print pattern. Each option should have a base price, and you should calculate and display the total cost based on user selections. Implement validation to ensure that all required options are selected before proceeding to checkout. Note that you do not need to write the checkout part of the application.

- o **Real-world applicability**: Customization is a key feature in many online businesses, especially in industries such as fashion, home decor, and personal goods.

- **Create a grading system**:

  - o **Objective**: Implement conditional logic to categorize performance.

  - o **Activity**: Create a Java program that accepts a student's score as input and categorizes their performance based on the following criteria:

    - **90 and above**: A

    - **80-89**: B

    - **70-79**: C

    - **60-69**: D

    - **Below 60**: F

      Use if-else statements to handle these conditions. Additionally, it allows users to input multiple student scores and generate a class performance report, indicating how many students fell into each grade category.

  - o **Real-world applicability**: Grading systems are used in academic settings worldwide, and automating the process ensures accurate, consistent results.

- **Create a temperature conversion tool**:

  - o **Objective**: Use methods and data types to solve real-world conversions.

  - o **Activity**: Write a program that converts temperatures between Celsius and Fahrenheit. Create two methods: one to convert from Celsius to Fahrenheit and one to convert from Fahrenheit to Celsius. The program should allow the user to select which conversion they want to perform and input the temperature value. After converting, display the result and offer the option to perform another conversion or exit.

  - o **Real-world applicability**: Conversion tools are commonly used in fields like science, engineering, and daily life, ensuring accuracy in different measurement systems.

- **Create a weekly work hours calculator**:

  - o **Objective**: Use loops, methods, and variables to calculate weekly work hours.

  - o **Activity**: Build a Java program that calculates the total hours worked by an employee during a week. The user should be able to input the hours worked for each day (Monday to Friday). The program should check that the total does not exceed 40 hours and display the total at the end. Additionally, if the total exceeds 40 hours, display a warning message.

    o **Real-world applicability**: Employee time tracking is essential in workforce management systems, ensuring compliance with labor laws and preventing overtime.

Self-assessment

The following questions are provided so you can self-assess your knowledge of the chapter's content and apply critical thinking to key concepts:

1. What is the difference between primitive and reference data types in Java? Provide examples of each?

2. Describe the purpose of the scope in Java. How does the scope of a variable impact its accessibility and lifetime in a program?

3. How could you modify a for loop to skip certain iterations? Provide a practical example where this might be useful.

4. Explain the difference between the while loop and the do-while loop. Under what circumstances would you use each?

5. Imagine a program where the use of conditional statements (if-else, switch) significantly affects the program's flow. How could these control structures improve the functionality, and could another approach be used?

Answers

1. Primitive data types hold simple values and are not objects. Examples include integer, float, Boolean, and character. They directly store the value in memory. Reference data types, on the other hand, refer to objects or more complex data structures like arrays, classes, and strings. For example, a string is a reference data type that points to an object containing a sequence of characters. Reference types store a memory address pointing to the object rather than the actual value.

2. The scope of a variable defines where it can be accessed within the program. In Java, there are three primary types of scope as follows:

    a. **Local variables**: Declared inside a method and only accessible within that method. They are destroyed after the method execution ends.

    b. **Instance variables**: Declared within a class but outside methods, making them accessible across different methods within the class.

    c. **Class variables**: Declared using the static keyword, these variables are shared across all instances of the class.

3. You can modify a for loop to skip specific iterations by using the continue statement. This statement forces the loop to jump to the next iteration, bypassing the rest of the code for the current iteration. The example uses continue to bypass a specific iteration in a loop.

```java
for (int i = 1; i <= 24; i++) {
    if (i == 8) {
        continue;  // Skip iteration when i equals 8
    }
    System.out.println(i);
}
```

4. A while loop checks the condition before executing the block of code, so if the condition is false from the start, the loop body will not execute. In contrast, a do-while loop checks the condition after executing the block of code, ensuring the code runs at least once, regardless of the initial condition. You would use a while loop when you only want to execute the loop if the condition is true at the start. Use a do-while loop when you need the code to execute at least once, even if the condition might not hold later.

5. Conditional statements allow for decision-making in programs by enabling different actions based on different inputs or conditions. For example, in a program that determines the shipping cost based on the destination country, an if-else statement could apply different logic for different regions:

```java
if (country.equals("USA")) {
    shippingCost = 12.00;
} else if (country.equals("Canada")) {
    shippingCost = 16.00;
} else {
    shippingCost = 24.00;
}
```

This conditional structure improves the program's functionality by applying dynamic logic based on the user's input. Alternatively, a switch statement could be used in place of if-else if there are multiple predefined categories to check, which could make the code cleaner in some situations.

CHAPTER 3
Object-oriented Programming Basics

Introduction

Object-oriented programming (**OOP**) is a framework used by Java for structuring and organizing code for scalability, readability, reusability, and maintainability. Java is an OOP language, and this chapter covers the basics of OOP to include the principles of abstraction, encapsulation, inheritance, and polymorphism. The OOP framework, also called a **programming paradigm**, empowers us to build complex Java programs efficiently.

In this chapter, we will cover the defining classes and objects, which are OOP building blocks. We will discuss the importance of constructors and method overloading and their contribution to flexible code. We will also cover how Java's **extends** keyword can be used to promote code reuse by enabling hierarchical relationships between classes. Additionally, the chapter will cover how to leverage OOP to manage data security and integrity in your Java applications securely. Topics related to security include access modifiers and encapsulation.

Structure

This chapter covers the following topics:

- Introduction to OOP principles
- Defining and using classes and objects

- Constructors and overloading

- Inheritance and the super keyword

- Polymorphism and method overriding

- Access modifiers and encapsulation

Objectives

By the end of this chapter, we will understand the fundamental principles of OOP, including encapsulation, inheritance, polymorphism, and abstraction. We will create and use classes and objects to structure your code with a modular, reusable approach. We will also create flexible and efficient code with constructors and method overloading. We will understand how to apply inheritance and the **extends** keyword to establish hierarchical relationships and promote code reuse. Additionally, we will use access modifiers to encapsulate data, ensuring data security and integrity within Java applications.

Introduction to OOP principles

OOP is an approach to programming, also referred to as a **programming paradigm**, that is based on the concept of objects. Objects are things that can contain data and code for manipulating that data. OOP is a foundational component of the Java programming language. This approach allows us to structure our applications so that they are modular, reusable, readable, and maintainable.

The concept of objects allows us to organize our code into objects, each with its own set of properties and behaviors. As this chapter explains, an object's properties are data, and its behaviors are methods (code modules). This programming approach makes development efficient and empowers us to write complex and scalable Java applications.

At the core of OOP are the objects, which we model after real-world entities using the principles of encapsulation, inheritance, polymorphism, and abstraction. Each of these principles is briefly explained in this section with more in-depth coverage, including examples later in this chapter.

Encapsulation

Encapsulation is a core OOP principle with the purpose of keeping data organized and safe. This is accomplished by bundling data and the code that manipulates it into a single unit called a class.

Note: **The terms data, properties, and attributes are essentially interchangeable in the context of OOP.**

This bundling serves several purposes, include the following:

- Ensures data integrity

- Can restrict access

- Protect sensitive data

- Prevent inadvertent interactions

Encapsulation is a critical part of software development in Java as it permits us to write applications that are both modular and secure, with great control over our data and how it flows throughout the application.

Inheritance

Inheritance in Java is modeled after real-world inheritance. Just as traits are passed down from grandparent to parent to child, classes in Java can inherit from other classes. This promotes code reuse, which means less programming. We establish a hierarchical relationship between classes, starting with a base class, also referred to as a **parent class**, and extending that class with specialized classes, also referred to as **child classes**. This inheritance has the child classes inheriting basic properties while also having their own unique attributes and behaviors.

Consider the hierarchy in the animal kingdom, partially illustrated in *Figure 3.1,* as follows:

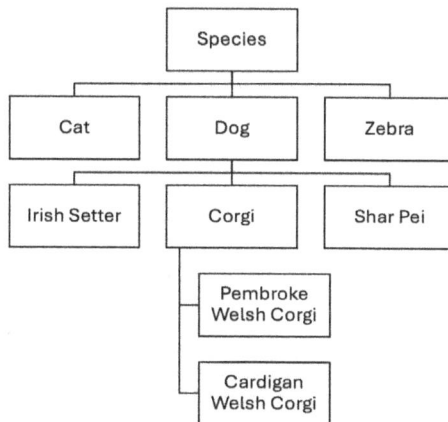

Figure 3.1: Four-layer inheritance hierarchy

In this example, **Species** is the base class, representing multiple animals, including **Dog**. The **Corgi** class inherits from **Dog**, which inherits from **Species**. The **Dog** class has three subclasses, or children, **Irish Setter**, **Pembroke Welsh Corgi**, and **Cardigan Welsh Corgi**.

Later in this chapter, we will create these classes and subclasses in Java.

Polymorphism

The term polymorphism, in programming, means many forms. Specifically, an object can be an instance of a parent class while also having its own unique attributes and behaviors. This allows us to write code that deals with objects of different classes in a standardized manner. This gives our programs great flexibility and extensibility.

Let us consider our dog example from the previous section. Using polymorphism, we can treat both `PembrokeWelshCorgi` and `CardiganWelshCorgi` as instances of their `Corgi` parent class. Furthermore, we can even treat them as instances of the broader `Dog` class. Although each of these child classes might share some methods, each subclass can override these methods to exhibit its own unique behaviors. As an example, both `PembrokeWelshCorgi` and `CardiganWelshCorgi` classes might have a `herd()` method, and each could implement that method differently as appropriate for their unique herding style; maybe one barks and the other nips at ankles.

Polymorphism is an essential OOP principle that allows us to create code that is flexible, adaptable, and scalable. Leveraging Java's polymorphism capabilities allows us to create systems where new object types can be easily created based on existing code. This mandates that the new objects must follow the structure and behavior expected by the parent class.

Abstraction

Abstraction is the fourth core OOP principle, and it allows us to hide the details of an object's implementation, only exposing what is necessary for the required functionality. The term abstraction comes from the act of abstracting or hiding implementation from functionality. We achieve this in Java by defining classes and interfaces with simplistic views of the overall class and encapsulating its complexities.

Back to our dog example, we could create an `Animal` abstract class that contains some basic methods such as `eat()`, `sleep()`, `walk()`, and `jump()`, but not provide any details for them. Then, the `Dog` class would extend the `Animal` class and provide implementation details for each of the four methods as they pertain to dogs. Classes for each sub-breed could contain additional method customization as appropriate.

Abstraction allows us to work on simplified representations of objects without needing to understand all the details. This is especially helpful when working on large-scale applications. Complexity hiding helps make our code more readable and maintainable.

Defining and using classes and objects

At this point, you should understand that classes and objects are core to Java's OOP implementation. This section explains how to define and use classes and objects. Our goal is to use the OOP approach to creating structured, modular applications. We create objects from classes, which means classes are the blueprints for objects. They define the attributes and methods that objects can have. We will continue with our dog example to help you contextualize how to define and use classes and objects.

Defining a class

Unsurprisingly, to create a class in Java, we use the **class** keyword followed by its name and a pair of curly brackets like this: **public class Dog {}**. Inside the curly brackets is where we define the **attributes**, also referred to as **fields**, and the **methods**, also referred to as **behaviors**. Let us write the **Dog** class and then discuss its components:

```
public class Dog {
    // attributes / fields
    private String name;
    private String breed;
    private int age;
    private double weight;
    // methods / behaviors
    public void bark() {
        System.out.println(name + " is currently barking!");
    }
    public void eat() {
        System.out.println(name + " is currently eating.");
    }
    public void sleep() {
        System.out.println(name + " is currently sleeping.");
    }
}
```

As you can see in our example, the **Dog** class contains attributes and methods. The attributes are **name**, **breed**, **age**, and **weight**. These are the characteristics of a dog created using the **Dog** class. Each dog can have its own values for these attributes. For example, one dog's name might be *Muzz*, and another is *Java*. Each of the methods was created using the **private** access modifier.

As we discussed in encapsulation, this is an example of it in action. This means that the attributes are only accessible from methods within this class. We will cover methods later in this chapter.

The **Dog** class currently contains three methods: **bark()**, **eat()**, and **sleep()**. They have not done anything impressive yet, other than output a message.

Creating an object

Now that we have a **Dog** class, we can create new objects using the class as a template. To do this, we will use the **new** keyword in Java. An object is a unique instance of a class. It has its own memory location and unique attribute values. The **new** keyword results in memory being allocated for the object. It also calls the class's constructor method, which is how the object is initialized.

Let us look at the following example:

```java
public class CorgiLove {
    public static void main(String[] args) {
        // Creating an object of the Dog class
        Dog myDog = new Dog();

        // Setting attributes
        myDog.name = "Basil";
        myDog.breed = "Corgi";
        myDog.age = 3;
        myDog.weight = 12.5;

        // Calling methods
        myDog.bark();
        myDog.eat();
        myDog.sleep();
    }
}
```

The key line of code is **Dog myDog = new Dog();** as it is how we create a **Dog** object. The **myDog** variable name is up to you. We could have easily used **myFirstDog** or **dadsDog**. In the attributes sections, we use dot notation (**.**) to access the object's attributes and methods. This is how we can ensure the attributes or methods are specifically referencing this specific object.

Initializing an object

When we used the new keyword to create **myDog**, an instance of the **Dog** class, Java used the constructor method in the class to create the instance. Constructors are automatically called when an object is created. These constructors are used to establish default attributes and their values. As you will see in the following example, constructors have the same name as the class. The following example is an updated **Dog** class that includes a constructor to initialize instances of the class and initialize its fields:

```java
public class Dog {
```

```
    // attributes / fields
    private String name;
    private String breed;
    private int age;
    private double weight;
    // Constructor
    public Dog(String name, String breed, int age, double weight) {
        this.name = name;
        this.breed = breed;
        this.age = age;
        this.weight = weight;
    }
    // methods / behaviors
    public void bark() {
        System.out.println(name + " is currently barking!");
    }
    public void eat() {
        System.out.println(name + " is currently eating.");
    }
    public void sleep() {
        System.out.println(name + " is currently sleeping.");
    }
}
```

Now that our **Dog** class has a constructor, we can modify our **CorgiLove** class and provide attribute values as part of the object creation process. The following is the code:

```
public class CorgiLove {
    public static void main(String[] args) {
        // Creating an object of the Dog class
        Dog myDog = new Dog("Basil", "Corgi", 3, 12.5);

        // Calling methods
        myDog.bark();
        myDog.eat();
        myDog.sleep();
    }
}
```

As you can see, the constructor allows us to create fully initialized objects with just one line of code.

Manipulating attributes

Now that we have an object with attributes, we need to be able to retrieve and change the values. For each attribute, we typically write a getter method to retrieve the value and a setter method to change the value. These getters and setters use the **get** and **set** prefixes to the method **name**. For example, we have a name attribute to create **getName()** and **setName()** methods. This naming convention is a best practice and helps make our code readable and maintainable.

The following is an updated **Dog** class with the getters and setters added:

```java
public class Dog {
    // attributes / fields
    private String name;
    private String breed;
    private int age;
    private double weight;
    // Constructor
    public Dog(String name, String breed, int age, double weight) {
        this.name = name;
        this.breed = breed;
        this.age = age;
        this.weight = weight;
    }
    // Getter and Setter for 'name'
    public String getName() {
        return name;
    }
    public void setName(String name) {
        this.name = name;
    }
    // Getter and Setter for 'age'
    public int getAge() {
        return age;
    }

    public void setAge(int age) {
        this.age = age;
```

```
    }
    // methods / behaviors
    public void bark() {
        System.out.println(name + " is currently barking!");
    }
    public void eat() {
        System.out.println(name + " is currently eating.");
    }
    public void sleep() {
        System.out.println(name + " is currently sleeping.");
    }
}
```

Next, we must modify our **CorgiLove** class to use the getters and setters. The following is an example where we use the **getName()**, **getAge()**, and **setAge()** methods:

```
public class CorgiLove {
    public static void main(String[] args) {
        // Creating an object of the Dog class
        Dog myDog = new Dog("Basil", "Corgi", 3, 12.5);
        // Accessing attributes with getters
        System.out.println("Dog's name is " + myDog.getName());
        System.out.println("Dog's age is " + myDog.getAge());
        // Modifying attributes with setters
        myDog.setAge(8);
        System.out.println("Updated age: " + myDog.getAge());
    }
}
```

Creating and using getters and setters gives us clear control of how our class attributes are accessed and modified. This is not only a best practice but also a great technique for keeping our data safe.

Constructors and overloading

In Java, we use constructor methods to initialize new objects, giving them their initial attribute values. We rely on constructors to properly initialize our objects before they are used in our applications. This is an important OOP construct. The concept of overloading constructors is an OOP feature that allows us to create multiple versions of a constructor, each with a unique set of parameters. This introduces great flexibility in how we create our objects.

Before we dive into constructor overloading, let us revisit our rules about constructors:

- They must have the same name as the class.

- They do not have a return type; this includes the **void** keyword.

- Their only purpose is to initialize objects.

In the previous section, we wrote the **Dog** class, which included this constructor method:

```java
public Dog(String name, String breed, int age, double weight) {
    this.name = name;
    this.breed = breed;
    this.age = age;
    this.weight = weight;
}
```

The method above ensures that whenever a **Dog** object is initialized, it will have attributes for **name**, **breed**, **age**, and **weight**. The use of Java's **this** keyword differentiates the parameter names and the class's fields.

Constructor overloading use case

In the previous section, we established that we could use the following code to create an instance of a **Dog** and establish the initial values for the object's attributes:

```java
Dog myDog = new Dog("Basil", "Corgi", 3, 12.5);
```

What if we do not have all four attribute values available to use when we create an object? Consider the scenario where our application is used at an animal clinic; the **name** and **breed** are entered into the system, and **age** and **weight** values are entered later during the animal's appointment. We do not want to be forced to put **age** and **weight** values; instead, we want to initialize the object with just two of the four attributes.

Each constructor has a unique parameter list, giving us the flexibility we need. So, let us overload our current constructor by creating a new constructor method with just the two attributes, as follows:

```java
public Dog(String name, String breed) {
    this.name = name;
    this.breed = breed;
    this.age = 0; // default value
    this.weight = 0.0; // default value
}
```

As you can see in the preceding code, the constructor's definition only includes two attributes, and the other two are given default values by the method.

Next, let us write another constructor that has no parameters as follows:

```java
public Dog() {
    this.name = "Unknown";
    this.breed = "Unknown";
    this.age = 0;
    this.weight = 0.0;
}
```

Note: Constructors with no parameters are referred to as default constructors.

The full **Dog** class code, with all constructors, getters, and setter methods included, is provided as follows:

```java
public class Dog {
    // attributes / fields
    private String name;
    private String breed;
    private int age;
    private double weight;
    // Constructor
    public Dog(String name, String breed, int age, double weight) {
        this.name = name;
        this.breed = breed;
        this.age = age;
        this.weight = weight;
    }

    // Constructor with only name and breed
    public Dog(String name, String breed) {
        this.name = name;
        this.breed = breed;
        this.age = 0; // default value
        this.weight = 0.0; // default value
    }
    // Constructor with no parameters (default constructor)
    public Dog() {
        this.name = "Unknown";
        this.breed = "Unknown";
        this.age = 0;
```

```java
        this.weight = 0.0;
    }
    // Getter and Setter for 'name'
    public String getName() {
        return name;
    }
    public void setName(String name) {
        this.name = name;
    }
      // Getter and Setter for 'breed'
      public String getBreed() {
        return breed;
    }
    public void setBreed(String breed) {
        this.breed = breed;
    }
    // Getter and Setter for 'age'
    public int getAge() {
        return age;
    }
    public void setAge(int age) {
        this.age = age;
    }
    // Getter and Setter for 'weight'
    public double getWeight() {
        return weight;
    }
    public void setWeight(double weight) {
        this.weight = weight;
    }
    // methods / behaviors
    public void bark() {
        System.out.println(name + " is currently barking!");
    }
    public void eat() {
        System.out.println(name + " is currently eating.");
    }
    public void sleep() {
```

```
        System.out.println(name + " is currently sleeping.");
    }
}
```

In the next section, we will explore how to call these different constructor methods.

Calling constructors

When we create a new **Dog** object, Java will know which constructor method to call based on our arguments. Remember, each constructor has a unique parameter list.

The following is an example of using all three constructors:

```java
public class AnimalClinic {
    public static void main(String[] args) {
        // Using the full constructor
        Dog dog1 = new Dog("Java", "Corgi", 10, 48.3);
        // Using the partial constructor
        Dog dog2 = new Dog("Brandy", "Irish Setter");
        // Using the default constructor
        Dog dog3 = new Dog();
        // Output example
        System.out.println(dog1.getName() + ", " + dog1.getBreed() + ", " +
dog1.getAge() + " years, " + dog1.getWeight() + " lbs");
        System.out.println(dog2.getName() + ", " + dog2.getBreed() + ", " +
dog2.getAge() + " years, " + dog2.getWeight() + " lbs");
        System.out.println(dog3.getName() + ", " + dog3.getBreed() + ", " +
dog3.getAge() + " years, " + dog3.getWeight() + " lbs");
    }
}
```

The following is the output of the **AnimalClinic** application:

```
Java, Corgi, 10 years, 48.3 lbs
Brandy, Irish Setter, 0 years, 0.0 lbs
Unknown, Unknown, 0 years, 0.0 lbs
```

We can see that each new **Dog** object was created with a different argument list, each corresponding to a different constructor based on the matching parameter list.

Once an object is created, it does not matter which constructor method was used. All getter and setter methods work on the objects regardless of how they were created.

Benefits

As we conclude our coverage of constructor overloading, let us recap the top three benefits of implementing this in our programs:

- Constructor overloading gives us great flexibility in creating objects because we can work with different data sets, each having its own list of available attributes.

- This approach results in less code because we do not need to duplicate methods for creating objects in various ways; rather, we can simply overload the constructor method in the class.

- Constructor overloading results in our code being more readable and maintainable.

Inheritance and the super keyword

Inheritance is a core OOP principle that allows a class to inherit attributes and methods from another class, forming a hierarchical relationship between classes. These relationships often model real-world relationships, as shown in *Figure 3.1* earlier in this chapter. This section demonstrates how to implement inheritance with Java's **extends** keyword and explains the role the **super** keyword plays in managing inherited attributes and methods. We will use the hierarchical structure of **Species**, **Animal**, **Canine**, and **Corgi** classes throughout this section.

Note: **Since we previously implemented a Dog class without inheritance, we will use a Canine class in this section to illustrate the hierarchical structure.**

Implementing inheritance

At the core of inheritance is the ability to define a class based on an existing class. The existing class is referred to as a **parent class** or **superclass**. The new class is a child class, also referred to as a subclass. The subclass inherits all the attributes and methods of the superclass, but is not limited to what it inherits; new attributes and methods can exist in subclasses.

Before we write our classes, we need to review the hierarchical structure to ensure we fully understand which attributes and methods are needed at each level. *Table 3.1* details the hierarchy we will implement as follows:

Class	Inherits from	Details
Species		This is the top-level class, representing the broad biological categories.
Animal	Species	It will represent characteristics common to all animals.
Canine	Animal	It will contain properties and behaviors specific to dogs.
Corgi	Canine	Further specializes the **Canine** class, distinguishing between types of Corgis: **Pembroke Welsh Corgi** and **Cardigan Welsh Corgi**.

Table 3.1: Class hierarchy based on real-world taxonomy

To implement this hierarchy, let us start by writing the **Species** class, the most general class in our hierarchy:

```
public class Species {
    // Attributes
    protected String scientificName;
    // Constructor
    public Species(String scientificName) {
        this.scientificName = scientificName;
    }
    // Method
    public void displayInfo() {
        System.out.println("Species: " + scientificName);
    }
}
```

As seen in the preceding code, the **Species** class has a single attribute, **scientificName** that is a common attribute for all species. The class contains a constructor and a method that displays the value of the **scientificName** attribute.

Next, we will write the **Animal** class, which will inherit from **Species**.

```
public class Animal extends Species {
    // Attributes
    protected String habitat;
    // Constructor
    public Animal(String scientificName, String habitat) {
        super(scientificName); // Calls the constructor of Species
        this.habitat = habitat;
    }
    // Method
    public void move() {
        System.out.println("The animal moves in its habitat.");
    }
}
```

Using the **extends** keyword tells Java that the **Animal** class inherits from **Species**. The **super(scientificName)** line calls the **Species** class constructor to initialize **scientificName**. The **move()** method is specific to **Animal**; it does not exist as part of the **Species** class.

Next, let us implement our **Canine** class and have it **extends** the **Animal** class as follows:

```
public class Canine extends Animal {
    // Attributes
```

```java
    protected String breed;
    // Constructor
    public Canine(String scientificName, String habitat, String breed) {
        super(scientificName, habitat); // Calls the constructor of Animal
        this.breed = breed;
    }
    // Method
    public void bark() {
        System.out.println("The dog barked.");
    }
}
```

Our **Canine** class uses the **super(scientificName, habitat)** code to call the **Animal** class constructor, which in turn calls the **Species** class constructor. The **bark()** method is specific to the **Canine** class; it was not inherited from **Animal** or **Species**.

```java
public class Corgi extends Canine {
    // Attributes
    private String subBreed;

    // Constructor
    public Corgi(String scientificName, String habitat, String breed, String subBreed) {
        super(scientificName, habitat, breed); // Calls the Canine constructor
        this.subBreed = subBreed;
    }

    // Method
    public void herd() {
        System.out.println("The " + subBreed + " Corgi is herding.");
    }

    // Overriding the displayInfo method
    @Override
    public void displayInfo() {
        super.displayInfo(); // Calls displayInfo of Species
        System.out.println("Breed: " + breed + ", Sub-breed: " + subBreed);
    }
}
```

Our **Corgi** class has the **subBreed** attribute, so we can specify one of the two **Corgi** types: **Pembroke Welsh Corgi** or **Cardigan Welsh Corgi**. The **herd()** method is specific to the **Corgi** class. Lastly, the **displayInfo()** method is overridden to display additional information about both the **breed** and **subBreed**.

Note: **The super keyword is used when a subclass needs to refer to its superclass. This can be used to call the superclass constructor or access superclass methods.**

Full inheritance demonstration

With our **Species**, **Animal**, **Canine**, and **Corgi** classes written, we are ready to create instances of these classes to demonstrate inheritance and use of the **super** keyword as follows:

```
public class PetGrooming {
    public static void main(String[] args) {
        // Creating a Corgi object
        Corgi myCorgi = new Corgi("Canis lupus familiaris", "Domestic",
"Corgi", "Pembroke Welsh Corgi");

        // Calling methods
        myCorgi.displayInfo(); // Calls the overridden method in Corgi
        myCorgi.move(); // Calls the method from Animal
        myCorgi.bark(); // Calls the method from Canine
        myCorgi.herd(); // Calls the method in Corgi
    }
}
```

The following is the output of the **PetGrooming** application:

Species: Canis lupus familiaris
Breed: Corgi, Sub-breed: Pembroke Welsh Corgi
The animal moves in its habitat.
The dog barked.
The Pembroke Welsh Corgi Corgi is herding.

Our **PetGrooming** application calls for four methods:

- **displayInfo()** in **Corgi** calls **super.displayInfo()** to access the superclass's version of the method. It then appends additional details specific to the **Corgi** class.

- **move()** is inherited from **Animal**.

- **bark()** is inherited from **Canine**.

- **herd()** is specific to **Corgi**.

Benefits

As we conclude our coverage of inheritance and the super keyword, let us recap the top three benefits of implementing this in our programs:

- **Code reusability**: We can put common attributes and functionality in a superclass and allow multiple subclasses to inherit from it. This reduces code duplication.

- **Logical organization**: We use inheritance to closely model real-world hierarchies and taxonomies for ease of understanding.

- **Extendibility**: We can add subclasses without the need to modify superclasses. This contributes to scalability.

Polymorphism and method overriding

Polymorphism, a core OOP principle, means many forms. In the context of Java, a single action can behave differently, specific to the object performing the action. This represents the opportunity to create highly flexible and extensible code. We can implement polymorphism in Java through method overriding and dynamic method dispatch. Both implementation approaches are covered in this section.

We will continue with the **Species**, **Animal**, **Canine**, and **Corgi** classes used earlier in this chapter. Our **Animal** class includes a **move()** method. Animals move in different ways. For example, a **Canine** class might *run*, a **Bird** class might *fly*, and a **Fish** class might *swim*. Polymorphism allows us to call a single **move()** method on any object inheriting from **Animal**, and each subclass can define its own implementation of that method.

Method overriding

In Java, we use method overriding so a subclass can provide a specific method implementation of a method that is already defined by its superclass. The overridden method in the subclass must have the same name, return type, and parameters as the method in the superclass. This is core to our ability to implement polymorphism. This allows the subclass to define its own unique behavior for a method while maintaining its accessibility through the superclass.

To illustrate method overriding, we will modify the **move()** method in our **Animal** class so it has an output message that is appropriate for a generic implementation. Then, we will override the **move()** method in the **Canine** and **Corgi** classes.

The following is the modified **move()** method for the **Animal** class:

```
public void move() {
    System.out.println("The animal moves appropriately in its habitat.");
}
```

Next, we need to override the **move()** method in the **Canine** class. The following is the code we will add to our **Canine** class:

```
@Override
public void move() {
    System.out.println("The dog runs around playfully in its habitat.");
}
}
```

As aforementioned, we used the **@Override** annotation to let Java know the method is overridden. The **move()** method in the **Canine** class is more specific than what is available in the **Animal** class.

Next, let us further specialize the **move()** method in the **Corgi** class. The following is the code:

```
@Override
public void move() {
    System.out.println("The " + subBreed + " trots with short, bounding
steps.");
}
```

Now, our **Corgi** class overrides the **move()** method with an implementation specific to Corgis. This demonstrates how each class in the hierarchy can provide its own method of implementation.

Dynamic method dispatch

A second approach to implementing polymorphism in Java is dynamic method dispatch. This approach involves Java making a runtime determination regarding which overridden method to execute based on the actual object type rather than the reference type. This permits us to write code that operates on superclass references and invokes subclass-specific behavior.

We will use our **Animal** hierarchy to demonstrate polymorphism with dynamic method dispatch.

The following is the code for an **AnimalSanctuary** application:

```
public class AnimalSanctuary {
    public static void main(String[] args) {
        Animal genericAnimal = new Animal("Generic species", "various
habitats");
        Animal dogAnimal = new Canine("Canis lupus familiaris", "Domestic",
"Mixed breed");
        Animal corgiAnimal = new Corgi("Canis lupus familiaris", "Domestic",
"Corgi", "Pembroke Welsh Corgi");
        genericAnimal.move(); // Calls Animal's move() method
```

```
        dogAnimal.move();       // Calls Canine's move() method due to
polymorphism
        corgiAnimal.move();     // Calls Corgi's move() method due to
polymorphism
    }
}
```

The output of this application is provided as follows:

The animal moves appropriately in its habitat.

The dog runs around playfully in its habitat.

The Pembroke Welsh Corgi trots with short, bounding steps.

In our example, we created three objects (**genericAnimal**, **dogAnimal**, and **corgiAnimal**) and declared them all as **Animal** types. A runtime, Java determines which **move()** method to call based on the type of the object:

- **genericAnimal.move()** calls the **move()** method in the **Animal** class.

- **dogAnimal.move()** calls the overridden **move()** method in the **Canine** class.

- **corgiAnimal.move()** calls the overridden **move()** method in the **Corgi** class.

The dynamic method dispatch approach empowers us to write highly flexible code. We can write methods that use superclass references, and Java will use the most specific implementation available at runtime.

Full implementation

Let us bring all the pieces together and demonstrate how polymorphism can simplify our code. Consider an **animalMovement()** method that accepts an **Animal** parameter and calls its **move()** method. With polymorphism, we can pass any subclass of **Animal** to this method, and it will exhibit the behavior specific to that subclass. We will start with a new **Zoo** class as follows:

```
public class Zoo {
    public void animalMovement(Animal animal) {
        animal.move();
    }
}
```

Now we will create a **NashvilleZoo** application to call the **AnimalMovement()** method with different types of animals:

```
public class NashvilleZoo {
    public static void main(String[] args) {
```

```
        Zoo zoo = new Zoo();

        Animal genericAnimal = new Animal("Generic species", "various
habitats");
        Animal dog = new Canine("Canis lupus familiaris", "Domestic", "Mixed
breed");
        Animal corgi = new Corgi("Canis lupus familiaris", "Domestic",
"Corgi", "Pembroke Welsh Corgi");

        zoo.animalMovement(genericAnimal);
        zoo.animalMovement(dog);
        zoo.animalMovement(corgi);
    }
}
```

The following is the output from this program:

The animal moves appropriately in its habitat.

The dog runs around playfully in its habitat.

The Pembroke Welsh Corgi trots with short, bounding steps.

In our example, we created an **animalMovement()** method in a **Zoo** class that can accept any **Animal** object. It relies on polymorphism to call the appropriate **move()** method. If we were to add a new animal type, such as **Bird** or **Fish**, the **animalMovemet()** method would not need to be changed as long as **Bird** and **Fish** were subclasses of **Animal** and override the **move()** method.

Benefits

As we conclude our coverage of polymorphism and method overriding, let us recap the top three benefits of implementing this in our programs:

- **Simplified code**: Polymorphism allows us to use common interfaces, making our code less bloated and easier to read and maintain.

- **Code reusability**: When we write generic code that can be used by several classes, we reduce code duplication. This makes our code both more readable and easier to maintain.

- **Flexibility**: Using polymorphism, we can introduce new subclasses without the need to modify existing code. This is a common theme among OOP principles.

Access modifiers and encapsulation

Encapsulation is a core OOP principle that enables us to write Java programs that keep data safe from misuse. In Java, we use access modifiers such as private and protected to set the accessibility of classes, attributes, and methods. With encapsulation, we can restrict how certain parts of our code are allowed to interact with other parts. This results in code that is secure, modular, and maintainable.

In Java, we implement encapsulation with an access modifier. These modifiers control where classes and their components (attributes and methods) can be accessed from. The default is referred to as package-private and enforces that, without an explicit access modifier, entities are only accessible within the same package. Let us examine the primary access modifiers as follows:

- The **public** access modifier is the least restrictive. Components declared as **public** are accessible from any other class.

- The **private** access modifier is the most restrictive modifier. Components declared as **private** are accessible only within the class in which they are defined.

- The **protected** access modifier allows components to be accessible within the same package and by subclasses, even if they are in different packages.

Each of these modifiers plays a key role in encapsulation. In the next section, we will put encapsulation into practice, focusing on the **private** access modifier.

Private

Our primary approach to implementing encapsulation is to make our class attributes private. This restricts direct access from outside the class. When we write our classes, we can include public getter and setter methods, providing controlled access to the class's attributes. This is an important aspect of OOP as it allows us to protect the internal state of any object, only exposing necessary information. It also permits data validation before any attribute value changes.

Let us look at encapsulation in the **Animal2** and **Canine2** classes. We are using new classes, so the original classes remain unchanged from the previous section. The following is the **Animal2** class:

```java
public class Animal2 extends Species {
    // Private attributes (encapsulation)
    private String habitat;
    private double weight;
    // Constructor
    public Animal2(String scientificName, String habitat, double weight) {
```

```
        super(scientificName);
        this.habitat = habitat;
        this.weight = weight;
    }
    // Getter and setter for habitat
    public String getHabitat() {
        return habitat;
    }
    public void setHabitat(String habitat) {
        this.habitat = habitat;
    }
    // Getter and setter for weight
    public double getWeight() {
        return weight;
    }
    public void setWeight(double weight) {
        if (weight > 0) { // Simple validation
            this.weight = weight;
        }
    }
}
```

We implemented encapsulation in our **Animal2** class by declaring the **habitat** and **weight** attributes as **private**. This prevents direct access to them from outside of the class. Controlled access is provided via the getter and setter methods for those attributes. We also implemented a simple validation in our **setWeight()** method, ensuring that no value below zero is applied.

Next, we will create a **Dog2** class to demonstrate encapsulating attributes in a subclass. The following is the code:

```
public class Dog2 extends Animal2 {
    private String breed;
    public Dog2(String scientificName, String habitat, double weight, String
breed) {
        super(scientificName, habitat, weight);
        this.breed = breed;
    }
    // Getter and setter for breed
    public String getBreed() {
        return breed;
    }
```

```
    public void setBreed(String breed) {
        this.breed = breed;
    }
}
```

Our **Dog2** class contains a breed attribute with a **private** access modifier. This means it can only be accessed via its getter and setter methods. This encapsulation protects the attributes from unintended changes from outside the class.

Protected

We now turn to the **protected** access modifier. It allows attributes and methods to be accessible in the same package and by subclass, regardless of whether they are in the same package or not.

> Note:A package in Java is like a file folder on your computer. Keeping related classes and subclasses together is a smart organizational approach.

The **protected** access modifier is especially important when it comes to inheritance, where subclasses need access to certain attributes and methods in the superclass. The following **Bird2** class extends **Animal2**:

```
public class Bird2 extends Animal2 {
    protected String featherColor;
    public Bird2(String scientificName, String habitat, double weight, String featherColor) {
        super(scientificName, habitat, weight);
        this.featherColor = featherColor;
    }
    public void fly() {
        System.out.println("The bird flies through the " + getHabitat());
    }
}
```

The **Bird2** class has a single attribute, **featherColor**, that is marked as **protected**. This means it can be accessed by any subclass of **Bird2** or other classes in the same package. The **fly()** method uses the **public getHabitat()** getter method in the **Animal2** class. As our examples illustrate, the **protected** modifier is the perfect balance between inheritance and access control.

Full implementation

Let us create a **Zoo2** application to demonstrate how access modifiers interact in a program. We will use **Animal2**, **Dog2**, and **Bird2** classes. First, we need to add a **move()** method in our **Animal2** class. The following is the code:

```
    // Method
    public void move() {
        System.out.println("The animal moves appropriately in its habitat.");
    }
```

Next, we create our **Zoo2** class as follows:

```
public class Zoo2 {
    public static void main(String[] args) {
        // Creating instances
        Animal2 genericAnimal = new Animal2("Canis lupus", "Forests", 70.5);
        Dog2 dog = new Dog2("Canis lupus familiaris", "Domestic", 12.5,
"Labrador");
        Bird2 bird = new Bird2("Corvus corax", "Mountains", 1.2, "Black");

        // Accessing public methods
        System.out.println("Animal habitat: " + genericAnimal.getHabitat());
        System.out.println("Dog breed: " + dog.getBreed());
        System.out.println("Bird feather color: " + bird.featherColor); //
Allowed because of protected access

        // Modifying attributes through public setters
        genericAnimal.setWeight(75.0);
        System.out.println("Updated weight: " + genericAnimal.getWeight());

        // Attempting direct access to private attribute (will result in an
error if uncommented)
        // dog.weight = 15.0;

        // Calling public methods
        dog.move();
        bird.fly();
    }
}
```

The output from the **Zoo2** class is as follows:

```
Animal habitat: Forests
Dog breed: Labrador
Bird feather color: Black
Updated weight: 75.0
The animal moves appropriately in its habitat.
```

The bird flies through the Mountains

In our example, the `getHabitat()` and `getWeight()` methods provide controlled access to the `habitat` and `weight` attributes. We also see that the `bird.featureColor` attribute is accessible in the `Zoo2` class because the `protected` method was used, giving us access within the same package.

Conclusion

By the end of this chapter, we explored the basics of OOP and how to implement them in Java. The four key principles of OOP (abstraction, encapsulation, inheritance, and polymorphism) were covered with explanations and code examples. You had the opportunity to learn how these principles can help us write highly structured code that is modular, reusable, readable, and maintainable.

The chapter also examined how to define and use classes and objects, which laid the framework for our ability to build complex programs. Constructors and constructor overloading were covered in detail, highlighting how to create and initialize objects. The chapter explored inheritance and demonstrated how to enable code reuse through hierarchical class relationships and the super keyword. Polymorphism and method overriding demonstrated Java's flexibility by allowing the same method to behave differently based on the calling object's class. Finally, the chapter demonstrated how encapsulation and access modifiers such as private, protected, and public can be used to create secure, well-organized code.

In the next chapter, *Chapter 4, Advanced OOP Concepts,* we will build on the basics of OOP and explore advanced topics like interfaces and abstract classes. As you can learn, they give us great flexibility and extensibility with our Java applications. The chapter will demonstrate how to implement multiple inheritance using interfaces and explore functional interfaces as well as default methods. Additional advanced topics include lambdas and method references for simplified functional programming.

Points to remember

- Access modifiers control the visibility and accessibility of classes, attributes, and methods.

- Abstraction hides the complexity of class implementations, exposing only the necessary parts of an object's functionality.

- An object is an instance of a class created using the new keyword.

- Class hierarchies represent real-world relationships and allow organized, reusable code structures.

- Constructor overloading allows for multiple constructors with different parameter lists, providing flexibility in how we initialize objects.

- Constructors are special methods used to initialize new objects, establishing their initial attribute values.

- Dynamic method dispatch enables Java to choose the appropriate overridden method based on the object's type at runtime.

- Encapsulation bundles data and methods within a class and restricts access to the class's attributes, ensuring data integrity.

- Getter methods provide controlled access to private attributes, allowing external classes to safely retrieve attribute values.

- Inheritance allows a class to inherit attributes and methods from a parent class, promoting code reuse.

- Method overriding allows a subclass to provide a specific implementation of a method that exists in its superclass.

- Objects created from the same class are unique, each occupying its own memory space and holding its own attribute values.

- Polymorphism enables objects of different classes to be treated as instances of a common superclass.

- Private access restricts members to the same class, ensuring they are not accessible outside of it.

- Protected access allows members to be accessible within the same package and by subclasses, even if they are in different packages.

- Public access allows members to be accessible from any other class, creating a clear interface for interacting with objects.

- Setter methods enable controlled modification of private attributes, often including validation to ensure data integrity.

- The super keyword allows a subclass to call its superclass's constructor and access its methods.

- Using classes and objects as building blocks in Java enables the creation of structured, modular, and reusable code.

Case studies

These case studies provide realistic scenarios that encourage you to think critically about applying OOP principles like encapsulation, access control, inheritance, and polymorphism in a variety of contexts.

The key case studies are provided as follows:

- **Managing access to sensitive data**: *StarTech Solutions* is a software development company that builds applications for managing data security in cloud environments. Their team recently started using OOP to create secure and scalable client applications. The lead developer designed a basic class hierarchy, including User, Admin, and SuperAdmin classes, which inherit from a base Person class. However, as the project evolves, the team struggles with management's access to sensitive data. They need to determine the best access modifiers and encapsulation strategies to protect user information across their application.

  o **For your consideration**: How can the team use private, protected, and public access modifiers to encapsulate sensitive user information while allowing appropriate access for different roles? What potential benefits could they realize if they implemented getter and setter methods to control access to critical data?

- **Constructor overloading for efficiency**: *Andromeda Analytics* is developing a new application to analyze user behavior for an e-commerce platform. They created a Product class with several attributes, including name, price, description, and stockQuantity. The team also plans to implement a DiscountedProduct subclass that adjusts prices dynamically based on seasonal discounts. Currently, they are using constructor overloading to provide different ways to initialize Product and DiscountedProduct objects. However, the development team is unsure if their overloaded constructors align with future requirements and if there is a more efficient way to initialize DiscountedProduct objects.

  o **For your consideration**: What are the advantages of using constructor overloading for initializing products with and without discount information? How could the team use the super keyword effectively to initialize attributes in the DiscountedProduct subclass without duplicating code from the Product class?

- **The need for polymorphism**: *Hyperion Robotics* specializes in building software for autonomous robots used in space exploration. They have developed an Entity class as a base for all robots, from which they inherit subclasses like Rover, Drone, and Orbiter. Each robot type has unique capabilities: rovers navigate rough terrain, drones fly, and orbiters monitor the atmosphere. The engineering team implemented a move() method in the Entity class and used polymorphism to allow each subclass to define specific movement behaviors. However, they are struggling to manage method overriding for different movement types effectively, as each subclass requires highly customized behaviors.

  o **For your consideration**: How can the team use method overriding to define unique movement behaviors for each robot type while maintaining a common interface for the move() method? What role does polymorphism play in allowing the development team to add new robot types in the future without major codebase changes?

- **Balance between encapsulation and controlled access**: *Celestial Insights* provides astrological data analysis and has recently launched a new project to create a client-facing platform for customized horoscope predictions. The platform includes classes such as Customer, Subscription, and Prediction. To secure customer data, the team has implemented private access modifiers on all sensitive information within the Customer class. However, they need to allow the Subscription class to access specific customer details for billing purposes. The team is considering different approaches to balance encapsulation and controlled data access.

  o **For your consideration**: How can the team leverage getter methods to provide controlled access to private customer data for the Subscription class? What alternatives could the development team explore, such as using the protected modifier or extending the Customer class, to manage access across related classes?

- **Maintaining data privacy**: *Orion Genomics* is building an application to store and analyze genomic data for medical research. The development team has implemented an OOP structure with Sample, DNASequence, and Gene classes. Each Sample object includes sensitive patient data, requiring strict data protection through private access modifiers. The DNASequence class, which inherits from Sample, needs access to non-sensitive sample information for analysis. The development team wants to use encapsulation and inheritance effectively to maintain data privacy while providing appropriate access for analysis.

  o **For your consideration**: How might the development team use encapsulation with private and protected modifiers to control access to sensitive patient data in Sample while allowing necessary access for DNASequence? What are the advantages of creating getter and setter methods for non-sensitive data in the Sample class, and how might they enforce data privacy across subclasses?

Multiple choice questions

1. **Which access modifier allows members to be accessible only within the same class?**

   a. Public

   b. Private

   c. Protected

   d. Default

2. **What is the main purpose of encapsulation in Java?**

   a. To allow all classes to access private data

   b. To support inheritance among classes

   c. To hide implementation details and protect data from misuse

   d. To make all attributes publicly accessible

3. **When is the super keyword most commonly used?**

   a. To call the superclass's constructor and access superclass methods

   b. To create overloaded constructors in a subclass

   c. To declare a class's private attributes

   d. To implement interfaces in a class

4. **Which OOP principles allow objects of different classes to be treated as objects of a common superclass?**

   a. Encapsulation

   b. Abstraction

   c. Inheritance

   d. Polymorphism

5. **What is the purpose of a getter method in Java?**

   a. To initialize an object's attributes

   b. To access private attributes in a controlled way

   c. To allow subclasses to inherit superclass attributes

   d. To enforce polymorphism in a superclass

Answers

1.	b.
2.	c.
3.	a.
4.	d.
5.	b.

Questions

1. How does encapsulation improve the security and maintainability of a Java application? Share an example where failing to use encapsulation might lead to unintended issues.

2. In what scenarios would you prefer to use private access modifiers over protected access modifiers and vice versa? Provide examples of situations that illustrate the importance of choosing the appropriate access level.

3. Constructor overloading allows for multiple ways to initialize objects in a class. What are the benefits and potential drawbacks of using overloaded constructors, especially in complex classes?

4. Polymorphism enables a single method call to produce different behaviors depending on the class that implements it. How does this principle make code more flexible, and what are some specific examples of where you might use polymorphism in a real-world application?

5. Java supports inheritance through the extends keyword, allowing one class to inherit from another. What are some potential pitfalls of using inheritance extensively? How would you balance inheritance with other OOP principles to ensure a clean, manageable code structure?

6. The super keyword is often used to call the superclass's constructor and access its methods. Why is this useful in subclasses, and how does it support the overall structure of the class hierarchy?

7. What are the pros and cons of creating getter and setter methods to access private fields in a class? Share a scenario where you might choose not to provide these methods for specific attributes.

8. How might the concept of method overriding help in designing a class hierarchy that includes general and specific classes, such as Animal and Dog? Describe a situation where method overriding might be more useful than creating entirely separate methods.

9. Access modifiers help control the visibility of attributes and methods. In an application with sensitive data, how would you design a class structure to ensure that only necessary classes can access specific data? Consider a scenario involving a customer database.

10. Reflect on the four main OOP principles: encapsulation, inheritance, polymorphism, and abstraction. Which principle do you find most challenging to implement effectively, and why? How would you explain its importance to someone new to programming?

Challenges

The following questions are provided to self-assess your knowledge of the chapter's content and apply critical thinking to key concepts:

- **Secure data encapsulation**:

- o **Objective**: Implement encapsulation to protect sensitive data within a class.

- o **Activity**: Perform the following actions:

  - Create a Student class with private attributes such as name, id, grade, and socialSecurityNumber.

  - Use **public** getter and setter methods to provide controlled access to all attributes.

  - Add validation in the setter methods to prevent invalid data (e.g., grades must be between 0 and 100).

  - Test your class by creating Student objects and attempting to set invalid values.

- o **Real-world applicability**: Encapsulation is crucial for protecting sensitive data in applications. This challenge is intended to help you understand how to control access to data and enforce data integrity through the proper use of access modifiers and validation.

- **Constructor overloading in action**:

  - o **Objective**: Implement constructor overloading for flexible object initialization.

  - o **Activity**: Perform the following actions:

    - Create a **Book** class that includes attributes such as title, author, ISBN, and price.

    - Implement three overloaded constructors:

      - ◆ One that takes all attributes.

      - ◆ One that only takes the title and author.

      - ◆ A default constructor with no parameters.

    - Write a test program that creates Book objects using all three constructors and displays their details.

  - o **Real-world applicability**: Constructor overloading allows Java developers to create objects with varying levels of detail, adapting to different use cases. This challenge is designed to help you practice designing flexible initialization options for classes.

- **Designing a class hierarchy**:

  - o **Objective**: Build a simple class hierarchy to demonstrate inheritance and method overriding.

- **Activity**: Perform the following actions:

  - Create a base class Vehicle with a move() method that prints a generic message about moving.

  - Create subclasses Car and Bicycle, each overriding the move() method to print a vehicle-specific movement message.

  - Instantiate both Car and Bicycle objects and call their move() methods to see the different outputs.

- **Real-world applicability**: Inheritance models real-world relationships and reduces code duplication by allowing subclasses to inherit common behavior from a base class. This challenge is designed to help you understand how inheritance and method overriding can lead to more organized and maintainable code.

- **Implementing polymorphism with dynamic method dispatch**:

  - **Objective**: Use polymorphism to create flexible methods that handle different subclasses.

  - **Activity**: Perform the following actions:

    - Create a Pet class with a makeSound() method that prints a generic message.

    - Extend the Pet class to create Dog and Cat subclasses, each overriding makeSound() to print their specific sounds (e.g., *The dog barks.* and *The cat purrs.*).

    - Write a method playWithPet(Pet pet) that calls makeSound() on a Pet object.

    - Test this method with both Dog and Cat objects.

  - **Real-world applicability**: Polymorphism allows us to write methods that operate on a superclass while enabling subclass-specific behavior. This challenge demonstrates the power of dynamic method dispatch in creating adaptable and reusable code.

- **Using access modifiers to create secure classes**:

  - **Objective**: Apply different access modifiers to create a secure class structure.

  - **Activity**: Perform the following actions:

    - Design a BankAccount class with private attributes accountNumber, balance, and ownerName.

- Add public methods to deposit and withdraw money, ensuring that the withdrawal method checks for sufficient funds before allowing the transaction.

- Use protected access for a calculateInterest() method that calculates monthly interest based on a protected interestRate attribute.

- Write a test program to interact with the BankAccount object, showing how the different access modifiers work in practice.

- o **Real-world applicability**: Managing access to class members is crucial in software applications that deal with sensitive data. This challenge is designed to help you understand how to use access modifiers to control what information is exposed and what remains protected.

Self-assessment

The following questions are provided to self-assess your knowledge of the chapter's content and apply critical thinking to key concepts:

1. What is the main purpose of encapsulation in OOP, and how does Java enforce it?

2. Explain the difference between method overloading and method overriding. Provide an example of when you might use each.

3. Why is the super keyword important in inheritance? Describe a situation where you would use it.

4. Imagine you are designing a class hierarchy for a transportation system. You create a superclass Vehicle and subclasses Car, Bicycle, and Boat. How could you use polymorphism to write a method that handles all types of vehicles without modifying the method for each new vehicle type?

5. Reflect on the access modifiers in Java (public, protected, private, and default). Why is it generally good practice to make class attributes private? How does this impact the security and maintainability of your code?

Answers

1. The main purpose of encapsulation is to restrict direct access to an object's data and to control how that data is modified or accessed. Java enforces encapsulation by making class attributes private and providing public getter and setter methods to access and modify the values safely. This protects the internal state of an object, prevents accidental modification, and helps maintain data integrity.

2. Method overloading occurs when multiple methods in the same class have the same name but different parameter lists. This permits multiple ways to call a method based on different inputs. This is often used in constructors to initialize objects with varying data. Method overriding, on the other hand, allows a subclass to provide a specific implementation of a method already defined in its superclass. This is useful when a subclass needs to modify the behavior of a method inherited from the parent class, such as defining unique behavior in a move() method for different animal types.

3. The super keyword allows a subclass to call the constructor or methods of its superclass, which provides a way to initialize inherited attributes or invoke parent methods. It is important because it helps avoid code duplication and maintains a clear link between superclass and subclass functionality. For instance, if a subclass Dog inherits from a superclass Animal, the Dog constructor might use super(habitat) to initialize the inherited habitat attribute, ensuring that the superclass's constructor is called and the attribute is correctly initialized.

4. Polymorphism allows us to create a single method in the Vehicle superclass, such as move(), and then override this method in each subclass (Car, Bicycle, Boat) to define specific movement behavior. For example, the move() method in Car might print, The car drives, while Bicycle might print, The bicycle pedals. You could then write a method like testVehicle(Vehicle v) that calls v.move(). Due to polymorphism, Java will automatically call the appropriate move() method based on the actual object type, allowing testVehicle to work with any Vehicle subclass without modification.

5. Making class attributes private is a good practice because it restricts direct access to those attributes from outside the class. This allows the class itself to control how and when they are modified through public methods. This protects the integrity of the data and prevents accidental modification or misuse. By controlling access with private attributes, we improve the security and maintainability of our code. This approach ensures that only specific methods (e.g., getters and setters) can modify them, allowing validation and error handling to be centralized. Encapsulating data this way makes the code more readable and maintainable.

Join our Discord space

Join our Discord workspace for latest updates, offers, tech happenings around the world, new releases, and sessions with the authors:

https://discord.bpbonline.com

CHAPTER 4
Advanced OOP Concepts

Introduction

The **object-oriented programming (OOP)** framework is core to Java development. It provides us with a robust framework and set of tools and practices to develop applications that are modular, scalable, safe, and maintainable. *Chapter 3, Object-oriented Programming Basics,* introduced the foundational principles of OOP, including encapsulation, inheritance, and polymorphism. This chapter will discuss the advanced OOP concepts in detail to help you exploit the full power of Java's OOP capabilities.

This chapter explores advanced OOP concepts, including interfaces and abstract classes, which give us tremendous flexibility and extensibility in our software designs. Coverage includes how interfaces enable multiple inheritances in Java, functional interfaces, and default methods. Lambda expressions and method references are also covered in this chapter.

Our goal is to use these advanced OOP concepts to help us write cleaner, more concise code while, at the same time, simplifying modern Java coding. By the end of this chapter, you should have a thorough understanding of OOP and gain practical skills for structuring complex applications with advanced design patterns.

Structure

This chapter covers the following topics:

- Introduction to interfaces
- Working with abstract classes
- Multiple inheritance in Java via interfaces
- Functional interfaces and default methods
- Lambdas and method references
- Object lifecycle

Objectives

This chapter was designed to help you understand and gain experience with implementing interfaces to enable flexibility in Java. As you work through this chapter, be mindful of the differences between abstract classes and interfaces, as it is important that you understand when to use each. By the end of this chapter, you should have confidence in your abilities to utilize functional interfaces and default methods to simplify your coding practices. You will have the opportunity to write and apply lambda expressions and method references for streamlined functional programming. Lastly, once you complete this chapter, you should be able to manage the lifecycle of objects in Java and apply advanced OOP concepts to design scalable and maintainable Java applications.

Introduction to interfaces

Interfaces in Java allow us to define contracts (requirements) for implementing classes. This is a foundational component of our ability to write flexible and scalable software applications. We accomplish this by enabling multiple inheritance, abstractions, and supporting polymorphism. The use of interfaces empowers us to design systems that are easy to read, maintain, and extend.

An interface in Java is a reference type with some similarities to classes. Interfaces can only contain the following components:

- Constants
- Method signatures
- Default methods
- Static methods

- Nested types

Interfaces cannot contain the following:

- Instance variables

- Constructors

Note: Interfaces cannot instantiate objects directly.

Interfaces cannot instantiate objects directly; instead, they define a contract that other classes must adapt by implementing the interface. To fully understand this concept, think of an interface as a blueprint for designing different types of buildings. For example, every building must have a foundation, roof, walls, and a way to get in and out of it, but the specific implementation of these components can vary widely depending on the builder, location, and type of building.

This section introduces the concept of interfaces, their syntax, and their use cases, along with practical examples drawn from the architecture of buildings and hierarchies to clarify the concepts.

Note: The previous chapter introduced OOP using the animal kingdom hierarchy to support knowledge transfer. The chapter uses architectural hierarchy to further your understanding of OOP. This should provide you with additional context when studying OOP and advanced OOP concepts.

Syntax and implementation

To create an interface, we simply need to use the **interface** keyword in its definition. The following **Building** interface shows the basic structure of an interface:

```java
public interface Building {
    void buildFoundation();
    void constructWalls();
    void addRoof();
}
```

In this example, **Building** is the name of our interface. Classes that implement this interface will be required to honor the contract, which consists of creating abstract **buildFoundation()**, **constructWalls()**, and **addRoof()** methods.

Let us look at two examples where classes use the **implements** keyword to implement our **Building** interface:

```java
public class Skyscraper implements Building {
    @Override
    public void buildFoundation() {
```

```
        System.out.println("Laying a deep concrete foundation for the
skyscraper.");
    }
    @Override
    public void constructWalls() {
        System.out.println("Constructing industrial steel and glass walls for
the skyscraper.");
    }
    @Override
    public void addRoof() {
        System.out.println("Adding a rooftop terrace for the skyscraper.");
    }
}
```

In the aforementioned example, you can see the **Skyscraper** class implements the **Building** interface and, therefore, has to define the same methods that are in the interface.

Now, let us look at a second implementation of the **Building** interface:

```
public class House implements Building {
    @Override
    public void buildFoundation() {
        System.out.println("Laying a shallow concrete foundation for the
house.");
    }
    @Override
    public void constructWalls() {
        System.out.println("Constructing brick and mortar walls for the
house.");
    }
    @Override
    public void addRoof() {
        System.out.println("Adding a gable roof for the house.");
    }
}
```

In our second example, we see the **House** class implements the **Building** interface and overrides the methods as per the interface's contract.

In both the **Skyscraper** and **House** implementations of the **Building** interface, all three methods were defined, just differently.

Multiple inheritance

Java gives us the flexibility to implement multiple interfaces at once. When we design our systems, we can have individual classes adopt behaviors from multiple interfaces. To demonstrate this, let us create two additional interfaces for building categories, **Commercial** and **Residential**:

```java
public interface Commercial {
    void addConferenceRooms();
    void addReceptionAreas();
}
public interface Residential {
    void addBedrooms();
    void addKitchen();
}
```

As you can see, we now have two additional interfaces, both with a contract of two methods. Next, let us write a class to implement multiple interfaces:

```java
public class DualUseBuilding implements Building, Residential, Commercial {
    @Override
    public void buildFoundation() {
        System.out.println("Laying a shared foundation for mixed-use
building.");
    }
    @Override
    public void constructWalls() {
        System.out.println("Constructing walls for mixed-use spaces.");
    }
    @Override
    public void addRoof() {
        System.out.println("Adding a shared roof for mixed-use building.");
    }
    @Override
    public void addBedrooms() {
        System.out.println("Adding residential apartments.");
    }
    @Override
    public void addConferenceRooms() {
        System.out.println("Adding office spaces with conference rooms.");
    }
    @Override
```

```
    public void addReceptionAreas() {
        System.out.println("Adding reception areas for each suite.");
    }
    @Override
    public void addKitchen() {
        System.out.println("Adding kitchen area for each suite.");
    }
}
```

In our example aforementioned, we created a **DualUseBuilding** class that implements three interfaces, each separated by a comma. All methods from the three interfaces must be defined; otherwise, you cannot compile and run your program.

Polymorphism

Interfaces allow objects of different classes to be treated as objects of the same interface type; thereby supporting polymorphism. This is the same thing as simply referring to buildings of all types (i.e., skyscrapers, houses, museums, etc.) as buildings.

The preceding example demonstrates runtime polymorphism. At compile time, the compiler only knows that the **building** is of type **Building**. However, at runtime, the actual method implementations in **Skyscraper** and **House** are called due to the object's true type.

Let us look at the following example in code:

```
public class ConstructionSite {
    public static void constructBuilding(Building building) {
        building.buildFoundation();
        building.constructWalls();
        building.addRoof();
    }
}
public class ConstructionCompany {
    public static void main(String[] args) {
        Building skyscraper = new Skyscraper();
        Building house = new House();
        ConstructionSite.constructBuilding(skyscraper);
        ConstructionSite.constructBuilding(house);
    }
}
```

Default and static methods

Let us continue our exploration of interfaces. We can extend their functionality by including default methods and static methods. When we create a default method in an interface, implementing classes can use it; they can also override it.

In the following example, we will update our **Building** interface by adding a **default** method:

```
public interface Building {
    void buildFoundation();
    void constructWalls();
    void addRoof();
    default void addBathrooms() {
        System.out.println("Adding bathrooms to the building.");
    }
}
```

Next, let us update a new class, **HouseBuilder**, that uses the **House** class, which takes advantage of the new **bathrooms() default** method in the **Building** interface:

```
public class HouseBuilder {
    public static void main(String[] args) {
        Building house = new House();
        house.addBathrooms();  // Invokes the default implementation
    }
}
```

Java also permits us to write utility methods within interfaces that are not tied to any instance. The following is an example implementation:

```
public interface BuildingUtilities {
    static void printBuildingInfo() {
        System.out.println("Buildings must be approved by the local Codes
office.");
    }
}
public class BuildingDriver {
    public static void main(String[] args) {
        BuildingUtilities.printBuildingInfo();
    }
}
```

Working with abstract classes

So far, we have explored classes and interfaces. One end of the spectrum we have fully implemented classes and, on the other end, pure abstraction with interfaces. In the middle of those are abstract classes. Abstract classes can have both concrete methods and abstract methods. Concrete methods are implemented, and abstract methods are not implemented. This pair of method types (concrete and abstract) allows us to both share code with related classes and mandate that certain methods are implemented in all subclasses.

Using this chapter's persistent architectural example, you can think of abstract classes as partially constructed building templates. One of these templates might specify how to create a foundation and add utilities, but leave the creation of walls and roofs up to the specific type of building. So, the foundation and utilities would be concrete methods, and the walls and roofs would be abstract methods.

We can declare classes with the **abstract** keyword, making them an abstract class. Objects of abstract classes cannot be instantiated directly; instead, subclasses can extend the abstract class and then provide concrete implementations of the methods in the abstract class.

The following is the syntax and structure of an abstract class:

```java
public abstract class BuildingTemplate {
    // Concrete Method: Shared implementation
    public void constructFoundation() {
        System.out.println("Constructing a standard concrete foundation.");
    }

    // Abstract Methods: Must be implemented by subclasses
    public abstract void constructWalls();

    public abstract void addRoof();
}
```

In the example code aforementioned, we declare **BuildingTemplate** as an abstract class using the **abstract** keyword. We define **constructFoundation()** as a concrete method, which is implemented in this class and shared across all building types. We also defined **constructWalls()** and **addRoof()** as abstract methods, which require specific implementation by each subclass.

Abstract class implementation

As we previously covered, subclasses inherit abstract methods from abstract classes, and they must implement them.

The following examples show how different building types can implement the **BuildingTemplate** abstract class:

```java
public class Restaurant extends BuildingTemplate {
    @Override
    public void constructWalls() {
        System.out.println("Consstructing brick and mortar walls for the
restaurant.");
    }
    @Override
    public void addRoof() {
        System.out.println("Adding a flat-top roof to the restaurant.");
    }
}
public class Bank extends BuildingTemplate {
    @Override
    public void constructWalls() {
        System.out.println("Constructing reinforced steel walls for the
bank.");
    }
    @Override
    public void addRoof() {
        System.out.println("Adding a steel and concrete roof to the bank.");
    }
}
```

With our **Restaurant** and **Bank** classes created and the abstract method implemented, we can use these classes to build specific types of buildings, as shown:

```java
public class ConstructionSite {
    public static void constructBuilding(BuildingTemplate building) {
        building.constructFoundation();
        building.constructWalls();
        building.addRoof();
    }
    public static void main(String[] args) {
        BuildingTemplate restaurant = new Restaurant();
        BuildingTemplate bank = new Bank();
        constructBuilding(restaurant);
        constructBuilding(bank);
```

```
        }
    }
```

Wrapping up abstract classes

As we have seen, abstract classes are a powerful OOP concept, allowing us to create both concrete and abstract methods. Concrete methods are shared across all subclasses, which helps reduce code duplication. Abstract methods are the ones that subclasses must implement. Each subclass can have its own unique abstract method implementation, and they must be implemented; otherwise, you will not be able to compile your program.

Abstract classes are useful when you want to share code with closely related classes, when you want to define both shared (concrete methods) and enforced behaviors (abstract classes), and when you want the shared base class to house instance variables or constructors.

Multiple inheritance in Java via interfaces

Multiple inheritance occurs when a class implements multiple interfaces. Java does not support multiple inheritance with classes because it introduces too much complexity. We can still implement multiple inheritance in Java using interfaces. This allows us to create programs where a single class can inherit attributes and behaviors from unrelated sources without introducing conflicts. Much like a child can inherit different attributes and behaviors from each of their biological parents, we can implement this in Java using interfaces.

Considering our architectural analogy, we can design a hybrid building that combines features from, for example, both residential and commercial buildings. We might construct a building that has a coffee shop on the first floor and apartments on the second and higher floors.

The following is an example code for a mixed-use building that combines behaviors from both the **Residential** and **Commercial** interfaces:

```java
public interface Residential {
    void addBedrooms();
    void addKitchen();
}
public interface Commercial {
    void addConferenceRooms();
    void addReceptionAreas();
}
public class MixedUseBuilding implements Residential, Commercial {
    @Override
    public void addConferenceRooms() {
        System.out.println("Adding a conference room and office spaces.");
```

```
    }
    @Override
    public void addReceptionAreas() {
        System.out.println("Adding a reception area near the front
entrance.");
    }
    @Override
    public void addBedrooms() {
        System.out.println("Adding residential apartments with bedrooms.");
    }
    @Override
    public void addKitchen() {
        System.out.println("Adding kitchens for each apartment.");
    }
}
```

Advantages and use cases

There are multiple advantages to using interfaces to implement multiple interfaces in Java. The first advantage and best practice is that interfaces separate contracts from the implementations. This allows us to create combinations of behaviors. Interfaces, in general, provide an organized approach to our code. We can encapsulate specific behaviors, improving the modularity of our code. Additionally, using interfaces to implement multiple interfaces in Java reduces code ambiguity, makes it easier to read, and, therefore, easier to troubleshoot and maintain.

The following are the primary use cases that warrant the use of multiple interfaces:

- When you want to avoid ambiguity, for example, you want to ensure there are no method name conflicts.

- We can enforce distinct custom behaviors when we implement multiple interfaces, making classes implement methods from multiple domains, such as with our **Residential** and **Commercial** interface example.

- When we want to define single responsibility interfaces.

Practical application

Let us put our use of multiple inheritance with interfaces to practical use. We will simulate building a smart building that inherits behaviors from multiple interfaces.

The following is the code:

```
public interface Sustainable {
```

```
    void installSolarPanels();
}
public interface Security {
    void addSurveillance();
}
public interface SmartSystems {
    void enableSmartLighting();
}
public class SmartBuilding implements Sustainable, SmartSystems, Security {
    @Override
    public void installSolarPanels() {
        System.out.println("Installing rooftop solar panels.");
    }
    @Override
    public void enableSmartLighting() {
        System.out.println("Enabling smart lighting for energy efficiency.");
    }
    @Override
    public void addSurveillance() {
        System.out.println("Adding high-resolution surveillance cameras.");
    }
}
```

As you can see, we created a **SmartBuilding** class that implements three interfaces (**Sustainable**, **Security**, and **SmartSystems**).

Let us look at one more practical example. We will simulate building a multipurpose event venue with interfaces such as **Concert**, **Conference**, and **Exhibition**.

```
public interface Concert {
    void setupAcousticSystem();
}
public interface Conference {
    void setupProjectionSystem();
}
public interface Exhibition {
    void configureOpenFloorPlan();
}
public class EventVenue implements Concert, Conference, Exhibition {
    @Override
    public void setupAcousticSystem() {
```

```
        System.out.println("Setting up acoustic panels for the concert.");
    }
    @Override
    public void setupProjectionSystem() {
        System.out.println("Setting up projection system for conference.");
    }
    @Override
    public void configureOpenFloorPlan() {
        System.out.println("Providing an open floor plan for exhibitions.");
    }
}
```

Functional interfaces and default methods

Functional interfaces are special interfaces that only contain a single abstract method. They serve as a core component of Java's functional programming model and, as you will see later in this chapter, as well as in *Chapter 8, Streams and Functional Programming*, they are used extensively with method references and lambda expressions.

Java requires functional interfaces to follow these rules:

- They can have multiple default or static methods.

- They can only have one abstract method.

We identify functional interfaces with the optional **@FunctionalInterface** annotation as shown:

```
@FunctionalInterface
public interface RoomDesigner {
    void designRoom(String roomType);
}
```

In the preceding example, the **designRoom(String roomType)** is the abstraction method that defines the functional interface's contract.

Note: **While the @FunctionalInterface annotation is optional, it is considered a best practice to always include it.**

Default methods

Default methods allow interfaces to include method implementations. This empowers us to maintain a balance between abstraction and reusability.

To define a default method in an interface, we use the **default** keyword as shown:

```
public interface Building {
    default void addBathrooms() {
        System.out.println("Adding bathrooms to the building.");
    }
}
```

Now, let us create a class **OfficeBuilding** to implement the **Building** interface and use its default method:

```
public class OfficeBuilding implements Building {
    @Override
    public void buildFoundation() {
        System.out.println("Constructing a deep foundation for the office
building.");
    }
    @Override
    public void constructWalls() {
        System.out.println("Constructing steel and glass walls for the
officebuilding.");
    }
    @Override
    public void addRoof() {
        System.out.println("Adding a roof to the office building.");
    }
    public static void main(String[] args) {
        Building office = new OfficeBuilding();
        office.addBathrooms(); // Uses the default implementation
    }
}
```

The output of this program is as follows:

Adding bathrooms to the building.

As you can see, our **OfficeBuilding** class did not implement the **addBathrooms()** method, but it can be called because it is a default method in the **Building** interface that the **OfficeBuilding** class implements.

Lambdas and method references

Lambdas and method references are among the advanced OOP constructs that Java offers us. As you will see in this section, lambdas enable us to write concise, reliable, and modular code when implementing abstract methods. Method references allow us to use shorthand for an existing method when implementing a functional interface. We will explore both constructs in this section.

Lambdas

A lambda expression is a way to implement a single abstract method of a functional interface. Java introduced this to eliminate boilerplate code and give us a concise approach to single abstract method implementation. This helps make our code more readable and, therefore, maintainable. It also supports functional programming, which we will explore in *Chapter 8, Streams and Functional Programming*.

The lambda expression syntax has three parts:

- Parameters encased in parentheses.

- The arrow operator (`->`), which separates the parameters and the body.

- The body, which is a code block enclosed in curly brackets.

The following is the syntax in the code:

```
(parameters) -> { body }
```

Using our architectural example from this chapter, consider lambdas as a flexible blueprint for specialized rooms (i.e., bedrooms). Instead of recreating a detailed blueprint for every variation, we can use lambdas to quickly create a reusable design.

Let us look at an example of designing a room within a building:

```
RoomDesigner designer = (roomType) -> {
    System.out.println("Designing a " + roomType);
};
designer.designRoom("Bedroom");
```

Compare the example below, which does not use a lambda expression:

```
RoomDesigner designer = new RoomDesigner() {
    @Override
    public void designRoom(String roomType) {
        System.out.println("Designing a " + roomType);
    }
};
designer.designRoom("Living Room");
```

Now, let us look at how we can concisely write the same code using a lambda expression:

```
RoomDesigner designer = roomType -> System.out.println("Designing a " +
roomType);

designer.designRoom("Living Room");
```

Method references

Java allows us to use the `::` operator as shorthand for existing methods.

Let us look at four examples, each with a different form.

The first form is with a static method reference. The syntax is **`ClassName::staticMethod`**.

The following is an example:
```java
public class Utilities {
    public static void designRoom(String roomType) {
        System.out.println("Designing a " + roomType + " using utilities.");
    }
}
RoomDesigner designer = Utilities::designRoom;

designer.designRoom("Office");
```

We can also use method reference shorthand with an instance method reference. This works with a specific object. The syntax is **`instance::instanceMethod`**.

The following is an example:
```java
BuildingPlanner planner = new BuildingPlanner();
RoomDesigner designer = planner::planRoom;

designer.designRoom("Library");
```

If we want to use the method reference shorthand for an instance method reference, with an arbitrary object, we would use this syntax: **`ClassName::instanceMethod`**.

The following is an example:
```java
Function<String, String> toUpperCase = String::toUpperCase;

System.out.println(toUpperCase.apply("building"));
```

The fourth method reference shorthand form is used for a constructor reference. The syntax is **`ClassName::new`**.

The following is an example:
```java
Supplier<BuildingPlanner> plannerSupplier = BuildingPlanner::new;

BuildingPlanner planner = plannerSupplier.get();
```

Use cases

Using lambdas and method references helps us write concise code, making our code more readable and maintainable. These techniques can seem daunting for beginning programmers, but as a developer's Java expertise increases, so should the use of lambdas and method references.

Generally, we should look to use lambdas when we need to define custom behaviors in line with the method call. Method references can be used when an existing method already provides the desired functionality.

Here are examples of using these techniques with our architectural analogy.

This first example uses a lambda as an approach to designing rooms with great flexibility:

```
RoomDesigner bedroomDesigner = room -> System.out.println("Designing a " +
room + " with modern furniture.");
bedroomDesigner.designRoom("Bedroom");
```

The following code is an example of a static method reference that leverages pre-defined utility methods:

```
public class RoomUtilities {
    public static void designStandardRoom(String roomType) {
        System.out.println("Designing a standard " + roomType);
    }
}
RoomDesigner standardDesigner = RoomUtilities::designStandardRoom;
standardDesigner.designRoom("Kitchen");
```

Our code snippet is an instance method reference example, which uses an existing object's method:

```
public class CustomRoomPlanner {
    public void customizeRoom(String roomType) {
        System.out.println("Customizing a " + roomType + " with user
preferences.");
    }
}
CustomRoomPlanner planner = new CustomRoomPlanner();
RoomDesigner customDesigner = planner::customizeRoom;
customDesigner.designRoom("Living Room");
```

We will explore lambdas in greater detail in *Chapter 8, Streams and Functional Programming*.

Object lifecycle

You should recall that the premise of OOP is that everything is an object. An object's lifecycle starts when it is created and ends with its destruction. Objects consume system memory, which is not released until the object is destroyed. To ensure our code runs efficiently and does not cause out-of-memory situations, we need to understand the object lifecycle.

This section continues with our architectural analogy. We can think of the lifecycle as a tiny building; it starts with construction (object creation), followed by its use (active lifecycle), and ends when the tiny building is demolished or repurposed (object destruction and **garbage collection (GC)**). Each stage in the lifecycle presents unique challenges and opportunities for us to optimize our code.

This section reviews each stage in the object lifecycle.

Object creation

The first stage of an object's lifecycle is object creation. We create objects using Java's **new** keyword or factory methods. When an object is created, memory is allocated in the **Java Virtual Machine (JVM)** heap. The heap is reserved for dynamic memory allocation. In addition, a reference to the object is stored in the stack memory. This is what holds method call information and local variables. The constructor is then called to initialize the object's state.

The following is an example:

```java
public class TinyBuilding {
    private String type;

    public TinyBuilding(String type) {
        this.type = type;
        System.out.println(type + " is constructed.");
    }
}
public class BuildTinyBuilding {
    public static void main(String[] args) {
        TinyBuilding cottage = new TinyBuilding("Cottage");
    }
}
```

The output from this example follows:

Cottage is constructed.

Next, let us review how to use the object.

Object use

Once an object is created, we can perform operations on it, store data, have it interact with other objects, and more.

The following is an example where we use the **Cottage** object we created in the previous lifecycle stage:

```
public class TinyBuilding {
    private String type;
    public TinyBuilding(String type) {
        this.type = type;
    }
    public void openDoor() {
        System.out.println("Opening the door of the " + type);
    }
}
```

As you can see, we added an **openDoor()** method to our **TinyBuilding** class.

Next, let us put that to use in our **BuildTinyBuilding** class, where our application's **main()** method exists:

```
public class BuildTinyBuilding {
    public static void main(String[] args) {
        TinyBuilding cottage = new TinyBuilding("Cottage");
        cottage.openDoor();
    }
}
```

The output of this program is shown as follows:

Opening the door of the Cottage

The following section covers the final lifecycle stage, destruction.

Object destruction

The object destruction stage of the object lifecycle is taken care of for us. Java automatically destroys objects when they are no longer referenced. If there are no references to an object, it cannot be reached or used, so it makes sense to free up (release) the memory those objects use.

This automatic resource reclamation is called GC. Java has a robust GC system that supports efficiency.

Let us explore Java's GC system, which is often abbreviated as GC.

As you can see in our following example code, we create a **TinyBuilding** object called **shed**. As it is set to **null**, there are no references to it, and Java will automatically reclaim the associated memory. The object will be destroyed. We can also explicitly call the garbage collector using the **System.gc()** method. This is how we get Java to run its garbage collector, although it does not guarantee that the **shed** will be destroyed.

```java
public class GarbageCollectionDemo {
    public static void main(String[] args) {
        TinyBuilding shed = new TinyBuilding("Shed");
        shed = null; // Eligible for garbage collection
        System.gc(); // Suggest garbage collection (not guaranteed)
    }
}
```

Best practices

It is important not to simply rely on Java's automatic GC system to keep our software running efficiently. This section reviews three best practices for managing the lifecycle of objects in our applications.

Minimize object creation

One of the easiest best practices to implement is to minimize object creation. We should avoid creating unnecessary objects regardless of application size. This is especially true for frequently used data types.

The following is an example:

```java
String tinyHome1 = "TinyHome";
String tinyHome2 = "TinyHome"; // Reuses the object from the string pool
```

Manage object references

We should strive to release references to objects when we no longer need them. This helps us avoid memory leaks.

Refer to the following code:

```java
public class Room {
    private TinyBuilding building;
    public void assignBuilding(TinyBuilding building) {
        this.building = building;
    }

    public void releaseBuilding() {
        this.building = null; // Release reference
    }
}
```

As you can see above, we set our object to **null**, releasing the object's reference and making it eligible for GC.

Explicitly close resources

We can explicitly close resources using the try-with-resources schema, which automatically closes the resource when the code block finishes execution.

Refer to the following code:

```
try (BufferedReader reader = new BufferedReader(new FileReader("tinyhome.
txt"))) {
    System.out.println(reader.readLine());
} catch (IOException e) {
    e.printStackTrace();

}
```

Using the try-with-resources schema is ideal for resources such as files, streams, and sockets.

Example

Let us look at a full example in code. We simulate the lifecycle of a **TinyBuilding2** object as follows:

```
public class TinyBuilding2 {
    private String name;
    public TinyBuilding2(String name) {
        this.name = name;
        System.out.println(name + " is constructed.");
    }
    public void useBuilding() {
        System.out.println(name + " is in use.");
    }
    @Override
    protected void finalize() throws Throwable {
        System.out.println(name + " is demolished.");
    }
}
```

The **TinyBuilding2Manager** application is our driver program. The following is the code:

```
public class TinyBuilding2Manager {
    public static void main(String[] args) {
        TinyBuilding2 tinyOffice = new TinyBuilding2("Tiny Office");
```

```
        tinyOffice.useBuilding();
        // De-reference the object to make it eligible for garbage collection
        tinyOffice = null;
        // Suggest garbage collection
        System.gc();
    }
}
```

The output of our program is shown as follows:

Tiny Office is constructed.

Tiny Office is in use.

As seen in the preceding code, we can use Java's **finalize()** method, which is called just before the object is garbage collected. The actual timing of the GC and the object's finalization is not guaranteed. It is, therefore, discouraged to use the **finalize()** method. The better alternative is to use the try-with-resources schema.

To drive this point home, the previous code might have provided the following output, but as you can see above, it did not. This speaks to the unpredictable behavior of the **finalize()** method.

Tiny Office is constructed.

Tiny Office is in use.

Tiny Office is demolished.

Conclusion

By the end of this chapter, we explored advanced OOP concepts that we can implement to create scalable and maintainable software systems. We started by covering interfaces and abstract classes; we examined how these constructs can enable flexibility and extensibility in our systems. We also looked at functional interfaces, default methods, lambdas, and method references. Additionally, we had the opportunity to understand how to use these constructs to make your Java code concise, easy to read, and maintainable. We concluded the chapter with a review of the object lifecycle and the critical role GC plays in memory management.

This chapter and its code examples were designed to provide insights into writing modular and reusable code while maintaining efficiency. The examples demonstrated how to leverage Java's advanced OOP capabilities to solve complex problems, implement best practices, manage resources effectively, and design systems that are robust and scalable.

The next chapter, *Chapter 5, Handling Errors and Exceptions*, introduces Java's sophisticated exception handling system. Effective error handling is crucial for creating robust Java applications, and this chapter explores the difference between checked and unchecked exceptions, how to use try-catch-finally blocks, and how to throw and handle exceptions in your code. Additionally, you can learn how to create custom exceptions and implement best practices for handling errors. The aim of this chapter is to help ensure you can handle unexpected issues gracefully and build applications that fail safely and informatively.

Points to remember

- Abstract classes allow the sharing of common code among related classes while enforcing the implementation of abstract methods in subclasses.

- Abstract methods in abstract classes must be implemented by subclasses, ensuring specific behaviors while sharing reusable code.

- An object's lifecycle consists of creation, active use, and destruction, with Java automatically managing memory through GC.

- Concrete methods in abstract classes provide shared implementations that help reduce code duplication across subclasses.

- Default methods in interfaces allow implementing classes to inherit and use method implementations while retaining the option to override them.

- Functional interfaces define a single abstract method, serving as the foundation for lambda expressions and method references.

- GC automatically reclaims memory used by objects that are no longer referenced, improving memory efficiency.

- Interfaces enable multiple inheritance in Java by allowing classes to implement multiple interfaces, combining distinct behaviors without conflicts.

- Lambdas provide a concise syntax for implementing functional interfaces, reducing boilerplate code, and improving readability.

- Method references offer a shorthand for referring to existing methods, enhancing code readability, and promoting reuse.

- Multiple inheritance through interfaces supports modularity by allowing classes to adopt behaviors from unrelated sources without ambiguity.

- Object creation occurs in the JVM heap, and memory is allocated using constructors or factory methods.

- Polymorphism allows objects of different classes to be treated as objects of the same interface type, enabling flexibility in design.

- Releasing references to objects when they are no longer needed can help prevent memory leaks and ensure objects become eligible for GC.

- The finalize() method is called before an object is destroyed by GC, but is deprecated due to its unpredictability.

- Try-with-resources ensures the automatic release of resources like files and sockets, making it a reliable alternative to finalize() for cleanup.

- Using interfaces promotes loose coupling and extensibility, which helps make code more readable and maintainable.

Case studies

These case studies provide realistic scenarios that encourage you to think critically about the concepts discussed in this chapter. Each scenario offers a realistic context for applying advanced OOP principles and promotes critical thinking about how to design and implement Java applications.

- **Starforge residential systems**: It is a startup that designs modular homes for off-world colonies. The company wants to develop a system where different types of homes, ranging from small domes to multi-unit habitats, share common features like a foundation and insulation, but have unique designs for walls and roofs based on planetary conditions. They also want to add optional components like solar panels or smart home controls.

  o **For your consideration**: How would you use abstract classes to define the common features (e.g., foundation and insulation)? How could you use interfaces to add optional features like solar panels or smart controls without impacting the core design? What role could polymorphism play in handling the construction process for different habitats?

- **Andromeda Event Center**: The Andromeda Event Center operates a multipurpose venue that can host concerts, conferences, and art exhibitions. Each event type has specific setup requirements, such as acoustic panels for concerts, projection systems for conferences, and open floor plans for exhibitions. The management wants a modular software design that allows them to dynamically configure the venue for different events.

  o **For your consideration**: How would you design interfaces for the specific requirements of each event type? Could multiple inheritance using interfaces be used effectively here? How would you ensure there is no ambiguity in method implementations? How might lambdas and method references simplify the scheduling and configuration of these events?

- **Galactic Bank secure systems**: Galactic Bank provides highly secure vaults and ATMs for its interplanetary customers. The company needs a software system that enforces strict security protocols for its bank buildings while also supporting modular expansion for residential or commercial components (e.g., an ATM in a commercial area). They also need to monitor and manage the lifecycle of vault objects to ensure they are properly released when no longer in use.

> ○ **For your consideration**: How could abstract classes be used to implement shared functionality for the core security features of bank buildings? How would you use interfaces to allow the modular expansion of residential or commercial components? What strategies would you use to manage the lifecycle of vault objects and ensure proper memory management?

- **Nebulae smart structures**: They develop smart buildings that adapt dynamically to usage patterns. The company's software must combine behaviors such as enabling smart lighting, adjusting climate control, and monitoring security cameras. Each smart feature should be independently modifiable and extendable for future updates.

  > ○ **For your consideration**: How would you use functional interfaces to model the independent behaviors of smart lighting, climate control, and security monitoring? Could default methods in interfaces be useful for adding shared functionality across multiple smart features? How would you implement this? How might GC impact the performance of this system, especially with dynamic changes in smart features? How would you use functional interfaces to model the independent behaviors of smart lighting, climate control, and security monitoring? Could default methods in interfaces be useful for adding shared functionality across multiple smart features? How would you implement this? How might GC impact the performance of this system, especially with dynamic changes in smart features?

- **Chronos modular construction**: They builds prefabricated structures that are assembled on-site. Each module, such as walls, roofs, and doors, has a specific design based on the customer's requirements. The company wants to create a system where each module can be defined independently but still adhere to a shared blueprint for compatibility.

  > ○ **For your consideration**: How would you use interfaces to enforce compatibility between different modules? What advantages would lambdas and method references offer for customizing the modules during assembly? How would you ensure that unused module objects are properly destroyed to optimize memory usage?

Multiple choice questions

1. **Which of the following best describes an abstract class in Java?**

   a. A class that can only have static methods.

   b. A class that cannot be instantiated and may contain both concrete and abstract methods.

   c. A class that defines a single abstract method.

   d. A class that implements multiple interfaces.

2. **What is the primary purpose of a functional interface?**

   a. To define a single abstract method for use with lambdas and method references.

   b. To provide multiple abstract methods for functional programming.

   c. To serve as a superclass for all Java classes.

   d. To prevent multiple inheritance in Java.

3. **Which of the following statements about interfaces in Java is true?**

   a. Interfaces can have constructors but cannot have static methods.

   b. Interfaces allow for multiple inheritance but cannot have instance variables.

   c. Interfaces are used to define concrete methods for shared behaviors.

   d. Interfaces can only have a single method to qualify as a functional interface.

4. **What happens to an object when it becomes eligible for GC in Java?**

   a. It is immediately destroyed by the JVM.

   b. Its finalize() method is always invoked.

   c. Its memory is reclaimed, although the exact timing is not guaranteed.

   d. The System.gc() method must be explicitly called to destroy it.

5. **Which feature allows Java to support multiple inheritance?**

   a. Abstract classes with concrete methods

   b. Method overloading

   c. Interfaces with default methods

   d. Static methods in functional interfaces

Answers

1.	b.
2.	a.
3.	b.
4.	c.
5.	c.

Questions

1. How do abstract classes and interfaces differ in terms of their use cases? Provide examples of when you would choose one over the other in a software design project.

2. Discuss the advantages and potential challenges of using multiple inheritance via interfaces in Java.

3. Reflect on the role of default methods in interfaces. How do they balance the need for abstraction and reusability? Share a scenario where using a default method might lead to design challenges.

4. Lambdas are designed to simplify code and improve readability. Do you find them intuitive, or do they make code harder to understand? Why might beginners struggle with lambdas?

5. In what scenarios would you prefer to use method references over lambdas? How do method references improve code maintainability?

6. Discuss the importance of managing the lifecycle of objects in Java. How does understanding GC help you write more efficient applications?

7. Polymorphism allows Java objects of different classes to be treated as objects of the same interface type. How does this capability contribute to modular and scalable software designs?

8. Explore the concept of functional interfaces. How do they enable the use of lambdas and method references? Provide examples where functional interfaces enhance code flexibility.

9. The finalize() method has been deprecated in modern Java. Why do you think it is no longer recommended? What alternatives are more reliable for resource cleanup?

10. Think about the architectural analogy used throughout this chapter. How did it help you understand the advanced OOP concepts? Propose another analogy that might also be effective for learning these topics.

Challenges

The following questions are provided to self-assess your knowledge of the chapter's content and apply critical thinking to key concepts:

- **Design a modular TinyHome system**:
  - o **Objective**: Implement multiple inheritance using interfaces to define distinct behaviors for a modular home system.
  - o **Activity**: Perform the following actions:
    - ▪ Create three interfaces: BasicModule, ResidentialFeatures, and CommercialFeatures.
    - ▪ Define methods in each interface that specify behaviors unique to those modules, such as addKitchen() in ResidentialFeatures and addReceptionArea() in CommercialFeatures.
    - ▪ Implement a TinyHome class that combines features from all three interfaces to create a mixed-use modular home.
    - ▪ Write a driver program to instantiate and use your TinyHome class, demonstrating its functionality.
  - o **Real-world applicability**: This challenge demonstrates how modularity in software design mirrors real-world requirements for flexible, scalable systems, such as housing projects with mixed functionalities.

- **Create a smart TinyOffice**:
  - o **Objective**: Develop a program that uses default methods in interfaces to provide shared functionality for smart features in a TinyOffice.
  - o **Activity**: Perform the following actions:
    - ▪ Create an interface SmartFeatures with default methods such as enableSmartLighting() and addSurveillance().
    - ▪ Implement a TinyOffice class that uses these default methods without overriding them.
    - ▪ Add a custom method setupOffice() in the TinyOffice class to demonstrate the use of smart features.
    - ▪ Write a driver program to instantiate and use the TinyOffice class, ensuring the default methods are invoked.
  - o **Real-world applicability**: This challenge highlights the benefits of reusability and modular design in building systems that incorporate cutting-edge features, such as smart offices or homes.

- **Abstracting TinyBuilding construction**:
  - o **Objective**: Design and implement an abstract class to streamline the construction of different types of tiny buildings.
  - o **Activity**: Perform the following actions:
    - ▪ Create an abstract class TinyBuildingTemplate with concrete methods like layFoundation() and abstract methods like buildWalls() and addRoof().
    - ▪ Implement two subclasses, TinyHouse and TinyCafe, that provide specific implementations for the abstract methods.
    - ▪ Write a driver program that uses a single method to construct both types of buildings using polymorphism.
  - o **Real-world applicability**: Abstract classes are essential in real-world software design, enabling code reuse while enforcing specific behaviors across related objects.

- **Managing the TinyBuilding lifecycle**:
  - o **Objective**: Simulate the lifecycle of a TinyBuilding, focusing on object creation, usage, and destruction with GC.
  - o **Activity**: Perform the following actions:
    - ▪ Create a class TinyBuildingLifecycle with methods to simulate construction (build()), use (operate()), and destruction (finalize()).
    - ▪ Instantiate the object in your main program, use its methods, and then set the reference to null to make it eligible for GC.
    - ▪ Explicitly suggest GC using System.gc(), and observe whether the finalize() method is called.
  - o **Real-world applicability**: Understanding the lifecycle of objects ensures efficient memory management in Java, which is critical for applications that handle dynamic resources.

- **Functional interfaces for room customization**:
  - o **Objective**: Use functional interfaces and lambdas to create a customizable room design system.
  - o **Activity**: Perform the following actions:
    - ▪ Create a functional interface RoomCustomizer with a single abstract method customizeRoom(String roomType).
    - ▪ Use lambdas to define room customization logic for at least three types of rooms (e.g., Bedroom, Kitchen, Office).

- Write a program that applies these lambda implementations to customize multiple rooms.

- Experiment with method references to replace one of the lambdas.

o **Real-world applicability**: Functional interfaces and lambdas allow developers to write concise, reusable logic, which is invaluable in scenarios like UI customization or event handling in modern applications.

Self-assessment

The following questions are provided so you can self-assess your knowledge of the chapter's content and apply critical thinking to key concepts as follows:

1. What are the key differences between abstract classes and interfaces in Java? In what situations would you choose one over the other?

2. Write an interface RoomFeatures with methods addLighting() and addHeating(). Then, create a class LivingRoom that implements this interface and provides specific implementations for the methods.

3. Given the following code snippet, identify and explain the purpose of the default keyword in the **Building** interface:

```
public interface Building {
    default void addBathrooms() {
        System.out.println("Adding bathrooms to the building.");
    }
}
```

4. How would you use functional interfaces and lambdas to dynamically add features to a tiny building during runtime? Provide a brief example.

5. If a class implements multiple interfaces with methods of the same signature, how should the class handle the ambiguity? Write a short example to demonstrate your solution.

Answers

1. Abstract classes can include both concrete and abstract methods, instance variables, and constructors. They are ideal when closely related classes share behavior. Interfaces can only include abstract methods (before Java 8) or default/static methods (from Java 8 onward). They are better suited for defining contracts that unrelated classes can implement. Use abstract classes when you want to share code among related classes. Use interfaces when you want to enforce a contract across unrelated classes or enable multiple inheritance.

2. See the code block as follows:

```
public interface RoomFeatures {
    void addLighting();
    void addHeating();
}
public class LivingRoom implements RoomFeatures {
    @Override
    public void addLighting() {
        System.out.println("Adding dimmable LED lighting.");
    }
    @Override
    public void addHeating() {
        System.out.println("Installing underfloor heating.");
    }
}
```

3. The default keyword allows interfaces to provide a concrete method implementation. This helps ensure backward compatibility when adding new methods to an interface. In the given example, the **addBathrooms()** method provides a default implementation, which can be inherited or overridden by implementing classes.

4. Functional interfaces and lambdas simplify adding features dynamically. For example:

```
@FunctionalInterface
public interface FeatureAdder {
    void addFeature(String feature);
}
public class TinyBuilding {
    public void applyFeature(FeatureAdder featureAdder, String feature)
    {
        featureAdder.addFeature(feature);
    }
}
public static void main(String[] args) {
    TinyBuilding building = new TinyBuilding();
    building.applyFeature(feature -> System.out.println("Adding " +
feature), "solar panels");
}
```

This allows for dynamic feature addition without hardcoding methods.

5. When implementing multiple interfaces with methods of the same signature, the class must override the conflicting method and provide its own implementation.

```java
public interface Residential {
    default void describe() {
        System.out.println("This is a residential building.");
    }
}
public interface Commercial {
    default void describe() {
        System.out.println("This is a commercial building.");
    }
}
public class MixedUseBuilding implements Residential, Commercial {
    @Override
    public void describe() {
        System.out.println("This is a mixed-use building.");
    }
}
```

By overriding **describe()**, **MixedUseBuilding** resolves the conflict and provides its own implementation.

Join our Discord space

Join our Discord workspace for latest updates, offers, tech happenings around the world, new releases, and sessions with the authors:

https://discord.bpbonline.com

CHAPTER 5
Handling Errors and Exceptions

Introduction

We spend a lot of time writing Java applications, and there are multiple things that can go wrong when our applications are run, including errors and exceptions. In the context of Java, errors are critical issues encountered that are beyond our application's control. Exceptions are recoverable problems that our code can handle. The ability to handle exceptions is the focus of this chapter.

Effective error-handling is a critical component of modern software development. As we write our programs, we have a good sense of what could go wrong, such as a missing file, and Java empowers us to manage those errors gracefully. We start by examining Java's exception hierarchy and understanding the differences between checked and unchecked exceptions. From there, the chapter demonstrates how to implement error-handling mechanisms using try-catch-finally blocks and explores exception propagation. As you will discover, exception propagation determines how errors travel through our application.

This chapter also introduces techniques for creating custom exceptions, which we can use to effectively communicate application-specific issues. You can discover how to test error-handling code to ensure robustness and reliability. The chapter concludes with best practices for designing fail-safe applications. The ability to gracefully handle exceptions is especially important when dealing with complex application components, such as file input/output, concurrency, and databases, each featured in later chapters in this book.

Structure

This chapter covers the following topics:

- Understanding Java exception hierarchy
- Checked vs. unchecked exceptions
- Try-catch-finally blocks
- Throwing exceptions and exception propagation
- Creating custom exceptions
- Testing exception handling

Objectives

This chapter aims to help the readers understand the structure and purpose of Java's exception hierarchy, differentiate between checked and unchecked exceptions and their use cases, and implement error-handling mechanisms using try-catch-finally blocks. By the end of this chapter, we will be able to utilize exception propagation and the throws keyword effectively, create custom exceptions tailored to specific application needs, and test exception handling code.

Understanding Java exception hierarchy

At the core of Java's exception handling framework is the ability to catch exceptions at runtime and handle them gracefully. This puts us in control of how our application responds to exceptions. This capability is built around Java's **Throwable** class. It is important to understand the structure and hierarchy of exception handling.

This section explores these concepts, starting with a look at the **Throwable** class.

Throwable class

Java includes the **Throwable** class to represent any object that can be thrown by the **Java Virtual Machine (JVM)**. In this context, thrown means that the JVM encountered an exceptional condition, such as an error, at runtime. The JVM signals this by creating an instance of the **Throwable** class, or one of its subclasses, and passing that instance to the JVM to handle the exception. So, in layman's terms, throwing an object means creating and signaling an error or exceptional condition to our program. We can catch what is thrown to gracefully handle the errors and exceptions.

As indicated in *Figure 1.1*, the **Throwable** class has two primary subclasses, **Error** and **Exception**, as follows:

Throwable			
	Error	InternalError	
		OutOfMemoryError	
		StackOverflowError	
	Exception	IOException	EOFException
			FileNotFoundException
			SocketException
		RuntimeException	ArithmeticException
			ArrayIndexOutOfBoundsException
			NullPointerException
		SQLException	

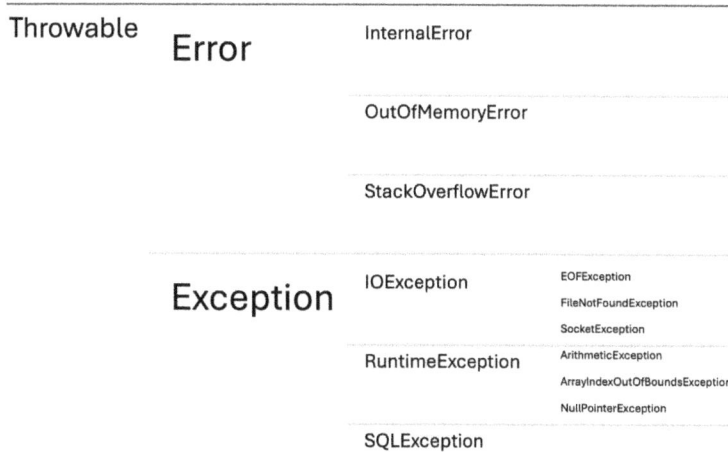

Figure 5.1: Java's exception hierarchy

In the next section, we will take a closer look at the differences between errors and exceptions in Java.

Errors vs. exceptions

We established that errors in Java are significant problems that are typically outside the control of our application, such as with hardware failures or critical resource exhaustion. Prime examples include **OutOfMemoryError**, which indicates the JVM ran out of memory, and **StackOverflowError**, which occurs when there is excessive recursion leading to a stack overflow.

Exceptions, on the other hand, are conditions that our application can recover from. They are further divided into checked and unchecked exceptions.

Checked exceptions must be declared in a method's **throws** clause or handled using try-catch. Examples include **IOException** for file or network I/O failures and **SQLException** for database operation failures.

Unchecked exceptions, also referred to as runtime exceptions, do not need to be declared or handled explicitly. Examples include **NullPointerException**, which occurs when accessing an object reference that is null, and **IndexOutOfBoundsException**, which occurs when accessing an invalid array or list index.

Note: **When to use checked vs. unchecked exceptions. Use checked exceptions for predictable issues that must be addressed at compile time (e.g., file not found, invalid user input). Use unchecked exceptions for programming errors that indicate bugs in your logic (e.g., null pointer, division by zero).**

Checked and unchecked exceptions are covered in greater detail later in this chapter.

Let us look at an example in code:

```java
import java.io.File;
import java.io.FileNotFoundException;
import java.util.Scanner;

public class ExceptionHierarchyExample {
    public static void main(String[] args) {
        try {
            // Checked Exception: Must handle or declare
            readFromFile("this_file_does_not_exist.txt");
            // Unchecked Exception: No requirement to handle
            int result = divide(10, 0);
        } catch (FileNotFoundException e) {
            System.out.println("File not found: " + e.getMessage());
        } catch (ArithmeticException e) {
            System.out.println("Math error: " + e.getMessage());
        } finally {
            System.out.println("Cleanup actions can go here.");
        }
    }
    public static void readFromFile(String fileName) throws
FileNotFoundException {
        File file = new File(fileName);
        Scanner scanner = new Scanner(file); // Throws FileNotFoundException
        while (scanner.hasNextLine()) {
            System.out.println(scanner.nextLine());
        }
    }
    public static int divide(int a, int b) {
        return a / b; // Throws ArithmeticException for b = 0
    }
}
```

The code aforementioned handles the **FileNotFoundException** checked exception. The **readFromFile** method declares that it may throw a **FileNotFoundException**. This must either be caught or declared in the calling method, which, in our case, is **main()**. The try-catch block ensures that a missing file does not crash the program.

We also handled the **ArithmeticException** unchecked exception. As you can see, the division by zero error is not declared or handled explicitly but is caught in the try-catch block. In our **finally** block, we would implement cleanup actions, such as closing resources.

We will explore the try-catch block in greater detail later in this chapter.

Throwable methods

Java's **Throwable** class includes several methods that we can use to inspect and respond to exceptions. The **getCause()** method retrieves the cause of the throwable, if there is one. The **getMessage()** method is perhaps the most used method because it returns a description of the exception. The **printStackTrace()** method can be used to print the exception's stack trace.

The following is a code snippet that demonstrates how some of these methods could be used:

```
try {
    int[] arr = new int[3];
    System.out.println(arr[19]); // IndexOutOfBoundsException
} catch (ArrayIndexOutOfBoundsException e) {
    System.out.println("Exception: " + e.getMessage());
    e.printStackTrace();
}
```

Best practices

This section provides the following best practices when handling exceptions in Java:

- Identify key areas of your applications where exception handling should be included. This can include areas when you open databases, communicate over a network, or work with files.

- Analyze your code to determine if it is likely to encounter errors, which are unrecoverable, or exceptions, which are recoverable.

- Implement an appropriate strategy, such as using try-catch for recovery or **throws** for propagation.

- Use **finally** to gracefully close files, databases, connections, and other resources.

- Document your exception handling with in-code comments.

- To the extent possible, test your exception handling before your application goes live.

- It is also a best practice to avoid common pitfalls. Here are the three most common pitfalls, all of which should be avoided.

- Avoid using **catch (Exception e) {}** as it suppresses all exceptions, making it difficult to debug.

- Avoid using **catch (Exception e) {}** without including handling code. We should always log or act on exceptions.

- Do not overuse checked exceptions. This can bloat our code and make it less readable.

Checked vs. unchecked exceptions

As previously mentioned, Java exceptions are either checked or unchecked. It is important for us to fully understand the distinction between these types so we can write reliable and maintainable applications. This section takes a closer look at checked and unchecked exceptions, use cases, and how to handle them effectively.

Checked exceptions

Checked exceptions are those that we should be able to anticipate and therefore recover from. They occur at runtime and are typically related to external resources or predictable issues involving operations such as:

- File handling

- Database connections

- Network operations

The Java compiler ensures that checked exceptions are handled by either using a try-catch block or declaring they are declared in the method signature with the **throws** keyword. The purpose is for us to handle problems that are predictable and recoverable.

The three most common checked exceptions are **FileNotFoundException**, **IOException**, and **SQLException**. The **FileNotFoundException** was demonstrated earlier in this chapter, so here we will demonstrate the **SQLException**.

The following is the code:

```
import java.sql.Connection;
import java.sql.DriverManager;
import java.sql.SQLException;

public class SQLExceptionExample {
    public static void main(String[] args) {
        Connection connection = null;
        try {
            // Trying to connect to the database
            connection = DriverManager.getConnection("jdbc:mysql://
localhost:3306/test", "user", "password");
            // Database operations would go here
```

```
        } catch (SQLException e) {
            // Handle the SQLException
            System.out.println("Database access error:");
            e.printStackTrace();
        } finally {
            // Close the connection (if it was established)
            if (connection != null) {
                try {
                    connection.close();
                } catch (SQLException e) {
                    System.out.println("Error closing the connection:");
                    e.printStackTrace();
                }
            }
        }
    }
}
```

In the example aforementioned, the **SQLException** can be thrown during the attempt to establish a database connection or when closing the connection. In both cases, we have a **catch** block to handle the exception. We also use **e.printStackTrace()** to display the details of the exception.

Unchecked exceptions

Unchecked exceptions can be a result of programming logic errors or bugs. In those cases, the exceptions could have been avoided with more thorough testing and quality assurance. These are unchecked because there is no compile-time enforcement by the Java compiler. We are not required to handle or declare unchecked exceptions. This designation of exceptions is to identify programming logic flaws, such as null references or invalid arguments.

Common examples of unchecked exceptions are **ArithmeticException**, such as division by zero; **ArrayIndexOutOfBoundsException**, such as when attempting to access an invalid array index; and **NullPointerException**, which occurs when accessing a null reference.

Let us understand how to handle an instance when we call a method with the following null reference:

```
public class NullPointerExceptionExample {
    public static void main(String[] args) {
        String myString = null;
        try {
            // Here we attempt to call a method with a null reference
```

```
        int length = myString.length();
    } catch (NullPointerException e) {
        System.out.println("We caught a NullPointerException:");
        e.printStackTrace();
    }
  }
}
```

In the aforementioned code, we declared a **String** variable called **myString** and set it to null. When we attempt to call the **length()** method on **myString**, a **NullPointerException** is thrown because **myString** does not reference any object. The **catch** block caught the exception and printed its stack tracking using the **printStackTrace()** method.

Table 5.1 summarizes the differences between checked and unchecked exceptions:

Component	Checked exceptions	Unchecked exceptions
Purpose	For recoverable problems	For programming errors
Compile-time enforcement	Must be handled or declared using throws	Not required
Examples	`FileNotFoundException`	`ArithmeticException`
	`IOException`	`ArrayIndexOutOfBoundsException`
	`SQLException`	`NullPointerException`

Table 5.1: Checked and unchecked exception comparison

Try-catch-finally blocks

So far, in this chapter, we have seen multiple instances of the try-catch-finally block. This section takes a deeper look at this construct, which is core to Java's ability to handle exceptions. It allows us to gracefully recover and maintain control of our application's flow.

Structure of try-catch-finally block

The try-catch-finally exception handling construct is comprised of three distinct blocks.

Let us examine each one in the following sections.

Try block

The **try** block contains the code that we think will throw an exception. The block attempts (tries) to execute the code. It passes any exceptions to the corresponding **catch** block. Here is the structure:

```
try {
    // the code in this block might throw an exception
}
```

Catch block

The **catch** block is where you handle exceptions thrown by the **try** block. Each catch block is associated with a specific exception type. We will look at multiple catch blocks later in this section.

The following is the structure:

```
catch {
    // the code to handle the exception
}
```

Finally block

The **finally** block is optional, but highly recommended. It is executed regardless of whether an exception occurred or not. It is considered cleanup code and is commonly used for closing files, databases, and connections.

Note: **The finally block always executes even if a return statement appears in the try or catch blocks.**

The following is the structure:

```
finally {
    // cleanup code goes here
}
```

Let us look at an example that uses all three blocks in the try-catch-finally construct:

```java
import java.io.File;
import java.io.FileNotFoundException;
import java.util.Scanner;
public class TryCatchFinallyExample {
    public static void main(String[] args) {
        Scanner scanner = null;
        try {
            File file = new File("unlikelyfile.txt");
            scanner = new Scanner(file); // Might throw FileNotFoundException
            while (scanner.hasNextLine()) {
                System.out.println(scanner.nextLine());
            }
        }
```

```
        } catch (FileNotFoundException e) {
            System.out.println("Error: The designated file was not found.");
        } finally {
            if (scanner != null) {
                scanner.close(); // Ensures resource is released
            }
            System.out.println("Finished file operations.");
        }
    }
}
```

In the aforementioned example, the **try** block attempted to open and read a file; the **catch** block handled the **FileNotFoundException**; and the **finally** block closed the **Scanner** resource to prevent resource leaks.

Multiple catch blocks

The try-catch-finally exception handling construct can be expanded beyond its three distinct blocks. Specifically, we can include multiple **catch** blocks, each handling a different exception type. If the **try** block throws multiple exceptions, Java will execute the first matching **catch** block.

The following is a code snippet to demonstrate this approach:

```
try {
    int[] array = new int[3];
    System.out.println(array[19]); // Throws ArrayIndexOutOfBoundsException
    int result = 19 / 0; // Throws ArithmeticException
} catch (ArrayIndexOutOfBoundsException e) {
    System.out.println("Array index out of bounds: " + e.getMessage());
} catch (ArithmeticException e) {
    System.out.println("Math error: " + e.getMessage());
} finally {
    System.out.println("Execution completed.");
}
```

The output of this code snippet will be as follows:

```
Array index out of bounds: Index 19 out of bounds for length 3
Execution completed.
```

Best practices and pitfalls

The importance of gracefully handling exceptions cannot be overstated. When implementing this in your applications, consider the following best practices:

- Be specific in the exceptions you catch. Instead of catching generic exceptions (i.e., **Exception** or **Throwable**), catch the specific exceptions you anticipate so you can handle them in a meaningful way.

- Minimize the code you put in your try blocks. Only put code in that block that might throw exceptions. This will make your troubleshooting and code maintenance efforts more efficient.

- Always release resources in your **finally** block to prevent resource leaks.

- Leverage the try-with-resources block to simplify cleanup.

Note: We will cover this in Chapter 9, Input/Output.

In addition, we should strive to avoid these common pitfalls when handling exceptions in our applications:

- Do not use empty catch blocks. This swallows exceptions without taking any action. This hides bugs and makes troubleshooting extremely difficult.

  The following is an example:

```
try {
    int result = 19 / 0;
} catch (ArithmeticException e) {
    // Avoid doing nothing here!
    // Handle the exception in a meaningful way!
}
```

- Use the **finally** block for what it was intended for. Do not overuse it. Instead, only use it for resource cleanup specific to the corresponding **try** block.

- While Java supports nesting try-catch blocks, it makes your code difficult to read and maintain. This should be avoided.

Throwing exceptions and exception propagation

So far, we have explored exceptions and the need to predict and handle them. We can also throw them intentionally. Java provides us with the ability to intentionally throw exceptions and propagate them up the call stack. This allows us to signal and manage exceptions effectively.

In this section, we will look at how and why we can generate exceptions in our code and how to propagate them. We will also cover exception management strategies.

Throwing exceptions

To intentionally throw an exception, we merely need to use Java's **throw** keyword. This can be useful when our program encounters a situation that it is unable to handle on its own, such as invalid user input or illegal method arguments.

The syntax for this is as follows:

```
throw new ExceptionType("Error message");
```

Here is an example of it in-code:

```
public class IntentionalThrowExample {
    public static void main(String[] args) {
        try {
            validateAge(119); // Will throw an exception
        } catch (IllegalArgumentException e) {
            System.out.println("Exception caught: " + e.getMessage());
        }
    }
    public static void validateAge(int age) {
        if (age > 99) {
            throw new IllegalArgumentException("Maximum age allowed is 99.");
        }
    }
}
```

The output of this program is as follows:

```
Exception caught: Maximum age allowed is 99.
```

In the aforementioned example, we used the **throw** keyword to create and throw an **IllegalArgumentException** when the **age** is greater than **99**. The exception carries a descriptive message to help identify the issue.

Exception propagation

When an exception is thrown in a method, we can either handle it within the method or propagate it to the caller. With propagation, we can keep pushing an exception up the call stack until it is caught by a try-catch block. So, if a method **throws** an exception that is not caught within itself, that exception propagates to the method that called it. This propagation continues until the exception is caught or the program ends.

The following is an example in-code:

```java
public class PropagationExample {
    public static void main(String[] args) {
        try {
            methodA();
        } catch (Exception e) {
            System.out.println("Caught exception: " + e.getMessage());
        }
    }
    public static void methodA() throws Exception {
        methodB(); // Propagates exception
    }
    public static void methodB() throws Exception {
        throw new Exception("Something went wrong in methodB.");
    }
}
```

The output of this application is as follows:

Caught exception: Something went wrong in methodB.

In the aforementioned example, the **methodB()** method throws an exception. The **methodA()** method declares to throw an exception but does not handle it. The **main()** method catches the propagated exception in a try-catch block.

Closer look at the throws keyword

As we saw in the previous section, methods must declare exceptions in their signature to propagate exceptions. This declaration is done with the **throws** keyword. This is only mandatory for checked exceptions; it is optional for unchecked exceptions.

The following is the syntax:

```java
returnType methodName(parameters) throws ExceptionType {
    // Method logic goes here
}
```

The following is a code snippet to demonstrate a method with the appropriate signature for exception propagation to occur:

```java
public static void readTheFile(String fileName) throws FileNotFoundException {
    File file = new File(fileName);
    Scanner scanner = new Scanner(file); // Throws FileNotFoundException
}
```

Note: Use the throws keyword for exceptions that you do not want to handle within a method.

So, what approach is better: catch or propagate? When we are designing our programs, we must grapple with that question. Do we want to handle exceptions locally or propagate them to the caller?

Table 5.2 provides a summary review of the two approaches:

Approach	Purpose	Example
Catch locally	• Handle exceptions close to the source • Recover or take specific actions	Retrying a database connection after a temporary failure.
Propagate	• When the method itself cannot resolve the issue • When the caller is better suited to handle it	Throwing an **SQLException** from a data access layer to an application layer for user notification.

Table 5.2: Summary of catch and propagation approaches

Best practices

The following are the best practices for throwing and propagating exceptions:

- Use specific exception types instead of generic ones. We should strive to provide meaningful error information for our logs and users.

  Table 5.3 provides the following examples:

Bad example	`throw new Exception("Error");`
Good example	`throw new IllegalArgumentException("Invalid argument");`

Table 5.3: Bad and good examples of specific error messages

- Whenever possible, avoid propagating runtime exceptions, such as **NullPointerExceptions**. Instead, fix the underlying logic.

- Thoroughly document your exceptions with in-code comments.

  The following code snippet provides an exemplar regarding the clarity and depth of comments:

```
/**
 * The readTheFile method reads a file and prints its content to the
console.
```

```
 * @param fileName the name of the file to read
 * @throws FileNotFoundException if the file does not exist at the given
path
 */
public void readFile(String fileName) throws FileNotFoundException {
    // Implementation would go here

}
```

- It is okay to create custom exceptions (covered in the next section), but do so sparingly. It is important to keep our code readable and maintainable.

Creating custom exceptions

Java's built-in exceptions are not always sufficient for our needs. Especially with complex programs, we could encounter scenarios where the built-in exceptions provide insufficient information about specific errors. In these cases, we can create our own exceptions, specifically tailored to our application's needs.

Custom exceptions allow us to:

- Provide more context about errors to our users and for our logs.

- Improve our code's readability by differentiating between standard and application-specific errors.

- Enforce specific error-handling by signaling critical issues unique to our application.

This section demonstrates how to design, create, and use custom exceptions effectively.

Designing custom exceptions

Java makes it easy for us to create custom extensions. We simply need to extend either the **Exception** class or the **RuntimeException** class, depending on whether we are working on a checked or unchecked exception.

The following is the three-step process:

1. First, we need to ensure we extend the appropriate base class. Here are the basic guidelines:

    a. Use the **Exception** class for checked exceptions (must be declared or handled).

    b. Use the **RuntimeException** class for unchecked exceptions (optional to declare or handle).

2. Next, we define a default constructor along with another one that accepts a custom error message. Although not required, we can also include a constructor that accepts a cause, which is great support for debugging.

3. Lastly, we can add fields to store additional information, such as error codes and user-friendly output messages. This third step is optional but highly recommended.

The following is an example of a custom checked exception:

```
/*
 * This class is a
 * custom checked
 * exception example
 */
public class InvalidInputException extends Exception {
    private int errorCode;
    // Default Constructor
    public InvalidInputException() {
        super("Invalid input provided.");
    }
    // Constructor with Custom Message
    public InvalidInputException(String message) {
        super(message);
    }
    // Constructor with Custom Message and Error Code
    public InvalidInputException(String message, int errorCode) {
        super(message);
        this.errorCode = errorCode;
    }
    // Getter for Error Code
    public int getErrorCode() {
        return errorCode;
    }
}
```

In our example above, the custom exception includes constructors for flexibility. The **errorCode** field provides additional context about the error.

Using a custom checked exception

In the previous section, we created a custom checked exception called **InvalidInputException** with a custom error message.

The following code demonstrates how we can implement a custom exception in a program:

```
public class CustomExceptionImplementation {
    public static void main(String[] args) {
        try {
            processInput(-5);
        } catch (InvalidInputException e) {
            System.out.println("Error: " + e.getMessage());
            System.out.println("Error Code: " + e.getErrorCode());
        }
    }
    public static void processInput(int input) throws InvalidInputException {
        if (input <= 0) {
            throw new InvalidInputException("Input must be positive.", 1001);
        }
        System.out.println("Valid input: " + input);
    }
}
```

Here is the output of our program:

```
Error: Input must be positive.
Error Code: 1001
```

Custom unchecked exceptions

The following example demonstrates how to create a custom unchecked exception:

```
/*
 * This class is a
 * custom unchecked
 * exception example
 */
public class ConfigurationException extends RuntimeException {
    public ConfigurationException(String message) {
        super(message);
    }
    public ConfigurationException(String message, Throwable cause) {
        super(message, cause);
    }
}
```

As you can see in our example, we extend the **RuntimeException** because our exception is unchecked. We also included two constructors: the default constructor and a second one that accepts a cause for greater insights.

Now, let us use our custom unchecked exception in a program:

```
public class CustomUncheckedExceptionImplementation {
    public static void main(String[] args) {
        try {
            loadConfiguration(null);
        } catch (ConfigurationException e) {
            System.out.println("Configuration error: " + e.getMessage());
        }
    }
    public static void loadConfiguration(String configPath) {
        if (configPath == null) {
            throw new ConfigurationException("Configuration file path cannot be
null.");
        }
        System.out.println("Loading configuration from: " + configPath);
    }
}
```

The following is the output of our program:

Configuration error: Configuration file path cannot be null.

Best practices

Here are several best practices for creating and using custom exceptions:

- If a standard exception suffices, use it.
- Give your custom exceptions self-describing names.
- Provide meaningful error messages.
- Thoroughly document your exceptions with in-code comments.

Testing exception handling

Like with any component of our applications, we need to thoroughly test our exception handling code to help ensure our applications gracefully manage errors. We spend a lot of time modeling our exception handling, and we want to ensure it behaves predictably under adverse conditions.

The following are the primary reasons to test our exception handling:

- Ensure our applications are robust.
- Ensure our applications are reliable.
- Verify that our program can recover from failures.
- Ensure we provide meaningful feedback to users and logs.
- Catch improperly handled or propagating exceptions to prevent runtime errors.
- Ensure our error-handling logic adheres to best practices.
- Ensure our error-handling does not introduce new issues.

There are several techniques available to support our testing efforts. JUnit is a framework for unit testing. It allows us to write and run repeatable tests to help ensure our code behaves as expected. We will cover JUnit thoroughly in *Chapter 13, Debugging, Testing, and Deployment*. In this section, we will implement testing without the use of JUnit.

The following are some benefits of testing exceptions without using JUnit:

- We can conduct self-contained testing without needing to install or configure external libraries.
- It can lead to a greater understanding of testing principles.
- It is a lightweight solution for simple projects.

Our testing techniques include the use of try-catch blocks, exception properties validation, and simulating error conditions.

Let us examine examples of testing checked and unchecked exceptions, both standard and custom.

Testing checked exceptions

Let us test a method that throws a **FileNotFoundException**.

The following is the code we want to test:

```java
import java.io.File;
import java.io.FileNotFoundException;
import java.util.Scanner;

public class MyFileReader {
    public String readMyFile(String fileName) throws FileNotFoundException {
        File file = new File(fileName);
        Scanner scanner = new Scanner(file);
        return scanner.nextLine();
```

```
        }
    }
```

Now, let us write a test case.

```
import java.io.FileNotFoundException;

public class MyFileReaderTest {
    public static void main(String[] args) {
        MyFileReader fileReader = new MyFileReader();
        try {
            fileReader.readMyFile("nonexistentfile.txt");
            System.out.println("Test failed: No exception was thrown.");
        } catch (FileNotFoundException e) {
            System.out.println("Test passed: Caught FileNotFoundException.");
            System.out.println("Exception message: " + e.getMessage());
        }
    }
}
```

The following is the output from our test:

Test passed: Caught FileNotFoundException.

Exception message: nonexistentfile.txt (No such file or directory)

As you can see in our example, the **try** block calls the **readMyFile()** method; that is the method we are testing. The **catch** block confirms that the expected exception is thrown and checks the output message. We have messages to tell us if the exception was thrown or not.

Testing unchecked exceptions

To test an unchecked exception, will write a method that throws an **IllegalArgumentException** for invalid input.

The following is the code we want to test:

```
public class MyMathToolkit {
    public int divide(int numerator, int denominator) {
        if (denominator == 0) {
            throw new IllegalArgumentException("Denominator cannot be zero.");
        }
        return numerator / denominator;
    }
}
```

The following is code we can use to test the unchecked exception:

```java
public class MyMathToolkitTest {
    public static void main(String[] args) {
        MyMathToolkit mathToolkit = new MyMathToolkit();
        try {
            mathToolkit.divide(19, 0);
            System.out.println("Test failed: No exception was thrown.");
        } catch (IllegalArgumentException e) {
            System.out.println("Test passed: Caught
IllegalArgumentException.");
            System.out.println("Exception message: " + e.getMessage());
        }
    }
}
```

The following is the output of our test:

Test passed: Caught IllegalArgumentException.

Exception message: Denominator cannot be zero.

In the preceding example, we validated that the **IllegalArgumentException** was thrown when we attempted to divide by zero. We also provided the exception message so we can validate it for correctness.

Testing custom exceptions

The following is a custom exception called **InvalidMathInputException**:

```java
public class InvalidMathInputException extends Exception {
    public InvalidMathInputException(String message) {
        super(message);
    }
}
```

Let us write code that throws that exception:

```java
public class MyInputValidator {
    public void validateTheAge(int age) throws InvalidMathInputException {
        if (age < 21) {
            throw new InvalidMathInputException("Minimum age allowed is 21.");
        }
    }
}
```

The following is code we can use to test our **validateTheAge()** method:

```java
public class MyInputValidatorTest {
    public static void main(String[] args) {
        MyInputValidator validator = new MyInputValidator();
        try {
            validator.validateTheAge(15);
            System.out.println("Test failed: No exception was thrown.");
        } catch (InvalidMathInputException e) {
            System.out.println("Test passed: Caught
InvalidMathInputException.");
            System.out.println("Exception message: " + e.getMessage());
        }
    }
}
```

The output of our test is as follows:

Test passed: Caught InvalidMathInputException.

Exception message: Minimum age allowed is 21.

Our test confirmed the exception type, and it validated our custom message.

Exception properties validation

For our final testing example, let us test a custom exception that has additional fields. Here is the code we want to test:

```java
public class MyCustomException extends Exception {
    private int errorCode;
    public MyCustomException(String message, int errorCode) {
        super(message);
        this.errorCode = errorCode;
    }
    public int getErrorCode() {
        return errorCode;
    }
}
```

Now, we can write a test case:

```java
public class MyCustomExceptionTest {
    public static void main(String[] args) {
        try {
            throw new MyCustomException("Custom error occurred.", 404);
```

```
        } catch (MyCustomException e) {
            System.out.println("Test passed: Caught MyCustomException.");
            System.out.println("Message: " + e.getMessage());
            System.out.println("Error Code: " + e.getErrorCode());
        }
    }
}
```

The following is the output of our test:

Test passed: Caught MyCustomException.

Message: Custom error occurred.

Error Code: 404

Our test ensured that our custom exception's message and additional property (**errorCode**) were correct.

Best practices

The following are the best practices for testing exception handing in our Java applications:

- Use descriptive output with your test cases so it is clear whether the test passed or failed.

- Simulate realistic scenarios for your tests with a focus on edge cases such as null values, empty inputs, etc.

- Validate messages and any additional properties.

- Explicitly verify the exception type.

This section featured manual testing instead of using a framework such as JUnit. This approach is usually sufficient for small programs, but a lack of automation would make testing larger programs difficult and inefficient. Manual testing can also introduce human errors, so, for larger systems, it is recommended that testing use a framework such as JUnit, which is covered in *Chapter 13, Debugging, Testing, and Deployment*.

Conclusion

By the end of this chapter, we established exception handling as a fundamental skill for writing robust, maintainable, and user-friendly Java applications. We explored Java's robust framework for managing errors and exceptions, which allows us to anticipate, handle, and gracefully recover from both predictable and unforeseen issues. The chapter examined Java's exception hierarchy, including the distinction between errors, checked exceptions, and unchecked exceptions. You had the opportunity to learn how to throw and propagate exceptions, allowing flexibility in how our programs handle errors.

The chapter also introduced the creation of custom exceptions, which allows us to encapsulate application-specific issues with greater clarity and precision. Finally, the chapter explored techniques for testing exception handling, helping to ensure that our applications can handle errors predictably and reliably under a variety of conditions.

In the next chapter, we will discuss data structures to include arrays and array lists and extend them into the Java Collections Framework. Our coverage will include how to work with lists, sets, maps, and queues. The chapter will also cover sorting and searching collections and the role of iterators and enhanced for loops. Mastering these structures can help enable you to write efficient, scalable code for handling large datasets.

Points to remember

- A custom exception can provide additional context about specific errors and is created by extending the Exception or RuntimeException class.

- Always validate exception properties such as messages and custom fields when testing exception handling.

- Avoid common pitfalls such as using empty catch blocks, catching generic exceptions, and overusing checked exceptions, which can obscure meaningful error-handling.

- Checked exceptions are enforced at compile time and should be used for predictable, recoverable issues, such as file I/O or database operations.

- Closing resources like files or database connections should be done in a finally block or using try-with-resources for better resource management.

- Custom exceptions should be given self-describing names and meaningful messages to improve code clarity and debugging.

- Document exceptions in method signatures using the throws keyword to propagate checked exceptions when they cannot be handled locally.

- Errors, such as OutOfMemoryError and StackOverflowError, represent serious issues that our applications typically cannot recover from and should not be handled in code.

- Exception propagation allows an exception to get passed up the call stack until it is caught and handled or the program terminates.

- Exception testing helps ensure that our applications can handle errors gracefully and recover predictably under adverse conditions.

- Gracefully handling exceptions ensures that applications remain robust, user-friendly, and maintainable.

- Java's exception hierarchy is rooted in the Throwable class, which is divided into Error and Exception subclasses.

- Multiple catch blocks can be used to handle different exception types, with Java executing the first matching block.

- The Throwable class provides useful methods, such as getMessage(), printStackTrace(), and getCause(), for inspecting and diagnosing exceptions.

- The finally block is executed regardless of whether an exception occurs and is often used for cleanup actions.

- Throwing exceptions intentionally using the throw keyword helps signal and manage application-specific issues that cannot be resolved directly.

- Try-catch-finally blocks form the foundation of Java's exception handling framework, allowing for error recovery and resource cleanup.

- Unchecked exceptions, such as NullPointerException and IllegalArgumentException, result from programming errors and are not enforced at compile time.

- Use descriptive test output messages to clearly indicate whether an exception handling test has passed or failed.

- Use specific exception types, such as IllegalArgumentException, instead of generic exceptions like Exception, to improve debugging and clarity.

Case studies

These case studies provide realistic scenarios that encourage you to think critically as follows:

- **File processing at TerraLogix Analytics**: TerraLogix Analytics specializes in processing large data files for geological surveys and environmental studies. Their flagship application imports raw data files, analyzes them, and generates reports for clients. During routine operations, TerraLogix encountered frequent errors when clients uploaded corrupted or incompatible files. The application crashes without notifying the user, leaving the file partially processed and the database in an inconsistent state.

  o **For your consideration**: How would you implement exception handling for the file import process to:

    - Validate file type and file size before processing.

    - Catch and handle exceptions like FileNotFoundException and IOException.

    - Ensure the database rolls back transactions when errors occur.

    - Use a custom exception to notify users about unsupported file formats.

- How would you use the try-catch-finally construct to ensure resources like file streams and database connections are properly closed? What custom exception would you create to represent file format issues, and what properties would you include?

- **Payment gateway at NebulaPay Systems**: NebulaPay Systems is a financial technology startup offering payment gateway services for small businesses. Merchants recently reported that the system occasionally fails during high-traffic periods, causing incomplete transactions. These failures are often due to network timeouts or invalid payment credentials, but the system does not log sufficient details to diagnose the problem.

  o **For your consideration**: How could you enhance exception handling in the payment processing module to handle SocketTimeoutException and SQLException separately? How would you implement exception propagation to ensure critical failures are logged and alert the monitoring system? Does it make sense to use a custom exception, like PaymentProcessingException, to encapsulate error details like transaction ID and error code? How would you test the handling of network-related exceptions without relying on an active network? What best practices would you apply to log sufficient details about exceptions without exposing sensitive user information?

- **Configuration management at Hyperdyne Robotics**: Hyperdyne Robotics designs autonomous robots for space exploration. Its robots rely on configuration files to operate in extreme environments. During a mission simulation, a configuration file was accidentally deleted. This caused a NullPointerException during initialization, leaving the robot in an unsafe state.

  o **For your consideration**: How could you refactor the configuration module to check for missing files and throw a custom ConfigurationException, handle scenarios where default values can be used to continue execution safely, and ensure the application terminates gracefully if critical configurations are missing? How can exception propagation be used to alert operators about missing configuration files during initialization? What fallback strategies could you implement to keep the robot operational when configuration files are unavailable?

- **Data validation at OrionBio Solutions**: OrionBio Solutions is developing an application for processing patient data in clinical trials. The application occasionally receives invalid data inputs, such as negative ages or missing patient IDs, causing errors downstream in reporting and data analysis.

  o **For your consideration**: How could you implement input validation with robust exception handling to use a custom InvalidInputException for invalid patient data, log the details of invalid inputs for audit purposes, and prevent invalid data from propagating to subsequent processes? How would you design a test suite to validate input data and handle edge cases like empty strings or special characters? What exception handling strategies could you use to notify administrators about frequent input errors while minimizing performance overhead?

- **Concurrency issues at Starfleet Logistics**: Starfleet Logistics provides real-time inventory tracking for space stations and starships. Their inventory application uses multithreading to handle concurrent updates from various devices. Starfleet engineers noticed data inconsistencies in inventory records caused by race conditions. These issues often lead to NullPointerException and IllegalStateException during concurrent updates.

  - **For your consideration**: How could you refactor the inventory update system to handle exceptions caused by race conditions gracefully, use synchronized blocks or locks to prevent data corruption, and log and propagate exceptions for debugging and monitoring? How would you structure your try-catch blocks to ensure critical inventory updates are always completed or rolled back? What tools or strategies could you use to test exception handling in a multithreaded environment?

Multiple choice questions

1. **What is the primary difference between errors and exceptions in Java?**
   a. Errors are critical issues outside of the application's control, while exceptions are recoverable.
   b. Errors are recoverable, while exceptions are not.
   c. Errors occur only during compilation, while exceptions occur only at runtime.
   d. Errors and exceptions are handled using different programming languages.

2. **Which of the following is an example of a checked exception?**
   a. NullPointerException
   b. IOException
   c. ArrayIndexOutOfBoundsException
   d. ArithmeticException

3. **What is the purpose of the finally block in Java's try-catch-finally construct?**
   a. To catch any exceptions not handled by the catch block.
   b. To define cleanup code that runs regardless of whether an exception occurs.
   c. To specify the exceptions a specific method can throw.
   d. To propagate exceptions to the calling method.

4. **Which statement is true about Java's throws keyword?**

    a. It is used to catch exceptions within a method.

    b. It is only used with runtime exceptions.

    c. It automatically handles exceptions thrown by the method.

    d. It declares exceptions that a method can propagate to its caller.

5. **When is it appropriate to create a custom exception in Java?**

    a. When an exception requires additional properties.

    b. When a standard exception provides sufficient information about the error.

    c. When an exception needs to be caught at compile time.

    d. When you want to avoid using unchecked exceptions.

Answers

1.	a.
2.	b.
3.	b.
4.	d.
5.	a.

Questions

1. How does the hierarchy of Java's exceptions (Throwable, Error, Exception) influence the way exceptions are handled in applications? Why is it important to differentiate between errors and exceptions?

2. When designing an application, how would you decide whether to use checked or unchecked exceptions? Share situations where one is more suitable than the other.

3. Discuss the role of try-catch-finally blocks in designing applications that are both robust and user-friendly. How does this construct balance error recovery and resource management?

4. Reflect on a real-world scenario in which a custom exception might be more useful than a standard Java exception. What properties or methods would you add to your custom exception?

5. What are the advantages and disadvantages of propagating exceptions up the call stack instead of handling them immediately? Provide examples of when propagation might be the better choice.

6. How would you design a test case to validate that an exception is thrown correctly? What additional steps would you take to test the message and properties of custom exceptions?

7. Discuss how exception handling might be implemented differently in critical systems (e.g., healthcare or financial applications) compared to less critical systems (e.g., a personal to-do list app).

8. In your opinion, what is the most important best practice for exception handling mentioned in the chapter? Explain your selection.

9. How can exception handling be used to improve debugging and monitoring in complex applications? What considerations should be made when logging exceptions to ensure security and efficiency?

10. In what ways can poor exception handling negatively impact users? For example, how might inadequate error messages or unhandled exceptions affect user trust or data security?

Challenges

The following questions are provided to self-assess your knowledge of the chapter's content and apply critical thinking to key concepts:

- **Validating user input**:

  o **Objective**: Ensure that user input meets predefined criteria and gracefully handles invalid inputs.

  o **Activity**: Write a Java program that accepts user input for a password. If the password does not meet the criteria listed below, throw a custom exception named InvalidPasswordException with an appropriate message. Ensure the program handles the exception and prompts the user to enter the password again until it is valid. The password must meet the following criteria:

    ▪ At least eight characters long.

    ▪ Contains at least one upper case letter.

    ▪ Contains at least one lowercase letter.

    ▪ Contains at least one digit.

  o **Real-world applicability**: User input validation is a common requirement in applications, especially for securing accounts and protecting sensitive data.

- **Processing missing configuration files**:
    - **Objective**: Handle the absence of a required configuration file and provide a fallback mechanism.
    - **Activity**: Accomplish the following:
        - Write a Java program that attempts to read a configuration file named config.txt.
        - If the file is missing, catch the FileNotFoundException and create a default configuration file with placeholder settings.
        - Log a message to the console indicating that the default file was created.
        - Use a try-catch-finally block to ensure any open file resources are closed.
    - **Real-world applicability**: Handling missing or corrupted configuration files is essential for ensuring application stability in diverse deployment environments.

- **Simulating payment processing errors**:
    - **Objective**: Simulate and handle exceptions during a simulated payment processing workflow.
    - **Activity**: Accomplish the following:
        - Create a class named PaymentProcessor with a method processPayment(double amount) that.
        - Throws an IllegalArgumentException if the amount is less than or equal to zero.
        - Simulates a NullPointerException if a required payment method (e.g., credit card object) is null.
        - Write a main program that tests this method, ensuring all exceptions are handled gracefully and meaningful messages are logged to the console.
    - **Real-world applicability**: Exception handling in financial systems helps maintain reliability and ensures errors are communicated clearly to users or administrators.

- **Logging multiple errors**:
    - **Objective**: Implement multiple catch blocks to handle different types of exceptions in a single workflow.
    - **Activity**: Accomplish the following:
        - Write a Java program that performs the following operations:

- ◆ Read an integer from the user.
- ◆ Divide a fixed value (e.g., 319) by this integer.
- ◆ Access an array with a size of 5 using the integer as the index.
- ▪ **Use multiple catch blocks to handle**:
  - ◆ ArithmeticException for division by zero.
  - ◆ ArrayIndexOutOfBoundsException for invalid array indices.
  - ◆ Any other unforeseen exceptions using a generic exception block.
- ▪ Log appropriate messages for each exception, and ensure the program continues execution after handling each exception.
- ○ **Real-world applicability**: Managing multiple error scenarios in a single workflow is essential for applications with complex data processing requirements.

- • **Custom exception for order processing**:
  - ○ **Objective**: Use custom exceptions to represent application-specific errors in a realistic scenario.
  - ○ **Activity**: Accomplish the following:
    - ▪ Write a Java program for a simple order management system and implement the following:
      - ◆ A placeOrder(int quantity) method that throws a custom exception, InsufficientStockException, if the quantity exceeds the available stock (set the stock limit to 100).
      - ◆ Ensure the exception includes a custom error message and a method getStockAvailable() that returns the remaining stock.
      - ◆ Test the method in the main program, handle the exception, and print a user-friendly message indicating the stock shortfall.
  - ○ **Real-world applicability**: Custom exceptions are crucial for building applications that communicate specific problems in a clear and structured way, such as inventory management systems.

Self-assessment

The following questions are provided to self-assess your knowledge of the chapter's content and apply critical thinking to key concepts as follows:

1. What is the primary purpose of the try-catch-finally construct, and how does each block contribute to effective exception handling? Provide an example of a situation where all three blocks would be used.

2. How do checked exceptions differ from unchecked exceptions in terms of usage and enforcement? Describe a scenario where a checked exception would be more appropriate than an unchecked exception.

3. Why might you choose to propagate an exception rather than handle the exception locally? Provide an example where exception propagation would be a better approach than immediate handling.

4. When creating a custom exception, what factors should you consider when your goal is to ensure it is effective and meaningful? Provide a brief example of a custom exception and explain why it is useful in the given context.

5. Imagine you are developing a file processing application that occasionally fails when the file is missing or corrupted. How would you apply the concepts from this chapter to ensure the application handles these errors gracefully and provides meaningful feedback to users?

Answers

1. The try block contains code that might throw an exception. The catch block handles specific exceptions that occur during the execution of the try block. The finally block is used for cleanup actions, such as closing resources, regardless of whether an exception was thrown. The following is an example:

   a. The try block attempts to open and read a specific file.

   b. The catch block handles errors such as FileNotFoundException.

   c. The finally block ensures the file is closed to avoid resource leaks.

2. Checked exceptions are enforced at compile time. We must handle them explicitly or declare them in the method signature (e.g., IOException). They are used for predictable, recoverable issues. Unchecked exceptions are not enforced at compile time. They typically represent programming errors like NullPointerException or ArithmeticException.

3. Propagation allows exceptions to be handled by a method higher in the call stack, which may have more context or capability to deal with the error. As an example, consider a multi-layered application where a data access method may throw an SQLException to the business logic layer. The business logic layer can decide whether to log the error, retry the operation, or notify the user, depending on the context.

4. When creating custom exceptions, we should consider the following factors:

   a. Does a standard exception suffice, or is additional information needed?

   b. What specific properties (e.g., error codes) are necessary to describe the problem?

   c. Is the exception self-explanatory?

Example:
```
public class InvalidInputException extends Exception {
    private int errorCode;
    public InvalidInputException(String message, int errorCode) {
        super(message);
        this.errorCode = errorCode;
    }
    public int getErrorCode() {
        return errorCode;
    }
}
```

Why is this custom exception useful? This exception is tailored to input validation, allowing us to provide detailed feedback such as an error code for debugging or user notifications.

5. Applying concepts presented in this chapter to the file processing application scenario could include the following:

   a. Implement a try-catch block to handle exceptions like FileNotFoundException and IOException.

   b. Use a custom exception (e.g., InvalidFileException) to signal issues specific to file processing, such as unsupported file formats.

   c. Log the errors to a file or console for debugging and display user-friendly messages to notify the user of the problem.

   d. Include a finally block to close file streams and release resources, even when an exception occurs.

Join our Discord space

Join our Discord workspace for latest updates, offers, tech happenings around the world, new releases, and sessions with the authors:

https://discord.bpbonline.com

CHAPTER 6
Data Structures and Collections

Introduction

Data structures are how we store data in Java, and there is a different structure for every type of data. Data structures are fundamental building blocks in programming, allowing efficient storage, retrieval, and manipulation of data. This chapter introduces essential data structures and Java's built-in collections framework. We will cover how to work with arrays and ArrayLists, as well as advanced structures like lists, sets, maps, and queues, each optimized for specific use cases.

Key to our coverage of data structures is the JCF, a powerful library that Java provides, so we can standardize data structures and related algorithm implementations. You will have the opportunity to learn how to use iterators for traversing collections and enhanced for loops for simplicity. We will also leverage the Comparable and Comparator interfaces as we explore sorting and searching.

Structure

This chapter covers the following topics:

- Introduction to arrays and ArrayLists
- Java Collection Framework

- Working with iterators and enhanced for loops

- Sorting and searching collections

- Comparable vs. Comparator

- Using Java's utility classes

Objectives

By the end of this chapter, you should be able to explain the purpose and functionality of key data structures in Java. Furthermore, you should be able to implement and manipulate arrays and ArrayLists, utilize the **Java Collections Framework (JCF)** to work with lists, sets, maps, and queues. Based on hands-on activities, you will have the opportunity to practice traversing collections using iterators and enhanced for loops in your Java applications and perform sorting and searching operations on collections using the Comparable and Comparator interfaces. Lastly, by the chapter's end, you should be able to apply Java's utility classes to simplify collection management and operations.

Introduction to arrays and ArrayLists

All programs deal with some sort of data, and modern applications typically deal with very large and complex datasets. It is important to implement efficient data access and storage in our applications. Fortunately, Java includes extensive capabilities that make it easy for us to manage our application's data, specifically collections of data, referred to as **data collections**.

Arrays and ArrayLists are among the most used structures for storing and manipulating collections of data in Java. Both can be used to organize and index data, and there are differences that we must understand so we ensure we use the data structure most suited to our application's needs.

Arrays offer a fixed-size container for elements that are of the same type. They have the following characteristics:

- They have a fixed size

- Fast access to elements

- Zero-based indices

Arrays are particularly useful for applications where memory efficiency and performance are crucial. They have minimal overhead, especially compared to ArrayLists.

ArrayLists are part of the JCF. Unlike arrays, ArrayLists can dynamically grow or shrink in size. Remember, arrays have a fixed size. So, ArrayLists are well-suited for handling varying amounts of data. ArrayLists also have built-in methods for operations like adding, removing, and searching for elements. This reduces the need for us to manually implement this functionality.

Figure 6.1 illustrates the core difference between arrays and ArrayLists, with the plus sign indicating that ArrayLists can shrink and increase in size:

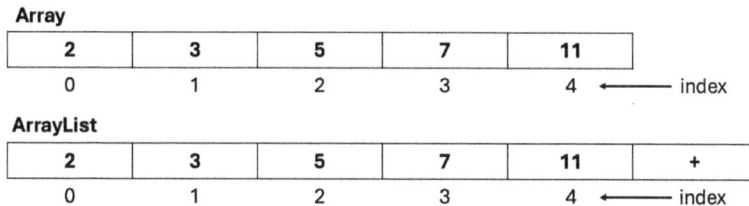

Figure 6.1: Difference between array and ArrayList

Implementing arrays

When we declare an array in Java, we must specify the data type it will contain and the fixed size. Following is an example where we create an array to store five integers:

```
int[] jerseys= new int[5];
```

Once the array is established, we can assign values to the elements. Remember, array indices start with zero. The following example assigns values to the first two elements in the **jerseys** array:

```
jerseys[0] = 8;
jerseys[1] = 24
```

We can access specific array elements. The following is how that is done:

```
System.out.println("The first jersey number is " + jerseys[0]);
```

We can iterate through our array to access all elements. Following is an example:

```
for (int i = 0; i < jerseys.length; i++) {
   System.out.println("The jersey at index " + i + ": " + jerseys[i]);
}
```

In the preceding example, we used the **length()** method to determine how many elements are there.

Implementing ArrayLists

ArrayLists are more dynamic in that we do not need to have a predetermined size. All the elements must be of the same data type, so that needs to be declared. Let us look at the following example where we declare, populate, access, and iterate through an **ArrayList**:

```
import java.util.ArrayList;
```

```java
public class PlanetArrayListExample {
    public static void main(String[] args) {
        // Declare and initialize an ArrayList
        ArrayList<String> planets = new ArrayList<>();
        // Add elements to the ArrayList
        planets.add("Mercury");
        planets.add("Venus");
        planets.add("Earth");
        planets.add("Mars");
        planets.add("Jupiter");
        planets.add("Saturn");
        planets.add("Uranus");
        planets.add("Neptune");
        planets.add("Pluto");
        // Access and print elements
        System.out.println("First planet: " + planets.get(0));
        // Remove an element
        planets.remove("Pluto");
        // Iterate through the ArrayList
        for (String planet : planets) {
            System.out.println(planet);
        }
    }
}
```

The output of our example follows:

First planet: Mercury

Mercury

Venus

Earth

Mars

Jupiter

Saturn

Uranus

Neptune

As a summary of arrays and ArrayLists, refer to *Table 6.1*:

Characteristic	Array	ArrayList
Performance	Faster	Slower
Size	Fixed	Dynamic
Flexibility	Low	High

Table 6.1: Array and ArrayList comparison

Java Collection Framework

The JCF is a collection of classes and interfaces that provides us with a tremendous set of data handling capabilities. The JCF helps simplify how our applications store and manipulate data. Without the JCF's classes and interfaces, we would spend a lot of time writing code that helps us manage data.

The JCF contains several types of collections. They are organized by root interfaces (collection and map). Following is a brief look at the JCF hierarchy and the most commonly used collections, maps, and other data structures:

- **Collection**:

  o **Lists**: Ordered collections that provide precise control over element positions. Notably, lists allow duplicate elements. Common examples include:

    ▪ **ArrayList**: A dynamic array that grows as needed.

    ▪ **LinkedList**: A list that provides efficient insertion and deletion operations.

  o **Queues**: This type of collection is designed for holding elements prior to processing, often in a specific order. Common examples include:

    ▪ **PriorityQueue**: A queue where elements are ordered based on their natural order or a custom Comparator (more on Comparators later in this chapter).

  o **Sets**: These collections ensure that all elements are unique. Common examples include:

    ▪ **HashSet**: This type of set uses a hash table for fast lookups.

    ▪ **TreeSet**: This type of set maintains elements in sorted order.

- **Maps**: Collections that store key-value pairs. We use the key for efficient retrieval of its value pair. Common examples include:

  o **HashMap**: Known for constant-time performance of basic operations.

  o **TreeMap**: Maintains keys in sorted order.

Collection operations

The four most common collection operations we are apt to need for our applications are adding, removing, searching, and sorting. *Table 6.2* lists some methods for each of those operations:

Operation	Example methods
Adding elements	`add()` `addAll()`
Removing elements	`remove()` `clear()`
Searching elements	`contains()` `indexOf()`
Sorting elements	`sort()` `filter()`

Table 6.2: Example methods for collection operations

As we progress through the remainder of the chapter, we will explore these collection operations with code examples.

Working with iterators and enhanced for loops

Once we have a collection, such as an ArrayList or LinkedList, we need to be able to access elements in that collection. This section focuses on traversing collections in an efficient manner. We will explore the two primary mechanisms provided by the JCF for sequencing through collections: iterators and enhanced for loops. These tools allow us to inspect each element in a collection without having to manually manage index positions. When we understand the proper use of iterators and enhanced for loops, we can write readable and error-free code.

Iterators

In Java, an iterator is an object that permits us to run through elements in a collection in a sequential manner. This is called sequential traversal and is an important operation to know how to implement. As you will see in an upcoming example, an iterator is a part of **java.util** package and includes several methods, including the ones listed in *Table 6.3*:

Method	Purpose
`hasNext()`	Checks if the collection contains at least one more element, returning true or false.
`next()`	Retrieves (gets) the next element in the collection.
`remove()`	Removes the element the iterator returned.

Table 6.3: Iterator methods

The benefit of using Iterators in our code is that they work with all types of collections and that they provide some flexibility to modify elements while iterating (that is, with the **remove()** method). Let us look at a sample code that uses an iterator with a list:

```java
import java.util.ArrayList;
import java.util.Iterator;
public class MyIteratorExample {
    public static void main(String[] args) {
        ArrayList<String> names = new ArrayList<>();
        names.add("Kobe");
        names.add("Magic");
        names.add("Kareem");
        names.add("Shaq");
        // Create an iterator for the list
        Iterator<String> iterator = names.iterator();
        // Iterate through the list
        while (iterator.hasNext()) {
            String name = iterator.next();
            System.out.println("Name: " + name);
            // Remove an element (optional)
            if (name.equals("Shaq")) {
                iterator.remove();
            }
        }
        System.out.println("Updated List: " + names);
    }
}
```

Here is the output of our code:

```
Name: Kobe
Name: Magic
Name: Kareem
Name: Shaq
Updated List: [Kobe, Magic, Kareem]
```

Enhanced for loops

Another approach to iterate through a collection is to use the for each loop, also referred to as the **enhanced for loop**. This is a simplified approach that abstracts the interior for loop components. As you can see in the following example, it is a concise way to iterate through a collection:

```java
import java.util.ArrayList;
public class MyEnhancedForLoopExample {
    public static void main(String[] args) {
        ArrayList<String> names = new ArrayList<>();
        names.add("Kobe");
        names.add("Magic");
        names.add("Kareem");
        // This is an enhanced for loop
        for (String name : names) {
            System.out.println("Name: " + name);
        }
    }
}
```

The output of our example follows:

```
Name: Kobe
Name: Magic
Name: Kareem
```

The advantage of using this approach is the cleaner, more readable code. If you need to iterate through a collection and you do not need to make modifications to the collection during the iteration, then this is the best approach to use.

Sorting and searching collections

Sorting and searching are two of the most fundamental operations we perform on collections. The purpose of these operations is not merely to find data; it is to organize and retrieve data efficiently. The JCF provides us with several tools to sort and search collections, making it easy for us to implement that functionality in our programs.

Sorting collections

We will leverage the utilities provided in Java's collections class. Specifically, we will use the **sort()** method to perform two sorts:

- **Natural order**: This is ascending numerical order and alphabetical order for numbers and strings, respectively.

- **Reverse order**: This is the opposite of natural order.

The following is our example code:

```java
import java.util.ArrayList;
import java.util.Collections;
public class SpacecraftSortingExample {
    public static void main(String[] args) {
        // Create and populate the ArrayList
        ArrayList<String> spacecraft = new ArrayList<>();
        spacecraft.add("Voyager");
        spacecraft.add("Apollo");
        spacecraft.add("Perseverance");
        spacecraft.add("Hubble");
        spacecraft.add("Artemis");
        // Sort in 'natural' order
        Collections.sort(spacecraft);
        System.out.println("Spacecraft (Natural Order): " + spacecraft);
        // Sort in reverse order
        spacecraft.sort(Collections.reverseOrder());
        System.out.println("Spacecraft (Reverse Order): " + spacecraft);
    }
}
```

The output of this application follows:

Spacecraft (Natural Order): [Apollo, Artemis, Hubble, Perseverance, Voyager]

Spacecraft (Reverse Order): [Voyager, Perseverance, Hubble, Artemis, Apollo]

Next, let us consider a **TreeSet** collection, which automatically maintains its elements in natural order:

```java
import java.util.TreeSet;
public class TreeSetExample {
    public static void main(String[] args) {
        // Create and populate a TreeSet
        TreeSet<String> spacecraft = new TreeSet<>();
        spacecraft.add("Voyager");
        spacecraft.add("Apollo");
        spacecraft.add("Perseverance");
        spacecraft.add("Hubble");
        spacecraft.add("Artemis");
        // Print the sorted TreeSet
        System.out.println("Sorted Spacecraft: " + spacecraft);
```

```
        // Attempt to add a duplicate item
        spacecraft.add("Apollo");
        System.out.println("After Adding Duplicate: " + spacecraft);
    }
}
```

The output of this program follows:

Sorted Spacecraft: [Apollo, Artemis, Hubble, Perseverance, Voyager]

After Adding Duplicate: [Apollo, Artemis, Hubble, Perseverance, Voyager]

As you can see, a **TreeSet** does not allow duplicate values.

Now, let us examine how we can use a **TreeMap** collection. **TreeMap** stores key-value pairs and keeps its keys sorted in natural order. This differs from a **TreeSet** that has unique elements and does not use key-value pairs. Following is our example **TreeMap** implementation:

```
import java.util.TreeMap;
public class TreeMapExample {
    public static void main(String[] args) {
        // Create and populate TreeMap
        // with spacecraft names and  launch years
        TreeMap<String, Integer> spacecraft = new TreeMap<>();
        spacecraft.put("Voyager", 1977);
        spacecraft.put("Apollo", 1968);
        spacecraft.put("Perseverance", 2020);
        spacecraft.put("Hubble", 1990);
        spacecraft.put("Artemis", 2022);
        // Print the sorted TreeMap
        System.out.println("Sorted Spacecraft (by Name): " + spacecraft);
    }
}
```

Here is the output of our example program:

Sorted Spacecraft (by Name): {Apollo=1968, Artemis=2022, Hubble=1990, Perseverance=2020, Voyager=1977}

As demonstrated, Java's collections utility class makes it easy for us to sort our collections.

Searching collections

Java makes searching collections equally as easy as sorting them. For our example, we will use the collections class. Following is how we can implement a search for a specific item in a collection:

```
import java.util.ArrayList;
import java.util.Collections;
public class SpacecraftSearchExample {
    public static void main(String[] args) {
        // Create and populate the ArrayList
        ArrayList<String> spacecraft = new ArrayList<>();
        spacecraft.add("Voyager");
        spacecraft.add("Apollo");
        spacecraft.add("Perseverance");
        spacecraft.add("Hubble");
        spacecraft.add("Artemis");
        // Sort ArrayList
        Collections.sort(spacecraft);
        // Simulate obtaining input from a user
        String missingSpacecraft = "Hubble";
        // Search for specific spacecraft
        int index = Collections.binarySearch(spacecraft, missingSpacecraft);
        if (index >= 0) {
            System.out.println("Found " + missingSpacecraft + " at index: " +
index);
        } else {
            System.out.println(missingSpacecraft + " not found in the list.");
        }
    }
}
```

The output of our application follows:

Found Hubble at index: 2

Note: **You must first sort the collection before searching. Although you will not receive an error, you are not apt to get reliable results. The output of the preceding example application, if the `Collections.sort(spacecraft)` line was removed, would be `Hubble not found in the list`.**

Next, let us revisit our **TreeSet** and demonstrate how to use the **contains()** method to conduct a search operation:

```
import java.util.TreeSet;
public class TreeSetSearchExample {
    public static void main(String[] args) {
        TreeSet<String> spacecraft = new TreeSet<>();
        spacecraft.add("Voyager");
```

```
        spacecraft.add("Apollo");
        spacecraft.add("Perseverance");
        spacecraft.add("Hubble");
        spacecraft.add("Artemis");
        // Search for a spacecraft
        if (spacecraft.contains("Hubble")) {
            System.out.println("Hubble is in the TreeSet.");
        } else {
            System.out.println("Hubble is not in the TreeSet.");
        }
    }
}
```

The following is the output of our example program:

Hubble is in the TreeSet.

Our final example for this section demonstrates how to search a **TreeMap**. In the following example implementation, we use the **containsKey()** and **containsValue()** methods that are part of the **TreeMap** utility class:

```
import java.util.TreeMap;
public class TreeMapSearchExample {
    public static void main(String[] args) {
        TreeMap<String, Integer> spacecraft = new TreeMap<>();
        spacecraft.put("Voyager", 1977);
        spacecraft.put("Apollo", 1968);
        spacecraft.put("Perseverance", 2020);
        spacecraft.put("Hubble", 1990);
        spacecraft.put("Artemis", 2022);
        // Search for a spacecraft by name
        if (spacecraft.containsKey("Hubble")) {
            System.out.println("Hubble is in the TreeMap.");
        } else {
            System.out.println("Hubble is not in the TreeMap.");
        }
        // Search for a launch year
        if (spacecraft.containsValue(1990)) {
            System.out.println("A spacecraft in our collection launched in
1990.");
        } else {
            System.out.println("No spacecraft in our collection launched in
```

```
1990.");
        }
    }
}
```

Here is the output of our example application:

Hubble is in the TreeMap.

A spacecraft in our collection launched in 1990.

As a final note on sorting and searching, let us review some best practices:

- Always sort your collection before using the **binarySearch()** method.
- Ensure you are using the appropriate data structures for your data.

Comparable vs. Comparator

As mentioned in the previous section, sorting is an extremely common operation in Java. We already demonstrated the natural order of collections, and that is sufficient for many programming requirements, but not all. Sometimes, we need to sort in a custom order. Java provides us with two tools (interfaces) to address this need: **Comparable** and **Comparator**. As you will see, these interfaces allow us to define custom ordering for objects in collections such as **ArrayList**, **TreeSet**, and **TreeMap**.

This section explains the **Comparable** and **Comparator** interfaces and demonstrates their use.

Comparable

Java's **Comparable** interface allows us to create classes with a custom natural order definition. These classes implement the **Comparable** interface and must override the **compareTo()** method. We use this method to define the order of objects by comparing the current object (**this**) with another object passed as an argument. Following is the syntax:

```
public interface Comparable<T> {
    int compareTo(T o);
}
```

The **compareTo()** method has three return options, as indicated in *Table 6.4*:

Return type	Description
0	If this and the object being compared are equal
Negative integer	If this is less than the object being compared
Positive integer	If this is greater than the object being compared

Table 6.4: compareTo() method return types

Let us look at an example in code. The **Dog** class in the following is **Comparable** because it implements the **Comparable** interface:

```java
class Dog implements Comparable<Dog> {
    private String name;
    public Dog(String name) {
        this.name = name;
    }
    public String getName() {
        return name;
    }
    @Override
    public int compareTo(Dog other) {
        return this.name.compareTo(other.name); // Natural order by name
    }
    @Override
    public String toString() {
        return name;
    }
}
```

The following code drives the **Dog** class to demonstrate the sorting using **Comparable**:

```java
import java.util.ArrayList;
import java.util.Collections;
public class ComparableExample {
    public static void main(String[] args) {
        ArrayList<Dog> dogs = new ArrayList<>();
        dogs.add(new Dog("Corgi"));
        dogs.add(new Dog("Beagle"));
        dogs.add(new Dog("Labrador"));
        dogs.add(new Dog("Dalmatian"));
        dogs.add(new Dog("Poodle"));
        Collections.sort(dogs); // Sort using Comparable
        System.out.println("Sorted Dogs by Name: " + dogs);
    }
}
```

The output of our program follows:

Sorted Dogs by Name: [Beagle, Corgi, Dalmatian, Labrador, Poodle]

In our example application, we used the **compareTo()** method to ensure our dog breeds are sorted alphabetically.

Comparator

While the **Comparable** interface allows a class to define its natural order, the **Comparator** interface allows us to define multiple custom sorting orders without modifying the class itself. This can be especially useful when we do not have to modify the class we are sorting. Following is the syntax:

```
public interface Comparator<T> {
    int compare(T o1, T o2);
}
```

The **compare()** method compares two objects and has three return options, as indicated in *Table 6.5*:

Return type	Description
0	If the two objects are equal
Negative integer	If **o1** is less than **o2**
Positive integer	If **o1** is greater than **o2**

Table 6.5: compareTO() method return types

Let us look at an example in the following code, where we sort cat breeds by custom order (name length):

```
class Cat {
    private String breed;
    public Cat(String breed) {
        this.breed = breed;
    }
    public String getBreed() {
        return breed;
    }
    @Override
    public String toString() {
        return breed;
    }
}
```

Next, we will write a **ComparatorExample** application to use in class:

```java
import java.util.ArrayList;
import java.util.Collections;
import java.util.Comparator;
public class ComparatorExample {
    public static void main(String[] args) {
        ArrayList<Cat> cats = new ArrayList<>();
        cats.add(new Cat("Exotic Shorthair"));
        cats.add(new Cat("Maine Coon"));
        cats.add(new Cat("Devon Rex"));
        cats.add(new Cat("Persian"));
        cats.add(new Cat("Ragdoll"));
        // Custom Comparator for sorting by cat breed name length
        Comparator<Cat> lengthComparator = new Comparator<Cat>() {
            @Override
            public int compare(Cat c1, Cat c2) {
                return Integer.compare(c1.getBreed().length(), c2.getBreed().
length());
            }
        };
        Collections.sort(cats, lengthComparator);
        System.out.println("Sorted Cats by Breed Name Length: " + cats);
    }
}
```

Following is our program's output:

Sorted Cats by Breed Name Length: [Persian, Ragdoll, Devon Rex, Maine Coon, Exotic Shorthair]

As you can see in our example, the custom **Comparator** orders our cat breeds based on the length of their names.

Combined use

We covered the **Comparable** and **Comparator** interfaces and demonstrated why and how you might use each of them. We can use both interfaces in the same application. For example, we can sort a list of zoo animals first by their natural order (alphabetically by name) and then by their age using a custom **Comparator**. Let us see this in the code:

```java
class Animal implements Comparable<Animal> {
    private String name;
```

```
    private int age;
    public Animal(String name, int age) {
        this.name = name;
        this.age = age;
    }
    public String getName() {
        return name;
    }
    public int getAge() {
        return age;
    }
    @Override
    public int compareTo(Animal other) {
        return this.name.compareTo(other.name); // Natural order by name
    }
    @Override
    public String toString() {
        return name + " (" + age + " years)";
    }
}
```

Next, we will write a driver program called **CombinedComparableComoparatorExample**, that uses the **Animal** class:

```
import java.util.ArrayList;
import java.util.Collections;
import java.util.Comparator;
public class CombinedComparableComparatorExample {
    public static void main(String[] args) {
        ArrayList<Animal> animals = new ArrayList<>();
        animals.add(new Animal("Elephant", 25));
        animals.add(new Animal("Zebra", 12));
        animals.add(new Animal("Lion", 15));
        animals.add(new Animal("Giraffe", 10));
        // Sort by natural order (name)
        Collections.sort(animals);
        System.out.println("Sorted Animals by Name: " + animals);
        // Custom Comparator to sort by age
        Comparator<Animal> ageComparator = new Comparator<Animal>() {
            @Override
```

```
            public int compare(Animal a1, Animal a2) {
                return Integer.compare(a1.getAge(), a2.getAge());
            }
        };
        Collections.sort(animals, ageComparator);
        System.out.println("Sorted Animals by Age: " + animals);
    }
}
```

Following is the output of our example application:

Sorted Animals by Name: [Elephant (25 years), Giraffe (10 years), Lion (15 years), Zebra (12 years)]

Sorted Animals by Age: [Giraffe (10 years), Zebra (12 years), Lion (15 years), Elephant (25 years)]

As a conclusion to this section, let us review the similarities and differences between the **Comparable** and **Comparator** interfaces. As you can see in *Table 6.6*, the two interfaces are related in that they provide object sorting but are different in their implementation:

Characteristic	Comparable	Comparator
Java package	`java.lang`	`java.util`
Implementation method	`compareTo(T o)`	`Compare(T o1, T o2)`
Use case	Defines natural order	Permits multiple custom orders
Class modification required?	Yes. We must implement Comparable.	No.

Table 6.6: Comparable and Comparator interface comparison

Using Java's utility classes

Java's utility package (**java.util**) provides us with a set of classes that simplify common operations. These classes help streamline tasks like managing collections, generating random numbers, and handling dates. In this section, we will recap the utility classes already covered in this chapter and introduce additional essential classes, providing coding examples for each of them.

Primary utility classes

Following is a recap of the utility classes already featured in this chapter:

- **ArrayList**: A dynamic array implementation that allows elements to be added or removed without predefined size limitations.

- **HashMap**: A `HashMap` stores key-value pairs, allowing for the fast retrieval of values based on keys. They are not sorted, and duplicate keys are not allowed.

- **HashSet**: A `HashSet` is a collection that does not allow duplicate elements and provides constant-time performance for basic operations like add, remove, and contains.

- **Collections**: This utility class has static methods for operations like sorting, reversing, and shuffling lists and searching within them using `binarySearch()`.

- **LinkedList**: A `LinkedList` is a collection that internally uses a doubly linked list. It is ideal when we have frequent insertions and deletions.

- **TreeMap**: A map implementation that keeps keys sorted in natural order or according to a specified `Comparator`.

- **TreeSet**: A set implementation that maintains elements in a natural order or a specified order. It also prevents duplicates.

As you saw, these classes are key to our ability to efficiently manage collections. The sections that follow cover additional utility classes.

Date

The **Date** class gives us access to a specific instant in time with millisecond precision. We typically use this when working with timestamps, displaying times in an interface, logging, and reporting. The following is a simple implementation example:

```
import java.util.Date;
public class DateExample {
    public static void main(String[] args) {
        // Get the current date and time
        Date currentDate = new Date();
        System.out.println("Current Date and Time: " + currentDate);
    }
}
```

The output of this example is based on the local computer's system time and displayed as indicated in the following:

```
Current Date and Time: Sat Dec 07 18:09:42 CST 2024
```

Calendar

Java's **Calendar** class gives us a flexible way to handle dates and times. This allows us to work with fields like year, month, and day. The following is an example:

```
import java.util.Calendar;
public class CalendarExample {
```

```java
    public static void main(String[] args) {
        // Create a calendar instance and set a specific date
        Calendar calendar = Calendar.getInstance();
        calendar.set(2025, Calendar.MARCH, 9);
        System.out.println("Custom Date: " + calendar.getTime());
    }
}
```

The output of this example is based on the custom date of March 9, 2025:

Custom Date: Sun Mar 09 18:14:22 CDT 2025

Random

The **Random** class generates pseudo-random numbers. It can generate random integers, doubles, Booleans, and more. Following is an example that generates three random integers, each based on a different range, and a random double:

```java
import java.util.Random;
public class RandomExample {
    public static void main(String[] args) {
        // Create an instance of Random
        Random random = new Random();
        // Generate random numbers
        int randomInt1 = random.nextInt(10); // Random integer between 0 and 9
        int randomInt2 = random.nextInt(100); // Random integer between 0 and 99
        int randomInt3 = random.nextInt(1000); // Random integer between 0 and 999
        double randomDouble = random.nextDouble(); // Random double between 0.0 and 1.0
        System.out.println("Random Integer (0 - 9): " + randomInt1);
        System.out.println("Random Integer (0 - 99): " + randomInt2);
        System.out.println("Random Integer (0 - 999): " + randomInt3);
        System.out.println("Random Double (0.0 - 1.0): " + randomDouble);
    }
}
```

Following is a sample output from our code:

Random Integer (0 - 9): 6
Random Integer (0 - 99): 27
Random Integer (0 - 999): 461
Random Double (0.0 - 1.0): 0.45391356008501416

Note: Pseudo-random refers to numbers that are generated using algorithms designed to simulate randomness. While they appear random, they are not truly random because they are calculated using deterministic processes, typically starting from an initial value called a seed.

Scanner

The **Scanner** class is a versatile utility class that enables us to read input from various sources, including files, the console, and more. It also supports parsing strings and primitives such as integers and doubles, making it an essential tool for handling user input in our Java applications. We will explore the **Scanner** class in detail in *Chapter 9, Input/Output,* where we will focus on its role in reading and processing input effectively.

Conclusion

This chapter explored the foundations of data structures and collections in Java, covering their implementation, functionality, and practical applications. We started with arrays and ArrayLists, examining their differences, use cases, and performance characteristics. The chapter then introduces the JCF, highlighting its key components, such as lists, sets, maps, and queues, and their practical utility in Java application development.

The chapter also demonstrated traversal techniques using iterators and enhanced for loops, enabling efficient navigation and manipulation of collections. Sorting and searching operations were covered using examples that demonstrated both built-in utilities and custom ordering using the Comparable and Comparator interfaces. The chapter concludes with a review of Java's utility classes, including HashMap, HashSet, LinkedList, Date, Calendar, and Random, providing tools for effective data management and manipulation.

The goal of the chapter was to give you a solid foundation for working with data structures in Java. These skills are essential for writing efficient, scalable, and maintainable applications.

In the next chapter, we will cover concurrency and multithreading in Java. The chapter will start by explaining how to create and manage threads using the Thread class and the Runnable interface. From there, the chapter explores synchronization, locks, and the Executor framework, which simplifies concurrent programming. The chapter also covers Java's concurrency utilities like CountDownLatch and CyclicBarrier, giving you tools to manage complex thread interactions. Best practices for writing thread-safe code are emphasized to help you avoid common pitfalls in concurrent programming.

Points to remember

- Adding elements to collections can be done using methods like add() and addAll(), available in classes such as ArrayList and LinkedList.

- ArrayLists are part of the JCF and provide dynamic resizing capabilities, making them suitable for applications with varying data sizes.

- Arrays are fixed-size collections that offer fast access to elements but lack the flexibility of dynamic resizing.

- Binary search requires a collection to be sorted beforehand to ensure accurate results when using methods like Collections.binarySearch().

- The Collections utility class provides static methods for operations such as sorting, reversing, shuffling, and searching in collections.

- Comparator interface allows for defining multiple custom orders for sorting objects without modifying their classes.

- Comparable interface enables objects to define their natural order by implementing the compareTo() method.

- Data structures like lists, sets, maps, and queues are key components of the JCF, each optimized for specific use cases.

- Enhanced for loops provide a cleaner and more readable way to traverse collections when modifications during traversal are not required.

- HashMap stores key-value pairs and is useful for fast lookups, but it does not guarantee any specific order.

- HashSet ensures unique elements and provides constant-time performance for basic methods such as add(), remove(), and contains().

- Iterators provide sequential traversal of collections and allow modifications during traversal using methods like remove().

- JCF simplifies data storage and manipulation through standardized implementations of data structures and algorithms.

- LinkedList is ideal for scenarios requiring frequent insertions and deletions due to its underlying doubly linked list implementation.

- Natural order sorting for collections like strings or numbers uses ascending order by default, which is handled efficiently by methods like Collections.sort().

- Random class generates pseudo-random numbers and supports methods for generating integers, doubles, Booleans, and more.

- Searching in collections can be performed using methods like contains() for sets and binarySearch() for sorted lists.

- Sorting collections can be achieved using methods like sort() in the collections utility class, supporting both natural and custom orders.

- TreeMap maintains key-value pairs with keys sorted in natural order or using a specified Comparator.

- TreeSet maintains elements in sorted order and prevents duplicates, making it suitable for collections requiring unique elements.

- Utility classes like Date and Calendar provide tools for handling dates and times, enabling flexibility in working with timestamps and scheduling.

Case studies

These case studies provide realistic scenarios that encourage you to think critically about the following:

- **Optimizing fleet management for StarNet Logistics**: StarNet Logistics, an intergalactic delivery company, maintains a fleet of spacecraft for transporting goods between colonies. Each spacecraft has a unique identifier, and the fleet manager needs a program to track which spacecraft are operational, under maintenance, or retired. The manager wants to store the list of spacecraft and perform the following operations: add new spacecraft identifiers dynamically as the fleet grows, remove retired spacecraft from the list, sort the identifiers alphabetically for display, and search for a specific spacecraft to check its status.

   o **For your consideration**: Explain which data structure you would use to manage the list of spacecrafts. How would you implement sorting and searching operations? What methods or utility classes from the JCF would simplify these tasks?

- **Inventory management for Andromeda Outfitters**: Andromeda Outfitters is a retailer specializing in clothing for space travelers. They manage a product catalog, and each product contains a name, unique **stock keeping unit (SKU)**, and price. The store's software needs to maintain a mapping between SKUs and product names, ensure that all product SKUs are unique, provide a sorted view of products by their names for customer browsing, and quickly check if a specific SKU is already in the catalog.

   o **For your consideration**: Which collection type would you use to store SKUs and product names? How would you implement sorting of the products by name while ensuring SKUs remain unique? What are the benefits of using a TreeMap over a HashMap for this scenario?

- **Real-time sensor monitoring for Cyberdyne Systems**: Cyberdyne Systems develops AI-driven robotics and needs to monitor data from thousands of sensors deployed across its machines. Each sensor sends data at regular intervals, and the company needs a system to: maintain a list of active sensors; identify duplicate sensor IDs to avoid processing redundant data; remove sensor IDs for sensors that go offline; and retrieve the most recently added sensor ID for debugging.

- **For your consideration**: Which collection type would be best suited for managing the list of active sensor IDs? How would you efficiently identify duplicates in the sensor data? How could you use a LinkedList to retrieve the most recently added sensor ID?

- **Membership management for Vulcan Academy**: The Vulcan Academy tracks its students by their names and membership numbers. The administration system must store membership numbers along with student names, allow efficient searching for a student by membership number, sort the list of students alphabetically by name for reporting, and identify duplicate student names to prevent registration errors.

  - **For your consideration**: How would you store the mapping between membership numbers and student names? How would you implement sorting the list of students by name while maintaining the mapping? Which Java utility classes and methods would help with duplicate detection and avoidance?

- **Butterfly observation tracker for Gamma Conservancy**: Gamma Conservancy tracks butterfly species in various habitats. For each species, it records the habitat, species name, and number of sightings. The system must store the species names and their respective habitats, allow sorting of species by their names within each habitat, and retrieve the total number of sightings for a specific species.

  - **For your consideration**: How would you organize the species names and their habitats for efficient management? What approach would you use to sort the species names within each habitat? Which data structures and methods would you recommend for retrieving and updating the total number of sightings?

Multiple choice questions

1. **Which of the following is true about ArrayLists in Java?**
   a. They have a fixed size.
   b. They allow duplicate elements.
   c. They do not support dynamic resizing.
   d. They are not part of the JCF.

2. **What method from the Collections class can be used to sort a list in natural order?**
   a. binarySearch()
   b. reverse()
   c. shuffle()
   d. sort()

3. **Which collection automatically maintains its elements in natural order and does not allow duplication?**

    a. ArrayList

    b. HashMap

    c. TreeSet

    d. LinkedList

4. **What is the primary purpose of the Comparable interface in Java?**

    a. To define the natural order of objects in a collection.

    b. To prevent duplicate elements in a collection.

    c. To provide faster access to elements in a collection.

    d. To allow objects to be compared using custom logic without modifying their class.

5. **Which of the following methods is not provided by the Iterator interface?**

    a. hasNext()

    b. next()

    c. remove()

    d. binarySearch()

Answers

1.	b.
2.	d.
3.	c.
4.	a.
5.	d.

Questions

1. What are the primary differences between arrays and ArrayLists in Java? In what scenarios would you choose one over the other?

2. The JCF includes several types of collections, such as lists, sets, and maps. Discuss how the choice of a collection type impacts the performance and functionality of an application.

3. TreeSet and TreeMap maintain elements in sorted order. How does this feature influence their use in applications, and what trade-offs might it introduce?

4. Iterators provide flexibility in traversing collections, while enhanced for loops simplify the process. Compare and contrast these two approaches and discuss when each would be most appropriate.

5. The Collections utility class provides methods like sort(), reverse(), shuffle(), and binarySearch(). How do these methods enhance the usability of Java collections, and what limitations should developers be aware of?

6. The Comparable and Comparator interfaces both enable sorting in Java. Discuss the differences between these interfaces and provide examples of when each would be the best choice for a project.

7. HashSet, TreeSet, and LinkedHashSet all enforce uniqueness but have different internal structures and behaviors. How do these differences affect their performance and suitability for various use cases?

8. Date and Calendar classes are both used for handling dates in Java. How do these classes compare, and what modern alternatives might be better suited for working with dates and times?

9. Random is a simple and versatile utility for generating random numbers in Java. Discuss potential pitfalls or considerations when using this class in applications that require secure or predictable random values.

10. How does the concept of pseudo-randomness affect the reliability and applicability of random number generators in programming? Discuss scenarios where pseudo-randomness is sufficient and others where true randomness or cryptographically secure randomness might be necessary.

Challenges

The following questions are provided to self-assess your knowledge of the chapter's content and apply critical thinking to key concepts:

- **Spacecraft roster management**:
  - **Objective**: Use data structures to manage a dynamic list of spacecraft.
  - **Activity**: Write a Java program that maintains a list of spacecraft names using an ArrayList. The program should allow the user to:
    - Add new spacecraft to the list.
    - Remove a spacecraft from the list
    - Display the list of spacecraft in alphabetical order.
    - Search for a specific spacecraft by name.

- o **Real-world applicability**: This challenge mirrors scenarios where organizations need to maintain and manipulate dynamic datasets, such as employee rosters or inventory systems.

- **Product catalog sorting**:

  - o **Objective**: Apply sorting techniques to organize a catalog of products.

  - o **Activity**: Create a Java program using a TreeSet to manage a catalog of product names. The program should:

    - ▪ Add product names to the catalog.

    - ▪ Display the product names in alphabetical order.

    - ▪ Prevent duplicate product names from being added.

  - o **Real-world applicability**: This challenge demonstrates how sorted collections can be used in e-commerce or retail systems to maintain clean and organized catalogs.

- **Student registration system**:

  - o **Objective**: Use maps to associate data pairs to handle duplicates effectively.

  - o **Activity**: Write a program that uses a HashMap to store student IDs (keys) and names (values). The program should:

    - ▪ Allow the user to add a student ID and name to the system.

    - ▪ Check if a student ID already exists before adding it to prevent duplicates.

    - ▪ Retrieve and display the name of a student based on their ID.

  - o **Real-world applicability**: This challenge mimics real-world applications like school management systems, where unique IDs are used to track individuals.

- **Randomized quiz generator**:

  - o **Objective**: Use random number generation to create a simple quiz system.

  - o **Activity**: Develop a program that:

    - ▪ Uses the Random class to generate five random integers between 1 and 100.

    - ▪ Prompts the user to guess each number, providing feedback on whether their guess is too high, too low, or correct.

    - ▪ Displays the total number of correct guesses at the end of the quiz.

○ **Real-world applicability**: This challenge introduces randomization and user interaction, which are common in gaming and educational applications.

- **Calendar event reminder**:

  ○ **Objective**: Practice date manipulation and scheduling with the Calendar class.

  ○ **Activity**: Write a Java program that:

    ▪ Creates a Calendar instance and sets a future date (e.g., a project deadline).

    ▪ Displays the current date and the future date.

    ▪ Calculates and displays the number of days remaining until the future date.

  ○ **Real-world applicability**: This challenge demonstrates how to use date and time utilities for scheduling and deadline tracking, which are essential in project management applications.

Self-assessment

The following questions are provided so you can self-assess your knowledge of the chapter's content and apply critical thinking to key concepts:

1. What are the key differences between arrays and ArrayLists in terms of size, performance, and flexibility? Provide examples where each would be the most appropriate choice.

2. Explain how the Collections.sort() method works. What requirements must be met for it to function correctly, and how would you use it to sort a list of strings?

3. How does a HashSet differ from a TreeSet in terms of functionality and performance? Provide an example scenario where each would be the preferred choice.

4. Why is it necessary to sort a collection before using Collections.binarySearch()? What could happen if the collection is unsorted?

5. Imagine you are tasked with maintaining a log of unique usernames for an application. Which data structure would you use and why? How would you handle checking for duplicate usernames and adding new ones efficiently?

Answers

1. Arrays have a fixed size, making them faster and more memory-efficient for static datasets where the number of elements is known in advance. For example, an array is ideal for storing the days of the week.

ArrayLists, on the other hand, provide dynamic resizing, making them suitable for scenarios where the size of the dataset changes frequently, such as maintaining a list of items in an e-commerce shopping cart. ArrayLists, being part of the JCF, also offer built-in methods for operations like adding and removing elements.

2. The Collections.sort() method sorts a list in natural order (ascending for numbers, alphabetical for strings). For it to function correctly, the list must contain elements that are either primitive types or implement the Comparable interface.

3. A HashSet uses a hash table for storing elements, ensuring constant-time performance for basic operations like add and remove. It does not maintain any order. Use it when performance is critical, and order is irrelevant, such as tracking user session IDs.

4. A TreeSet stores elements in sorted order and supports range queries. Use it when order is important, like storing and retrieving product names in alphabetical order.

5. The Collections.binarySearch() method requires a sorted collection because it relies on the divide-and-conquer algorithm to efficiently locate an element. If the collection is unsorted, the results may be unpredictable or incorrect. For example, if you search for Zebra in an unsorted list, the method might not find it even if it exists. Always use Collections.sort() before binarySearch().

6. Use a HashSet to store usernames since it ensures uniqueness and provides constant-time performance for add and contains operations.

Join our Discord space

Join our Discord workspace for latest updates, offers, tech happenings around the world, new releases, and sessions with the authors:

https://discord.bpbonline.com

CHAPTER 7

Concurrency and Multithreading

Introduction

Concurrency enables programs to simultaneously handle multiple tasks and is at the heart of modern software applications. This is a performance improvement programming construct and is the focus of this chapter. The chapter starts by introducing the foundational concepts of multithreading in Java. The goal is to equip you with the tools and techniques needed to build efficient, thread-safe applications. Following the fundamentals, the chapter covers the basics of creating threads using the **Thread** class and the **Runnable** interface. It also covers synchronization and locks, which can help us achieve data consistency in concurrent environments.

The chapter also introduces the Executor framework, which simplifies thread management. It also covers Java's concurrency utilities like **CountDownLatch** and **CyclicBarrier** for coordinating complex thread interactions. Lastly, the chapter explores best practices for writing thread-safe code, helping you to avoid common pitfalls such as deadlocks and race conditions.

Structure

This chapter covers the following topics:

- Introduction to Java multithreading
- Thread class and Runnable interface

- Synchronization and locks
- Executor framework
- Concurrency utilities
- Best practices for writing concurrent code

Objectives

By the end of this chapter, you should understand the basics of multithreading and its importance in modern software development. Following the examples provided in this chapter should enable you to create and manage threads using the **Thread** class and the **Runnable** interface. You should also be able to apply synchronization and locks to maintain data consistency in concurrent applications, use the Executor framework to manage threads effectively, and implement advanced thread coordination with Java's concurrency utilities, include **CountDownLatch** and **CyclicBarrier**. Finally, by the end of this chapter, you should be able to effectively implement best practices for writing thread-safe Java code.

Introduction to Java multithreading

In Java, our applications can perform tasks within separate threads. Modern computers have multiple cores in their **central processing units (CPUs)**, allowing them to handle multiple threads simultaneously. This capability is known as multithreading. It makes efficient use of modern multi-core processors.

As you will see later in this chapter, we implement multithreading in Java by using the **java.lang.Thread** class and the **java.lang.Runnable** interface, making it easy for us to create and manage threads. One of the great benefits of multithreading is that it allows us to execute different parts of our application concurrently. This can significantly improve the performance and responsiveness in a variety of application types, including real-time systems, modern games, data processing pipelines, and more.

As you progress through this chapter and its Java code examples, you should form a foundational understanding of multithreading. It is recommended that you focus on its importance and practical implementation in Java. One of the early concepts to understand is the difference between processes and threads. For example, threads share memory space within a single process. *Figure 7.1* illustrates the concepts of threads and multithreading:

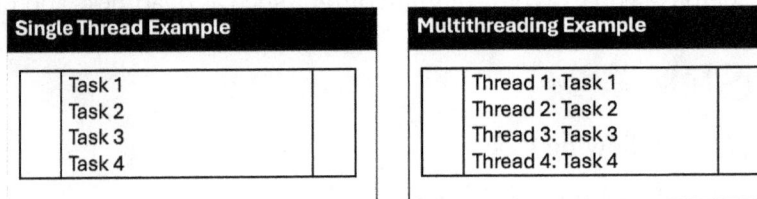

Figure 7.1: Threads and multithreading

As illustrated in *Figure 7.1*, the single-threaded approach involves each task being executed in sequence; the second one starts when the first one ends, and so on. In the multithreading example, each task is handled by a separate thread, allowing them to run at the same time (concurrently).

Let us look at a common use case for multithreading in modern video games. Multithreading is used in video games to improve the game's performance and responsiveness. *Figure 7.2* shows a basic game architecture with five distinct threads, each running concurrently:

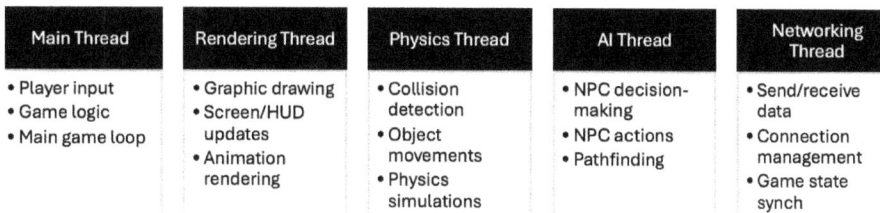

Main Thread	Rendering Thread	Physics Thread	AI Thread	Networking Thread
• Player input • Game logic • Main game loop	• Graphic drawing • Screen/HUD updates • Animation rendering	• Collision detection • Object movements • Physics simulations	• NPC decision-making • NPC actions • Pathfinding	• Send/receive data • Connection management • Game state synch

Figure 7.2: Video game multithreading example

As you can see in *Figure 7.2*, modern video games can make great use of multithreading. In this example, there are five primary threads. By separating, for example, the Rendering Thread from the Main Thread, the game can continue to process player inputs and the game logic without being slowed down or introducing lag while performing rendering tasks. A dedicated Physics Thread can allow the game to perform complex calculations while not impacting the game's performance. The AI Thread handles the **non-player characters** (**NPCs**) and their actions. It makes sense to have AI in its own thread. The Networking Thread might handle a game server and be especially important in massively multiplayer games.

An enterprise application might have the following primary threads:

- Main thread
- Database thread
- Networking thread
- User interface thread
- Logging thread
- Cache management thread
- Security thread
- Task scheduling thread
- Program or infrastructure health thread
- Background thread

In the next section, you can learn how to create and start threads using the **Thread** class and implement custom behavior by overriding its run method or by providing a **Runnable** instance.

Thread class and Runnable interface

The **Thread** class and the **Runnable** interface are the building blocks of multithreading in Java. They provide two distinct ways to create and manage threads, which empower us to execute tasks concurrently in our programs. The **Thread** class represents a single thread of execution. To use it, we simply create a subclass of **Thread** and override its run method to define the task the thread will execute.

The sections that follow use the use cases of a video game and an enterprise banking application to demonstrate how to use the **Thread** class and implement the **Runnable** interface.

Video game use case

Using a video game use case, consider a scenario where multiple components of a game (that is, rendering graphics, processing player input, and playing background music) need to operate simultaneously. Each of these tasks can run on a separate thread to ensure a smooth gaming experience. Let us look at two approaches: one using the **Thread** class and another using the **Runnable** interface.

Thread class in a video game

The **BackgroundRenderer** class in the following extends Java's **Thread** class. It simulates rendering 24 frames of background graphics:

```java
class BackgroundRenderer extends Thread {
    @Override
    public void run() {
        for (int i = 0; i < 24; i++) {
            System.out.println("Rendering background frame " + i);
            try {
                Thread.sleep(300); // Simulate rendering time
            } catch (InterruptedException e) {
                System.out.println("Rendering interrupted");
            }
        }
    }
}
```

The **GameThreadsDemo1** class contains a **start()** method that begins the thread by invoking its **run()** method in a separate thread of execution:

```java
public class GameThreadsDemo1 {
    public static void main(String[] args) {
        BackgroundRenderer renderer = new BackgroundRenderer();
```

```
        renderer.start(); // Start the background rendering thread
    }
}
```

Next, let us look at an example of our video game using the **Runnable** interface.

Runnable interface in a video game

In the previous section, we demonstrated how straightforward subclassing the **Thread** class can be. It is typically better to implement the **Runnable** interface, especially when we need to separate the task logic from thread management. This is a more flexible approach because it allows our class to extend to another class while still running as a thread.

The following is an example of processing player input using the **Runnable** interface:

```
class PlayerInputHandler implements Runnable {
    @Override
    public void run() {
        for (int i = 0; i < 24; i++) {
            System.out.println("Processing player input " + i);
            try {
                Thread.sleep(300); // Simulate input processing delay
            } catch (InterruptedException e) {
                System.out.println("Input processing interrupted");
            }
        }
    }
}
```

The **PlayerInputHandler** class above implements the **Runnable** interface. The **GameThreadsDemo2** class as follows, defines the task logic and allows the **Thread** class to manage execution:

```
public class GameThreadsDemo2 {
    public static void main(String[] args) {
        Thread inputThread = new Thread(new PlayerInputHandler());
        inputThread.start(); // Start the input handling thread
    }
}
```

In our video game example, we might need both background rendering and input processing to run simultaneously. The following example demonstrates how to combine multiple threads:

```
public class GameThreadsDemo3 {
    public static void main(String[] args) {
```

```
    Thread renderer = new BackgroundRenderer();
    Thread inputThread = new Thread(new PlayerInputHandler());

    renderer.start();
    inputThread.start();
  }
}
```

With both threads running concurrently, our game can process player input while continuously rendering graphics. This ensures a smooth, responsive gaming experience.

Enterprise banking use case

This section demonstrates how to use the **Thread** class and the **Runnable** interface with an enterprise banking application. Multithreading would be essential for handling complex operations (that is, processing multiple customer transactions, generating reports, managing notifications, etc.) in that type of application. Using the **Thread** class and **Runnable** interface would allow us to execute these tasks concurrently, ensuring responsiveness and efficiency in a high-demand environment.

Let us look at two approaches: one using the **Thread** class and another using the **Runnable** interface.

Thread class in enterprise banking

Let us suppose we are working on an enterprise banking application and need it to generate transaction reports. Each report involves heavy computations, so it can be assigned to a separate thread using the **Thread** class. The following is an example:

```
class TransactionReportGenerator extends Thread {
    private String accountNumber;

    public TransactionReportGenerator(String accountNumber) {
        this.accountNumber = accountNumber;
    }

    @Override
    public void run() {
        System.out.println("Generating transaction report for account: " +
accountNumber);
        try {
            Thread.sleep(2400); // Simulate time-consuming report generation
        } catch (InterruptedException e) {
```

```
            System.out.println("Report generation interrupted for account: " +
accountNumber);
        }
        System.out.println("Report generated for account: " + accountNumber);
    }
}
public class BankingThreadsDemo1 {
    public static void main(String[] args) {
        TransactionReportGenerator report1 = new
TransactionReportGenerator("12345");
        TransactionReportGenerator report2 = new
TransactionReportGenerator("67890");

        report1.start(); // Start the first report thread
        report2.start(); // Start the second report thread
    }
}
```

The preceding example demonstrates how multiple threads can be used to generate transaction reports for different accounts simultaneously. This will assuredly improve efficiency in our multi-user banking system.

Next, let us look at an example of enterprise banking using the **Runnable** interface.

Runnable interface in enterprise banking

When processing customer transactions, using the **Runnable** interface would allow us to decouple the business logic from thread management. Following is how we can implement that:

```
class TransactionProcessor implements Runnable {
    private String transactionId;
    public TransactionProcessor(String transactionId) {
        this.transactionId = transactionId;
    }
    @Override
    public void run() {
        System.out.println("Processing transaction: " + transactionId);
        try {
            Thread.sleep(2400); // Simulate transaction processing delay
        } catch (InterruptedException e) {
            System.out.println("Transaction interrupted: " + transactionId);
```

```
        }
        System.out.println("Transaction completed: " + transactionId);
    }
}
public class BankingThreadsDemo2 {
    public static void main(String[] args) {
        Thread transaction1 = new Thread(new TransactionProcessor("TXN001"));
        Thread transaction2 = new Thread(new TransactionProcessor("TXN002"));
        transaction1.start(); // Start the first transaction thread
        transaction2.start(); // Start the second transaction thread
    }
}
```

This approach allows our application to process multiple transactions concurrently, ensuring the system remains responsive.

In a real-world banking system, multiple threads would likely be required to manage tasks like generating transaction reports, processing payments, and sending notifications simultaneously. The following is how that can be done:

```
public class BankingThreadsDemo3 {
    public static void main(String[] args) {
        Thread reportThread = new TransactionReportGenerator("12345");
        Thread transactionThread = new Thread(new
TransactionProcessor("TXN001"));
        reportThread.start();
        transactionThread.start();

        System.out.println("Banking system is handling tasks concurrently.");
    }
}
```

By combining threads, our banking system can efficiently handle diverse tasks. This should result in an enhanced user experience even during peak load times.

Synchronization and locks

We have established the benefits of enabling multiple threads in the programs we write. These threads often need to access shared resources like game data or bank accounts. If we do not manage their access to these resources, the threads can interfere with each other, resulting in a race condition.

Note: **A race condition is when two or more threads competing for resources cause inconsistencies or data corruption.**

Synchronization and locks are programming constructs that help us manage thread access to shared resources. Our goal is to use multiple threads while ensuring data remains consistent and safe. This section explores both constructs.

Using synchronization

Synchronization, in the context of Java programming, refers to the coordination of multiple thread execution to ensure access to shared resources is available and prevents data corruption, errors, or eroding the user experience. Let us explore this a bit further with examples from our video game and banking application scenarios featured in this chapter.

Video games often implement a health bar to visually communicate health to the player. This is a shared resource with, as an example, a thread that manages the health bar to decrease health and another thread that restores health to simulate in-game healing. Without synchronization, simultaneous health bar updates could result in incorrect health values due to race conditions.

Now, consider our banking application, where separate threads are attempting to process withdrawals from the same account. This could occur when the account owner is processing a transaction, and while a scheduled electronic bill pay is simultaneously processed. Without proper synchronization, the account balance could be miscalculated, leading to overdrafts or other inconsistencies.

Synchronization example

To demonstrate how to implement synchronization, we will create a **GameHealthBar** class that manages a game player's health. The most straightforward approach to ensuring thread-safety is with the use of the synchronized keyword. In the following example, we use the synchronized keyword for the **takeDamage()** and **heal()** methods. This ensures only one thread can execute the method at a time.

Following is the **GameHealthBar** class:

```
class GameHealthBar {
    private int health = 100;
    public synchronized void takeDamage(int damage) {
        if (health > 0) {
            health -= damage;
            System.out.println("You took damage. Health: " + health);
        }
    }
    public synchronized void heal(int amount) {
```

```
        if (health < 100) {
            health += amount;
            System.out.println("You healed. Health: " + health);
        }
    }
}
```

Next, we create a class with the game's **main()** method. As you can see in the following, we create separate threads for the damage and healing functions:

```
public class GameSynchronizationDemo1 {
    public static void main(String[] args) {
        GameHealthBar healthBar = new GameHealthBar();
        Thread damageThread = new Thread(() -> {
            for (int i = 0; i < 5; i++) {
                healthBar.takeDamage(10);
                try {
                    Thread.sleep(50);
                } catch (InterruptedException e) {
                    e.printStackTrace();
                }
            }
        });
        Thread healThread = new Thread(() -> {
            for (int i = 0; i < 5; i++) {
                healthBar.heal(5);
                try {
                    Thread.sleep(70);
                } catch (InterruptedException e) {
                    e.printStackTrace();
                }
            }
        });
        damageThread.start();
        healThread.start();
    }
}
```

The output of the program is shown in the following. This is because we used the **synchronized** keyword; our updates to the **health** variable are consistent, even when it is being simultaneously accessed by multiple threads:

```
You took damage. Health: 90
You healed. Health: 95
You took damage. Health: 85
You healed. Health: 90
You took damage. Health: 80
You healed. Health: 85
You took damage. Health: 75
You took damage. Health: 65
You healed. Health: 70
You healed. Health: 75
```

Next, we will look at locks, a second approach to help avoid race conditions in a multithreaded environment.

Using locks

When necessary, we can implement a more advanced approach to synchronization. Specifically, we can implement Java's **java.util.concurrent.locks.Lock** interface, which gives us greater control over thread access. A **ReentrantLock**, for example, can explicitly lock and unlock critical sections of code. This allows for more sophisticated thread management, such as trying to acquire a lock with a timeout or checking if the lock is held by any thread. Additionally, **ReentrantLock** provides better performance under high contention compared to **synchronized** blocks, making it a preferred choice for complex multithreaded applications.

Locks example

To demonstrate locks, we will write a **BankAccount1** class that includes a **balance** variable and a lock using the **ReentrantLock** class from **java.util.concurrent.locks**. The **BankAccount1** class has a constructor to set the initial **balance** and a **withdraw** method to withdraw an amount from the account. When the **withdraw** method is called, it obtains the lock to ensure that only one thread can modify the balance at a time. Inside the **try** block, it checks if there are sufficient funds. If there are, it subtracts the withdrawal amount from the balance and prints the remaining balance. If not, it prints a message indicating there are insufficient funds. Finally, the lock is released in the final block to ensure it always gets released, even if an exception occurs. This code ensures thread-safety by using a lock to control access to the shared balance resource.

Following is the **BankAccount1** class:

```
import java.util.concurrent.locks.Lock;
import java.util.concurrent.locks.ReentrantLock;
class BankAccount1 {
    private double balance;
```

```
    private final Lock lock = new ReentrantLock();
    public BankAccount1(double initialBalance) {
        this.balance = initialBalance;
    }
    public void withdraw(double amount) {
        lock.lock(); // Obtain lock
        try {
            if (balance >= amount) {
                System.out.println("Withdrawing: " + amount);
                balance -= amount;
                System.out.println("Remaining Balance: " + balance);
            } else {
                System.out.println("Low funds; cannot withdraw: " + amount);
            }
        } finally {
            lock.unlock(); // Release lock
        }
    }
}
```

Our use of **ReentrantLock** ensures that only one thread can access the critical section of our code at a time, preventing race conditions. Following is the driver program for the **BankAccount1** class:

```
public class BankingLocksDemo1 {
    public static void main(String[] args) {
        BankAccount1 account = new BankAccount1(1500);
        Thread user1 = new Thread(() -> account.withdraw(900));
        Thread user2 = new Thread(() -> account.withdraw(700));
        user1.start();
        user2.start();
    }
}
```

Following is the output of the program:

```
Withdrawing: 900.0
Remaining Balance: 600.0
Low funds; cannot withdraw: 700.0
```

Avoiding deadlocks with tryLock

While synchronization and locks can be used to solve many concurrency issues, they can also introduce new problems. One such problem is with deadlocks, which occur when two or more threads are waiting indefinitely for each other's locks.

To avoid deadlocks, we should be consistent in the order in which we acquire our locks across all threads. It is also advisable to minimize the scope of **synchronized** code to help reduce contention. We can also use the **tryLock()** method, which is part of the **java.util. concurrent.locks.Lock** interface. This is especially useful when we want to avoid deadlocks by attempting to acquire a lock without blocking it indefinitely. The method returns a Boolean indicating whether the lock was successfully acquired. Following is the basic syntax of **tryLock()** and an example of how to use it:

```
boolean tryLock();
```

We can also use **tryLock()** with a timeout. Following is the syntax for that version:

```
boolean tryLock(long timeout, TimeUnit unit) throws InterruptedException;
```

The **timeout** parameter is the maximum time to wait. This version of the method returns **true** if the lock is acquired within the specified time or false if the timeout expires before the lock can be acquired.

The next sections provide examples of both versions of **tryLock()**, one without blocking and one with a **timeout**.

Example without blocking

In our banking application example, consider that two threads are trying to access the same account for different transactions. We can implement **tryLock()** to prevent one thread from waiting indefinitely for the lock. The following is an example:

```
import java.util.concurrent.locks.Lock;
import java.util.concurrent.locks.ReentrantLock;
class BankAccount2 {
    private double balance;
    private final Lock lock = new ReentrantLock();
    public BankAccount2(double initialBalance) {
        this.balance = initialBalance;
    }
    public void withdraw(double amount) {
        if (lock.tryLock()) {
            try {
                if (balance >= amount) {
```

```
                    System.out.println("Withdrawing: " + amount);
                    balance -= amount;
                    System.out.println("Remaining Balance: " + balance);
                } else {
                    System.out.println("Low funds; cannot withdraw: " +
amount);
                }
            } finally {
                lock.unlock();
            }
        } else {
            System.out.println("Unable to acquire lock. Transaction
skipped.");
        }
    }
}
```

Following is the driver code for our example:

```
public class BankingLocksDemo2 {
    public static void main(String[] args) {
        BankAccount2 account = new BankAccount2(1500);

        Thread user1 = new Thread(() -> account.withdraw(900));
        Thread user2 = new Thread(() -> account.withdraw(700));

        user1.start();
        user2.start();
    }
}
```

Example of time out

We can also implement **tryLock()** when we want a thread to wait for a specific time period before giving up on acquiring the lock. To do this, we use the timeout version of **tryLock()**. Following is an example implementation using our banking application:

```
import java.util.concurrent.TimeUnit;
import java.util.concurrent.locks.Lock;
import java.util.concurrent.locks.ReentrantLock;
class BankAccount3 {
    private double balance;
```

```java
    private final Lock lock = new ReentrantLock();
    public BankAccount3(double initialBalance) {
        this.balance = initialBalance;
    }
    public void withdraw(double amount) {
        try {
            if (lock.tryLock(3, TimeUnit.SECONDS)) {
                try {
                    if (balance >= amount) {
                        System.out.println("Withdrawing: " + amount);
                        balance -= amount;
                        System.out.println("Remaining Balance: " + balance);
                    } else {
                        System.out.println("Low funds; cannot withdraw: " +
amount);
                    }
                } finally {
                    lock.unlock();
                }
            } else {
                System.out.println("Unable to acquire lock within the timeout.
Transaction skipped.");
            }
        } catch (InterruptedException e) {
            System.out.println("Thread interrupted while waiting for lock.");
        }
    }
}
```

Following is the driver code for our example:

```java
public class BankingLocksDemo3 {
    public static void main(String[] args) {
        BankAccount3 account = new BankAccount3(1500);

        Thread user1 = new Thread(() -> account.withdraw(900));
        Thread user2 = new Thread(() -> account.withdraw(700));

        user1.start();
        user2.start();
```

```
    }
}
```

Executor framework

Our thread management thus far has been manual, and that can quickly become challenging. This is especially true when dealing with many tasks and when we want to optimize thread usage. The Executor framework simplifies thread management in Java by decoupling task submission from the mechanics of how threads are managed. Instead of creating and managing threads manually, as we have done up to this point, we can use the Executor framework to efficiently handle concurrent tasks in our applications.

The Executor framework is part of the **java.util.concurrent** package. It offers a set of flexible tools for managing thread pools, scheduling tasks, and optimizing resource usage. To identify the usefulness of this framework, let us consider our two application examples (video game and banking app) used throughout this chapter.

In our video game, we need to handle multiple tasks, including rendering graphics, processing player inputs, managing NPC behaviors, and more. Manually creating and managing threads for each of those tasks would be inefficient and likely introduce errors.

Our banking application needs to handle multiple concurrent requests, such as balance inquiries, withdrawals, and transaction history generation. This can easily overload the system if each request is handled by a new thread. A thread pool provided by the Executor framework allows the system to manage requests efficiently without exhausting resources.

The Executor framework consists of several key components, as indicated in *Table 7.1*:

Component	Explanation
Executor interface	This is the base interface.
ExecutorService interface	This is a more advanced interface that includes lifecycle management as well as methods for task submission.
ScheduledExecutorService interface	This can be used for scheduling tasks periodically or after a delay.
ThreadPoolExecutor class	Used for managing thread pools.

Table 7.1: Executor framework components

Let us look at how to implement the Executor framework using our video game and banking application examples.

Executor example for a video game

To demonstrate the usefulness of the executor framework, we will start with our video game example. Our game has several tasks (that is, rendering graphics, processing player input, and spawning NPCs that run concurrently using the Executor framework.

The following are three classes, each simulating a different task:

```java
public class GameRenderTask implements Runnable {
    @Override
    public void run() {
        System.out.println("Rendering graphics...");
    }
}
public class GameInputTask implements Runnable {
    @Override
    public void run() {
        System.out.println("Processing player input...");
    }
}
public class GameSpawnNPCTask implements Runnable {
    @Override
    public void run() {
        System.out.println("Spawning NPC...");
    }
}
```

Following is the driver program where we use **Executors.newFixedThreadPool(3)** to create a thread pool with three threads:

```java
import java.util.concurrent.ExecutorService;
import java.util.concurrent.Executors;

public class GameExecutorDemo1 {
    public static void main(String[] args) {
        ExecutorService executor = Executors.newFixedThreadPool(3);
        executor.execute(new GameRenderTask());
        executor.execute(new GameInputTask());
        executor.execute(new GameSpawnNPCTask());
        executor.shutdown();
    }
}
```

As seen in the preceding code, the **execute()** method is used to submit tasks to the thread pool for execution, and the **shutdown()** method stops the thread pool after all tasks have completed.

Executor example for a banking application

Now, let us consider how we would use the **Executor** class in our banking application. Our application might be required to concurrently process multiple customer transactions. Following is an example implementation:

```java
public class BankTransactionTask implements Runnable {
    private String transactionId;
    public BankTransactionTask(String transactionId) {
        this.transactionId = transactionId;
    }
    @Override
    public void run() {
        System.out.println("Processing transaction: " + transactionId);
    }
}
```

Following is the driver program where **Executors.newCachedThreadPool()** is used to create a thread pool that dynamically adjusts the number of threads based on the demand:

```java
import java.util.concurrent.ExecutorService;
import java.util.concurrent.Executors;
public class BankingExecutorDemo {
    public static void main(String[] args) {
        ExecutorService executor = Executors.newCachedThreadPool();
        executor.execute(new BankTransactionTask("BTXN000001"));
        executor.execute(new BankTransactionTask("BTXN000002"));
        executor.execute(new BankTransactionTask("BTXN000003"));
        executor.execute(new BankTransactionTask("BTXN000004"));
        executor.execute(new BankTransactionTask("BTXN000005"));
        executor.shutdown();
    }
}
```

ScheduledExecutorService example

Java's Executor framework also includes **ScheduledExecutorService**, which is a specialized **Executor** that allows tasks to run periodically or after a specified delay. Let us implement this in our banking application. We will implement regularly scheduled balance notifications. Following is the code:

```java
public class BankBalanceNotifications implements Runnable {
    @Override
    public void run() {
        System.out.println("Sending balance notification to customers...");
    }
}
```

Following is the driver class:

```java
import java.util.concurrent.Executors;
import java.util.concurrent.ScheduledExecutorService;
import java.util.concurrent.TimeUnit;

public class BankScheduledExecutorDemo {
    public static void main(String[] args) {
        ScheduledExecutorService scheduler = Executors.
newScheduledThreadPool(1);

        // Schedule the task to run every 10 seconds
        scheduler.scheduleAtFixedRate(new BankBalanceNotifications(), 0, 10,
TimeUnit.SECONDS);
    }
}
```

Our example uses **Executors.newScheduledThreadPool(1)** to create a scheduled thread pool with one thread. The **scheduleAtFixedRate** method runs **BankBalanceNotifications** every 10 seconds.

Concurrency utilities

The **java.util.concurrent** package contains a multitude of concurrency utilities that are designed to help us develop multithreaded applications. We have already covered several of them, including **ExecutorService**, **ScheduledExecutorService**, and **ReentrantLock**. This section explores three additional utilities: **CountDownLatch**, **CyclicBarrier**, and **Semaphore**. These tools provide us with advanced control over thread coordination and thread synchronization. This enables us to handle complex interactions between threads. Understanding these tools can result in code that is readable and efficient.

CountDownLatch

A **CountDownLatch** is a synchronization tool we can use to allow one or more threads to wait until a set of operations in other threads finishes. When the latch reaches zero, all waiting threads are released. This is a simple and powerful construct.

The following implementation uses our video game example. Here we program a **GameResourceLoader** class that uses a **CountDownLatch** to ensure the game does not start until all resources are loaded:

```java
import java.util.concurrent.CountDownLatch;
class GameResourceLoader implements Runnable {
    private final CountDownLatch latch;
    private final String resource;
    public GameResourceLoader(CountDownLatch latch, String resource) {
        this.latch = latch;
        this.resource = resource;
    }
    @Override
    public void run() {
        System.out.println("Loading " + resource);
        try {
            Thread.sleep(1000); // Simulate loading time
        } catch (InterruptedException e) {
            e.printStackTrace();
        }
        System.out.println(resource + " loaded.");
        latch.countDown();
    }
}
```

Following is the driver class:

```java
import java.util.concurrent.CountDownLatch;

public class GameCountDownLatchDemo {
    public static void main(String[] args) throws InterruptedException {
        CountDownLatch latch = new CountDownLatch(3);

        new Thread(new GameResourceLoader(latch, "Textures")).start();
        new Thread(new GameResourceLoader(latch, "Sounds")).start();
        new Thread(new GameResourceLoader(latch, "Models")).start();
```

```
        new Thread(new GameResourceLoader(latch, "Levels")).start();

        latch.await(); // Wait for all resources to load
        System.out.println("All resources loaded. Game starting...");
    }
}
```

Note: **If you have ever played a video game that had a loading screen, the developers used this approach to ensure all Textures, Sounds, Models, Levels, etc., were loaded before the game could be played.**

As you can see in our example implementation, the game waits for all resources to be loaded before starting.

Next, let us look at another implementation, this time using our baking application example. Consider that transactions over a specified threshold might require approvals from multiple banking officials or departments. We can use a **CountDownLatch** to ensure the transaction processing thread waits until all required approvals are received. Following is how that could be implemented:

```
import java.util.concurrent.CountDownLatch;

class BankApprovalTask implements Runnable {
    private final CountDownLatch latch;
    private final String department;

    public BankApprovalTask(CountDownLatch latch, String department) {
        this.latch = latch;
        this.department = department;
    }

    @Override
    public void run() {
        System.out.println("Approval from " + department + " in progress...");
        try {
            Thread.sleep(1500); // Simulate approval time
        } catch (InterruptedException e) {
            e.printStackTrace();
        }
        System.out.println(department + " approved.");
        latch.countDown();
    }
```

```
}
```

Following is the driver class:

```java
import java.util.concurrent.CountDownLatch;
public class BankCountDownLatchDemo {
    public static void main(String[] args) throws InterruptedException {
        CountDownLatch latch = new CountDownLatch(3);
        new Thread(new BankApprovalTask(latch, "Finance")).start();
        new Thread(new BankApprovalTask(latch, "Risk Management")).start();
        new Thread(new BankApprovalTask(latch, "Compliance")).start();
        latch.await(); // Wait for all approvals
        System.out.println("Transaction approved by all departments.");
    }
}
```

CyclicBarrier

A **CyclicBarrier** can be used to synchronize multiple threads, making them wait at a common point until all threads reach the barrier. Once all threads reach the barrier, they are released to continue their respective execution. This construct is especially useful in scenarios where threads must wait for each other to reach a certain point before proceeding. Because this can be reused after the threads are released, it is ideally suited for iterative tasks. Let us look at a sample implementation using our video game example. Consider that the game is a multiplayer racing game, and players must wait at a starting line before the game begins. We can use a **CyclicBarrier** to ensure all players are ready before the race starts. The following is how that can be implemented:

```java
import java.util.concurrent.CyclicBarrier;
class GamePlayer implements Runnable {
    private final CyclicBarrier barrier;
    private final String name;
    public GamePlayer(CyclicBarrier barrier, String name) {
        this.barrier = barrier;
        this.name = name;
    }

    @Override
    public void run() {
        try {
            System.out.println(name + " is ready.");
            barrier.await(); // Wait for all players to be ready
```

```
            System.out.println(name + " starts playing!");
        } catch (Exception e) {
            e.printStackTrace();
        }
    }
}
```

Following is the driver class:

```
import java.util.concurrent.CyclicBarrier;
public class GameCyclicBarrierDemo {
    public static void main(String[] args) {
        CyclicBarrier barrier = new CyclicBarrier(3, () -> System.out.
println("All players are ready. Game starts!"));
        new Thread(new GamePlayer(barrier, "Player 1")).start();
        new Thread(new GamePlayer(barrier, "Player 2")).start();
        new Thread(new GamePlayer(barrier, "Player 3")).start();
    }
}
```

Next, let us look at another implementation of **CyclicBarrier**, this time using our baking application example. We might need to add the ability to generate comprehensive financial reports in our banking application. This might require data from multiple departments. We can use a **CyclicBarrier** to ensure that all departments complete their data preparation before the report is generated. Following is how that could be implemented:

```
import java.util.concurrent.CyclicBarrier;
class BankDepartmentTask implements Runnable {
    private final CyclicBarrier barrier;
    private final String department;
    public BankDepartmentTask(CyclicBarrier barrier, String department) {
        this.barrier = barrier;
        this.department = department;
    }
    @Override
    public void run() {
        try {
            System.out.println(department + " department is preparing data.");
            Thread.sleep(2000); // Simulate data preparation time
            System.out.println(department + " department has finished.");
            barrier.await(); // Wait for other departments
        } catch (Exception e) {
```

```
            e.printStackTrace();
        }
    }
}
```

Following is the driver class:

```
import java.util.concurrent.CyclicBarrier;
public class BankCyclicBarrierDemo {
    public static void main(String[] args) {
        CyclicBarrier barrier = new CyclicBarrier(3, () -> System.out.
println("All departments have finished. Generating financial report."));
        new Thread(new BankDepartmentTask(barrier, "Finance")).start();
        new Thread(new BankDepartmentTask(barrier, "Risk")).start();
        new Thread(new BankDepartmentTask(barrier, "Compliance")).start();
    }
}
```

Semaphore

A **Semaphore** controls access to a resource by allowing a limited number of threads to acquire it at the same time. It is useful for managing access when there is a fixed number of resources. It is a synchronization aid that restricts the number of concurrent threads that can access a particular resource. A **Semaphore** maintains a set of permits and uses two primary methods:

- **acquire()** blocks, if necessary, until a permit is available, and then take it.

- **release()** adds a permit, potentially releasing a blocking acquirer.

Following is an example implementation for a video game that needs to limit the number of players who can log in at the same time:

```
import java.util.concurrent.Semaphore;

class GameLoginTask implements Runnable {
    private final Semaphore semaphore;
    public GameLoginTask(Semaphore semaphore) {
        this.semaphore = semaphore;
    }
    @Override
    public void run() {
        try {
            semaphore.acquire();
```

```
                System.out.println(Thread.currentThread().getName() + " logged
in.");
                Thread.sleep(2000); // Simulate gameplay
            } catch (InterruptedException e) {
                e.printStackTrace();
            } finally {
                System.out.println(Thread.currentThread().getName() + " logged
out.");
                semaphore.release();
            }
        }
    }
}
```

Following is the driver class:

```
import java.util.concurrent.Semaphore;
public class GameSemaphoreDemo {
    public static void main(String[] args) {
        Semaphore semaphore = new Semaphore(2); // Limit to 2 concurrent
logins
        for (int i = 1; i <= 5; i++) {
            new Thread(new GameLoginTask(semaphore), "Player " + i).start();
        }
    }
}
```

Best practices for writing concurrent code

Modern Java applications have an emphasis on efficiency, underscoring the importance of writing concurrent code. Creating functionality so our applications can simultaneously handle multiple tasks introduces challenges such as race conditions, deadlocks, and resource contention. This section presents several best practices to help mitigate these risks and help you ensure your multithreaded Java applications are both reliable and maintainable.

The following best practices should always be followed when writing concurrent code:

- **Avoid blocking operations**: Blocking operations, such as waiting for a thread to complete or acquiring a lock indefinitely, can cause performance bottlenecks. To avoid blocking issues, we can use non-blocking algorithms where possible, use **tryLock()** with a timeout to prevent indefinite blocking, and use asynchronous tasks to improve responsiveness.

- **Avoid deadlocks**: A deadlock can occur when two or more threads are waiting on each other to release locks, resulting in a standstill. To prevent deadlocks, we should always acquire locks in a consistent order, use `tryLock()` to avoid indefinite waiting, and break large tasks into smaller, independent tasks that do not require holding multiple locks simultaneously.

- **Document concurrency requirements**: To ensure our code is maintainable, we should thoroughly document which resources are shared between threads, what synchronization mechanisms are used to protect shared resources, and any potential deadlock scenarios and how they are mitigated.

- **Handle exceptions gracefully**: Regardless of the programming construct, we should always handle our exceptions gracefully. Unhandled exceptions in one thread can cause the entire application to fail or leave shared resources in an inconsistent state. Graceful exception handling includes always wrapping concurrent code in try-catch blocks and using custom exception handlers for thread pools. Refer to *Chapter 5, Handling Errors and Exceptions,* for additional insights.

- **Profile and monitor concurrent code**: Concurrency issues often arise under specific conditions, such as high load or specific timing sequences. Use monitoring tools, such as **Java VisualVM (JVisualVM)** and **Java Mission Control (JMC)**, to monitor thread behavior. **Application performance monitoring** (APM) tools can be used to detect deadlocks, race conditions, and bottlenecks in production. Refer to *Chapter 13, Debugging, Testing, and Deployment,* for additional insights.

- **Protect critical sections**: Identify critical sections of code that modify shared resources and protect them to ensure data consistency. Use appropriate synchronization mechanisms as outlined in this chapter.

- **Thoroughly test concurrent code**: Concurrency issues are often hard to detect through informal testing. To ensure your concurrent code is reliable, you should use stress testing tools to simulate high concurrency loads, test your code under different environments and hardware configurations, and use concurrency testing frameworks. Refer to *Chapter 13, Debugging, Testing, and Deployment,* for additional insights.

- **Use higher-level concurrency utilities**: Instead of manually managing threads, use the Executor framework and concurrency utilities provided in the `java.util.concurrent` package. This approach can result in Java handling many of the complexities of thread management for us. Specifically, use `ExecutorService` for task management and use `CountDownLatch`, `CyclicBarrier`, and `Semaphore` to coordinate thread interactions.

Writing concurrent code requires us to adopt a performance-maximization mindset. By following the best practices presented above, you should be able to build robust multithreaded applications that are efficient, maintainable, and free from common concurrency pitfalls.

Conclusion

This chapter explored the essential concepts and tools for building concurrent applications in Java. Starting with the basics of multithreading using the Thread class and Runnable interface, you had the opportunity to learn how to create and manage threads effectively. The chapter also covered synchronization techniques, such as using locks and the synchronized keyword, to maintain data consistency and prevent race conditions.

The Executor framework was introduced and established as a powerful abstraction for managing thread pools, and various concurrency utilities like CountDownLatch, CyclicBarrier, and Semaphore. Those utilities were shown to simplify complex thread interactions and enable us to build scalable and efficient applications by handling concurrent tasks with ease.

The concepts, practices, and examples covered in this chapter were intended to equip you to tackle real-world concurrency challenges.

The next chapter focuses on functional programming in Java, particularly the streams **application programming interface** (**API**) introduced in Java 8. This chapter explains how to work with streams, performing operations like filtering, mapping, and reducing data in a functional style. The chapter also explores functional interfaces such as Predicate, Consumer, and Supplier, which power much of modern Java's functional capabilities. Hands-on opportunities are provided for working with lambdas and parallel streams to handle large datasets efficiently. By mastering these techniques, you can be better prepared to write cleaner, more efficient code.

Points to remember

- acquire() and release() methods in Semaphore control the number of concurrent threads accessing a shared resource.

- APM tools can help detect deadlocks, race conditions, and performance bottlenecks in production systems.

- Blocking operations can cause performance bottlenecks; use non-blocking algorithms or tryLock() to avoid indefinite waiting.

- Concurrency improves performance by allowing multiple tasks to execute simultaneously, especially in multi-core systems.

- Concurrency issues, such as race conditions and deadlocks, arise when multiple threads access shared resources without proper synchronization.

- Concurrency utilities, such as CountDownLatch, CyclicBarrier, and Semaphore, simplify complex thread interactions and coordination.

- CountDownLatch allows threads to wait until a set number of operations are completed before continuing execution.

- CyclicBarrier enables multiple threads to wait at a common point until all threads reach the barrier, making it useful for iterative tasks.

- Deadlocks occur when two or more threads wait indefinitely for each other's locks; consistent lock ordering and **tryLock()** can help prevent them.

- Documenting shared resources and synchronization mechanisms is essential for maintaining concurrent code.

- Executor framework provides tools to manage thread pools, task scheduling, and resource optimization, improving scalability and maintainability.

- ExecutorService offers lifecycle management and task submission methods, such as execute() and shutdown().

- Java's Thread class allows you to create a thread by extending the class and overriding the run() method.

- Lock interfaces, like ReentrantLock, offer more granular control over synchronization compared to synchronized blocks.

- Methods protected by synchronization ensure only one thread can access critical sections at a time.

- Multithreading enables programs to execute tasks concurrently, improving performance and responsiveness.

- Non-blocking algorithms can be used to avoid issues caused by threads waiting for resources indefinitely.

- Proper exception handling in concurrent code ensures applications remain stable even when unexpected issues occur.

- Runnable interface provides a more flexible way to define tasks for threads, allowing your class to extend other classes while still being runnable by threads.

- ScheduledExecutorService allows tasks to be scheduled to run periodically or after a delay.

- Semaphore controls access to a limited number of permits, ensuring that only a fixed number of threads can access a shared resource simultaneously.

- Synchronization using synchronized methods or locks ensures that shared resources remain consistent when accessed by multiple threads.

- Test concurrent code thoroughly using stress testing tools and concurrency frameworks to identify potential issues under high loads.

- tryLock() provides a way to acquire a lock without blocking indefinitely; it can be used with or without a timeout.

Case studies

These case studies provide realistic scenarios that encourage you to think critically about how concurrency and multithreading can be used to solve real-world challenges. These scenarios are based on fictitious companies and are designed to help you apply the concepts covered in this chapter to practical situations. Each case study includes guiding questions to encourage critical thinking and problem-solving.

- **Optimizing game performance**: *ExoGame Studios* is a gaming company developing a popular massively multiplayer online game called *Galactic Conquest*. The game features complex graphics rendering, real-time player interactions, and AI-driven NPCs. Recently, players have complained about performance issues such as input lag and rendering delays during large multiplayer battles. The game currently uses a single-threaded architecture for handling most game components. The development team is considering adopting multithreading to improve performance by separating tasks such as graphics rendering, input processing, AI, and networking.

  o **For your consideration**: Which tasks in the game should be handled by separate threads to optimize performance? How could the Executor framework be used to manage thread pools for different game components? What concurrency utilities (e.g., CountDownLatch or CyclicBarrier) would be useful in coordinating game start events or synchronizing player actions? What precautions should the team take to avoid race conditions or deadlocks when multiple threads access shared game data?

- **Preventing transaction conflicts**: *Nova Bank Ltd.* is a digital bank with millions of customers. The bank's transaction processing system has recently faced issues with concurrent withdrawals and deposits on the same account, leading to inconsistent account balances. The current system processes each transaction in its own thread without proper synchronization, which has caused race conditions when multiple transactions occur simultaneously on the same account. NovaBank's IT department has been tasked with redesigning the transaction system to ensure accurate account balances, even during high-traffic periods. They are considering using locks and synchronization to manage access to account data.

  o **For your consideration**: How would you use locks to ensure that only one thread can modify an account balance at a time? What role could the tryLock() method play in preventing deadlocks during transaction processing? How might the bank use a Semaphore to limit the number of concurrent transactions processed on a single account? What best practices from this chapter would you recommend to ensure thread-safety and prevent performance bottlenecks?

- **Managing large-scale data processing**: *Cygnus Data Corp* specializes in processing large datasets for scientific research. The company's flagship product, StellarAnalysis, processes astronomical data from space observatories to detect patterns in cosmic phenomena. The current version of the software struggles with performance issues due to its single-threaded data processing pipeline. The engineering team at Cygnus Data Corp wants to redesign the data pipeline using multithreading to improve performance. They are exploring the use of the Executor framework to distribute data processing tasks across multiple threads and are considering using concurrency utilities to manage dependencies between different stages of the pipeline.

- o   **For your consideration**: How could the Executor framework be used to manage the different stages of the data processing pipeline? In what situations would CountDownLatch be useful for ensuring that all data is loaded before starting the analysis? How might Cygnus Data Corp use CyclicBarrier to synchronize different stages of the data processing pipeline? What challenges might arise from using multithreading in this scenario, and how would you address them?

- **Scheduling patient notifications**: Andromeda Health is a healthcare provider that sends patients automated appointment reminders and health tips via its mobile app. The system currently processes notifications in a batch job, but delays are causing patients to receive reminders late. The company wants to move to a real-time notification system using scheduled threads. The IT team is considering implementing a ScheduledExecutorService to handle real-time notifications and ensure that reminders are sent on time. They are also exploring the possibility of limiting the number of concurrent notifications sent to avoid overwhelming the server.

- o   **For your consideration**: How could ScheduledExecutorService be used to send periodic notifications to patients? What steps would you take to ensure that the notification system does not become overloaded during peak times? How could Andromeda Health use a Semaphore to limit the number of concurrent notifications sent? What additional measures could be taken to ensure that notifications are sent reliably and without duplication?

- **Synchronizing distributed systems**: *QuantumCom* is a telecommunications provider that manages distributed systems across multiple data centers. These systems must remain synchronized to ensure consistent data across all locations. The company has been facing synchronization issues that lead to inconsistent records when data is updated concurrently from different locations. The IT team at QuantumCom is looking to implement synchronization mechanisms to ensure that data updates are coordinated across data centers. They are considering using CyclicBarrier to synchronize data updates and CountDownLatch to ensure that all data centers have received updates before committing changes.

- o   **For your consideration**: How could CyclicBarrier be used to ensure that all data centers are ready before synchronizing updates? What role could CountDownLatch play in ensuring that all data centers have processed updates before confirming data consistency? How might QuantumCom handle scenarios where a data center fails to synchronize within a specified timeframe? What other concurrency utilities or best practices from this chapter could be applied to ensure reliable distributed synchronization?

Multiple choice questions

1. **Which of the following is an advantage of using the Executor framework in Java?**

   a. It allows for infinite thread creation without resource management.

   b. It simplifies thread management by providing thread pools and task scheduling.

   c. It eliminates the need for synchronization in concurrent applications.

   d. It prevents all types of concurrency issues automatically.

2. **In a banking application, which concurrency utility would be most appropriate to ensure that a transaction processing thread waits until approvals from multiple departments are received?**

   a. CountDownLatch

   b. Semaphore

   c. CyclicBarrier

   d. ScheduledExecutorService

3. **Which method from the Lock interface allows a thread to attempt to acquire a lock without blocking indefinitely?**

   a. acquire()

   b. release()

   c. tryLock()

   d. lockInterruptiblity()

4. **What is the key difference between the synchronized keyword and the ReentrantLock class?**

   a. Synchronized provides. More control over locks than ReentrantLock.

   b. ReentrantLock allows for timed attempts to acquire a lock, while synchronized does not.

   c. Synchronized can be used with tryLock(), but RenentrantLock cannot.

   d. Reentrantock does not require a final block for unlocking.

5. **Which concurrency utility is best suited for ensuring that all players in a multiplayer game are ready before starting the game?**

   a. ScheduledExecutorService

   b. Semaphore

   c. CountDownLatch

   d. CyclicBarrier

Answers

1.	b.
2.	a.
3.	c.
4.	b.
5.	d.

Questions

1. Why is multithreading important in modern software applications, and how does it improve performance in both video games and enterprise systems? Discuss specific use cases from the chapter and share real-world examples of applications that benefit from multithreading.

2. What are some of the risks associated with using multiple threads to access shared resources? How do synchronization and locks help address these risks, and what best practices can be followed to prevent issues such as race conditions and deadlocks?

3. The Executor framework simplifies thread management by decoupling task submission from execution. How would you explain the advantages of using the Executor framework to someone who is unfamiliar with multithreading? Provide examples from the video game and banking application scenarios.

4. In the chapter, the CountDownLatch and CyclicBarrier utilities were introduced as tools for coordinating threads. How do these utilities differ in terms of their functionality and use cases? Which scenarios would benefit more from using CountDownLatch versus CyclicBarrier?

5. Locks provide more control over thread synchronization compared to the synchronized keyword. What are the key differences between ReentrantLock and synchronized blocks? When would you choose one over the other, and why?

6. Deadlocks can occur when multiple threads wait indefinitely for each other to release locks. What are some strategies you can implement to prevent deadlocks in a

multithreaded application? How does the tryLock() method help mitigate the risk of deadlocks?

7. Concurrency utilities such as Semaphore are used to control access to shared resources. How could a Semaphore be applied in a real-world system to limit the number of concurrent users accessing a critical resource? Discuss the potential advantages and disadvantages of using a Semaphore.

8. The chapter covered best practices for writing concurrent code, including the importance of exception handling and profiling. Why is it important to handle exceptions gracefully in multithreaded applications? How can tools like JVisualVM and JMC assist in identifying concurrency issues?

9. How would you design a multithreaded application to process high-volume transactions in a banking system? Discuss how you would use the concepts of thread pools, locks, and concurrency utilities to ensure both efficiency and accuracy in the system.

10. How would you decide whether to use a synchronized block, a ReentrantLock, or a Semaphore in a multithreaded application? Discuss the scenarios where each synchronization mechanism is best suited. Consider factors such as performance, ease of use, and thread coordination. Provide examples of when you might prefer one over the others and explain your reasoning.

Challenges

The following questions are provided to self-assess your knowledge of the chapter's content and apply critical thinking to key concepts:

*   **Improving a video game's performance with threads**:

    o   **Objective**: Learn to apply multithreading concepts to improve the responsiveness of a video game application.

    o   **Activity**: You are tasked with optimizing a simple video game that currently processes all tasks on a single thread. The game has three main tasks: rendering graphics, processing player input, and playing background music. Perform the following actions:

        ▪   Refactor the game by creating separate threads for each task.

        ▪   Use the Thread class and the Runnable interface to implement this.

        ▪   Ensure that the game runs smoothly by preventing any blocking operations in the main thread.

o **Real-world applicability**: This challenge mirrors real-world scenarios where video games and interactive applications must handle multiple tasks simultaneously to avoid lag and improve user experience.

- **Ensuring data consistency in a banking application**:

  o **Objective**: Practice using synchronization and locks to manage shared resources in a concurrent environment.

  o **Activity**: Perform the following actions:

    ▪ Write a Java program for a banking system that allows multiple users to withdraw funds from the same bank account simultaneously.

    ▪ Use a BankAccount class with a withdraw method.

    ▪ Use synchronization to ensure that only one thread can modify the account balance at a time.

    ▪ Test your program with multiple threads trying to withdraw funds concurrently and verify that the account balance remains accurate.

  o **Real-world applicability**: This challenge simulates a common issue in financial applications where concurrent transactions can cause inconsistent data if not properly synchronized.

- **Managing a thread pool for task scheduling**:

  o **Objective**: Learn to use the Executor framework to manage concurrent tasks efficiently.

  o **Activity**: Perform the following actions:

    ▪ Write a Java program to simulate a task scheduling system for a customer service center. The system should handle the following tasks:

      ◆ Processing customer requests

      ◆ Sending follow-up emails

      ◆ Generating daily reports

    ▪ Use the ExecutorService from the Executor framework to manage a fixed thread pool of three threads. Submit the tasks to the thread pool and ensure that all tasks are executed efficiently without creating unnecessary threads.

  o **Real-world applicability**: This challenge demonstrates how businesses can optimize resource usage by managing concurrent tasks through thread pools, reducing server load, and improving response times.

- **Coordinating multiple threads with** CountDownLatch:

  o **Objective**: Apply the CountDownLatch utility to ensure that multiple threads complete their tasks before proceeding.

  o **Activity**: Perform the following actions:

    ▪ Write a Java program to simulate a video game loading screen. The game should not start until all required resources are loaded:

      ◆ Textures

      ◆ Sounds

      ◆ Models

      ◆ Levels

    ▪ Use a CountDownLatch to coordinate the loading tasks. Each resource should be loaded by a separate thread, and the main thread should wait until all resources are loaded before starting the game.

  o **Real-world applicability**: This challenge highlights how concurrency utilities like CountDownLatch can be used to manage dependencies between tasks, ensuring that critical processes are completed before proceeding.

- **Avoiding deadlocks with** tryLock():

  o **Objective**: Learn how to prevent deadlocks by using the tryLock() method from the ReentrantLock class.

  o **Activity**: Perform the following actions:

    ▪ Write a Java program that simulates two users trying to access two shared resources (e.g., a file and a printer) at the same time. Without proper locking, this can cause a deadlock.

    ▪ Use two ReentrantLock objects to represent the resources.

    ▪ Implement a solution using tryLock() to prevent deadlocks.

    ▪ Test your solution by simulating concurrent access from multiple threads.

  o **Real-world applicability**: This challenge addresses a common issue in software systems where multiple processes compete for the same resources. Learning to avoid deadlocks is essential for building reliable and efficient concurrent applications.

Self-assessment

The following questions are provided so you can self-assess your knowledge of the chapter's content and apply critical thinking to key concepts:

1. What is the primary difference between using the Thread class and implementing the Runnable interface to create a thread in Java?

2. How does the CountDownLatch utility work, and when would you use it in a real-world application? Provide a practical scenario where it would be beneficial.

3. Explain how the Executor framework helps optimize thread management. What are the key benefits of using a thread pool over manually managing threads?

4. Imagine you are developing a file-processing system where multiple threads need to read and update the same file simultaneously. What synchronization techniques would you use to ensure data consistency, and why?

5. Reflect on a situation where a deadlock could occur in a multithreaded application. How would you use tryLock() to prevent deadlocks? Provide an example scenario to support your answer.

Answers

1. The primary difference is that when you use the Thread class, you create a new class that extends Thread and overrides its run method. This approach marries the task logic with thread management, which can be limiting. On the other hand, implementing the Runnable interface separates the task logic from thread management, allowing more flexibility, such as extending other classes while still running tasks on threads. The Runnable interface is generally preferred for cleaner design and greater reusability.

2. The CountDownLatch utility allows one or more threads to wait until a set of operations in other threads are completed. It works by counting down from a given number, and when the count reaches zero, all waiting threads are released. A practical scenario would be a video game loading screen that waits for all resources (textures, sounds, models, levels) to be fully loaded before starting the game. The main thread can wait on the latch until all loading tasks are complete.

3. The Executor framework provides an abstraction for managing thread pools, allowing us to submit tasks without worrying about the underlying thread management. The key benefits of using a thread pool include:

    a. Reducing the overhead of creating and destroying threads repeatedly.

    b. Managing a fixed number of threads to prevent resource exhaustion.

    c. Simplifying task scheduling and execution.

4. To ensure data consistency in a file-processing system with multiple threads accessing the same file, you could use synchronized blocks or a ReentrantLock. A ReentrantLock offers more control over thread synchronization, such as the ability to attempt a lock with a timeout (tryLock()). By locking critical sections of code where the file is being read or written, you can prevent race conditions and ensure that only one thread modifies the file at a time, maintaining data integrity.

5. A deadlock could occur if two threads try to acquire two different locks in a different order. For example, Thread 1 locks Resource A and waits to lock Resource B, while Thread 2 locks Resource B and waits to lock Resource A. Both threads would be stuck waiting indefinitely. Using tryLock() with a timeout can prevent this by allowing threads to attempt to acquire a lock and give up if they cannot acquire it within a certain timeframe. This way, threads can back off and retry, avoiding deadlock situations.

Join our Discord space

Join our Discord workspace for latest updates, offers, tech happenings around the world, new releases, and sessions with the authors:

https://discord.bpbonline.com

CHAPTER 8
Streams and Functional Programming

Introduction

In programming, streams are channels or pipelines through which data flows from a source, such as a file or an array. When we use a stream, we can process and manipulate it. The concept is that data flows smoothly from the source to the finish, allowing us to handle the data efficiently. Java includes a stream of **application programming interface** (**API**) and functional programming features that represent a unique approach to how we handle and process data.

Java's streams API allows us to write both expressive and concise code to query and manipulate data collections. This chapter explores functional programming with a focus on the Streams API and the foundational concepts of functional interfaces, lambdas, and parallel processing.

This chapter aims to help you learn how to leverage intermediate and terminal stream operations and perform tasks such as filtering, mapping, and reducing datasets. The chapter also explores the power of parallel streams so you can handle large-scale data processing tasks more efficiently. Additionally, you can gain practical experience with handling optional objects to manage nulls gracefully.

Structure

This chapter covers the following topics:

- Introduction to Streams API
- Intermediate and terminal operations
- Functional interfaces
- Using lambdas with streams
- Parallel streams
- Optional class and handling nulls

Objectives

By the end of this chapter, you should understand the purpose and capabilities of Java's Streams API. This includes the ability to differentiate between intermediate and terminal operators in streams. You should also be able to use functional programming interfaces, use lambda expressions to simplify data processing, and implement parallel streams to help improve the performance of your Java applications. Finally, this chapter is aimed at helping you learn to apply the **Optional** class to handle null values safely and effectively.

Introduction to Streams API

Java's Streams API allows for efficient work with data collections in both a functional and declarative manner. Streams allow us to process data with a focus on handling the function of that data without being overly concerned as to how it is done. This approach is different from traditional iteration-based methods and results in more expressive and concise code that is easier to read and maintain.

In Java, a stream is a sequence of elements used for sequential and parallel operations. The streams do not store data; rather, they operate on data sources. These sources can be **input/output (I/O)** channels, arrays, or collections. Using the Streams API allows us to perform complex data manipulations on data without having to worry about explicit iteration logic.

We will look at an example in code later in this section.

Note:**There are two types of stream operations: intermediate to transform a stream into another stream, such as filtering, and terminal operations that produce a result, such as summing results.**

Streams API advantages

There are four primary advantages of using the Streams API, and each is described in the following list:

- Our code is more concise because iteration and data manipulation tasks are simplified with less code.

- Our code becomes more self-descriptive (declarative), which leads to code that is more readable and maintainable.

- The API supports parallel processing, leading to better performance for data-intensive tasks.

- The original data source is immutable; our operations do not modify the data source, supporting data integrity.

The Streams API enables us to simplify data processing tasks. Instead of writing explicit looks, we can define data operations in a declarative manner. This makes our code easier to debug, read, and maintain.

Examples

To illustrate the Streams API, this chapter uses a fictitious application called *Social Sense*, a social media data analysis tool. Social Sense processes user activity data, such as posts, likes, and followers, to generate insights for social media managers and business leaders.

Suppose that the Social Sense application tracks active users based on the number of posts they make daily. Following is how we can use streams to count active users (those who have made at least 10 posts) from a list of user activities:

```java
import java.util.*;
class UserActivity {
    private String username;
    private int posts;
    public UserActivity(String username, int posts) {
        this.username = username;
        this.posts = posts;
    }
    public String getUsername() {
        return username;
    }
    public int getPosts() {
        return posts;
    }
}
```

```
}
public class SocialSense1 {
    public static void main(String[] args) {
        List<UserActivity> activities = List.of(
            new UserActivity("Neo", 319),
            new UserActivity("Trinity", 3),
            new UserActivity("Morpheus", 7),
            new UserActivity("AgentSmith", 24),
            new UserActivity("Cypher", 1),
            new UserActivity("Oracle", 999)
        );
        long activeUsers = activities.stream()
            .filter(activity -> activity.getPosts() >= 10)
            .count();
        System.out.println("Active users: " + activeUsers);
    }
}
```

In the preceding example, we used the **.stream()** method to convert the list of user activities into a stream. We used the **.filter()** method to retain users who made at least 10 posts. Finally, we used the **.count()** terminal operation to calculate the number of remaining elements in the stream. The output of our application follows:

Active users: 3

Intermediate and terminal operations

At this point, we should understand that the Streams API employs the concept of intermediate and terminal operations. These operations define the computations and transformations our code performs on a data stream.

This section explores both types of operations.

Intermediate operations

Intermediate operations transform. Examples include **filter()**, **distinct()**, and **sorted()** methods. These are considered lazy because they do not process elements of the stream until we invoke a terminal operation, such as **collect()** or **forEach()**. Laziness, in this respect, is a positive thing because it allows for efficient processing. We can even chain intermediate operations together without evaluating the elements until necessary.

Let us look at an example using our Social Sense scenario. Suppose the application tracks user activities, and we want to extract the usernames of the most active users (those with 10 or more posts) and provide the results in alphabetical order.

Following is a code snippet demonstrating how we can accomplish that:

```
List<String> activeUsers = activities.stream()
    .filter(activity -> activity.getPosts() >= 10) // Retain active users
    .map(UserActivity::getUsername) // Extract usernames
    .sorted() // Sort alphabetically
    .collect(Collectors.toList()); // Collect into a list
System.out.println("Active Users: " + activeUsers);
```

In the preceding example, you can see that we used **filter()** to keep users with 10 or more posts; **map()** to extract the username from each **UserActivity**; **sort()** to put the names in alphabetical order; and **collect()** to put the results in a list.

Let us look at another example. Let us say that our Social Sense application tracks hashtags that appear in posts. Each **UserActivity** has a list of hashtags, and we want to find all unique hashtags.

The following is how that could be accomplished:

```
List<String> uniqueTags = activities.stream()
    // next line flattens all hashtags into a single stream
    .flatMap(activity -> activity.getTags().stream())
    .distinct() // Remove duplicates
    .sorted() // Sort alphabetically
    .collect(Collectors.toList()); // Collect into a list
System.out.println("Unique Tags: " + uniqueTags);
```

In our example aforementioned, we used **flatMap()** to convert a stream of lists into a single stream of hashtags, **distinct()** to ensure there are no duplicates, and **sort()** to provide results in alphabetical order.

Terminal operations

Terminal operations do the following:

- Consume the string
- Produce a result
- Trigger the execution of intermediate operations

Common terminal operations include **collect()**, **count()**, **forEach()**, and **reduce()**. Let us look at a couple of examples. This first example is how we could find the most active user based on their post count:

```
activities.stream()
```

```
    .max(Comparator.comparingInt(UserActivity::getPosts)) // Find user with
the max posts
    .ifPresent(user -> System.out.println("Most Active User: " + user.
getUsername()
        + " with " + user.getPosts() + " posts"));
```

In the example aforementioned, we used **max()** to find the user with the highest number of posts and **ifPresent()** to safely handle the optional result to print details.

Let us use another terminal operation example to calculate the average and total number of posts across all users.

Following is how we could implement that:

```
int totalPosts = activities.stream()
    .mapToInt(UserActivity::getPosts) // Convert UserActivity to an IntStream
of post counts
    .sum(); // Sum all post counts
double averagePosts = activities.stream()
    .mapToInt(UserActivity::getPosts)
    .average() // Calculate the average
    .orElse(0.0); // Provide a default value if no elements are present
System.out.println("Total Posts: " + totalPosts);
System.out.println("Average Posts per User: " + averagePosts);
```

For a final example, we will generate a detailed user report arranged by post count in descending order. We will include the usernames with the total posts in an easy-to-read format.

Following is the code:

```
activities.stream()
    .filter(activity -> activity.getPosts() >= 10) // Retain active users
    .sorted(Comparator.comparingInt(UserActivity::getPosts).reversed()) //
Sort by posts, descending
    .map(activity -> activity.getUsername() + " - " + activity.getPosts() + "
posts") // Format output
    .forEach(System.out::println); // Print each line
```

Final thoughts on terminal operators

The following is an overview version of our Social Sense application that includes all the examples from this section:

```
import java.util.*;
import java.util.stream.*;
class UserActivity2 {
    // private variables
```

```
        public UserActivity2(String username, int posts, List<String> tags) { }
        public String getUsername() { }
        public int getPosts() { )
        public List<String> getTags() { }
}
public class SocialSense2 {
        public static void main(String[] args) { }
}
```

Following is the output from our **SocialSense2.java** application:

Output from "Example: Active User Analysis"

Active Users: [AgentSmith, Neo, Oracle]

Output from "Example: Tag Analyticss with flatMap"

Unique Tags: [#architect, #code, #coding, #destroy, #fight, #free, #help, #java, #love, #merge, #phone, #ship, #spirit, #theone, #virus, #zion]

Output from "Example: Most Active User"

Most Active User: Oracle with 999 posts

Output from "Example: Aggregating Post Statistics"

Total Posts: 1353

Average Posts per User: 225.5

Output from "Example: Generating a Report"

Oracle - 999 posts

Neo - 319 posts

AgentSmith - 24 posts

Functional interfaces

Java has several interfaces in the **java.util.function** package that we can use to implement functional programming in our applications. Commonly used functional interfaces include **Consumer<T>**, **Function<T>**, **Predicate<T>**, and **Supplier<T>**. These interfaces enable us to write code that is expressive and concise, using method references and lambda expressions.

Note: Functional programming emphasizes the evaluation of mathematical functions for computation and does not change data.

A functional interface is defined as an interface that contains exactly one abstract method, which makes it eligible for use with lambdas. While functional interfaces can have multiple default or static methods, having only one abstract method is what defines them as functional interfaces.

The key advantages of using functional interfaces in Java include:

- They enable us to write concise code by simplifying complex logic with lambdas.

- We can encapsulate logic into reusable components.

- Functional programming easily integrates with Java's Streams API for processing data collections.

Note: **Lambdas are a way to represent a function without a name. They enable us to treat functionality as a method argument.**

Functional interface examples

Let us use our Social Sense application scenario to review several code snippets that use functional interfaces.

In our first example, we can identify active users (those with at least 10 posts) using **Predicate** to encapsulate the filtering logic:

```
Predicate<UserActivity> isActive = activity -> activity.getPosts() >= 10;
List<UserActivity> activeUsers = activities.stream()
    .filter(isActive)
    .collect(Collectors.toList());
System.out.println("Active Users: " + activeUsers);
```

As you can see in the example above, we used a **Predicate** to encapsulate the condition for identifying active users and **filter()** to apply the condition to retain matching elements.

This next example uses **Consumer** to define an action for displaying user details:

```
Consumer<UserActivity> displayUser = user ->
    System.out.println(user.getUsername() + " has " + user.getPosts() + "
posts");
activities.stream()
    .forEach(displayUser);
```

In the preceding example, we used **Consumer** to process each **UserActivity** by printing its details and **forEach()** to apply the action to all users in the stream.

This next example creates a list of usernames using a **Function**:

```
Function<UserActivity, String> extractUsername = UserActivity::getUsername;
List<String> usernames = activities.stream()
    .map(extractUsername)
    .collect(Collectors.toList());
System.out.println("Usernames: " + usernames);
```

In our example aforementioned, we used **Function** to transform each **UserActivity** into its username and the **map()** method to apply the transformation to each element.

Our final example provides default values using a **Supplier**:

```
Supplier<String> defaultMessage = () -> "No active users found.";
String message = activities.stream()
    .filter(activity -> activity.getPosts() >= 5)
    .findFirst()
    .map(UserActivity::getUsername)
    .orElseGet(defaultMessage);
System.out.println(message);
```

The preceding example uses a **Supplier** to provide a feedback message when no matching records are found and the **orElseGet()** method to invoke the **Supplier** if the stream is empty.

Using lambdas with streams

As mentioned in the previous section, lambda expressions are a key component of functional programming in Java. They are short blocks of code that can be passed as a parameter to perform a specific action. When we use lambdas with streams, it becomes easier to define data processing logic without lengthy code. The primary benefits of using lambdas with Streams are that our boilerplate code is reduced, making our code more concise; our code is more readable; and it works seamlessly with Java's functional interfaces.

The following is the structure of a lambda expression in Java:

```
(parameters) -> expression_or_block
```

Reviewing the preceding lambda expression, let us look at each component. First, **(parameters)** is the input to the lambda. The arrow **(->)** separates the **(parameters)** from the body. Lastly, the body is the code to be executed. The body can be a single statement or a block of code. Following is how we might implement a lambda expression in our Social Sense application:

```
activities.stream()
    .filter(activity -> activity.getPosts() >= 10)
    .forEach(System.out::println);
```

Lambada examples

Let us explore how lambdas integrate seamlessly with the Streams API, using Social Sense as our example application.

Our first example filters out inactive users (those with fewer than 10 posts):

```
List<UserActivity> activeUsers = activities.stream()
    .filter(activity -> activity.getPosts() >= 10) // Lambda defines the
```

```
condition
    .collect(Collectors.toList()); // Collect results into a list
System.out.println("Active Users: " + activeUsers);
```

For our second example, we extract usernames from a list of **UserActivities**:

```
List<String> usernames = activities.stream()
    .map(activity -> activity.getUsername()) // Transform each UserActivity to
a username
    .collect(Collectors.toList());
System.out.println("Usernames: " + usernames);
```

The following example sorts users by the number of posts in descending order:

```
List<UserActivity> sortedUsers = activities.stream()
    .sorted((a, b) -> Integer.compare(b.getPosts(), a.getPosts())) // Custom
Comparator using a lambda
    .collect(Collectors.toList());
System.out.println("Sorted Users: " + sortedUsers);
```

As illustrated in the following, we can use a lambda expression to print a summary for each user:

```
activities.stream()
    .forEach(activity -> System.out.println(
        activity.getUsername() + " - " + activity.getPosts() + " posts"));
```

Our final example combines filtering, aping, and sorting using lambdas to generate a detailed report of active users. The following is the code:

```
activities.stream()
    .filter(activity -> activity.getPosts() >= 5) // Retain active users
    .sorted((a, b) -> Integer.compare(b.getPosts(), a.getPosts())) // Sort by
posts, descending
    .map(activity -> activity.getUsername() + " - " + activity.getPosts() + "
posts") // Format output
    .forEach(System.out::println); // Print each line
```

Final thoughts on lambdas

The following is an updated version of our Social Sense application that includes all the examples from this section:

```
import java.util.*;
import java.util.stream.*;
class UserActivity3 {
    private String username;
```

```java
        private int posts;
        public UserActivity3(String username, int posts) {
            this.username = username;
            this.posts = posts;
        }
        public String getUsername() {
            return username;
        }
        public int getPosts() {
            return posts;
        }
        @Override
        public String toString() {
            return username + " - " + posts + " posts";
        }
    }
    public class SocialSense3 {
        public static void main(String[] args) {
            List<UserActivity3> activities = List.of(
                new UserActivity3("Neo", 319),
                new UserActivity3("Trinity", 3),
                new UserActivity3("Morpheus", 7),
                new UserActivity3("AgentSmith", 24),
                new UserActivity3("Cypher", 1),
                new UserActivity3("Oracle", 999)
            );
            // Filtering active users (5 or more posts)
            List<UserActivity3> activeUsers = activities.stream()
                .filter(activity -> activity.getPosts() >= 10)
                .collect(Collectors.toList());
            System.out.println("Active Users:");
            activeUsers.forEach(System.out::println);
            // Extracting and printing usernames
            List<String> usernames = activities.stream()
                .map(UserActivity3::getUsername)
                .collect(Collectors.toList());
            System.out.println("\nUsernames:");
            usernames.forEach(System.out::println);
```

```
        // Sorting users by post count (descending)
        List<UserActivity3> sortedUsers = activities.stream()
            .sorted((a, b) -> Integer.compare(b.getPosts(), a.getPosts()))
            .collect(Collectors.toList());
        System.out.println("\nSorted Users:");
        sortedUsers.forEach(System.out::println);
        // Generating and displaying user report
        System.out.println("\nUser Report:");
        activities.stream()
            .filter(activity -> activity.getPosts() >= 10)
            .sorted((a, b) -> Integer.compare(b.getPosts(), a.getPosts()))
            .map(activity -> activity.getUsername() + " - " + activity.
getPosts() + " posts")
            .forEach(System.out::println);
    }

}
```

Following is the output from our **SocialSense3.java** application:

```
Active Users:
Neo - 319 posts
AgentSmith - 24 posts
Oracle - 999 posts
Usernames:
Neo
Trinity
Morpheus
AgentSmith
Cypher
Oracle
Sorted Users:
Oracle - 999 posts
Neo - 319 posts
AgentSmith - 24 posts
Morpheus - 7 posts
Trinity - 3 posts
Cypher - 1 posts
User Report:
Oracle - 999 posts
```

```
Neo - 319 posts
AgentSmith - 24 posts
```

Parallel streams

It is undeniable that we live in a data-rich world. Datasets continue to grow larger, and as we strive for high-performance, processing data sequentially quickly becomes a bottleneck. Java's Streams API helps us with this challenge with the parallel streams construct. It allows us to process data across multiple threads, taking advantage of multi-core processors. We can reduce execution times by dividing the data processing workload into smaller tasks and handling them concurrently.

Note: **Parallel streams perform operations on data streams concurrently over multiple CPU cores.**

The primary benefit of using parallel streams is improved runtime performance. This is especially applicable for large datasets. A collateral benefit is that parallel streams have built-in thread management, saving us from manual thread management.

Considerations

There are several aspects of parallel streams that we need to consider. The most important consideration is the realization that not all tasks benefit from parallelization; in fact, improper implementation can lead to performance degradation and even unexpected behavior. We need to keep in mind that parallel streams are optimized and best suited for processing large datasets and tasks that require heavy computation.

Processing overhead is another consideration when using parallel streams. This approach adds overhead for thread management and combining processing results.

We also need to understand that data processing operations on parallel streams do not maintain the order of elements unless we explicitly include that in our implementation. This can be accomplished using a method such as **forEachOrdered()**.

Implementation

To create a parallel stream, we split a stream's data source into multiple chunks. Each chunk is processed in a separate thread. This is achieved in Java using a fork and join framework that handles both the workload distribution and thread management. The fork and join operations are taken care of for us by Java. All we need to do is use the **parallel()** method on a sequential stream and **parallelStream()** on a collection.

The following code calls **parallelStream()** instead of **stream()**, enabling parallel processing. This example uses a parallel stream to sum the numbers from the stream:

```
List<Integer> numbers = Arrays.asList(1, 2, 3, 4, 5, 6, 7, 8, 9, 10);
int sum = numbers.parallelStream()
                  .mapToInt(Integer::intValue)
                  .sum();
System.out.println("Sum: " + sum);
```

Parallel streams examples

Let us explore how parallel streams can be used in our Social Sense example application.

Our first example calculates the number of active users (those with at least ten pots) using a parallel stream. We use the **parallelStream()** method to process the filtering operation across multiple threads. This reduces execution time and is ideal for large datasets. Following is the code:

```
long activeUserCount = activities.parallelStream()
    .filter(activity -> activity.getPosts() >= 10)
    .count();
System.out.println("Active User Count: " + activeUserCount);
```

The second example in the following shows how to use a parallel stream to calculate the total number of posts across all users. We use the **reduce()** method to combine results from multiple threads as an efficient way to compute the final sum. Following is the code:

```
int totalPosts = activities.parallelStream()
    .mapToInt(UserActivity::getPosts)
    .reduce(0, Integer::sum);
System.out.println("Total Posts: " + totalPosts);
```

Our final example demonstrates how we can use a parallel stream to generate a report of active users sorted by their post counts.

Following is the code:

```
activities.parallelStream()
    .filter(activity -> activity.getPosts() >= 5)
    .sorted(Comparator.comparingInt(UserActivity::getPosts).reversed())
    .map(activity -> activity.getUsername() + " - " + activity.getPosts() + "
posts")
    .forEachOrdered(System.out::println);
```

Optional class and handling nulls

Java's **Optional** class gives us a way to gracefully handle null values. We do this by representing a value regardless of whether it exists. This helps us avoid **NullPointerException** errors. The **Optional** class represents a better approach than returning null values.

Note: **NullPointException errors occur when an attempt is made to use an object reference that has not been initialized.**

The **Optional** class can be empty or have a value. It provides us with methods to handle values without having to manually code checks for null values. This promotes a clear and methodical approach to handling absent values in our code. The three primary benefits of using the **Optional** class are:

- Helps us avoid the **NullPointException** error.

- Makes our code more readable and maintainable.

- Encapsulates the presence or absence of a value. This reduces the need to inculcate null checks throughout our code.

Implementing the Optional class

There are multiple ways to create an **Optional** instance. First, we can use **Optional.of(value)** to create an **Optional** with a specified non-null value; we can use **Optional.ofNullable(value)** to create an **Optional** that can hold a null value; and we can use **Optional.empty()** to create an **Optional** with no value. Following is the syntax for each method:

```
// Non-empty Optional
Optional<String> nonEmpty = Optional.of("Hello");
// Can hold null
Optional<String> nullable = OPTIONAL.ofNullable(null);
// Empty Optional
Optional<String> empty = Optional.empty();
```

Key methods in the **Optional** class include **isPresent()** for checking if a value is present; **ifPresent(Consumer)** that executes a code block if a value is present; and additional self-describing methods such as **orElse(defaultValue)**, **orElseGet(Supplier)**, **orElseThrow(Supplier)**, and more.

Optional class examples

Let us explore how to incorporate the **Optional** class and null handling in our Social Sense example application.

Our first example finds the most active user in the dataset. Instead of returning null when no users are present, we use an **Optional**. As you can see, the **max()** method returns an **Optional**.

We use this approach because the dataset could be empty. The **ifPresent()** method ensures the value is only processed if it exists.

Following is the code:

```
Optional<UserActivity> mostActiveUser = activities.stream()
    .max(Comparator.comparingInt(UserActivity::getPosts));


mostActiveUser.ifPresent(user -> System.out.println(
    "Most Active User: " + user.getUsername() + " with " + user.getPosts() + "
posts"
));
```

The next example addresses adding a default message if no active users are found. The **orElse()** method provides us with a fallback message when the stream is empty. Following is the code:

```
String message = activities.stream()
    .filter(activity -> activity.getPosts() >= 10)
    .findFirst()
    .map(UserActivity::getUsername)
    .orElse("No active users found");

System.out.println(message);
```

Our final example uses **Optional.ofNullable()** to safely process null values. This allows us to create an **Optional** even if the value is null. The **ifPresentOrElse()** method provides actions for both the case if a value is present as well as when the value is absent. Following is the code:

```
UserActivity user = getUserActivityById("319"); // This method might return
null
Optional<UserActivity> optionalUser = Optional.ofNullable(user);


optionalUser.ifPresentOrElse(
    u -> System.out.println("User found: " + u.getUsername()),
    () -> System.out.println("User not found")
);
```

Final thoughts on the Optional class

The following is an updated version of our Social Sense application that includes all the examples from this section:

```
import java.util.*;
class UserActivity4 {
    private String username;
```

```java
    private int posts;
    public UserActivity4(String username, int posts) {
        this.username = username;
        this.posts = posts;
    }
    public String getUsername() {
        return username;
    }
    public int getPosts() {
        return posts;
    }
    @Override
    public String toString() {
        return username + " - " + posts + " posts";
    }
}
public class SocialSense4 {
    public static void main(String[] args) {
        List<UserActivity4> activities = List.of(
            new UserActivity4("Neo", 319),
            new UserActivity4("Trinity", 3),
            new UserActivity4("Morpheus", 7),
            new UserActivity4("AgentSmith", 24),
            new UserActivity4("Cypher", 1),
            new UserActivity4("Oracle", 999)
        );
        // Example 1: Retrieving the most active user
        Optional<UserActivity4> mostActiveUser = activities.stream()
            .max(Comparator.comparingInt(UserActivity4::getPosts));
        mostActiveUser.ifPresent(user -> System.out.println(
            "Most Active User: " + user.getUsername() + " with " + user.
getPosts() + " posts"));

        // Example 2: Providing a default value if no active user is found
        String message = activities.stream()
            .filter(activity -> activity.getPosts() >= 10)
            .findFirst()
            .map(UserActivity4::getUsername)
```

```
            .orElse("No active users found");
        System.out.println(message);
        // Example 3: Avoiding NullPointerException with Optional.ofNullable
        UserActivity4 potentialUser = getUserActivityById("Charlie",
activities);
        Optional<UserActivity4> optionalUser = Optional.
ofNullable(potentialUser);
        optionalUser.ifPresentOrElse(
            u -> System.out.println("User found: " + u.getUsername()),
            () -> System.out.println("User not found")
        );
        // Example 4: Using orElseThrow to handle missing values
        try {
            UserActivity4 user = activities.stream()
                .filter(activity -> activity.getUsername().equals("Eve"))
                .findFirst()
                .orElseThrow(() -> new NoSuchElementException("User not
found"));
            System.out.println("Found user: " + user.getUsername());
        } catch (NoSuchElementException e) {
            System.out.println(e.getMessage());
        }
    }
    private static UserActivity4 getUserActivityById(String username,
List<UserActivity4> activities) {
        return activities.stream()
            .filter(activity -> activity.getUsername().equals(username))
            .findFirst()
            .orElse(null);
    }
}
```

Following is the output of our code:

Most Active User: Oracle with 999 posts
Neo
User not found
User not found

Conclusion

This chapter explored the power of Java's Streams API and functional programming features to help us efficiently process and manipulate data collections. It was established that these constructs enable us to create concise and declarative code that is readable and maintainable, specific to complex data operations. Attention was paid to stream basics, operation types, and their advantages, which include immutability and parallelism. Intermediate and terminal operations were also covered, demonstrating how to transform and aggregate data. Functional interfaces and lambdas were also explored, showing us how to define clear, reusable logic for various tasks. The chapter also examined parallel streams for concurrent data processing and the Optional class as a solution for safely handling null values.

The chapter used a fictitious Social Sense application as a consistent example. This helped demonstrate real-world applications of the chapter's concepts. Our examples included filtering active users, generating reports, and handling large-scale data processing tasks.

The next chapter focuses on I/O with an emphasis on file handling. The chapter explains why file handling is essential for many Java applications and introduces Java's I/O systems. The chapter explains how to read and write files using java.nio package and explore streams for handling both character and byte data. Serialization and deserialization for storing and retrieving objects from files are also covered. Buffered and data streams are introduced for optimizing performance, presenting the skills needed to manage files efficiently and securely in Java applications.

Points to remember

- A lambda expression is a short block of code that can be passed as an argument to perform a specific action.

- An Optional is a container object that may or may not contain a value, reducing the risk of NullPointerException.

- An Optional object can be created using methods such as Optional.of(value), Optional.ofNullable(value), or Optional.empty().

- Calling parallelStream() on a collection enables parallel processing by splitting the data source into multiple chunks, each processed in a separate thread.

- Chaining intermediate operations in streams, such as filter(), map(), and sorted(), allows for flexible and efficient data transformations.

- Common functional interfaces include Predicate, Consumer, Function, Supplier, and BiFunction, each serving a distinct purpose in functional programming.

- Functional interfaces are designed to work seamlessly with lambda expressions and method references.

- Intermediate operations in streams, such as filter() and map(), are lazy and do not execute until a terminal operation is invoked.

- Java's Streams API enables us to process collections of data in a functional and declarative manner.

- Method references, such as UserActivity::getUsername, provide a shorthand for writing lambdas that invoke a single method.

- Null values can be gracefully handled using the Optional class, which provides methods such as orElse(), orElseGet(), and orElseThrow() for handling absent values.

- Parallel streams are best suited for CPU-intensive operations on large datasets but may introduce overhead for smaller datasets.

- Parallel streams leverage the fork/join framework for thread management and workload distribution.

- Stream pipelines consist of a source, intermediate operations, and a terminal operation.

- Streams do not store data; they operate on data sources such as arrays or collections.

- Terminal operations, such as collect(), forEach(), and reduce(), consume the stream and trigger the execution of intermediate operations.

- The forEachOrdered() method can be used to maintain the order of elements in parallel streams.

- The map() method transforms elements of a stream, while flatMap() flattens nested structures into a single stream.

- The Optional.ifPresentOrElse() method provides a way to execute actions for both the presence and absence of a value.

- The Streams API promotes immutability by ensuring that operations do not modify the original data source.

- Using Predicate with filter() allows for condition-based filtering of stream elements.

- Using the Streams API results in concise, expressive, and readable code for data processing tasks.

Case studies

These case studies provide realistic scenarios that encourage you to think critically about how to apply the concepts covered in this chapter to realistic scenarios. Each case study includes a scenario description and critical thinking prompts to deepen your understanding of the Streams API, functional programming, parallel streams, and the Optional class:

- **LunarNet social analytics**: LunarNet, a social media analytics startup, collects data from thousands of posts made daily on its platform. The data includes user activity, hashtags, and timestamps. LunarNet needs to identify the top 10 trending hashtags while ensuring there are no duplicates. The results should be sorted alphabetically for easy reference.

  o **For your consideration**: How would you use flatMap() to process hashtags from multiple user posts into a single stream? Which combination of intermediate and terminal operations would you use to remove duplicates and sort the hashtags? How could the application leverage parallel streams to process a large dataset efficiently, and what considerations should be considered?

- **Nebula Retail insights**: Nebula Retail operates a loyalty program that tracks customer purchases and assigns points. Each customer's profile includes their name, total points, and a list of purchase categories. Nebula wants to identify its top five customers by points and display their names along with the categories where they spend the most.

  o **For your consideration**: How would you use max() to identify the top customers by their points? What role could map() and reduce() play in summarizing purchase categories for each customer? How could the Optional class be used to handle cases where no customers qualify for the top five?

- **StarForge Data Solutions**: StarForge Data Solutions processes large-scale telemetry data from sensors deployed on remote space stations. Each sensor reports metrics such as temperature, pressure, and operational status. StarForge must filter out sensors reporting faulty data, calculate the average temperature across all stations, and provide a summary of healthy sensors.

  o **For your consideration**: How would you use filter() to exclude faulty sensors based on their operational status? Which stream operations would be appropriate for calculating the average temperature? When would you use parallelStream() for processing the sensor data, and how would you ensure accuracy in combining results from multiple threads?

- **AstroCorp Logistics**: AstroCorp Logistics manages a fleet of interplanetary cargo ships. Each ship's activity log includes the captain's name, cargo type, and the number of successful deliveries. AstroCorp wants to create a report of captains with more than 50 deliveries, sorted by their performance, while ensuring the data is displayed in the order of processing.

  o **For your consideration**: Which combination of intermediate operations would you use to filter and sort captains based on deliveries? How would you use forEachOrdered() in this scenario to maintain the order of processing? How could functional interfaces, such as Predicate and Function, simplify the filtering and transformation tasks?

- **NovaMed Health Analytics**: NovaMed Health Analytics monitors patient activity through wearable devices. Each device records steps, heart rate, and sleep hours. NovaMed needs to determine which patients averaged fewer than four hours of sleep over the past week and send an alert. If no patients qualify, a default message should be displayed.

  o **For your consideration**: How could you use filter() and map() to isolate and analyze patients' sleep data? How would you implement orElse() or orElseGet() to handle cases where no patients meet the criteria? What advantages would the Optional class provide for ensuring null safety in processing patient data?

Multiple choice questions

1. **Which of the following is an advantage of using the Streams API?**

   a. Streams store data in memory for faster access

   b. Streams modify the original data source

   c. Streams enable concise and declarative code for data processing

   d. Streams automatically optimize all operations for large datasets

2. **What is the primary difference between intermediate and terminal operations in the Streams API?**

   a. Intermediate operations are lazy and transform the stream, while terminal operations consume the stream and produce a result

   b. Intermediate operations consume the stream, while terminal operations transform it

   c. Intermediate operations produce a result, while terminal operations trigger stream execution

   d. Intermediate operations are only available for parallel streams

3. **Which functional interface would you use to represent a function that accepts one input and returns a result?**

   a. Predicate

   b. Consumer

   c. Function

   d. Supplier

4. **In which scenario would using parallel streams not be ideal?**

   a. Processing a dataset with millions of records

   b. Sorting a large collection by a specific criterion

    c. Aggregating numerical data across a large dataset

    d. Performing I/O heavy operations

5. **How does the Optional class improve null handling in Java?**

    a. It allows developers to bypass null checks entirely

    b. It provides a clear and structured way to handle values that may be null

    c. It automatically converts null values to empty strings

    d. It eliminates the need for exception handling

Answers

1.	c.
2.	a.
3.	c.
4.	d.
5.	b.

Questions

1. In what ways does the Streams API enable a more declarative programming style compared to traditional iteration methods? Share examples where declarative code improves clarity and maintainability.

2. Discuss how intermediate operations like filter() and map() differ in their role within a stream pipeline. How can chaining these operations impact performance and readability?

3. Functional interfaces are a critical part of Java's functional programming model. How do they simplify the use of lambdas and method references in stream operations? Provide examples from the chapter.

4. The Optional class is designed to handle null values more gracefully. How does its usage promote safer programming practices compared to traditional null checks? What are the potential pitfalls when using optional?

5. Parallel streams are powerful for processing large datasets, but can introduce complexity. Under what circumstances would you choose parallel streams over sequential streams? What considerations must be made to ensure accurate results?

6. Java's flatMap() operation is often used when working with nested structures like lists of lists. Discuss a scenario from the chapter or your own experience where flatMap() provided a clear solution to a data processing challenge.

7. Compare the methods orElse(), orElseGet(), and orElseThrow() from the Optional class. How would you decide which one to use in a given situation? Discuss examples from the chapter.

8. The chapter emphasizes the importance of immutability when using the Streams API. Why is immutability critical in stream processing, and how does it affect the original data source?

9. Discuss the trade-offs of using forEach() versus forEachOrdered() in stream operations. In what situations is maintaining the order of elements essential, and why?

10. Reflecting on the Social Sense examples, how can the combination of functional interfaces, lambdas, and streams be applied to solve real-world challenges in fields such as data analytics, social media, or healthcare? Provide a hypothetical use case based on your field of interest.

Challenges

The following questions are provided to self-assess your knowledge of the chapter's content and apply critical thinking to key concepts:

-   **Identifying top performers**:

    o   **Objective**: Learn to use the Streams API to filter, sort, and transform data.

    o   **Activity**: You are tasked with analyzing employee performance data for a company called *GalaxyCorp*. Each employee has a name, department, and performance score. Write a Java program to identify and display the top three employees with the highest performance scores. If fewer than three employees are present, display all employees in descending order of their scores. Use the Streams API to filter, sort, and display the results.

    o   **Real-world applicability**: This challenge mimics common scenarios in **human resource (HR)** analytics and performance tracking, where top performers need to be identified from large datasets.

-   **Cleaning up duplicate entries**:

    o   **Objective**: Practice using distinct() and other intermediate operations to process data.

    o   **Activity**: You are managing a list of social media hashtags for the fictional platform *NovaTrends*. Some hashtags are duplicated, and your task is to clean the list. Write a Java program that removes duplicate hashtags, sorts the remaining ones alphabetically, and displays the clean list. Use Streams API operations such as distinct(), sorted(), and collect().

- o **Real-world applicability**: Data cleaning is a crucial step in preparing datasets for analysis, ensuring accuracy and efficiency in applications like social media monitoring or trend analysis.

- **Handling missing data**:

  - o **Objective**: Use the Optional class to safely handle potential null values in data processing.

  - o **Activity**: For a fictional e-commerce site called *StarMall*, create a method that retrieves product information based on its ID. The method should return an Optional<Product>. If the product is not found, print a product not found message. If the product exists, display its name and price. Use the Optional methods ifPresent() and orElse().

  - o **Real-world applicability**: This challenge mirrors real-world tasks in software development, where missing or incomplete data must be handled gracefully to maintain a seamless user experience.

- **Calculating averages**:

  - o **Objective**: Apply the Streams API to perform numerical calculations like averages.

  - o **Activity**: You are analyzing daily step count data from wearable devices for a health app called *HealthSphere*. Each user logs their step count for a day, and your task is to calculate the average step count across all users. Write a Java program that uses mapToInt() and average() to compute and display the average. If no users are found, display no data available.

  - o **Real-world applicability**: Calculating averages is a common requirement in data analysis for applications like fitness tracking, performance monitoring, and user behavior analysis.

- **Filtering and reporting**:

  - o **Objective**: Combine filtering, mapping, and terminal operations to generate meaningful reports.

  - o **Activity**: For a logistics company called *SkyFreight*, you are tasked with generating a report on active delivery drivers. Each driver has a name, completed deliveries, and status (active or inactive). Write a Java program to filter for active drivers, sort them by the number of completed deliveries (descending), and display their names along with the delivery counts.

  - o **Real-world applicability**: Generating filtered and sorted reports is a key skill in logistics, business analytics, and operational monitoring, where actionable insights are derived from raw data.

Self-assessment

The following questions are provided so you can self-assess your knowledge of the chapter's content and apply critical thinking to key concepts:

1. What are the primary differences between intermediate and terminal operations in the Streams API? Provide examples of each.

2. How does the Optional class help handle null values in Java? Describe its key methods and give a use case.

3. Explain the difference between map() and flatMap() in the Streams API. When would you use one over the other?

4. Why is immutability important when working with streams, and how does it impact the original data source?

5. Imagine you are tasked with processing a list of transactions for an e-commerce platform. Each transaction contains a customer ID, amount, and status (for example, completed, pending). How would you use streams to:

    a. Filter for completed transactions.

    b. Calculate the total transaction amount.

    c. Generate a list of unique customer IDs from the completed transactions.

Answers

1. Intermediate operations transform a stream into another stream and are lazy, meaning they do not execute until a terminal operation is invoked. Examples include filter(), map(), and sorted(). Terminal operations consume the stream and produce a result. Examples include collect(), forEach(), and count().

2. The Optional class provides a way to represent the presence or absence of a value, reducing the risk of a NullPointerException. Key methods include:

    a. orElse() returns the value if present; otherwise, it returns a default value.

    b. orElseGet() computes a value if none is present.

    c. orElseThrow() throws an exception if no value is present.

    d. ifPresent() executes an action if a value is present.

    A typical use case is the safe retrieval of a user profile:
    ```
    Optional<User> user = findUserById("319");

    user.ifPresent(u -> System.out.println("User: " + u.getName()));
    ```

3. map() transforms each element in a stream into another form, producing a one-to-one mapping. flatMap() flattens a stream of streams into a single stream, often used when working with nested structures.

4. Immutability ensures that stream operations do not modify the original data source, preventing unintended side effects. Streams operate on a copy of the data, leaving the original collection intact.

5. To filter, calculate, and generate the required data, we would combine filtering, mapping, and aggregation to produce the desired results. Following is a sample code:

```
List<Transaction> transactions = List.of(
    new Transaction("C1", 100, "Completed"),
    new Transaction("C2", 200, "Pending"),
    new Transaction("C1", 150, "Completed")
);
// Filter for completed transactions
List<Transaction> completed = transactions.stream()
    .filter(t -> t.getStatus().equals("Completed"))
    .collect(Collectors.toList());
// Calculate total transaction amount
int totalAmount = completed.stream()
    .mapToInt(Transaction::getAmount)
    .sum();
// Generate unique customer IDs
Set<String> uniqueCustomers = completed.stream()
    .map(Transaction::getCustomerId)
    .collect(Collectors.toSet());
System.out.println("Completed Transactions: " + completed);
System.out.println("Total Amount: " + totalAmount);
System.out.println("Unique Customers: " + uniqueCustomers);
```

Join our Discord space

Join our Discord workspace for latest updates, offers, tech happenings around the world, new releases, and sessions with the authors:

https://discord.bpbonline.com

CHAPTER 9

Input/Output

Introduction

Nearly every application has some **input/output (I/O)**. Whether it is user input or interactions with files, networks, or databases, we must learn how to enable this functionality both efficiently and securely. The chapter explores reading user input, processing text files, serializing and deserializing objects, and optimizing performance using buffered streams. This chapter is designed to provide you with a solid foundation for mastering file handling in Java.

Persistent data storage and retrieval are core to modern Java applications, so the chapter emphasizes practical approaches to managing character and byte streams. Serialization and deserialization techniques, essential for saving and restoring the state of objects, are also explored. In this chapter, you will understand how to handle a wide range of I/O tasks.

Structure

This chapter covers the following topics:

- Introduction to Java I/O
- Using the Scanner class for input
- File handling with java.nio

- Working with serialization and deserialization
- Buffered streams and data streams
- Handling character and byte streams

Objectives

By the end of this chapter, you should be able to explain the role of I/O operations in Java applications. Moreover, you will be able to implement the **Scanner** class to handle user inputs, read and write files using Java's nio package, and implement character streams and byte streams. You should also be able to use buffered and data streams to optimize the performance of the I/O components of your Java applications. Using the guided examples, you should be able to implement object persistence with serialization and deserialization. Finally, by the chapter's end, you should be able to apply best practices for secure and efficient file handling in your Java applications.

Introduction to Java I/O

It is common for modern Java applications to process data from and to a multitude of sources, including user input, various file formats, and databases. This is a core functionality, making it important to learn how to handle I/O operations efficiently so we can ensure our applications are responsive and scalable. Fortunately, Java provides us with a robust set of **application programming interfaces** (**APIs**) for managing I/O.

This section introduces Java's I/O capabilities, starting with an overview of I/O streams, which form the foundation of Java's I/O mechanisms.

> **Note:** To illustrate the concepts in this chapter, we will use Digitale, a fictitious digital media company that offers a streaming service for music and videos. Digitale's backend requires efficient file management to store metadata about media files, log user activity, and process customer preferences.

By applying Java's I/O features, we will develop components that handle user input, read and write media metadata, and manage application logs efficiently.

Overview of I/O streams

Streams are at the core of Java's I/O system. They provide flexible approaches to processing I/O. Java's I/O framework abstracts I/O operations, allowing us to work with files and data structures, network connections, and in-memory data structures with relative ease.

> **Note:** A stream is a sequence of data that flows from a source to its destination (from input to output).

Java's I/O system is built on the concept of streams, which provide a flexible way to process I/O data. A stream is a sequence of data that flows from a source (input) to a destination (output). There are two general categories of streams:

- **Character stream**: This is used for handling text data.
- **Byte stream**: This is used for handling binary data (that is, images, audio, video, etc.).

Let us examine each stream category and demonstrate its use in code.

Introduction to character streams

Character streams are efficient for handling text-based data. It helps us ensure that proper encoding and decoding of characters takes place. Common uses of data streams include working with log files, configuration files, and other text files.

Following is an example, using our Digitale example where we read media descriptions from a text file:

```java
import java.io.FileReader;
import java.io.IOException;
public class MediaDescriptionReader {
    public static void main(String[] args) {
        try (FileReader fr = new FileReader("descriptions.txt")) {
            int character;
            while ((character = fr.read()) != -1) {
                System.out.print((char) character);
            }
        } catch (IOException e) {
            System.err.println("Error reading description file: " +
e.getMessage());
        }
    }
}
```

In our example aforementioned, we use a **FileReader** to process the **descriptions.txt** file as a character stream. Our example also provides an early look at how to handle file access issues. We will look at that in detail later in this chapter.

Introduction to byte streams

When we have files such as audio, video, and images, we need to use a byte stream to handle their binary data. This type of stream is also useful when working with encrypted data.

Following is a Digitale example where we read metadata from a binary file:

```java
import java.io.FileInputStream;
import java.io.IOException;
public class MetadataReader {
    public static void main(String[] args) {
        try (FileInputStream fis = new FileInputStream("metadata.dat")) {
            int data;
            while ((data = fis.read()) != -1) {
                System.out.print((char) data);
            }
        } catch (IOException e) {
            System.err.println("Error reading metadata file: " +
e.getMessage());
        }
    }
}
```

In our example aforementioned, we use **FileInputStream** to read the **metadata.dat** binary file, which processes the file one byte at a time.

Importance of I/O in programming

Think of any of your favorite applications, whether it be a desktop application, a mobile app, something that runs on a tablet, or a media streaming application that runs on your smart TV, and think of the mix of I/O that is being processed. If you are a student or a faculty member, consider your **learning management system** (**LMS**) and how many I/O operations are involved. Nearly all modern applications include I/O operations. The key to these operations is efficiency.

Using our Digitale digital media company as an example, I/O operations are critical for managing user interactions, storing media metadata, processing logs, and streaming content efficiently. Whether we are reading media descriptions from a text file, logging playback histories, or writing user-generated playlists to external files, we must implement proper I/O management to ensure our application runs smoothly and reliably.

Let us look at five examples that demonstrate the importance of I/O in Java development.

Handling user input

Most applications require user input, whether from a keyboard, a touchscreen, or a network request. Java's **Scanner** class simplifies reading input from the console, which makes it especially useful for interactive applications.

Using our Digitale example, we can create functionality for users to enter their favorite songs through the console, which our application would process using the scanner:

The **Scanner** class is explored in the *Using the Scanner class for input* section later in this chapter.

Managing file storage

File storage is one of the primary methods of managing persistent data, which persists after an application terminates. We use persistent data to save system configurations, user data, logs, and more. In Java, we can use the **java.nio.file** package to implement efficient file operations, including reading, writing, and changing data.

Digitale, as an example, would use file storage to store recently played songs. This could be logged in a text file, which allows users to pause and resume their sessions.

The **java.nio.file** package is detailed in the *File handling with java.nio* section later in this chapter.

Buffered streams

One of the efficiency issues with persistent data storage is the number of physical disk access iterations. Large files, if not handled in an efficient manner, can significantly degrade an application's responsiveness and the user experience. To overcome this issue, we can use Java's buffered streams to improve performance. This is accomplished by minimizing the number of physical disk accesses.

In the context of our Digitale example, imagine that when a user plays a song, our application appends playback data to a log file. This would be accomplished using buffered writing.

Buffered streams are thoroughly explored in the *Buffered streams and data streams* section later in this chapter.

Object persistence

In Java applications, our data structures are complex, and we prefer to store them as objects instead of as text or raw data. Java empowers us to accomplish object persistence through serialization.

For instance, Digitale may want to save user profiles with their preferences and playlists as serialized objects.

Object persistence is covered in the *Working with serialization and deserialization* section later in this chapter.

Network communication

I/O operations also permit us to communicate over the Internet and other networks. Consider Digitale's backend, which might need to fetch media metadata from a remote server or stream audio to users. Java's socket programming and HTTP APIs enable these interactions.

We will explore network-based I/O in *Chapter 10, Database Connectivity*.

Using the Scanner class for input

This chapter has established that most applications rely on user input to some extent. This can be to enable interaction and personal experiences, capture login credentials, process text files, and more. With such a demand for this functionality, it is paramount that we read this input efficiently. Java's **Scanner** class does the heavy lifting for us so we can easily read data from various sources.

Continuing with our Digitale example, user input is essential for features like searching for songs, adding media to playlists, and customizing user preferences. This section explores how to leverage the **Scanner** class to read input effectively.

Overview of the Scanner class

The **Scanner** class is part of **java.util** package, and provides us with an efficient way to parse user input from different sources. It can be used to read both primitives (integers, doubles, etc.) and strings, making it a highly versatile tool for our applications. In addition to reading input from multiple sources, the **Scanner** class supports different data types, splits input into tokens, and handles input validation.

To use the **Scanner** class, we first import it and then create an instance. Following is an example:

```java
import java.util.Scanner;

public class ScannerExample {
    public static void main(String[] args) {
        Scanner scanner = new Scanner(System.in);
        System.out.print("Enter your favorite song: ");
        String song = scanner.nextLine();
        System.out.println("You entered: " + song);
        scanner.close();
    }
}
```

In this example, we used the **new Scanner(System.in)** statement to initialize a scanner to read from the console. The **nextLine()** method captures an entire line of text, allowing users to input song names with spaces. Our example ends with **scanner.close()** to release system resources after input is read.

Following is an example where we read multiple data types without the requirement for manual conversion:

```
import java.util.Scanner;
public class UserPreferences {
    public static void main(String[] args) {
        Scanner scanner = new Scanner(System.in);
        System.out.print("Enter your preferred music genre: ");
        String genre = scanner.nextLine();
        System.out.print("How many songs do you listen to daily? ");
        int dailySongs = scanner.nextInt();
        System.out.print("Do you prefer high-quality streaming? (true/false)
");
        boolean highQuality = scanner.nextBoolean();
        System.out.println("\nUser Preferences:");
        System.out.println("Genre: " + genre);
        System.out.println("Daily Songs: " + dailySongs);
        System.out.println("High-Quality Streaming: " + highQuality);
        scanner.close();
    }
}
```

In this example, we used **nextInt()** to read integer input and **nextBoolean()** to read Boolean values. We need to be careful when we mix **nextLine()** with other methods to avoid input skipping (we will discuss this later in this chapter's *Reading and parsing data from files* section).

Another common use of the **Scanner** class is to use it with files. This empowers us to load media descriptions, user preferences, or logs. The following is an example where we read a playlist file in Digitale:

```
import java.io.File;
import java.io.FileNotFoundException;
import java.util.Scanner;
public class PlaylistReader {
    public static void main(String[] args) {
        try {
            File file = new File("playlist.txt");
            Scanner scanner = new Scanner(file);
            while (scanner.hasNextLine()) {
                String song = scanner.nextLine();
```

```
            System.out.println("Now playing: " + song);
        }
        scanner.close();
    } catch (FileNotFoundException e) {
        System.err.println("Playlist file not found.");
    }
    }
}
```

Following is a sample output from our **PlaylistReader**:

Now playing: Whispering Pines - The Howling Wolves
Now playing: Ocean Breeze - The Soaring Eagles
Now playing: Golden Meadow - The Grazing Deer
Now playing: Thunder Over the Valley - The Roaring Lions
Now playing: River's Serenade - The Swimming Otters
Now playing: Dancing Leaves - The Playful Squirrels
Now playing: Moonlit Forest - The Silent Owls
Now playing: Snowfall Symphony - The Arctic Foxes
Now playing: Mountain Echo - The Wandering Bears
Now playing: Sands of Time - The Desert Tortoises

As you can see in our example aforementioned, we used **Scanner scanner = new Scanner(file)** to read data from a file. We used **hasNextLine()** to ensure all lines are read until the end. We also used a try-catch block for error handling, preventing crashes if the file is missing.

Reading input from the console

Java's **Scanner** class provides a straightforward way for us to read data from the console. This can be useful for capturing user preferences, search queries, and other interactive elements. For Digitale, user input is essential for song searches, playlist creation, and content filtering.

Let us demonstrate how to capture user input from the console efficiently. We will use the **Scanner** class to read input from **System.in**, as we did in an earlier section, allowing users to enter data through the keyboard. The example below takes this one step further by showing how this console input can be used to initiate additional functionality. Following is how we can implement that functionality using Digitale to search for a song:

```
import java.util.Scanner;
public class SongSearch {
    public static void main(String[] args) {
        Scanner scanner = new Scanner(System.in);
        System.out.print("Enter a song title to search: ");
```

```
        String songTitle = scanner.nextLine();
        System.out.println("Searching for: " + songTitle);
        scanner.close();
    }
}
```

In our example, **Scanner scanner = new Scanner(System.in)** is used to initialize the scanner to read user input. The **nextLine()** method captures an entire line, allowing users to enter song titles with spaces. Finally, **scanner.close()** releases resources after input is processed.

Let us look at another example where we obtain input from the console. In this example, we demonstrate how the **Scanner** class can read numbers and Boolean values, specifically so Digitale can obtain a user rating for a song. Following is the code:

```
import java.util.Scanner;
public class SongRating {
    public static void main(String[] args) {
        Scanner scanner = new Scanner(System.in);
        System.out.print("Enter your rating (1-5) for the song: ");
        int rating = scanner.nextInt();
        System.out.println("You rated this song: " + rating + " stars.");
        scanner.close();
    }
}
```

For our example aforementioned, we used **nextInt()** to read an integer input; this is ideal for rating features. Following is the output of our program:

Enter your rating (1-5) for the song: 3

You rated this song: 3 stars.

Reading and parsing data from files

It is common for our applications to use data that is stored in files and to write data to files. Java's **Scanner** class makes it easy for us to read and parse text-based data from files. With this, we can incorporate functionality in our applications to load configuration settings, process logs, and retrieve stored user preferences. For Digitale, reading media-related data from files allows users to access saved playlists, playback history, and song metadata. We demonstrated this earlier in the chapter with the PlaylistReader.java application.

Let us look at how we can process files that have structured data. We will use the **Scanner** class tokenization to parse song data from the **playlist.txt** file. For this example, we assume that each song's title and artist are separated by a hyphen. Following is the code:

```java
import java.io.File;
import java.io.FileNotFoundException;
import java.util.Scanner;
public class PlaylistParser {
    public static void main(String[] args) {
        try {
            File file = new File("playlist.txt");
            Scanner scanner = new Scanner(file);
            while (scanner.hasNextLine()) {
                String line = scanner.nextLine();
                String[] parts = line.split(" - "); // Splitting title and
artist
                if (parts.length == 2) {
                    System.out.println("Song: " + parts[0] + " | Artist: " +
parts[1]);
                }
            }

            scanner.close();
        } catch (FileNotFoundException e) {
            System.err.println("Playlist file not found.");
        }
    }
}
```

Our example aforementioned splits the data to extract meaningful information. We used the **split()** method to separate the song title and artist based on the hyphen delimiter. We ensure that our parsing is valid by checking if the line contains two elements. Following is the output of our application:

Song: Whispering Pines | Artist: The Howling Wolves

Song: Ocean Breeze | Artist: The Soaring Eagles

Song: Golden Meadow | Artist: The Grazing Deer

Song: Thunder Over the Valley | Artist: The Roaring Lions

Song: River's Serenade | Artist: The Swimming Otters

Song: Dancing Leaves | Artist: The Playful Squirrels

Song: Moonlit Forest | Artist: The Silent Owls

Song: Snowfall Symphony | Artist: The Arctic Foxes

Song: Mountain Echo | Artist: The Wandering Bears

Song: Sands of Time | Artist: The Desert Tortoises

Common pitfalls and best practices

As we have seen, the **Scanner** class simplifies reading input from the console and a file. If we use this class improperly, we might experience unexpected behavior, performance issues, or even data loss. Let us look at four of the most common pitfalls (mixing input methods, not closing the scanner, invalid inputs, inefficiencies) and four best practices using the **Scanner** class for input.

The following are the common pitfalls:

- **Mixing input methods**: The first common pitfall is mixing the **nextLine()** method with other input methods, for example, combining **nextLine()** with **nextInt()**. The problem with this mix is that **nextInt()** and other primitive input methods do not consume the new line character (**\n**), leaving it in the buffer. This causes **nextLine()** to skip input.

  In the following example, we attempt to obtain the user's age using **nextInt()**, followed by an attempt to obtain a song name using **nextLine()**. Following is the code:

  ```
  import java.util.Scanner;

  public class MixingInputMethodsPitfall {
      public static void main(String[] args) {
          Scanner scanner = new Scanner(System.in);
          System.out.print("Enter your age: ");
          int age = scanner.nextInt(); // Reads number but leaves \n in
  buffer
          System.out.print("Enter your favorite song: ");
          String song = scanner.nextLine(); // Skips input!
          System.out.println("Age: " + age + ", Favorite Song: " + song);
          scanner.close();
      }
  }
  ```

  As you can see in the output in the following, the user was never asked what their favorite song was:

  Enter your age: 24

  Enter your favorite song: Age: 24, Favorite Song:

  This logic error is a result of the **nextLine()** method immediately returning an empty string because it reads the leftover new line character (**\n**) left by **nextInt()**. The solution to this pitfall would be to always consume the extra new line before using **nextLine()** following numeric input. Following is the code that fixes the logic error:

```java
import java.util.Scanner;
public class MixingInputMethodsFixed {
    public static void main(String[] args) {
        Scanner scanner = new Scanner(System.in);
        System.out.print("Enter your age: ");
        int age = scanner.nextInt();
        scanner.nextLine(); // Fixed: Consume leftover newline
        System.out.print("Enter your favorite song: ");
        String song = scanner.nextLine();
        System.out.println("Age: " + age + ", Favorite Song: " + song);
        scanner.close();
    }
}
```

When we run the updated code, we see that both the age and song title can be obtained from the user. The output is as follows:

Enter your age: 24

Enter your favorite song: When Doves Cry

Age: 24, Favorite Song: When Doves Cry

- **Not closing the scanner**: All of our code examples that use the **Scanner** class include the **scanner.close()** method to release system resources after input is read. A common pitfall is neglecting to close the scanner. This can lead to resource leaks and needs to be avoided. The solution is to simply make this a matter of routine coding; always close your scanner. The ideal approach is to implement this with a try-with-resources block when dealing with files. The following is how that is done:

```java
try (Scanner scanner = new Scanner(new File("playlist.txt"))) {
    while (scanner.hasNextLine()) {
        System.out.println(scanner.nextLine());
    }
} catch (FileNotFoundException e) {
    System.err.println("File not found.");
}
```

- **Invalid input**: A third pitfall related to using the **Scanner** class is failing to check the validity of user input. Invalid user input, whether intentional or not, represents a significant threat to our systems. We should always validate user input. For example, if we are asking for an age, we only expect an integer for input. Also, it provides the user with appropriate feedback. The following code snippet demonstrates this implementation:

```
Scanner scanner = new Scanner(System.in);
System.out.print("Enter your rating (1-5): ");
if (scanner.hasNextInt()) {
    int rating = scanner.nextInt();
    System.out.println("Your rating: " + rating);
} else {
    System.out.println("Invalid input! Please enter a number.");
}
scanner.close();
```

- **Inefficiencies**: A fourth pitfall is being inefficient when we use the **Scanner** class for large files. Remember, the **Scanner** reads input one line at a time, and this works fine for small files. When we are working with large files, we need to use a different approach. In this instance, we should use **BufferedReader** for greater efficiency. Here is how that can be implemented:

```
import java.io.BufferedReader;
import java.io.FileReader;
import java.io.IOException;
public class BufferedReaderExample {
    public static void main(String[] args) {
        try (BufferedReader br = new BufferedReader(new
FileReader("large_playlist.txt"))) {
            String line;
            while ((line = br.readLine()) != null) {
                System.out.println(line);
            }
        } catch (IOException e) {
            System.err.println("Error reading file.");
        }
    }
}
```

Best practices

The best practices presented here are the same as the aforementioned solutions to avoiding the pitfalls. They are as follows:

- Consume new lines when mixing input types.

- Always close the scanner, or use try-with-resources for proper resource management.
- Always validate user input.
- Use **BufferedReader** for large files.

File handling with java.nio

The previous section introduced the ability to read files, and while the approach taken with **java.io** is sufficient for small files, it results in inefficiencies when larger files are involved. Our goal is to handle files for both I/O in an efficient manner. To accomplish this, we will use the capabilities available in Java's **java.nio.file** package. It provides us with a flexible and efficient way to work with files and directories.

For Digitale, our digital media company example, managing files efficiently is essential for storing user-generated playlists, processing media metadata, and handling application logs. This section demonstrates the capabilities of the **java.nio.file** package, with a focus on reading, writing, and managing files in a structured and efficient manner.

Basics of working with files in Java

The **java.nio.file** package consists of classes and methods that we can use to handle file operations efficiently, especially when compared to **java.io**. Core to this package is the **Path** class that is used to create objects that represent file or directory locations. Also core to **java.nio.file** is the **Files** class that includes utility methods that we can use to read, write, copy, and delete files.

It is a good practice to always check if a file exists before executing any file-related operation to prevent errors. Let us look at an example that demonstrates how to check if a file exists:

```
import java.nio.file.*;
public class FileCheckExampmle {
    public static void main(String[] args) {
        Path path = Paths.get("playlist.txt");
        if (Files.exists(path)) {
            System.out.println("File exists: " + path.toAbsolutePath());
        } else {
            System.out.println("File not found.");
        }
    }
}
```

In our example aforementioned, we used **Paths.get("filename")** to create a **Path** object for the file. We then used **Files.exists(path)** to check if the file exists. Unlike **java.io.File**, **java.nio.file** provides a simpler and more powerful suite of file operation methods.

Reading and writing text files using java.nio

We can use Java's **Files** class to read and write files in a more efficient manner than with the **Scanner** approach. In this section, we will demonstrate both reading and writing files using **java.nio**.

Let us start with an example of how to read a playlist file for Digitale. The following is the code:

```java
import java.nio.file.*;
import java.io.IOException;
import java.util.List;
public class ReadPlaylist {
    public static void main(String[] args) {
        Path filePath = Paths.get("playlist.txt");
        try {
            List<String> lines = Files.readAllLines(filePath);
            for (String line : lines) {
                System.out.println("Now playing: " + line);
            }
        } catch (IOException e) {
            System.err.println("Error reading the file: " + e.getMessage());
        }
    }
}
```

In our **ReadPlaylist.java** example aforementioned, we used **Files.readAllLines(filePath)** to read all lines of the file into a **List<String>**. This makes it easy for us to process. This approach is more concise and readable than using a **Scanner**. We also implemented exception handling to prevent a system crash if the file is missing.

Next, let us look at an example that saves a user's playlist to an output file. Following is the code:

```java
import java.nio.file.*;
import java.io.IOException;
import java.util.Arrays;
import java.util.List;
public class WritePlaylist {
    public static void main(String[] args) {
        List<String> playlist = Arrays.asList(
            "Whispering Pines - The Howling Wolves",
            "Ocean Breeze - The Soaring Eagles",
```

```
            "Golden Meadow - The Grazing Deer"
        );
        Path filePath = Paths.get("newPlaylist.txt");
        try {
            Files.write(filePath, playlist);
            System.out.println("Nw playlist saved successfully.");
        } catch (IOException e) {
            System.err.println("Error writing to file: " + e.getMessage());
        }
    }
}
```

In our aforementioned example, we wrote a list of strings directly to a file (**newPlaylist.txt**). This approach overwrites any existing content already in the file. In our example, the file did not already exist, so a new file was created. Let us look at an example where we show the user the current playlist, ask for a new song and author, append that to the list, and then display the updated list. The following is the code:

```
import java.io.IOException;
import java.nio.file.*;
import java.util.List;
import java.util.Scanner;
import java.util.Arrays;
import java.nio.charset.StandardCharsets;
import java.nio.file.StandardOpenOption;
public class AppendPlaylist {
    public static void main(String[] args) {
        Path filePath = Paths.get("myPlaylist.txt");
                // Display current playlist
        System.out.println("Current Playlist:");
        displayPlaylist(filePath);
        // Get user input
        Scanner scanner = new Scanner(System.in);
        System.out.print("\nEnter the song title: ");
        String songTitle = scanner.nextLine();
        System.out.print("Enter the artist name: ");
        String artist = scanner.nextLine();
        scanner.close();
        // Append new song to file
        String newEntry = songTitle + " - " + artist;
```

```
        appendToPlaylist(filePath, newEntry);
        // Display updated playlist
        System.out.println("\nUpdated Playlist:");
        displayPlaylist(filePath);
    }
    /**
     * Reads and displays the contents of the playlist file.
     */
    private static void displayPlaylist(Path filePath) {
        try {
            if (Files.exists(filePath)) {
                List<String> lines = Files.readAllLines(filePath,
StandardCharsets.UTF_8);
                if (lines.isEmpty()) {
                    System.out.println("Playlist is empty.");
                } else {
                    lines.forEach(System.out::println);
                }
            } else {
                System.out.println("Playlist file not found. Creating a new
one...");
                Files.createFile(filePath);
            }
        } catch (IOException e) {
            System.err.println("Error reading the playlist: " +
e.getMessage());
        }
    }


    /**
     * Appends a new song entry to the playlist file.
     */
    private static void appendToPlaylist(Path filePath, String newEntry) {
        try {
            Files.write(filePath, Arrays.asList(newEntry), StandardCharsets.
UTF_8, StandardOpenOption.APPEND);
            System.out.println("Song added successfully.");
        } catch (IOException e) {
            System.err.println("Error updating the playlist: " +
e.getMessage());
```

```
        }
    }
}
```

Following is the output of our code:

```
Current Playlist:
Whispering Pines - The Howling Wolves
Ocean Breeze - The Soaring Eagles
Golden Meadow - The Grazing Deer
Enter the song title: Ocean Wings
Enter the artist name: The Diving Pelicans
Song added successfully.
Updated Playlist:
Whispering Pines - The Howling Wolves
Ocean Breeze - The Soaring Eagles
Golden Meadow - The Grazing Deer
Ocean Wings - The Diving Pelicans
```

Our **AppendPlaylist.java** application uses **Files.readAllLines()** to read **myPlaylist.txt** and outputs its contents to the console. If the file does not already exist, a new one is created. Next, we prompt the user for a song title first, then the artist. We use **appendToPlaylist(filePath, newEntry)** from **java.nio.file.StandardOpenOption** to append the file with the new song and artist, using the title–artist format. Lastly, we read and print the new contents of the **myPlaylist.txt** file.

Working with serialization and deserialization

So far, this chapter has covered I/O via the console and text files. That functionality is sufficient for basic needs. However, it is not sufficient when we are dealing with more complex data structures. As demonstrated in this section, we can use serialization to convert Java objects into a binary format and save them to a file or transmit them over a network. When we want to retrieve these serialized objects, we reconstruct them into their original form via deserialization.

For Digitale, serialization is crucial for storing user playlists, media metadata, and playback histories. Instead of saving this data as raw text, serialization enables storing entire Java objects, preserving data structure and relationships.

Storing and retrieving objects from files

The technique of serializing and deserializing is useful for persisting things such as user settings, data caching, and saving the state of our application.

Note: Serialization allows objects to be converted into a byte stream and stored in a file. Deserialization reconstructs objects from the byte stream, preserving their original state and data structure.

For Digitale, serialization enables storing user-generated playlists, playback history, and media metadata as structured objects rather than plain text. This allows efficient retrieval and manipulation of data without manual parsing.

Serialization

To store and retrieve objects from a file, Java provides us with **ObjectOutputStream** to convert and write objects to a file, **ObjectInputStream** to read and reconstruct objects from a file, and the **Serializable** interface that enables serialization for a class. To make a class serializable, it must implement **Serializable**, allowing Java to handle the conversion automatically. The following is an example that stores song information for Digitale:

```java
import java.io.Serializable;
public class MediaMetadata implements Serializable {
    private static final long serialVersionUID = 1L; // Ensures compatibility during deserialization
    private String title;
    private String artist;
    private String genre;
    private double duration; // In minutes
    public MediaMetadata(String title, String artist, String genre, double duration) {
        this.title = title;
        this.artist = artist;
        this.genre = genre;
        this.duration = duration;
    }
    @Override
    public String toString() {
        return "Title: " + title + "\nArtist: " + artist + "\nGenre: " + genre + "\nDuration: " + duration + " mins\n";
    }
}
```

In our aforementioned example, we implemented **Serializable**, allowing instances to be written to and read from a file. We used **serialVersionUID** to ensure compatibility between different versions of the class. Finally, we used the **toString()** method to display object details after deserialization.

To save multiple song metadata entries to a file, we use **ObjectOutputStream**. The following is an example where we write media metadata to a file:

```java
import java.io.*;
import java.util.ArrayList;
import java.util.List;
public class MetadataWriter {
    public static void main(String[] args) {
        List<MediaMetadata> mediaList = new ArrayList<>();
        mediaList.add(new MediaMetadata("Whispering Pines", "The Howling
Wolves", "Folk", 4.35));
        mediaList.add(new MediaMetadata("Ocean Breeze", "The Soaring Eagles",
"Instrumental", 5.12));
        mediaList.add(new MediaMetadata("Golden Meadow", "The Grazing Deer",
"Acoustic", 3.48));
        try (FileOutputStream fos = new FileOutputStream("metadata.dat");
             ObjectOutputStream oos = new ObjectOutputStream(fos)) {
            oos.writeObject(mediaList);
            System.out.println("Media metadata saved successfully.");
        } catch (IOException e) {
            System.err.println("Error saving metadata: " + e.getMessage());
        }
    }
}
```

Our example aforementioned creates a list of **MediaMetadata** objects, then uses **ObjectOutputStream** to write the object list into **metadata.dat**. We used a try-with-resources block to ensure safe resource management.

> **Note: While most objects in Java can be serialized with the aforementioned approach, Java also provides us with the Externalizable interface for greater control over the serialization process.**

Deserialization

Next, let us look at how we can retrieve objects from a file. This requires us to deserialize the objects. Our following example reads media metadata from **metadata.dat**. Following is the code:

```java
import java.io.*;
import java.util.List;
public class DeserializationExample {
    public static void main(String[] args) {
```

```
    try (FileInputStream fis = new FileInputStream("metadata.dat");
        ObjectInputStream ois = new ObjectInputStream(fis)) {
        List<MediaMetadata> mediaList = (List<MediaMetadata>) ois.
readObject();
        System.out.println("Retrieved Media Metadata:");
        for (MediaMetadata media : mediaList) {
            System.out.println(media);
        }
    } catch (IOException | ClassNotFoundException e) {
        System.err.println("Error reading metadata: " + e.getMessage());
    }
    }
}
```

Our example, as aforementioned, uses **ObjectInputStream** to read objects from **metadata. dat**. We cast the deserialized data back to **List<MediaMetadata>**. Our example also handles exceptions properly, preventing crashes if the file is missing or corrupted.

Serialization and deserialization examples

Now that we have covered the basics of storing and retrieving objects, we can explore additional real-world scenarios where serialization can enhance file management. Serialization would be particularly useful for Digitale, where storing structured data such as user playlists, playback histories, and media metadata can contribute to seamless data persistence. This section provides practical examples of serialization and deserialization, covering appending serialized data, handling version changes, and improving performance with buffered streams.

Appending serialized data without overwriting

By default, **ObjectOutputStream** overwrites the file every time an object is serialized. This can be a desired behavior or problematic. If we want to retain current information, we need to append objects without erasing previous entries. To accomplish that, we must use a custom stream to avoid writing a new header when appending. This will ensure that previously written objects remain accessible.

The following is an example where we store user playback history in a **playback.dat** file:

```
import java.io.*;
import java.util.List;
import java.util.ArrayList;
class PlaybackHistory implements Serializable {
    private static final long serialVersionUID = 1L;
    private String songTitle;
```

```java
    private String timestamp;
    public PlaybackHistory(String songTitle, String timestamp) {
        this.songTitle = songTitle;
        this.timestamp = timestamp;
    }
    @Override
    public String toString() {
        return "Song: " + songTitle + " | Played at: " + timestamp;
    }
}
public class PlaybackLogger {
    private static final String FILE_NAME = "playback.dat";
    public static void main(String[] args) {
        PlaybackHistory newPlayback = new PlaybackHistory("Whispering Pines",
"2025-01-30 14:45");
        List<PlaybackHistory> playbackList = readPlaybackHistory(); // Load
previous records
        playbackList.add(newPlayback); // Append new record
        writePlaybackHistory(playbackList);
        System.out.println("Updated Playback History:");
        playbackList.forEach(System.out::println);
    }
    /**
     * Reads previous playback history from file.
     */
    private static List<PlaybackHistory> readPlaybackHistory() {
        try (FileInputStream fis = new FileInputStream(FILE_NAME);
             ObjectInputStream ois = new ObjectInputStream(fis)) {
            return (List<PlaybackHistory>) ois.readObject();
        } catch (IOException | ClassNotFoundException e) {
            return new ArrayList<>(); // Return empty list if file not found
        }
    }
    /**
     * Writes updated playback history to file.
     */
    private static void writePlaybackHistory(List<PlaybackHistory> history) {
        try (FileOutputStream fos = new FileOutputStream(FILE_NAME);
             ObjectOutputStream oos = new ObjectOutputStream(fos)) {
```

```
            oos.writeObject(history);
            System.out.println("Playback history updated.");
        } catch (IOException e) {
            System.err.println("Error writing playback history: " +
e.getMessage());
        }
    }
}
```

Our example, as aforementioned, reads existing records first, preventing the loss of previous data. It then writes the entire list back to **playback.dat**, ensuring all entries persist. If the file does not already exist, it starts fresh with an empty list.

The output of our example is as follows:

Playback history updated.

Updated Playback History:

Song: Whispering Pines | Played at: 2025-01-30 14:45

Handling class version changes

When our class structure changes, it introduces problems with our serialization implementation. An example is when we add a new field to our objects. The older serialized objects could become incompatible, leading to an **InvalidClassException** error. The solution to this challenge is to use **serialVersionUID** and transient fields. Let us look at an example that modifies **PlaybackHistory** to include a new field (device information). Following is the code:

```
import java.io.Serializable;
class PlaybackHistory implements Serializable {
    private static final long serialVersionUID = 2L; // Updated version
    private String songTitle;
    private String timestamp;
    private transient String deviceUsed; // New field (not serialized)
    public PlaybackHistory(String songTitle, String timestamp, String
deviceUsed) {
        this.songTitle = songTitle;
        this.timestamp = timestamp;
        this.deviceUsed = deviceUsed;
    }
    @Override
    public String toString() {
        return "Song: " + songTitle + " | Played at: " + timestamp + " |
Device: " + (deviceUsed != null ? deviceUsed : "Unknown");
```

```
        }
    }
```

In our example aforementioned, we use **serialVersionUID** to prevent compatibility issues. If the class is modified, older versions can still be read. The transient fields are not serialized, which prevents errors if a new field is added later.

Improving performance with buffered streams

Another challenge with serialization is that it can be slow if large objects are written without implementing buffering. **BufferedOutputStream** allows us to reduce disk write operations, thereby improving performance. Following is an example where we efficiently store large playlist data:

```java
import java.io.*;
import java.util.ArrayList;
import java.util.List;
class PlaylistEntry implements Serializable {
    private static final long serialVersionUID = 1L;
    private String title;
    private String artist;
    public PlaylistEntry(String title, String artist) {
        this.title = title;
        this.artist = artist;
    }
    @Override
    public String toString() {
        return "Song: " + title + " | Artist: " + artist;
    }
}
public class PlaylistSerializer {
    private static final String FILE_NAME = "playlist.dat";
    public static void main(String[] args) {
        List<PlaylistEntry> playlist = new ArrayList<>();
        playlist.add(new PlaylistEntry("Golden Meadow", "The Grazing Deer"));
        playlist.add(new PlaylistEntry("Ocean Breeze", "The Soaring Eagles"));
        writePlaylist(playlist);
        System.out.println("Playlist saved successfully.");
        List<PlaylistEntry> loadedPlaylist = readPlaylist();
        System.out.println("\nLoaded Playlist:");
        loadedPlaylist.forEach(System.out::println);
```

```
    }

    /**
     * Writes the playlist to a file using buffering.
     */
    private static void writePlaylist(List<PlaylistEntry> playlist) {
        try (FileOutputStream fos = new FileOutputStream(FILE_NAME);
             BufferedOutputStream bos = new BufferedOutputStream(fos);
             ObjectOutputStream oos = new ObjectOutputStream(bos)) {
            oos.writeObject(playlist);
        } catch (IOException e) {
            System.err.println("Error writing playlist: " + e.getMessage());
        }
    }
    /**
     * Reads the playlist from the file.
     */
    private static List<PlaylistEntry> readPlaylist() {
        try (FileInputStream fis = new FileInputStream(FILE_NAME);
             BufferedInputStream bis = new BufferedInputStream(fis);
             ObjectInputStream ois = new ObjectInputStream(bis)) {
            return (List<PlaylistEntry>) ois.readObject();
        } catch (IOException | ClassNotFoundException e) {
            return new ArrayList<>(); // Return empty list if file is missing
        }
    }
}
```

As you can see in our example, we used a **BufferedOutputStream** to speed up the writing process by reducing I/O operations. This reduces memory overhead compared to writing objects directly. Additionally, we used **BufferedInputStream** for optimized reading.

Buffered streams and data streams

We established the importance of efficient file handling for overall application performance, especially when dealing with large files or frequent read or write operations. In Java, we can implement buffered streams to improve efficiency by reducing direct disk access. The same is true for data streams, where we can allow reading and writing primitive data types in a compact binary format.

We should consider using buffered streams for the following use cases:

- For large files
- For frequent I/O operations
- When performance is a priority

For our ongoing Digitale example, these techniques are crucial for optimizing media metadata storage, log management, and playback history tracking. This section explores how buffered streams can enhance I/O performance and how data streams facilitate structured binary data handling.

Using buffered streams for efficiency

We previously covered Java's **FileInputStream** and **FileOutputStream**, both of which perform byte-by-byte operations. This can be extremely inefficient for large files. Buffered streams improve performance by storing data in memory before writing the data to disk or reading from it. This significantly reduces the number of I/O operations.

Buffered streams use an internal buffer to read/write chunks of data instead of reading and writing them one byte at a time. This significantly speeds up file operations. Let us look at a Digitale example where we want to efficiently log song playback histories without excessive disk write operations. We accomplish this using **BufferedOutputStream**. Following is the code:

```java
import java.io.BufferedOutputStream;
import java.io.FileOutputStream;
import java.io.IOException;
import java.nio.charset.StandardCharsets;
public class LargePlaybackLogger {
    public static void main(String[] args) {
        String logEntry = "User played: Symphony of the Stars - Aurora Sounds\n";
        String fileName = "playback_log.txt";
        try (FileOutputStream fos = new FileOutputStream(fileName, true);
            BufferedOutputStream bos = new BufferedOutputStream(fos)) {
            bos.write(logEntry.getBytes(StandardCharsets.UTF_8));
            bos.flush(); // Ensures data is written immediately
            System.out.println("Playback log updated.");
        } catch (IOException e) {
            System.err.println("Error writing log: " + e.getMessage());
        }
    }
}
```

As aforementioned, our example uses **BufferedOutputStream** to reduce the number of direct writes to the file, which will improve our application's performance. The **flush()** method ensures all buffered data is written, which prevents data loss in case of an unexpected shutdown. Lastly, we used **FileOutputStream(filename, true)** to append the file, ensuring new log entries are added without overwriting existing ones.

Let us look at a second example, which reads a large log file using **BufferedInputStream**. Following is the code:

```
import java.io.BufferedInputStream;
import java.io.FileInputStream;
import java.io.IOException;
public class LargePlaybackReader {
    public static void main(String[] args) {
        String fileName = "playback_log.txt";
        try (FileInputStream fis = new FileInputStream(fileName);
             BufferedInputStream bis = new BufferedInputStream(fis)) {
            int data;
            while ((data = bis.read()) != -1) {
                System.out.print((char) data);
            }
        } catch (IOException e) {
            System.err.println("Error reading log: " + e.getMessage());
        }
    }
}
```

In our aforementioned example, we used **BufferedInputStream** to read the data in chunks, making it faster than reading one byte at a time. Our implementation reduces the frequency of disk access, thereby improving efficiency when handling large logs or media metadata files.

Overview of DataInputStream and DataOutputStream

Data streams, provided by **DataInputStream** and **DataOutputStream**, allow us to implement reading and writing functionality for primitive data types (that is, **int**, **double**, etc.) in a structured binary format. This makes these streams ideal for storing structured information.

The benefits of data streams are efficient storage and data type preservation.

DataOutputStream

Let us look at an example where we write binary metadata using **DataOutputStream**. Our Digitale implementation will enable the storage of song metadata (title, duration, and rating) in a compact binary file. Following is the code:

```java
import java.io.DataOutputStream;
import java.io.FileOutputStream;
import java.io.IOException;
public class MediaMetadataWriter {
    public static void main(String[] args) {
        String fileName = "media_metadata.dat";
        try (FileOutputStream fos = new FileOutputStream(fileName);
            DataOutputStream dos = new DataOutputStream(fos)) {
            // Writing song metadata
            dos.writeUTF("Symphony of the Stars");  // Song Title
            dos.writeDouble(4.35);                   // Duration in minutes
            dos.writeInt(50000);                     // Popularity (play count)
            System.out.println("Media metadata saved successfully.");
        } catch (IOException e) {
            System.err.println("Error writing metadata: " + e.getMessage());
        }
    }
}
```

In our example aforementioned, we used **writeUTF()** to store strings efficiently in a binary format. We also used **writeDouble()** and **writeInt()** to store numerical values directly. This avoided the overhead that could have been needed for text conversion. Our application is efficient because the binary format is smaller and faster to read/write compared to plain text.

DataInputStream

Let us look at one more example, one that reads binary metadata using **DataInputStream**. Digitale needs to load stored metadata from a binary file and display it. The following is the code:

```java
import java.io.DataInputStream;
import java.io.FileInputStream;
import java.io.IOException;
public class MediaMetadataReader {
    public static void main(String[] args) {
        String fileName = "media_metadata.dat";
```

```java
        try (FileInputStream fis = new FileInputStream(fileName);
             DataInputStream dis = new DataInputStream(fis)) {
            // Reading song metadata
            String title = dis.readUTF();
            double duration = dis.readDouble();
            int popularity = dis.readInt();
            System.out.println("Media Metadata:");
            System.out.println("Title: " + title);
            System.out.println("Duration: " + duration + " mins");
            System.out.println("Play Count: " + popularity);
        } catch (IOException e) {
            System.err.println("Error reading metadata: " + e.getMessage());
        }
    }
}
```

In our aforementioned example, we used the **readUTF()** method to reconstruct stored strings. The **readDouble()** and **readInt()** methods were used to retrieve numbers efficiently. Our implementation does not require manual parsing, making it ideal for structured numeric data storage.

Handling character and byte streams

As we have seen in this chapter, Java provides us with two fundamental types of streams for reading and writing data, character streams and byte streams. We use character streams to handle text-based data using **Reader** and **Writer** classes and byte streams to handle binary data using **InputStream** and **OutputStream** classes.

These streams are crucial for Digitale's processing of media files, metadata, and user-generated content. Understanding the difference between character and byte streams can help us choose the most efficient approach for each task. We will be focusing on that in this section.

Difference between character and byte streams

The key difference between character streams and byte streams is the kind of data they handle and how they process it. Character streams handle text data (letters, numbers, and symbols). Byte streams handle raw binary data, which is ideal for working with non-text data such as images, audio, and video.

Let us explore both types of streams in more detail.

Character streams

We can use character streams to process text data using the **Reader** and **Writer** classes. These classes handle Unicode characters, making them ideal for reading and writing text files, configuration files, and logs. The key classes are **FileReader**, **FileWriter**, **BufferedReader**, **BufferedWriter**, and **PrintWriter**.

The following is an example of writing a text file using **FileWriter**:

```java
import java.io.FileWriter;
import java.io.IOException;
public class PlaylistWriter {
    public static void main(String[] args) {
        String fileName = "playlist.txt";
        try (FileWriter writer = new FileWriter(fileName)) {
            writer.write("Whispering Pines - The Howling Wolves\n");
            writer.write("Ocean Breeze - The Soaring Eagles\n");
            System.out.println("Playlist saved.");
        } catch (IOException e) {
            System.err.println("Error writing file: " + e.getMessage());
        }
    }
}
```

In our aforementioned example, we used **FileWriter** to write human-readable text. This approach automatically handles character encoding, which helps us avoid corruption in non-**American Standard Code for Information Interchange (ASCII)** text.

Byte streams

Byte streams are used to process binary data using Java's **InputStream** and **OutputStream** classes. These streams are typically used for media files, images, and encrypted data. The key classes used with byte streams are **FileInputStream**, **FileOutputStream**, **BufferedInputStream**, **BufferedOutputStream**, **DataInputStream**, and **DataOutputStream**.

Let us look at an example where we copy a binary file using **FileInputStream** and **FileOutputStream**. Following is the code:

```java
import java.io.FileInputStream;
import java.io.FileOutputStream;
import java.io.IOException;
public class MediaFileCopy {
    public static void main(String[] args) {
        String sourceFile = "original.mp3";
```

```
        String destinationFile = "copy.mp3";
        try (FileInputStream fis = new FileInputStream(sourceFile);
             FileOutputStream fos = new FileOutputStream(destinationFile)) {
            byte[] buffer = new byte[1024]; // 1KB buffer
            int bytesRead;
            while ((bytesRead = fis.read(buffer)) != -1) {
                fos.write(buffer, 0, bytesRead);
            }
            System.out.println("File copied successfully.");
        } catch (IOException e) {
            System.err.println("Error copying file: " + e.getMessage());
        }
    }
}
```

This approach is ideal for non-text files such as audio, video, and encrypted data. It works with raw bytes, thereby preserving the file structure without any encoding issues.

Use cases for each type of stream

When deciding which type of stream to use, it boils down to the type of data your application is dealing with. If you use text data, you will implement a character stream. You will implement a byte stream if you are working with non-text data such as images, audio, or video.

Usage of character streams

As we have seen, character streams are ideal for text files, structured text-based data files, and human-readable content. Here is a final character stream example using our Digitale scenario. The following example uses **BufferedReader** to read lyrics from a file:

```
import java.io.BufferedReader;
import java.io.FileReader;
import java.io.IOException;
public class LyricsReader {
    public static void main(String[] args) {
        String fileName = "song_lyrics.txt";
        try (BufferedReader br = new BufferedReader(new FileReader(fileName)))
{
            String line;
            while ((line = br.readLine()) != null) {
                System.out.println(line);
```

```
            }
        } catch (IOException e) {
            System.err.println("Error reading lyrics: " + e.getMessage());
        }
    }
}
```

Usage of byte streams

Byte streams are useful for binary files, performance-critical applications, and precise file control. In our final byte stream example, we implement streaming an audio file for Digitale, using **BufferedInputStream**. Following is the code:

```java
import java.io.BufferedInputStream;
import java.io.FileInputStream;
import java.io.IOException;
public class AudioStream {
    public static void main(String[] args) {
        String fileName = "audio.mp3";
        try (BufferedInputStream bis = new BufferedInputStream(new
FileInputStream(fileName))) {
            byte[] buffer = new byte[4096]; // 4KB buffer
            int bytesRead;
            while ((bytesRead = bis.read(buffer)) != -1) {
                System.out.println("Streaming " + bytesRead + " bytes...");
            }
        } catch (IOException e) {
            System.err.println("Error streaming audio: " + e.getMessage());
        }
    }
}
```

Conclusion

This chapter explored Java's I/O capabilities, covering the essential techniques required to manage I/O efficiently. We began with basic input handling using the Scanner class, learning how to read user input interactively from the console and parse structured text files. We also explored Java's java.nio package for improved file operations, including reading and writing text data efficiently. The chapter covered serialization and deserialization, a powerful technique for storing Java objects in a structured manner. The chapter demonstrated how it can enable applications like Digitale to implement persistent media metadata, user playlists, and playback histories while maintaining the integrity of object structures.

The chapter also considered performance optimization, using buffered streams to reduce direct disk access and data streams for efficient binary data storage. Finally, we examined character and byte streams.

The next chapter covers connecting Java applications to databases using **Java Database Connectivity** (**JDBC**). The chapter shows how to setup JDBC in your projects, establish connections to databases, and execute **Structured Query Language** (**SQL**) queries. The chapter also explains how to use prepared statements and callable statements for interacting with databases securely and efficiently. Additionally, the chapter explores how to handle database transactions in Java, ensuring consistency and reliability in your applications. Best practices for database operations are emphasized to ensure optimal performance.

Topics covered include an introduction to databases and JDBC, setting up JDBC, establishing connections, executing queries, prepared statements, callable statements, handling transactions in JDBC, and database operations best practices.

Points to remember

- Appending data to files should be done carefully to avoid unnecessary blank lines or overwriting existing content.

- Binary data, such as images and audio files, should be processed using byte streams rather than character streams.

- Buffered streams are recommended for handling large files efficiently by reducing the number of read or write operations.

- Character streams are designed for handling text data and automatically handle character encoding.

- Data streams allow for efficient storage and retrieval of primitive data types in a compact binary format.

- Deserialization can fail if the class structure has changed since the object was serialized, unless serialVersionUID is used properly.

- Exception handling should always be implemented when performing file I/O to prevent application crashes due to missing files or access issues.

- File handling in Java is more efficient and flexible using the java.nio.file package compared to older java.io methods.

- File reading operations should always close resources properly to prevent memory leaks, ideally using try-with-resources.

- File writing should be performed with appropriate StandardOpenOption settings to either overwrite or append data.

- Java serialization allows objects to be converted into a byte stream and saved to a file for later retrieval.

- Large files should be read and written using buffered streams to optimize performance.

- Mixing scanner methods can cause input skipping issues, so we should always consume the newline character after reading numbers.

- Object streams enable the storage and retrieval of complete Java objects from files.

- Performance issues can arise when processing large amounts of data without buffering.

- Reading files with BufferedReader improves efficiency by reading data in chunks instead of one character at a time.

- Serialization is useful for persisting complex objects, but should be used carefully to ensure compatibility across different versions of a class.

- Text-based data should be stored using character streams, while raw binary data should be stored using byte streams.

- The files class in java.nio.file provides utility methods for reading, writing, copying, and deleting files in a concise manner.

- The Scanner class is useful for reading user input from the console as well as parsing text files line by line.

- The try-with-resources statement should be used for managing file streams to ensure automatic resource closure.

- Writing to files with BufferedWriter improves efficiency and allows appending text without affecting existing content.

- When working with large data sets, structured binary storage using DataOutputStream and DataInputStream can significantly improve performance.

Case studies

These case studies provide realistic scenarios that encourage you to think critically about file handling, serialization, and I/O optimization:

- **Optimizing log file management**: *NebulaTunes*, a futuristic music streaming service, logs every song streamed by users to a file. The system writes millions of log entries daily, causing slow performance and excessive disk I/O. The company's current logging system writes each entry directly to a text file using FileWriter, but recent system monitoring shows that disk writes are slowing down the overall performance.

○ **For your consideration**: How can NebulaTunes improve logging performance while ensuring all data is written correctly? Would buffered writing be a suitable solution, and why? If the log files become too large, what strategy could be used to manage them efficiently?

• **Handling user preferences in a cross-version system for StarMap AI**: StarMap AI, a space exploration research platform, stores user preferences and configuration settings using Java serialization. The company recently introduced new settings that were not part of the original system, and now older serialized preference files fail to load properly, throwing InvalidClassException. Users who stored preferences in previous versions of the application can no longer load their settings because the class structure has changed.

○ **For your consideration**: What is causing this issue, and how can serialization be modified to allow backward compatibility? How does serialVersionUID help in maintaining class compatibility? Would **JavaScript Object Notation (JSON)** based storage be a better alternative to Java serialization in this case?

• **Efficiently processing large media files in the Andromeda Archives**: The Andromeda Archives, a digital library of interstellar broadcasts, stores massive audio and video files. The system frequently copies and transfers large binary media files, but has been experiencing slow performance due to inefficient file handling. Developers currently use FileInputStream and FileOutputStream, but have observed that processing speed decreases dramatically for large files (over 1GB).

○ **For your consideration**: How can buffered streams improve performance when handling large binary files? Would using byte streams or character streams be more appropriate for these media files? What is the best way to implement file copying while minimizing memory usage?

• **Structuring and storing high-frequency sensor data for QuantumMetrics**: QuantumMetrics, a deep-space data analysis company, collects real-time sensor data from satellites and deep-space probes. The data includes high-precision floating-point values (for example, temperature and radiation levels) recorded every second. Currently, the company writes sensor data as plain text to **comma-separated value (CSV)** files. However, they have noticed growing storage requirements and performance issues when reading the data back.

○ **Foryourconsideration**:WouldswitchingtobinarystoragewithDataOutputStream improve efficiency? Why or why not? How would structuring binary formats (for example, DataOutputStream) help in reading sensor data faster compared to text-based storage? What are the trade-offs between using human-readable formats (for example, CSV or JSON vs. binary formats (for example, serialized objects, binary streams)?

- **Implementing a secure user authentication system for CyberCore**: CyberCore, a cybersecurity firm, is developing a secure login system that encrypts user credentials before storing them in a file. They must ensure sensitive information (for example, usernames and hashed passwords) is stored securely without being accessible in plain text. Currently, user credentials are written to a simple text file using FileWriter, making them vulnerable to data breaches.

  o **For your consideration**: Why is storing user passwords in plain text a major security risk? Would using DataOutputStream or Java serialization provide better security? How can encryption be integrated with Java's I/O system to store credentials securely?

Multiple choice questions

1. **Which of the following best describes the purpose of buffered streams in Java?**
   a. They compress data before writing it to a file
   b. They improve performance by reducing direct disk I/O operations
   c. They encrypt data before writing it to a file
   d. They automatically convert binary data to text

2. **What happens if you serialize an object in Java and later change the class structure without defining serialVersionUID?**
   a. The deserialization process fails with an InvalidClassException
   b. The object is automatically updated to match the new class structure
   c. The old object data is ignored, and a new object is created
   d. The Java compiler detects the change and prevents serialization

3. **Which Java I/O class should you use to efficiently read a large text file line by line?**
   a. BufferedReader
   b. FileInputStream
   c. DataInputStream
   d. ObjectInputStream

4. **When should you use DataOutputStream instead of FileWriter?**
   a. When writing structured binary data
   b. When writing human-readable text files
   c. When storing serialized Java objects
   d. When appending data to an existing text file

5. **What is the primary difference between character streams and byte streams in Java?**

    a. Character streams process binary data, while byte streams handle text

    b. Byte streams automatically manage character encoding, while character streams do not

    c. Character streams handle text-based data, while byte streams handle binary data

    d. Byte streams are faster than character streams for all file operations

Answers

1.	b.
2.	a.
3.	a.
4.	a.
5.	c.

Questions

1. Java provides both java.io and java.nio.file for file handling. What are the key differences between these two approaches, and when would you choose one over the other?

2. Buffered streams are recommended for improving I/O performance. Explain how buffering works and provide a real-world scenario where using buffered streams would significantly enhance efficiency.

3. Serialization allows objects to be stored and retrieved from files, but it also introduces potential compatibility issues. What are some best practices to ensure backward compatibility when serializing objects?

4. In many applications, data can be stored as plain text (for example, JSON, CSV) or in binary format (for example, serialized objects, binary streams). What are the advantages and disadvantages of each approach, and how would you decide which one to use?

5. Java's Scanner class makes it easy to read user input from the console or from files. However, it has some known pitfalls, especially when reading mixed data types. What are some common issues developers face with the scanner, and how can they be avoided?

6. When working with large media files, such as high-quality audio or video, byte streams (InputStream, OutputStream) are often preferred over character streams (Reader, Writer). Why is this the case, and what would happen if you attempted to process a binary file using a character stream?

7. If you were developing an enterprise application that needed to store user-generated data (for example, playlists, reviews, or preferences), would you choose serialization or database storage? Explain the factors that would influence your decision.

8. The try-with-resources statement is widely recommended when working with file I/O operations in Java. Why is it considered best practice, and what risks does it help mitigate?

9. Data security is an important consideration when storing user information in files. What measures should be taken to ensure sensitive data (for example, passwords and personal information) is stored securely when using Java's file handling features?

10. Suppose you are designing a high-performance logging system for a cloud-based application. What file-handling techniques would you implement to ensure efficient logging, fast retrieval, and minimal disk usage? Would you use text-based logs, binary logs, or a combination of both?

Challenges

The following questions are provided to self-assess your knowledge of the chapter's content and apply critical thinking to key concepts:

- **Secure user preferences storage:**

  o **Objective**: Implement a system that securely stores and retrieves user preferences using serialization.

  o **Activity**: Perform the following actions:

    ▪ Create a UserPreferences class that includes fields for username, preferred theme (light/dark), and volume level (0-100).

    ▪ Implement serialization to store user preferences in a file.

    ▪ Implement deserialization to allow preferences to be loaded when the program starts.

    ▪ Ensure that if the file does not exist, the program initializes default preferences.

  o **Real-world applicability**: Many applications allow users to save their settings. This challenge reinforces how serialization can be used to persist configurations between program executions.

- **Playlist manager with gile I/O:**

  o **Objective**: Develop a Java application that allows users to create and manage a simple music playlist stored in a text file.

- ○ **Activity**: Perform the following actions:

  - ▪ Create a program that allows users to add, view, and remove songs from a playlist.

  - ▪ Store the playlist in playlist.txt, ensuring new songs are appended rather than overwriting the file.

  - ▪ Implement functionality to display the playlist contents to the user.

  - ▪ Handle cases where the file does not exist or is empty.

- ○ **Real-world applicability**: This exercise mimics real-world applications where user-generated content, such as music playlists or favorite lists, needs to be stored persistently.

- **Log analyzer for system events**:

  - ○ **Objective**: Process and analyze system log files efficiently using buffered streams.

  - ○ **Activity**: Perform the following actions:

    - ▪ Create a log file (system.log) with at least 10 sample log entries in the format:

      ```
      [2025-01-30 14:45:23] INFO - System started
      [2025-01-30 14:46:10] WARNING - Low disk space
      [2025-01-30 14:47:05] ERROR - Network connection lost
      ```

    - ▪ Write a program that reads the log file using BufferedReader and allows the user to:

      - ◆ View all log entries

      - ◆ Filter logs (display only error messages)

      - ◆ Count total occurrences of each log type (information, warning, and error)

  - ○ **Real-world applicability**: System administrators and developers often need to analyze log files for troubleshooting and system monitoring. This challenge helps students work with structured file data and efficient file reading techniques.

- **Binary storage for high scores**:

  - ○ **Objective**: Implement a game high score tracker using DataOutputStream and DataInputStream.

  - ○ **Activity**: Perform the following actions:

    - ▪ Create a HighScore class with fields for player name, score, and date.

- Write a program that allows users to enter new high scores and stores them in a binary file (highscores.dat).

- Implement functionality to read and display all stored high scores.

- Ensure data is stored in binary format rather than as plain text.

○ **Real-world applicability**: This challenge teaches students how to store structured numerical data efficiently in a way that avoids text-based parsing issues, like how games track scores.

- **Secure credential storage**:

  ○ **Objective**: Store and retrieve user login credentials securely without using plain text storage.

  ○ **Activity**: Perform the following actions:

    - Create a program that allows users to register a username and password.

    - Use DataOutputStream to store credentials in a binary file (credentials. dat).

    - Implement a login system that allows users to enter their credentials and verify them against stored data.

    - Ensure passwords are not stored in plain text by using a simple hashing mechanism (for example, Java's hashCode() method).

  ○ **Real-world applicability**: User authentication is a crucial aspect of application security. This challenge provides a foundational approach to securely storing and verifying user credentials without relying on plain text storage.

Self-assessment

The following questions are provided so you can self-assess your knowledge of the chapter's content and apply critical thinking to key concepts:

1. **Conceptual**: What are the key differences between character streams and byte streams in Java, and when should each be used?

2. **Practical**: Suppose you need to process a large log file containing system events. Which Java I/O classes would you use to read the file efficiently, and why?

3. **Scenario-based**: You are developing a high score tracking system for a game. The application needs to store and retrieve structured numerical data (for example, player names, scores, timestamps). Would you use plain text files, Java serialization, or data streams for this purpose? Explain your reasoning.

4. **Application-oriented**: Imagine you are working on a document editing application

where users need to save and load their work. Would it be better to store the document contents as serialized objects, plain text, or binary data? Justify your choice.

5. **Reflection**: Think about an application you use frequently (for example, a music streaming app, a file manager, or a social media platform). What types of Java I/O techniques do you think it relies on for handling data storage and retrieval? Explain how these concepts from the chapter might apply to its functionality.

Answers

1. Character streams are used for handling text-based data, ensuring proper character encoding. They are ideal for reading/writing plain text files, XML, or JSON. Byte streams handle binary data, such as audio, images, and video files, preserving raw byte structure without encoding conversions. Use character streams for human-readable text and byte streams for binary files.

2. To efficiently process a large log file, BufferedReader should be used with FileReader to read the file line by line, reducing memory usage. BufferedReader.readLine() ensures that only one line is loaded into memory at a time, making it ideal for large files. If further processing is needed (for example, filtering logs), a Scanner with token-based parsing could be used.

3. For a high score tracking system, data streams would be the best choice. They allow storing structured numerical data in a compact binary format, ensuring fast read/write operations without manual text parsing. Plain text (CSV, JSON) requires additional conversion, while serialization may lead to compatibility issues when the class structure changes.

4. In a document editing application, the best approach depends on the file format. If the application saves raw text (for example, .txt files), character streams are sufficient. If formatting and structure need to be preserved (for example, .docx or .pdf), binary streams are required. Serialization would only be useful for storing additional metadata (for example, recent edits, author details) in a proprietary format.

5. Applications like music streaming services rely on multiple Java I/O techniques:
   a. Buffered streams for efficient log handling (for example, play history tracking).
   b. Byte streams for audio file processing and downloading.
   c. Character streams for storing user preferences and metadata.
   d. Serialization or database integration for storing playlists and user settings.

CHAPTER 10
Database Connectivity

Introduction

Databases are a fundamental component of modern Java applications. The importance of efficient data retrieval, manipulation, and storage cannot be overstated, as they are important to Java applications, from small single-function tools to large enterprise systems. This chapter explores database connectivity and operations to help you build efficient and scalable database functionality in your Java applications. Specifically, this chapter explores how Java interacts with relational databases for handling structured data.

The chapter begins with an introduction to relational databases, focusing on how they are used in Java applications. We will examine how these databases are structured and how they store data. SQLite, an open-source, lightweight embedded database, will be used for hands-on examples of how to implement persistent data storage. Core database operations via **Structured Query Language** (**SQL**) queries will also be covered.

The advanced topic of executing SQL queries programmatically using **Java Database Connectivity** (**JDBC**) will also be explored. We look at the importance of databases and JDBC in application development. Key topics include setting up JDBC in a Java project, establishing connections to a database, executing SQL queries, and using prepared and callable statements. This chapter also addresses two underlying concerns with databases: secure and efficient data handling. Finally, we cover database transactions, best practices for database operations, and performance enhancement techniques.

Structure

This chapter covers the following topics:

- Introduction to databases for Java applications
- Working with databases in Java
- Using JDBC for database connectivity
- Transaction management
- Database operations best practices

Objectives

By the end of this chapter, you should understand how to implement relational databases in Java and perform basic SQL operations. Aided by the hands-on exercises, you should be able to setup, create, and interact with a database using the Java programming language. You should also understand the role JDBC has in database interactions and how it can help you manage database transactions. Finally, you should understand and be able to implement best practices for database interactions in Java, such as preventing SQL injections.

Introduction to databases for Java applications

Nearly every modern software development project involves manipulating, storing, and retrieving data efficiently. This is true for small, medium, and large applications. Even modern digital games require databases. We can develop Java applications that interact with databases, efficiently handle large volumes of data, and do so with security practices.

Consider how much data online retailers manage. Their systems often have user accounts, product information, order transactions, and inventories. They need to be able to store and retrieve data efficiently. This chapter features a fictitious online retailer that sells used books, Bougie Books, as our example application. Bougie Books maintains a catalog of books, customer orders, and reviews, all requiring structured storage in a relational database. As we explore database concepts and SQL queries, we will build out the database functionality that supports this bookstore's operations.

Overview of relational databases

Among the several types of databases, relational databases are the most widely used for modern application development. They are structured to support data consistency and data management efficiency.

> Note: **Relational databases organize data into structured tables with predefined relationships.**

Relational databases provide us with these benefits:

- Structured data storage
- Data integrity enforcement
- Efficient complex query support
- Transaction management
- Structured entity relationships
- Scalability

This type of database is easy to understand because of its table structure. Each table represents an entity. Each row is a record, and each column is a field. The columns hold a specific data type, such as a date, number, or text. We connect tables through **primary keys** (**PKs**) and **foreign keys** (**FKs**). These keys allow us to establish relationships between different entities.

Let us use our Bougie Books example. For that application, we will need to store information about books, customers, and orders.

Table 10.1 shows how we would organize Bougie Books data using a relational database:

Table name	Use
`Books`	Contains book details such as `title`, `author`, `price`, etc.
`Customers`	Store `name`, `email`, `address`, etc.
`Orders`	Used to track customer purchases
`Order_Items`	Itemized record of each order

Table 10.1: Bougie Books relational database tables

Figure 10.1 shows an abbreviated database schema to illustrate how the database tables are linked using PK and FK:

Table Name: Books

Name	Data Type	Description
book_id (PK)	INTEGER	Unique identifier for each book.
title	TEXT	Title of the book.
author	TEXT	Author of the book.
genre	TEXT	Genre/category of the book.
price	REAL	Price of the book.
stock_qty	INTEGER	Number of copies available.

Table Name: Orders

Name	Data Type	Description
order_id (PK)	INTEGER	Unique identifier for each order.
order_date	TEXT (ISO format)	Date when the order was placed.
customer_id (FK)	INTEGER	Links to customer_id in Customers.
total_price	REAL	Total cost of the order.

Table Name: Customers

Name	Data Type	Description
cust_id (PK)	INTEGER	Unique identifier for each customer.
name	TEXT	Full customer name
email	TEXT	Customer's email address
phone_nbr	TEXT	Customer phone number
address	TEXT	Street address
city	TEXT	City

Table Name: Order_Items

Name	Data Type	Description
order_item_id (PK)	INTEGER	Unique identifier for each order item.
order_id (FK)	INTEGER	Links to order_id in Orders.
book_id (FK)	INTEGER	Links to book_id in Books.
quantity	INTEGER	Number of copies of the book ordered.

Figure 10.1: Abbreviated Bougie Books database schema

When creating a database schema, several considerations are involved, including what data is needed, what its format will be, and what relationships we need between the tables. In our example, the **Orders** and **Books** tables have a many-to-many relationship. This is because a single order can contain multiple books, and a book can appear in multiple orders. We would manage that using our **Order_Items** table.

To implement our Bougie Books example, we will select data types that are compatible with SQLite.

Table 10.2 describes the data types we will use:

Data type	Description
INTEGER	Used for IDs to ensure indexing efficiency
REAL	This will be used for precise calculations
TEXT	Used for dates in the **YYYY-MM-DD HH:MM:SS** format

Table 10.2: Selected data types for Bougie Books

Our structured schema should permit the Bougie Books application to efficiently manage its book inventory, customer information, and orders. Implementing a relational database supports transaction integrity and scalability.

Storing and managing structured data

The core purpose of a database is to securely store structured data so applications can retrieve and manage the data. Our goal is for efficiencies in our database interactions. This is achieved with well-defined tables with relationships between them.

At Bougie Books, structured data is essential for tracking book inventories, processing customer orders, and managing user information. In a relational database, tables are the primary way to store structured data. As we covered in the previous section, each table represents an entity (e.g., **Books**, **Customers**, **Orders**), and each row in the table represents a record (e.g., an individual book or customer).

Data consistency

Our tables consist of columns, each with a specific data type. Their structured nature ensures data consistency.

> **Note: Data consistency means that every record follows the same format.**

As an example, in Bougie Books, the **Books** table stores information about available books, including their **title**, **author**, **genre**, **price**, and **stock_qty**. Refer to *Table 10.3* for sample data:

Book_id (PK)	title	author	genre	price	stock_qty
1	Mastering Agile for Enterprises	Aditi Agarawal	Software	12.99	24
2	Cloud Security for Beginners	Sasa Kovacevic	Security	14.99	8
3	Java 8 to 21	Shai Almog	Programming	9.99	32

Table 10.3: Sample data for the books table

As seen in the preceding table, each row represents a book, and each column defines properties of the book. This type of table might have additional fields (columns) to include publish date, edition, condition, binding, hard cover/soft cover, ISBN, etc. The **book_id** field is the PK, which is a unique identifier for each book.

Managing relationships

We previously mentioned FK as a mechanism to establish connections between tables. These relationships are important as they are intended to prevent data duplication and ensure consistency across all records.

Using our Bougie Books example, a customer order needs to keep track of which books were purchased. Since the book information is already in the **Books** table, we do not need to replicate it; instead, we can use the **Order_Items** table to link books and orders through FKs.

See *Table 10.4* for an example:

order_item_id (PK)	order_id (FK)	book_id (FK)	quantity
1	1001	1	2
2	1001	3	1
3	1--2	2	3

Table 10.4: Sample data for books table

In our example, **order_id 1001** contains two copies of **Mastering Agile for Enterprises** and one copy of **Java 8 to 21**. This structure allows Bougie Books to store order information efficiently without repeating book details in multiple tables.

Storing and managing data

SQL is how we interact with the structured data in a relational database. Let us look at some fundamental SQL operations using our Bougie Books database example.

To add data to tables, we use the **INSERT** statement. When Bougie Books receives a shipment of used books, it gets stored in the **Books** table with a statement such as this:

```
INSERT INTO Books (book_id, title, author, genre, price, stock_qty)
VALUES (4, 'Blender 3D for Jobseekers', 'Laurie Annis', 'Game Dev', 11.99, 8);
```

This **INSERT** statement adds a new record to the table, storing the book **Blender 3D for Jobseekers** by **Laurie Annis** in our inventory.

To update existing data, we use the **UPDATE** statement. Each time a customer purchases a book, the stock quantity needs to be updated.

The following is an example of how we would use the **UPDATE** statement to reduce a book's quantity by one:

```
UPDATE Books
SET stock_qty = stock_qty - 1
WHERE book_id = 1;
```

The query aforementioned decreases the stock of **Mastering Agile for Enterprises** by one copy after a successful purchase.

To display available books to customers or to generate reports for managers, we use a **SELECT** statement such as shown:

```
SELECT title, author, price, stock_qty
FROM Books
WHERE stock_qty > 0
ORDER BY title ASC;
```

Optimizing data storage

The concept of optimized data storage has the purpose of enabling efficient data management by our Java applications. This requires us to optimize our queries and storage techniques.

The following are some best practices to help us achieve optimized data storage:

- Determine which columns will be searched the most and index them. This will improve the speed of your queries.

- Where possible, use transactions for batch operations. We will cover transactions later in this chapter.

- Carefully design your database schema to avoid redundant data. This will improve consistency and reduce storage bloat.

- Use the most efficient data type for each field to reduce storage overhead.

Importance of databases in Java applications

The use of databases in Java applications gives us the ability to implement persistent storage. Users expect their data to be available each time they use an application. A simple example is a user profile. We do not require our users to create new accounts each time they use our system; instead, we store their credentials in a database for later retrieval.

The value of databases goes beyond simple user accounts and includes use cases such as product inventories, financial transactions, data analytics, and more. When databases are structured for efficient storage, our applications can use SQL statements to retrieve, manipulate, and store data.

For our Bougie Books online bookstore, a database is essential for managing the catalog of books, customer orders, transactions, and financial accounting. Without a database, the application would struggle to maintain a consistent and reliable record of business operations.

Let us explore several key reasons why databases are vital for Java applications.

Persistent data storage

As we established, Java applications usually require data to persist beyond a single runtime session. Without persistent storage, we would need to manage our data in volatile memory, which is lost when the application terminates. Relational databases allow our data to be stored permanently, making it available even after a system restart.

For example, at Bougie Books, we need to store customer purchase histories. We can retrieve that information anytime by storing order records in a database. Here is how we might store an order in our Bougie Books database:

```
INSERT INTO Orders (order_id, order_date, cust_id, total_price)
VALUES (1003, '2025-02-16', 202, 75.99);
```

This approach ensures order information remains in the system permanently.

Efficient searches

We designed our database with efficiency in mind. A well-structured database promotes fast data retrieval via SQL queries, allowing our Java applications to access and filter information efficiently.

A common example at Bougie Books is when a customer searches for books by a specific author. Instead of scanning an entire file or iterating through an in-memory list, we can instantly use a simple SQL query to retrieve relevant records.

The following is an example:

```
SELECT title, price FROM Books WHERE author = 'Neo Anderson';
```

This query quickly fetches all books by **Neo Anderson**, providing a seamless user experience.

Data consistency and integrity

Although we touched on data consistency earlier in this chapter, let us look at it again and use an example to solidify our understanding. Relational databases enforce data integrity primarily through constraints like PKs and FKs. This prevents issues such as duplicate records and missing data.

Using Bougie Books as an example, every order must be linked to a valid customer. An FK constraint ensures that an order cannot be created if the customer does not exist in the system.

Here is how we can establish a FK constraint in our **Orders** table:

```
CREATE TABLE Orders (
    order_id INTEGER PRIMARY KEY,
    order_date TEXT NOT NULL,
    cust_id INTEGER NOT NULL,
    total_price REAL CHECK (total_price > 0),
    FOREIGN KEY (cust_id) REFERENCES Customers(cust_id)
);
```

In your preceding SQL example, **FOREIGN KEY** ensures that a valid customer must exist before placing an order. The **CHECK (total_price > 0)** statement is another constraint, ensuring that negative order totals are not possible. Such constraints can prevent invalid data from corrupting the system.

Multi-user access

Most modern applications support multiple users accessing the system simultaneously. We use databases to handle concurrent operations efficiently. Our goal is to maintain data consistency even when multiple users read and write data at the same time.

As an example, imagine that we have multiple customers attempting to purchase the last available copy of a book at Bougie Books. The database will ensure that only one of the customers can successfully complete the transaction.

Let us look at how we can handle simultaneous purchases:

```
BEGIN TRANSACTION;
UPDATE Books
SET stock_qty = stock_qty - 1
WHERE book_id = 2 AND stock_qty > 0;
COMMIT;
```

In this example, it is critical that inventory levels are continually updated to prevent multiple customers from buying the same book at the same time. This avoids inventory conflicts.

Scalability

It is important to plan for the growth of our databases so we can efficiently handle increased data volumes without slowing down overall system performance. For Bougie Books, this means:

- Expanding the book catalog without performance issues.

- Managing thousands of customer orders without system crashes.

- Supporting multiple categories, discounts, and promotions.

A relational database can handle millions of records efficiently using indexes, optimized queries, and caching mechanisms.

Security

Another reason to implement relational databases is to leverage their built-in security mechanisms. It is important to restrict access to private and sensitive information. With relational databases, we can implement user roles and permissions to ensure that only authorized users can modify or view specific data.

For example, at Bougie Books, this might mean that customers can only see their own orders, and managers can manage inventory and view all orders.

Here is an example of how to grant read-only access to customers:

```
GRANT SELECT ON Orders TO customer_role;
```

The SQL statement above ensures customers can view orders but cannot modify them. Using a role-based access system can prevent unauthorized modifications to our application's data.

Working with databases in Java

The previous section covered the importance of databases in Java applications and explained how relational databases can be used for persistent data. This section applies knowledge from the previous section with practical hands-on examples. We will use SQLite to build database functionality for Bougie Books, our online retailer. We will cover basic SQL operations, demonstrate how to execute SQL queries with Java, and setup and interact with SQLite in a Java program.

Basic SQL operations

The four primary database interactions are **create, read, update, and delete (CRUD)**, and the four fundamental SQL operations are **SELECT**, **INSERT**, **UPDATE**, and **DELETE**. These operations allow us to retrieve and modify records in our database.

Let us look at how to use these SQL operations using Bougie Books for context.

Retrieving data

When a customer or other user searches for books on Bougie Books, we would use the **SELECT** statement to retrieve relevant data.

Here is an example where we retrieve all books currently in the inventory:

```
SELECT title, author, price, stock_qty
FROM Books
WHERE stock_qty > 0
ORDER BY title ASC;
```

This query returns all books currently available in the bookstore based on the inventory value being greater than zero. The query will return the book's **title**, **author**, **price**, and **stock_qty**. The number of books in stock. The results will be presented alphabetically by **title**.

Adding data

When a new book arrives, the Bougie Book staff will use the system to add it to the database. The functionality to add a new book to our **Books** table requires the use of **INSERT**. Here is how that is done:

```
INSERT INTO Books (book_id, title, author, genre, price, stock_qty)
VALUES (5, 'Master Flutter', 'Kevin Moore', 'Programming', 31.99, 24);
```

This adds the book **Master Flutter** to our inventory, with appropriate metadata to include the quantity added to the inventory.

Updating data

Updating existing data is a common database operation. This could be to update a book's price, fix a typographical error, or update the inventory after a book is purchased.

Here is an example of how we can reduce our stock after a sale:

```
UPDATE Books
SET stock_qty = stock_qty - 1
WHERE book_id = 5;
```

This decreases the stock count for **Mastering Flutter** by one copy after a sale.

Deleting data

If a book is sold out, we merely need to update the record to reflect zero for the quantity. If, however, a book is discontinued, we will need to remove it from our inventory.

Here is an example of how that can be done:

```
DELETE FROM Books
WHERE book_id = 5;
```

This will permanently delete the book **Mastering Flutter** from our database.

Executing SQL queries

Java provides the JDBC API to communicate with relational databases. We will explore how to use JDBC to send SQL queries from Java code to our database. For now, let us look at the basic mechanics for executing SQL queries in Java.

Our first task is to connect to a database, as follows:

```
public class DatabaseConnection {
    public static Connection connect() {
        Connection conn = null;
        try {
            String url = "bougie_books.db";
            conn = DriverManager.getConnection(url);
            System.out.println("Connected to Bougie Books database.");
        } catch (SQLException e) {
            System.out.println("Connection failed: " + e.getMessage());
        }
        return conn;
    }
}
```

This code snippet attempts to connect to our database. If the database does not already exist, then it will be created.

Next, we can test our connection with this line of code:

```
connect(); // Test the connection
```

Once connected to our database, we can execute SQL statements from Java using the **Statement** and **PreparedStatement** classes.

Here is an abbreviated example where we might retrieve all books from our database:

```
try (Connection conn = DatabaseConnection.connect();
```

```
    Statement stmt = conn.createStatement();
    ResultSet rs = stmt.executeQuery("SELECT * FROM Books")) {

  while (rs.next()) {
      System.out.println(rs.getInt("book_id") + " - " +
                         rs.getString("title") + " by " +
                         rs.getString("author") + " - $" +
                         rs.getDouble("price"));
  }
} catch (SQLException e) {
    System.out.println("Error fetching books: " + e.getMessage());
}
```

The preceding code snippet demonstrates how to use the **Statement** class to retrieve all books from the **Books** table and print them to the console.

Using SQLite

For simple programs and for testing, SQLite databases can be helpful. They are easy to implement and do not require a separate database server. SQLite databases are stored as a single **.db** file.

The following steps are used to setup and test SQLite:

1. Install the SQLite extension in VS Code.

2. Add the SQLite JDBC driver for our project. You can find the latest driver here: **https://mvnrepository.com/artifact/org.xerial/sqlite-jdbc**

3. Create a **/lib** folder in your VS Code project and put the **.jar** file there.

4. Create a **/.vscode** folder in your project.

5. Inside the **.vscode** folder, create a new **launch.json** file and add the following to that file:
    ```
    {
        "version": "3.49.0.0",
        "configurations": [
            {
                "type": "java",
                "name": "Launch Java Program",
                "request": "launch",
                "mainClass": "SQLiteConnection",
                "projectName": "SQLiteConnection",
    ```

```
                "classPaths": [
                    "${workspaceFolder}/lib/sqlite-jdbc-3.49.0.0.jar"
                ]
            }
        ]
    }
```

6. Write an **SQLConnection** class such as this:

```java
import java.sql.Connection;
import java.sql.DriverManager;
import java.sql.SQLException;
public class SQLiteConnection {
    public static void main(String[] args) {
        Connection connection = null;
        try {
            // Load the SQLite JDBC driver
            Class.forName("org.sqlite.JDBC");
            // db parameters
            String url = "jdbc:sqlite:./lib/test.db"; // Ensure this is
correct
            // create a connection to the database
            connection = DriverManager.getConnection(url);
            System.out.println("Connection to SQLite has been
established.");
        } catch (ClassNotFoundException e) {
            System.out.println("SQLite JDBC driver not found. " +
e.getMessage());
        } catch (SQLException e) {
            System.out.println(e.getMessage());
        } finally {
            try {
                if (connection != null) {
                    connection.close();
                }
            } catch (SQLException ex) {
                System.out.println(ex.getMessage());
            }
        }
    }
}
```

```
            }
```

7. Use **javac** in a terminal window to compile your program. For example:

    ```
    javac -cp .:./lib/sqlite-jdbc-3.49.0.0.jar SQLiteConnection.java
    ```

8. Use **java** in a terminal window to run your program. For example:

    ```
    java -cp .:./lib/sqlite-jdbc-3.49.0.0.jar SQLiteConnection
    ```

If everything works well, you should see the following output:

```
Connection to SQLite has been established.
```

Creating the Bougie Books database

Okay, now that we have SQLite working in VS Code, let us create a **Connection** class for our Bougie Books database.

The following is a sample class:

```java
import java.sql.Connection;
import java.sql.DriverManager;
import java.sql.SQLException;
public class BBDatabaseConnection {
    public static Connection connect() {
        Connection conn = null;
        try {
            // Connect to SQLite database file
            String url = "jdbc:sqlite:bougie_books.db";
            conn = DriverManager.getConnection(url);
            System.out.println("Connected to Bougie Books database.");
        } catch (SQLException e) {
            System.out.println("Connection failed: " + e.getMessage());
        }
        return conn;
    }
    public static void main(String[] args) {
        connect(); // Test the connection
    }
}
```

We will use this class for our database connection. Next, let us create a class to create our **Books** table:

```java
import java.sql.Connection;
```

```java
import java.sql.SQLException;
import java.sql.Statement;
public class BBCreateTables {
    public static void main(String[] args) {
        String sql = "CREATE TABLE IF NOT EXISTS Books ("
                + "book_id INTEGER PRIMARY KEY, "
                + "title TEXT NOT NULL, "
                + "author TEXT NOT NULL, "
                + "genre TEXT, "
                + "price REAL NOT NULL, "
                + "stock_qty INTEGER NOT NULL)";
        try (Connection conn = BBDatabaseConnection.connect();
             Statement stmt = conn.createStatement()) {
            stmt.execute(sql);
            System.out.println("Books table created successfully.");
        } catch (SQLException e) {
            System.out.println("Error creating table: " + e.getMessage());
        }
    }
}
```

To compile our program, we use **javac** as shown:

```
javac -cp .:./lib/sqlite-jdbc-3.49.0.0.jar BBDatabaseConnection.java
BBCreateTables.java
```

Now, we are ready to run our program to create the **Books** table. Run this from the terminal:

```
java -cp .:./lib/sqlite-jdbc-3.49.0.0.jar BBCreateTables
```

Our output should be as shown:

```
Connected to Bougie Books database.
```

```
Books table created successfully.
```

At this point, you can start adding data to your database using the **INSERT** SQL statement, as demonstrated earlier in this chapter.

Using JDBC for database connectivity

The previous section demonstrated the use of JDBC to provide us with a common interface for working with SQL queries and managing database connections.

Note: **JDBC is the standard API for working with relational databases in Java.**

So far, we have used SQLite for our Bougie Books examples, but JDBC also works with other databases like *MySQL*, *PostgreSQL*, and *Oracle*. The difference is that for each type of database, we need to obtain and use a specific driver.

Regardless of the database type, JDBC serves as the connector between our Java application and our database. As you have seen, JDBC enables us to connect to relational databases, execute SQL queries, and manage transactions.

Our implementations include the following components:

- JDBC driver
- Database connection
- **Statement** or **PreparedStatement** for SQL query execution
- **ResultSet** to store query results

We can refer to the previous section for implementation examples.

Let us look at how we can use JDBC to handle transactions.

> **Note: A transaction is a group of operations that succeeds or rolls back if it fails.**

To start a transaction, we first disable auto-commit:

```
conn.setAutoCommit(false);
```

If our transaction succeeds, we can save the changes to the database with this statement:

```
conn.commit();
```

If our transaction fails, we need to roll it back. The following statement will undo the changes:

```
conn.rollback();
```

Now that we understand transactions, let us move on to the next section, which focuses on managing them.

Transaction management

The purpose of transaction management is to help ensure data integrity in all database operations. This is especially important when we have multiple simultaneous users. We want to prevent corruption of our data, and transactions play an important role in ensuring our database operations are **atomic, consistent, isolated, and durable (ACID)**.

As a reminder, transactions are sequences of multiple database operations that are executed as a block or unit.

Table 10.5 contains descriptions of each of the ACID properties as well as use cases specific to Bougie Books:

Property	Description	Bougie Books use case
Atomic	All operations with a transaction must succeed for the transaction to succeed.	A transaction could consist of order creation and stock update; both must succeed.
Consistent	Transactions result in valid database states.	A book's quantity cannot be less than zero.
Isolated	Transactions do not collide.	Two customers trying to buy the last copy of a book at the same time can only result in one customer's purchase.
Durable	Transactions committed to the database are permanent.	Once an order is committed to the database, it remains stored.

Table 10.5: ACID properties with Bougie Books use cases

The key to successful transaction management is the use of commits and rollbacks. Many databases have built-in functionality for automatically committing transactions. To ensure consistency, we follow these transaction management steps:

1. Start the transaction with **conn.setAutoCommit(false);**

2. After successful database operations, commit the changes with **conn.commit();**

3. If an error occurs, rollback the changes with **conn.rollback();**

Using our Bougie Books example, let us look at how we might process an order using transactions:

1. A customer places an order.

2. Deduct the purchased quantity from the **Books** table.

3. Add the purchase to the **Orders** table.

4. Ensure that both operations (*Steps* 2 and 3 above) either both succeed or roll back the changes.

Here is a code snippet to demonstrate how that could be implemented:

```
try {
    conn.setAutoCommit(false);  // Begin transaction
    // Deduct stock
    String updateStock = "UPDATE Books SET stock_qty = stock_qty - ? WHERE
book_id = ?";
    PreparedStatement pstmt1 = conn.prepareStatement(updateStock);
    pstmt1.setInt(1, 2);  // Reduce stock by 2
    pstmt1.setInt(2, 1);  // Book ID = 1
```

```
    pstmt1.executeUpdate();
    // Insert order
    String insertOrder = "INSERT INTO Orders (order_id, order_date, cust_id,
total_price) VALUES (?, ?, ?, ?)";
    PreparedStatement pstmt2 = conn.prepareStatement(insertOrder);
    pstmt2.setInt(1, 101);  // Order ID
    pstmt2.setString(2, "2025-02-16");  // Order date
    pstmt2.setInt(3, 5);  // Customer ID
    pstmt2.setDouble(4, 79.98);  // Total price
    pstmt2.executeUpdate();
    conn.commit();  // Commit transaction
} catch (SQLException e) {
    conn.rollback();  // Rollback on error
    System.out.println("Transaction failed: " + e.getMessage());
}
```

As seen in the preceding code, we use a try-catch block to catch **SQLException** errors. An error with any atomic part of the transaction will result in the operation being rolled back, restoring the database to its previous state.

Database operations best practices

Inefficient, insecure, and poorly coded database queries can have devastating impacts on your Java applications. Symptoms of these problems can include performance bottlenecks, security vulnerabilities, logic errors, and code that is difficult to maintain.

This section explores several best practices when working with databases in Java, all within the context of our Bougie Books application.

Preventing SQL injection

SQL injection is one of the most prevalent security vulnerabilities related to databases. Malicious entities attempt to manipulate SQL statements by injecting harmful input.

As an example, consider the following code:

```
String userInput = "Java";  // Could be manipulated by the user
String query = "SELECT * FROM Books WHERE genre = '" + userInput + "'";
Statement stmt = conn.createStatement();
ResultSet rs = stmt.executeQuery(query);
```

If the user inputs **'' OR '1'='1'**, the original query becomes the following:

```
SELECT * FROM Books WHERE genre = '' OR '1'='1';
```

This would return all records, exposing the database in its entirety. To prevent this, we can implement parameterized queries using **PreparedStatement** instead of concatenating user input directly into SQL strings.

Here is an example:

```
String query = "SELECT * FROM Books WHERE genre = ?";
PreparedStatement pstmt = conn.prepareStatement(query);
pstmt.setString(1, userInput);

ResultSet rs = pstmt.executeQuery();
```

This approach ensures we treat user input as data, not part of the SQL statement. This is an effective approach for preventing SQL injection.

Optimizing query performance

Another best practice is to optimize our SQL queries for efficient performance. Poorly written SQL statements can lead to system lag, slow response times, and increased server load. To achieve our goal of optimized query performance, we can use four specific techniques.

First, we can use **PreparedStatement** for repeated queries. This technique's efficiency is due to the database caching execution, which reduces overhead. This results in safer and faster queries.

Here is an example:

```
String query = "SELECT * FROM Books WHERE price < ?";
PreparedStatement pstmt = conn.prepareStatement(query);
pstmt.setDouble(1, 50.00);  // First execution
pstmt.executeQuery();
pstmt.setDouble(1, 30.00);  // Second execution with new parameter
pstmt.executeQuery();
```

A second optimization approach is to only retrieve columns that are necessary. Instead of using **SELECT ***, specify only the columns needed by the system. Instead of **SELECT * FROM Books;** use something like **SELECT title, price FROM Books WHERE stock_qty > 0;**

A third query optimization approach is to use indices to implement faster searches. Here is how we can create an index on the **title** column:

```
CREATE INDEX idx_title ON Books (title);
```

This speeds up queries like:

```
SELECT * FROM Books WHERE title = 'Effective Java';
```

A final query optimization approach is to limit result sets, especially when dealing with large datasets. Limiting the number of results can avoid overwhelming the application. Here is an example:

```
SELECT * FROM Books ORDER BY title ASC LIMIT 10;
```

Managing database connections

It is important to realize that database connections are resource-intensive, underscoring the importance of managing them properly. Poorly managed database connections can lead to memory leaks and overall poor performance.

The three techniques can lessen this drain on resources:

- Use try-with-resources for automatic resource management. This approach was used throughout this chapter.

- Implement connection pooling to reuse existing connections instead of opening a new connection each time you have a database request. This will reduce overhead. You can use one of the following connection pooling libraries with Java:
  - Apache DBCP
  - C3P0
  - HikariCP

- Always close database connections when you are done with them. This will prevent connection leaks.

  Here is an example of how that is done:

  ```
  if (conn != null && !conn.isClosed()) {
      conn.close();
  }
  ```

Handling query results

Efficiently processing **ResultSet** data is a best practice that helps ensure optimal performance and readability of our application. We can take two recommended approaches in observance of this best practice.

First, we should ensure we iterate through **ResultSet** properly.

We can use a **while** loop to process results row by row, as demonstrated:

```
String query = "SELECT title, price FROM Books WHERE stock_qty > 0";
PreparedStatement pstmt = conn.prepareStatement(query);
ResultSet rs = pstmt.executeQuery();
while (rs.next()) {
```

```
    String title = rs.getString("title");
    double price = rs.getDouble("price");
    System.out.println(title + " - $" + price);
}
```

A second approach is to safely handle null values. After retrieving a value, we can use **wasNull()** to check for nulls.

Here is an example of how that is done:

```
int stockQty = rs.getInt("stock_qty");
if (rs.wasNull()) {
    stockQty = 0;   // Default value
}
```

Handle errors and exceptions

Our final best practice for working with databases in Java is to properly handle errors and exceptions. This will help ensure our application gracefully recovers from any unexpected failures.

One approach is to use specific exception handling to differentiate between SQL and general exceptions.

For example:

```
try {
    // Database code
} catch (SQLIntegrityConstraintViolationException e) {
    System.out.println("Duplicate entry: " + e.getMessage());
} catch (SQLException e) {
    System.out.println("Database error: " + e.getMessage());
} catch (Exception e) {
    System.out.println("Unexpected error: " + e.getMessage());
}
```

A second approach is implementing transaction rollbacks when any operation within a transaction fails.

Here is an example:

```
try {
    conn.setAutoCommit(false);
    // Execute multiple SQL statements
    conn.commit();
} catch (SQLException e) {
```

```
    conn.rollback();  // Rollback changes on error
    System.out.println("Transaction failed: " + e.getMessage());
}
```

A third approach is to log errors to support debugging. For example, you can log errors for debugging. There are logging frameworks (i.e., Log4j and SLF4J) that can help.

Lastly, we should always avoid exposing sensitive information. For example, displaying raw SQL errors to users should always be avoided. Instead, provide user-friendly messages and log the technical details.

For example:

```
System.out.println("An unexpected error occurred. Please try again later.");

logger.error("SQL Error", e);
```

Conclusion

This chapter explored foundational database concepts for Java applications. It emphasized the role of relational databases in modern Java applications and highlighted how structured data can support scalable and efficient data management. Using an online bookstore scenario, we demonstrated how to design database schemas, manage structured data using SQL, and implement CRUD operations to handle common data operations.

The chapter also explored how Java interacts with databases using JDBC. We also covered best practices for optimizing query performance, managing database connections, and handling errors and exceptions. You should now be able to build Java applications that leverage databases to provide users with persistent data, seamless interactions, and reliable performance.

The next chapter focuses on **graphical user interfaces** (**GUIs**), which allow users to interact with our applications visually. The chapter introduces JavaFX, Java's modern GUI framework. The chapter explains how to setup JavaFX and create visually appealing layouts with the scene graph. The chapter also covers handling user events, where you can learn to create controls like buttons and text fields, and binding properties to enhance your application's interactivity.

Points to remember

- ACID properties ensure reliable transaction management.

- Always close database connections after use to prevent resource leaks and maintain performance.

- Avoid using SELECT * in queries; specify only the columns you need to improve performance.

- Batch operations should be wrapped in transactions to ensure data integrity and consistency.

- Connection pooling improves performance by reusing database connections.

- Consistency in a relational database ensures that data remains accurate and follows defined rules and constraints.

- CRUD operations are the fundamental database interactions used in applications.

- Data integrity is enforced using constraints like PRIMARY KEY, FOREIGN KEY, NOT NULL, UNIQUE, and CHECK.

- Data persistence allows information to be stored beyond the application's runtime, ensuring data longevity.

- Disabling auto-commit mode allows for manual transaction control using commit and rollback.

- Efficient error handling includes catching specific SQL exceptions and logging technical details for debugging.

- FKs link related tables and enforce referential integrity between entities in a relational database.

- Indexing frequently searched columns improves query performance, especially for large datasets.

- JDBC is the standard API for connecting Java applications to relational databases.

- Parameterized queries using PreparedStatement prevent SQL injection and improve query security.

- PreparedStatement allows for precompiled SQL queries, improving performance and security.

- PKs uniquely identify each record in a table and serve as references in FK relationships.

- Proper transaction management ensures that related database operations either all succeed or all fail.

- Relational databases organize data into structured tables with defined relationships, ensuring data consistency.

- ResultSet is used to store and iterate through query results in Java database operations.

- Rollback undoes changes made during a transaction if an error occurs, maintaining database integrity.

- SQL injection is a critical security vulnerability that can be prevented by using parameterized queries.

- SQLite is a lightweight, embedded database ideal for small to medium-sized applications without requiring a separate server.

- SQL is used to interact with relational databases through commands like SELECT, INSERT, UPDATE, and DELETE.

- Transactions group multiple database operations into a single unit, ensuring atomicity and consistency.

- Use try-with-resources statements in Java to automatically close connections, statements, and result sets.

- Using CHECK constraints in table definitions ensures data follows specific rules (e.g., quantity < 0).

- Using PreparedStatement over Statement improves both security and performance in database operations.

- Using ResultSet efficiently involves iterating over rows with a while loop and retrieving data using appropriate getter methods.

Case studies

These case studies provide realistic scenarios that encourage you to think critically about JDBC and operations:

- **Vulcan Ventures, an inventory management system**: Vulcan Ventures is a startup that sells high-tech gadgets online. Their growing inventory requires a robust database system to manage product listings, stock levels, and supplier details. The development team at Vulcan Ventures has built a Java-based inventory management system using SQLite. However, they are facing challenges with data consistency. Occasionally, stock levels become negative due to concurrent updates when multiple users process orders simultaneously.

  o **For your consideration**: How would you redesign the inventory update process to prevent stock levels from going negative? What transaction management techniques (e.g., ACID properties) would you apply? How would you optimize queries for inventory lookups, especially for high-demand products?

- **Andorian Archives, a digital library program**: Andorian Archives offers a massive digital library, allowing users to rent and read books online. The system supports thousands of concurrent users and holds millions of book records. The library's search functionality has become sluggish, particularly when users search by book title or author. The current SQL query uses SELECT * on the entire books table without indexing. Users are also reporting occasional duplicate book entries.

- o **For your consideration**: How would you improve search performance and optimize the query? What indexing strategy would you implement to support fast lookups? How could you enforce data integrity to prevent duplicate book entries?

- **Romulan Retail, an e-commerce platform**: Romulan Retail is an e-commerce site selling collectibles and rare artifacts. The platform supports online shopping carts, user profiles, and order histories. A recent security audit revealed that the application is vulnerable to SQL injection attacks, especially on the login page. Malicious users have been able to bypass authentication using crafted input in the login form.

  - o **For your consideration**: How would you refactor the login functionality to prevent SQL injection? What best practices would you apply to secure other user input forms throughout the site? How can you implement proper error handling and logging to detect future injection attempts?

- **Betazoid Banking, a financial transactions system**: Betazoid Banking offers digital banking services, allowing customers to transfer funds, view statements, and manage accounts through their Java-based platform. The bank has encountered issues with incomplete transactions, where users transfer money, but only one account gets updated. For instance, the sender's account is debited, but the recipient's account is not credited due to a failure mid-transaction.

  - o **For your consideration**: How would you use transaction management to ensure atomicity and consistency during fund transfers? What steps would you take to implement proper rollback in case of errors? How could you log failed transactions to support troubleshooting and recovery?

- **Ferengi Foods, an online ordering system**: Ferengi Foods is a food delivery service that allows users to order meals from local restaurants. Their platform tracks orders, manages customer data, and processes payments. During peak hours, customers report that their orders are not being recorded properly. The development team suspects connection leaks are causing database timeouts, leading to dropped transactions.

  - o **For your consideration**: How would you implement connection pooling to manage database connections efficiently? What strategies would you use to ensure all connections are properly closed after use? How could you monitor and detect connection leaks in the system before they impact customers?

Multiple choice questions

1. **Which of the following statements about PreparedStatement in JDBC is true?**
   a. It automatically prevents SQL injection by parameterizing user inputs.
   b. It requires manual escaping of user inputs to prevent SQL injection.
   c. It is less efficient than using a statement for repeated queries.
   d. It can only execute SELECT queries.

2. **In a relational database, what is the primary role of an FK?**
   a. To ensure data within a table remains unique.
   b. To link records in one table to related records in another table.
   c. To speed up search queries through indexing.
   d. To auto-increment values in a column.

3. **Which of the following is not part of the ACID properties in transaction management?**
   a. Atomic
   b. Consistent
   c. Durable
   d. Scalable

4. **What is the primary purpose of connection pooling?**
   a. To avoid using JDBC drivers.
   b. To allow multiple databases to be accessed simultaneously.
   c. To reuse existing database connections.
   d. To prevent SQL injection attacks.

5. **What SQL command would you use to permanently remove a record from a table?**
   a. UPDATE
   b. DELETE
   c. REMOVE
   d. DROP

Answers

1.	a.
2.	b.
3.	d.
4.	c.
5.	b.

Questions

1. In the context of Java applications, why is it important to use prepared statements instead of regular statements when handling user input? Explain why failing to do so could lead to a security vulnerability.

2. Relational databases enforce data integrity using constraints like PKs and FKs. How do these constraints help maintain consistency in multi-user applications? Provide an example from an e-commerce platform.

3. Discuss the significance of ACID properties in transaction management. Why are these properties critical in applications that handle financial transactions, such as online banking?

4. Connection pooling is often recommended for improving the efficiency of database operations. What are the benefits of connection pooling, and how does it help with resource management in high-traffic applications?

5. SQL JOIN operations allow combining data from multiple tables. In the context of Bougie Books, how would you design a query to retrieve customer orders along with book titles and quantities? Why is understanding JOINs essential for complex data retrieval?

6. Indexing is a crucial optimization technique for improving query performance. What factors should be considered when deciding which columns to index? Can over-indexing negatively impact database performance?

7. Consider a situation where a Java application using SQLite starts to experience performance degradation as the dataset grows. What steps would you take to diagnose and address the issue? How does database design play a role in long-term scalability?

8. Reflect on the use of transactions in handling complex operations, such as processing an online order. What could go wrong if transactions are not properly managed? How would you implement error handling to ensure data consistency in such operations?

9. In multi-user applications, concurrency control is critical. Discuss how Java and relational databases handle concurrent data access. What strategies can be implemented to prevent issues like deadlocks or race conditions?

10. Security is a recurring theme in database management. Beyond preventing SQL injection, what other security practices would you implement when developing a Java application that interacts with a database? Consider aspects like encryption, access control, and secure error handling.

Challenges

The following questions are provided to self-assess your knowledge of the chapter's content and apply critical thinking to key concepts:

- **Designing a relational database schema**:
  - **Objective**: Apply your understanding of relational databases to design a structured schema with proper relationships and constraints.
  - **Activity**: Perform the following actions:
    - Design a relational database schema for an online art gallery, *Pixel Palace*, that sells digital artwork. The gallery sells individual art pieces, tracks artists, and manages customer orders.
    - Create tables for artists, artworks, customers, and orders.
    - Define appropriate PKs and FKs to establish relationships between tables.
    - Include at least five fields per table with appropriate data types (e.g., TEXT, INTEGER, REAL).
    - Write SQL statements to create these tables using SQLite.
  - **Real-world applicability**: Database schema design is essential in any application that manages structured data, such as e-commerce, content management systems, or social media platforms.

- **Implementing CRUD operations with JDBC**:
  - **Objective**: Demonstrate proficiency in using JDBC to interact with a database and perform basic CRUD operations.
  - **Activity**: Perform the following actions:
    - Create a Java application for a simple student management system using SQLite and JDBC.
    - Design a Student table with fields, student_id, name, major, and GPA.

- Implement the following functions using JDBC:

  - **Insert**: Add new student records.

  - **Read**: Display all students or search by major.

  - **Update**: Modify a student's GPA.

  - **Delete**: Remove a student from the database.

  - Use PreparedStatement for all queries to prevent SQL injection.

  o **Real-world applicability**: CRUD operations form the backbone of many applications, from content management systems to **customer relationship management (CRM)** software.

- **Managing transactions and ensuring data integrity**:

  o **Objective**: Implement transaction management to ensure data integrity during complex operations.

  o **Activity**: Perform the following actions:

    - Create a Java application for *Galaxy Bank* that allows users to transfer money between accounts.

    - Design an Accounts table with fields, account_id, account_holder, and balance.

    - Implement a transferFunds method that:

      - Deducts the transfer amount from the sender's account.

      - Adds the transfer amount to the recipient's account.

      - Ensures the transaction is atomic—either both operations succeed or neither.

      - Uses JDBC transactions with commit and rollback.

      - Check that the sender has sufficient funds before completing the transfer.

  o **Real-world applicability**: Banking and e-commerce systems rely heavily on transactions to ensure data accuracy during sensitive operations like fund transfers and order placements.

- **Optimizing query performance**:

  o **Objective**: Optimize SQL queries for efficiency and explore how indexing improves performance.

- o **Activity**: Perform the following actions:

  - Using the Bougie Books example, extend the database to include a Reviews table with fields review_id, book_id, customer_id, rating, and comment.

  - Write a SQL query to retrieve the top five highest-rated books, including their average rating and number of reviews.

  - Create an index on the rating field and compare the query execution time before and after indexing.

  - Reflect on the performance improvements and when indexing should be used.

- o **Real-world applicability**: Efficient query design and indexing are crucial for performance optimization in applications dealing with large datasets, such as online stores, social networks, or streaming platforms.

- **Securing user input and preventing SQL injection**:

  - o **Objective**: Demonstrate an understanding of SQL injection vulnerabilities and how to prevent them using parameterized queries.

  - o **Activity**: Perform the following actions:

    - Develop a simple Java login system for an online forum called *NexusChat*.

    - Design a user table with fields, user_id, username, and password.

    - Implement a login method that:

      - Uses user input for username and password.

      - Authenticates users securely using PreparedStatement to prevent SQL injection.

      - Includes a demonstration of how SQL injection could exploit an insecure query, followed by the secure, fixed version.

    - **Bonus**: Implement basic password validation (e.g., minimum length) before executing the query.

  - o **Real-world applicability**: Securing user inputs is critical in applications that handle sensitive data, such as user accounts, payment systems, or any public-facing services.

Self-assessment

The following questions are provided to self-assess your knowledge of the chapter's content and apply critical thinking to key concepts:

1. What are the ACID properties in transaction management, and why are they essential for maintaining data integrity in Java database applications?

2. Explain the difference between Statement and PreparedStatement in JDBC. Why is PreparedStatement generally preferred, especially when handling user inputs?

3. In a relational database, what is the role of a FK, and how does it help maintain data integrity? Provide an example using the Bougie Books database schema.

4. Imagine you are developing a Java application for an online bookstore. You notice that search queries for books by title are slow. What steps could you take to optimize query performance using techniques covered in this chapter?

5. Think of a real-world application (e.g., an e-commerce platform, banking system, or social network). How would you implement transaction management in that application to ensure data integrity during complex operations, like placing an order or transferring funds?

Answers

1. The following ACID properties are essential to prevent data corruption, especially in multi-user environments:

    a. Atomicity ensures that a transaction is treated as a single unit; either all operations succeed, or none do.

    b. Consistency guarantees that a transaction brings the database from one valid state to another, maintaining data integrity.

    c. Isolation ensures that concurrent transactions do not interfere with each other, preserving data accuracy.

    d. Durability guarantees that once a transaction is committed, its changes are permanent, even in the case of a system crash.

2. **Statement vs. PreparedStatement**:

    a. Statement executes static SQL queries directly, often leading to vulnerabilities like SQL injection when user inputs are concatenated into the query.

    b. PreparedStatement allows parameterized queries, where placeholders (?) are used, and user inputs are safely bound to these placeholders. This approach prevents SQL injection and often results in better performance, as the SQL execution plan can be reused.

3. A foreign key establishes a relationship between two tables, linking a column in one table to the primary key in another. This enforces referential integrity, ensuring that records in one table correspond to valid entries in another.

   a. **Example (Bougie Books)**:

   ```
   CREATE TABLE Orders (
       order_id INTEGER PRIMARY KEY,
       order_date TEXT NOT NULL,
       cust_id INTEGER,
       FOREIGN KEY (cust_id) REFERENCES Customers(cust_id)
   );
   ```

4. Using a banking system as an example, where users can transfer funds between accounts, we would ensure data integrity with these steps:

   a. Use transactions to wrap the deduction from one account and the addition to another in a single unit of work.

   b. Implement commit only if both operations succeed. Otherwise, use rollback to revert any partial changes.

Join our Discord space

Join our Discord workspace for latest updates, offers, tech happenings around the world, new releases, and sessions with the authors:

https://discord.bpbonline.com

CHAPTER 11

GUI Programming

Introduction

Graphical user interfaces (**GUIs**) are an important component of modern applications. They provide users with a visual interface to interact with our applications. It is part of user experience design with the goal of providing users with visually engaging and interactive experiences.

There are several approaches to building GUIs for our applications. We can use older libraries such as Swing and the **Abstract Window Toolkit** (**AWT**) or JavaFX, the de facto standard for building robust GUIs, especially for desktop applications. While there are newer frameworks like Electron and Qt, this chapter focuses on JavaFX as the primary Java GUI development approach.

This chapter explores the fundamentals of GUI development using JavaFX. Our coverage starts with an overview and setting up the JavaFX environment. Next, we will look at the core concepts of JavaFX, including the scene graph, layouts, and event handling mechanisms. The chapter will demonstrate how to create UI elements such as buttons, text fields, and menus, and how to handle user interactions through event-driven programming. You will be able to learn about property binding, which allows for seamless updates between UI elements and underlying data. We will also explore the concept of observables, enabling dynamic and responsive interfaces.

We will use a **Personal Finance Tracker** (**PFT**) desktop application to demonstrate JavaFX concepts.

Structure

This chapter covers the following topics:

- Basics of JavaFX
- Setting up a JavaFX environment
- Understanding the scene graph
- Layouts, controls, and event handling
- Binding properties and observables
- Completing the PFT application

Objectives

By the end of this chapter, you should be able to setup your local development environment to include JavaFX for GUI development. You should have a firm understanding of the JavaFX architecture and its layouts. By following the example and performing the hands-on activities, you should be able to implement user interface controls, handle user interactions, and apply property binding and observables. Furthermore, by the chapter's end, you should be able to create a basic JavaFX application.

Basics of JavaFX

Java has a long history of GUI development, which started with Swing and AWT toolkits. JavaFX was created by *Sun Microsystems* in late 2008. Two years later, *Oracle* acquired Sun Microsystems and supported JavaFX for approximately eight years. From that point on, JavaFX has been supported by the open-source community under the label of the OpenJFX project.

Note: **Sun Microsystems was the original creator of Java.**

JavaFX is a GUI framework that enables us to build interactive desktop applications in Java. It includes built-in tools for UI controls, the ability to bind data and style with **Cascading Style Sheet** (**CSS**), and multimedia support. JavaFX's predecessors are Swing and AWT.

JavaFX's advantage over those GUI frameworks includes:

- CSS support for styling.
- **FX markup language** (**FXML**) support for UI definitions.
- Multimedia support.

- Newer UI components, including charts.

- A scene graph model (covered later in this chapter).

- Cross-platform compatibility.

- Use of GPU acceleration.

A review of the above features should leave no doubt in your mind as to the reason why the JavaFX framework is so widely used for enterprise applications, desktop dashboards, and data visualization utilities.

Architecture

JavaFX uses a hierarchical structure, as illustrated in *Figure 11.1*.

The Stage is an application's main window and contains all UI elements; a Scene is a content area inside a Stage, and Nodes are individual UI components (i.e., buttons, labels, input boxes, etc.), as shown:

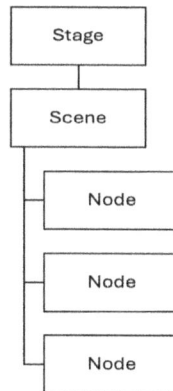

Figure 11.1: JavaFX hierarchical structure

Working with the hierarchical structure is one of the two important components. First is the event-driven programming model that has our code respond to user behaviors such as clicking buttons. Another important component is the binding properties that allow UI components to dynamically update when the underlying data changes.

Let us take a closer look at the core components of the JavaFX architecture. First, there must be an **Application** class that launches the GUI. The stage, the main window, displays the UI elements. While there is always a primary stage, we can create additional stages (additional windows). Within a stage are scenes. Scenes hold UI components and are organized into a scene graph (covered later in this chapter). The individual UI components are called nodes.

The event-driven programming model mentioned earlier is based on event listeners that allow our UI components to react to user clicks, capture user input in text boxes, respond to menu selections, and more. These event listeners, coupled with the ability to bind UI components to data, can result in highly dynamic and interactive application GUIs.

PFT planning

As we progress through this chapter, we will incrementally develop a PFT desktop application. Our application will allow users to track income and expenses and visualize financial trends. We will also implement data persistence.

The following is a plan for how we will create the PFT GUI using JavaFX:

- **Stage and scene**:
  o Define the main application window.
  o Organize UI elements.

- **Layouts and controls**:
  o Design structured user input forms.

- **Event handling**:
  o Capture button clicks.
  o Respond to form submissions.

- **Property binding**:
  o Dynamically synchronize UI elements based on user actions.

By the end of this chapter, you should have a functional JavaFX-based finance tracker that reflects a real-world application using Java.

Setting up a JavaFX environment

This section provides information on setting up your development environment for JavaFX development. We will use **Visual Studio Code** (**VS Code**).

Our goal is to use JavaFX to start developing our PFT desktop application. We will start with the prerequisites of the **Java Development Kit** (**JDK**), the JavaFX **software development kit** (**SDK**), and the required extensions. Next, we will create a JavaFX project to verify our setup.

Lastly, we will discuss the next steps and a plan for our PFT desktop application.

Prerequisites

JavaFX is not included in modern versions of the JDK, so we need to configure it in our project explicitly.

Note: JavaFX exclusion from the JDK reflects its support shift from Oracle to the OpenJFX project.

Java Development Kit

First, we need to ensure we have JDK 17 or later. Enter the `java -version` in a terminal window to display the version of Java installed on your computer.

The example output is provided as follows:

```
java version "23" 2024-09-17
Java(TM) SE Runtime Environment (build 23+37-2369)
Java HotSpot(TM) 64-Bit Server VM (build 23+37-2369, mixed mode, sharing)
```

If your version is earlier than JDK 17, follow the steps in *Chapter 1, Introduction to Java Programming,* to install a recent version.

JavaFX SDK

Our next step is to download the JavaFX SDK. *Gluon,* a software company, champions the open-source OpenJFX project.

The latest JavaFX SDK can be obtained from the following link on Gluon's site:

https://gluonhq.com/products/javafx/

Download the SDK specific to your operating system and **central processing unit (CPU)** architecture. Versions for Linux, macOS, and Windows are available.

After you download the SDK, extract the zip/archive file and place the contents in a location you can remember. There is no installation process; you merely need to have the JavaFX SDK available on your system.

VS Code and extensions

You should already have VS Code installed on your computer. If not, follow the steps in *Chapter 1, Introduction to Java Programming,* to install a recent version. Once VS Code is installed, you need to install the **Extension Pack for Java**.

Open VS Code and click the extensions icon at the bottom of the left navigation panel, as shown in *Figure 11.2*. Use the search bar to locate the **Extension Pack for Java** by *Microsoft*.

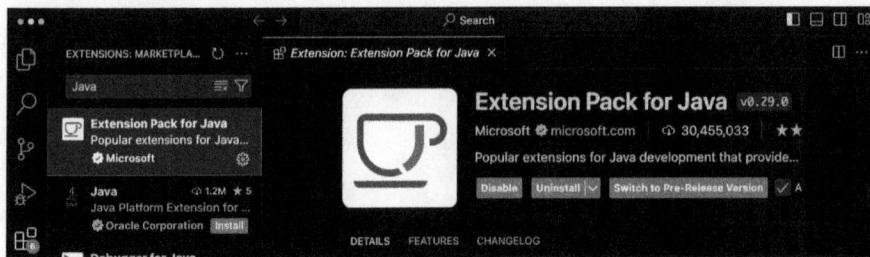

Figure 11.2: Top section of VS Code Extensions area with Extension Pack for Java selected

If the extension is not installed, click the installation button and follow the on-screen instructions.

Creating a JavaFX project

At this point, you should have the JDK, JavaFX SDK, and VS Code ready to use. This section walks through the setup of our PFT project in VS Code.

Undertake the following steps to create a new project, add dependencies, and verify the setup by running the PFT project:

1. Our first step is to create a new Java project:

    a. Create a folder for your PFT project.

    b. Open VS Code and press *Cmd + Shift + P* (on macOS) or *Ctrl + Shift + P* (on Windows) to open the command palette.

    c. Enter `Java: Create Java Project` and select that item.

    d. Select **No Build Tools** (we are taking this route for simplicity).

    e. Select the location where you want to save your project.

    f. Name your project **PFT**.

2. Next, we need to link JavaFX to our project. This adds a dependency to our project and is necessary because JavaFX is an external library.

    a. If VS Code did not automatically create a **lib** folder in your project directory, create it manually.

    b. Refer to your uncompressed **JavFX** folder and copy the **lib** folder into the **lib** folder of your project. You can accomplish this with your system's file folders or simply drag the **JavaFX** folder to the **lib** folder in the VS Code interface.

    c. Next, we need to create a **launch.json** file inside our project's **.vscode** directory. Sample content for that file is provided below. Be sure to update the path to match what you put in your **lib** folder, as shown:

```
{
    "version": "0.2.0",
    "configurations": [
        {
            "type": "java",
            "name": "Run JavaFX App",
            "request": "launch",
            "mainClass": "Main",
            "vmArgs": "--module-path lib --add-modules javafx.
controls,javafx.fxml"
        }
    ]
}
```

d. We are now ready to create a **Main.java** file in our **src** folder.

Here is a sample code:

```
import javafx.application.Application;
import javafx.scene.Scene;
import javafx.scene.control.Label;
import javafx.scene.layout.StackPane;
import javafx.stage.Stage;
public class Main extends Application {
    @Override
    public void start(Stage primaryStage) {
        Label label = new Label("\tCongratulations\n\nJavaFX is
setup correctly!");
        StackPane root = new StackPane(label);
        Scene scene = new Scene(root, 400, 300);
        primaryStage.setScene(scene);
        primaryStage.setTitle("JavaFX Setup Test");
        primaryStage.show();
    }
    public static void main(String[] args) {
        launch(args);
    }
}
```

3. Our last task is to run our application to verify that we have VS Code properly configured and can use JavaFX for development. If your test is successful, you should

see an application window displayed on your system (refer to *Figure 11.3*):

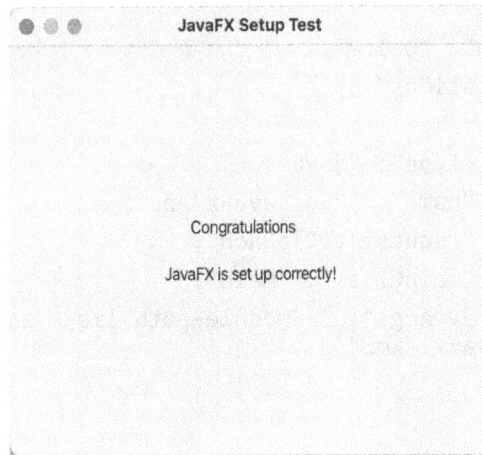

Figure 11.3: *JavaFX setup test window from Main.java*

Next steps and PFT

With JavaFX up and running, we can start building our PFT application. We will work on this progressively throughout the remainder of the chapter with the following goals:

- Design the application layout.

- Create UI components.

- Implement event handling.

- Use property binding and observables.

By the end of this chapter, our PFT application should be fully functional with a GUI that permits users to:

- Enter transactions

- View summaries

- Interact with financial data

Understanding the scene graph

The scene graph is an important part of JavaFX's UI framework; it organizes the graphical elements (nodes) in our application. Every UI component (e.g., button, labels, images, etc.) is a note with properties. The scene graph provides us with the ability to implement layouts and event handling for interactive interfaces.

As illustrated in *Figure 11.4*, scene graphs are part of JavaFX's hierarchy and are a child node of the stage. Scenes are content areas that group UI components (nodes).

Figure 11.4 shows a **Vertical Box (VBox)** as a Root Node that consists of a Label, input boxes for the Username and Password, and a Login button:

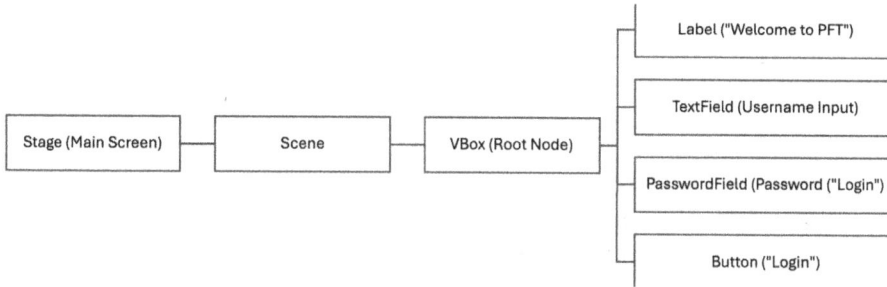

Figure 11.4: JavaFX example structure for a login interface

This section explores the scene graph and its components as we build out our PFT application.

Core components

Before we discuss the scene in depth, let us first look at the stage. The stage represents our application's window and is at the top of JavaFX's hierarchy. Our application's main window is referred to as the **primary stage**. We can also add additional stages for popup/modal windows.

Each stage can hold one active scene at a time. Scenes are UI containers that serve as a bridge between the stage and the individual UI components. We can dynamically swap scenes as needed.

Nodes are UI components in the scene graph. The three primary categories of nodes are explained in *Table 11.1*:

Category	Type	Examples
Parent nodes	Layout managers and containers	**Horizontal Box (HBox)**, VBox, GridePane, etc.
Leaf nodes	Basic UI elements	Buttons, labels, images, etc.
Shape nodes	Graphics	Circles, lines, rectangles

Table 11.1: JavaFX node categories and examples

Nodes are highly customizable and have a plethora of properties to include position, size, style, and event handling.

Setting up the PFT stage and scene

Let us setup the stage and scene for our PFT desktop application. First, we need to update our **launch.json** file as shown:

```json
{
    "version": "0.2.0",
    "configurations": [
        {
            "type": "java",
            "name": "PFTApp",
            "request": "launch",
            "mainClass": "PFTApp",
            "projectName": "PFT_94836854",
            "vmArgs": "--module-path lib --add-modules javafx.controls,javafx.fxml"
        },
        {
            "type": "java",
            "name": "Run JavaFX App",
            "request": "launch",
            "mainClass": "Main",
            "vmArgs": "--module-path lib --add-modules javafx.controls,javafx.fxml"
        }
    ]
}
```

As aforementioned, we added the **javafx.controls** and **javafx.fxml** modules to our project.

Note: The original launch.json file has been renamed _launch.json in case you want to revert to follow previous examples.

Next, let us add a simple logo named **pft_logo.png** and place it in a **/resource** folder in your project.

Now we can write our **PFTApp** class as shown:

```java
import javafx.application.Application;
import javafx.scene.Scene;
import javafx.scene.control.Label;
import javafx.scene.image.Image;
import javafx.scene.image.ImageView;
import javafx.scene.layout.VBox;
```

```java
import javafx.stage.Stage;
public class PFTApp extends Application {
    @Override
    public void start(Stage primaryStage) {
        // Set Application Title
        primaryStage.setTitle("Personal Finance Tracker");
        // Create a Label for the title
        Label titleLabel = new Label("\t\tWelcome to Personal Finance
Tracker!");
        titleLabel.setStyle("-fx-font-size: 16px; -fx-font-weight: bold;");
        // (Optional) Load a logo image
        ImageView logoView = new ImageView(new Image("file:resources/pft_logo.
png"));
        logoView.setFitWidth(125);
        logoView.setPreserveRatio(true);
        // Create a layout and add components
        VBox root = new VBox(3); // Vertical layout with spacing
        root.getChildren().addAll(logoView, titleLabel);
        // Create Scene and set it in the Stage
        Scene scene = new Scene(root, 400, 300);
        primaryStage.setScene(scene);
        // Show the application window
        primaryStage.show();
    }
    public static void main(String[] args) {
        launch(args);
    }
}
```

The preceding code is heavily commented to help you understand what each block of code does. As you can see, we created a primary stage, added a title, created a text label, and added a label.

When you run the application, you should see a window as shown in *Figure 11.5*:

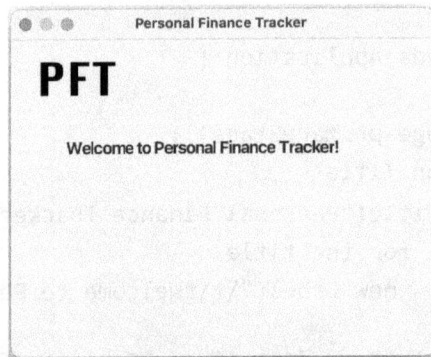

Figure 11.5: Initial PFT interface

In subsequent sections, we will continue to build out our PFT desktop application.

Layouts, controls, and event handling

The last section walked through the creation of a stage and scene for our PFT desktop application. We added a logo and a title. This section expands our application's GUI with the introduction of layouts, controls, and event handling. Specifically, we will explore how layouts are used to organize UI components purposefully, how to use controls to capture user input, and how to react to user behaviors with event handling.

Layouts

Layouts are an important aspect of GUIs. They are containers that efficiently arrange UI elements. Layout containers can automatically adjust elements based on the size of the screen and the content. The two most common JavaFX layout containers are VBox and HBox, which, as their names suggest, arrange elements vertically and horizontally.

> Note: **Layout containers can also be referred to as layout managers. The terms are interchangeable.**

Common uses of the VBox layout container include forms, menus, and content we want to align vertically. HBox is a common layout container for things like header and footer sections, toolbars, buttons, and input fields. BorderPane, another layout container, can be used to divide the UI into left, right, center, top, and bottom sections (see *Figure 11.6*). We have complete control over the size of these sections.

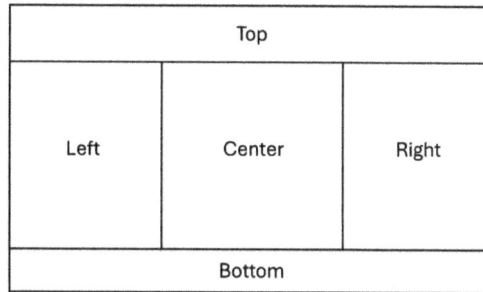

Figure 11.6: *JavaFX BorderPane sections*

The GridPane is another common layout manager. It is used for tables, forms, and other structured layouts.

Let us update our PFT application to include the following layout managers:

- A BorderPane as the main layout with these sections:

    o **Top**: We will place our logo and title here.

    o **Left and Right**: We will use these sections to pad the center.

    o **Center**: This will contain a VBox and an HBox.

    o **Bottom**: We will display a copyright label.

- **VBox**: We will use this for transactional input.

- **HBox**: We will use this for buttons.

- **GridPane**: We will use this for a data table.

Here is the code to implement our layout managers:

```
import javafx.application.Application;
import javafx.geometry.Insets;
import javafx.scene.Scene;
import javafx.scene.control.Label;
import javafx.scene.image.Image;
import javafx.scene.image.ImageView;
import javafx.scene.layout.BorderPane;
import javafx.scene.layout.GridPane;
import javafx.scene.layout.HBox;
import javafx.scene.layout.VBox;
import javafx.stage.Stage;


public class PFTApp extends Application {
```

```java
@Override
public void start(Stage primaryStage) {
    primaryStage.setTitle("Personal Finance Tracker");

    // BorderPane layout
    BorderPane root = new BorderPane();
    root.setPadding(new Insets(10));

    // BorderPane - Top
    Label titleLabel = new Label("Personal Finance Tracker");
    titleLabel.setStyle("-fx-font-size: 20px; -fx-font-weight: bold;");
    ImageView logoView = new ImageView(new Image("file:resources/pft_logo.
png"));
    logoView.setFitWidth(100);
    logoView.setPreserveRatio(true);

    HBox topBox = new HBox(10, logoView, titleLabel);
    topBox.setPadding(new Insets(10));
    root.setTop(topBox);

    // BorderPane - Left and Right
    root.setLeft(new Label("   "));
    root.setRight(new Label("   "));

    // BorderPane - Bottom
    Label copyrightLabel = new Label("© 2025 Personal Finance Tracker");
    HBox bottomBox = new HBox(copyrightLabel);
    bottomBox.setPadding(new Insets(10));
    bottomBox.setStyle("-fx-alignment: center;");

    // BorderPane - Center
    VBox vbox = new VBox(15);
    vbox.setPadding(new Insets(10));
    vbox.getChildren().add(new Label("Transaction Input Section (To Be
Added)")); // Placeholder
    root.setCenter(vbox);

    // GridPane
```

```
        GridPane accountTable = new GridPane();
        accountTable.setPadding(new Insets(10));
        accountTable.setHgap(10);
        accountTable.setVgap(10);

        // Table Column Headers
        accountTable.add(new Label("Account #"), 0, 0);
        accountTable.add(new Label("Account Name"), 1, 0);
        accountTable.add(new Label("Balance"), 2, 0);

        // VBox for the Bottom
        VBox bottomVBox = new VBox(10, accountTable, bottomBox);
        root.setBottom(bottomVBox);

        // Create Scene
        Scene scene = new Scene(root, 600, 400);
        primaryStage.setScene(scene);
        primaryStage.show();
    }

    public static void main(String[] args) {
        launch(args);
    }
}
```

Our PFT application now has some placeholder content inside layout managers (refer to *Figure 11.7*):

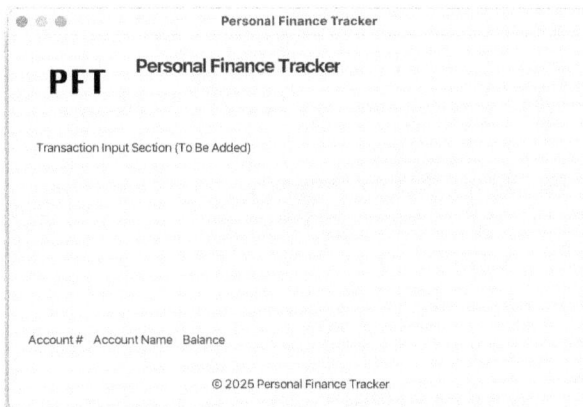

Figure 11.7: *Updated PFT application window*

Input controls

We are now ready to add input fields and buttons inside our PFT application's VBox and HBox.

Let us add the following code to our **PFTApp.java** class, replacing the placeholder content identified with the **// BorderPane - Center** in-code comment that we added in the previous section:

```
// BorderPane - Center
VBox vbox = new VBox(15);
vbox.setPadding(new Insets(10));
// VBox - Transaction Input
Label transactionLabel = new Label("Enter Transaction Details");
transactionLabel.setStyle("-fx-font-size: 16px; -fx-font-weight:
bold;");

TextField amountField = new TextField();
amountField.setPromptText("Enter amount");

TextField categoryField = new TextField();
categoryField.setPromptText("Enter category");

TextField descriptionField = new TextField();
descriptionField.setPromptText("Enter description");

vbox.getChildren().addAll(transactionLabel, amountField,
categoryField, descriptionField);

// HBox - Buttons
Button addButton = new Button("Add Transaction");
Button clearButton = new Button("Clear Fields");

HBox hbox = new HBox(10, addButton, clearButton);
hbox.setPadding(new Insets(10));

vbox.getChildren().add(hbox);
root.setCenter(vbox);
```

As you can see in *Figure 11.8,* we added three input fields and two buttons:

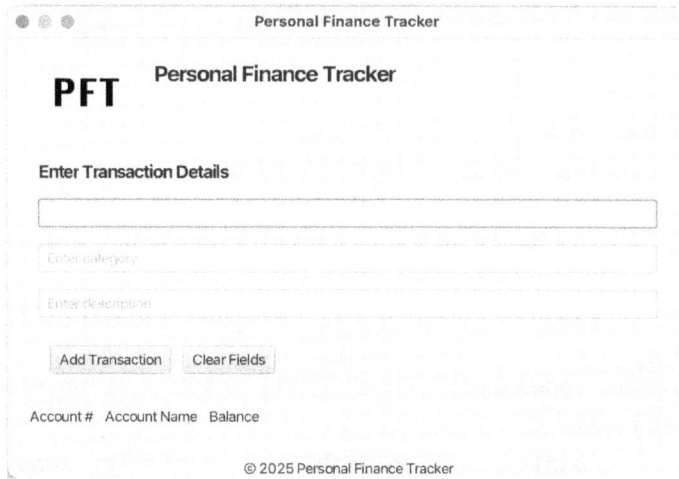

Figure 11.8: *Updated PFT application window with input fields and buttons*

Handling events

Event handling is how we design our JavaFX application to respond to user behaviors such as selecting an item from a dropdown menu, clicking a button, checking a box or radio button, inputting text, etc. The user-initiated event drives our application's actions. This is referred to as an event-driven programming model.

Our next task is handling events, specifically when clicking a button.

The following steps need to be taken to make this happen:

1. Add a **GridPane** named **accountTable** at the class-level. Here is that section of code:

   ```
   public class PFTApp extends Application {

       private GridPane accountTable;

       @Override
       public void start(Stage primaryStage) {
   ```

2. Add code to handle button clicks. Replace the section starting with the **// HBox – Buttons** in-code comment with the following:

   ```
   // HBox - Buttons
   Button addButton = new Button("Add Transaction");
   Button clearButton = new Button("Clear Fields");

   HBox hbox = new HBox(10, addButton, clearButton);
   ```

```
                    hbox.setPadding(new Insets(10));

                    // Event Handling
                    addButton.setOnAction(e -> {
                        String amount = amountField.getText();
                        String category = categoryField.getText();
                        String description = descriptionField.getText();

                        if (amount.isEmpty() || category.isEmpty() || description.
            isEmpty()) {
                            showAlert("Error", "All fields must be filled.");
                        } else {
                            addTransactionToTable(accountTable, amount, category,
            description);
                            amountField.clear();
                            categoryField.clear();
                            descriptionField.clear();
                        }
                    });

                    clearButton.setOnAction(e -> {
                        amountField.clear();
                        categoryField.clear();
                        descriptionField.clear();
                    });

                    // Add transaction input and buttons to VBox
            vbox.getChildren().add(hbox);
                root.setCenter(vbox);
```

3. Next, let us create a **showAlert()** method to display alert messages to the user. This will be inside the **start()** method, just below the **// Create Scene** section:

```
// Display alerts
private void showAlert(String title, String message) {
    Alert alert = new Alert(Alert.AlertType.INFORMATION);
    alert.setTitle(title);
    alert.setHeaderText(null);
    alert.setContentText(message);
    alert.showAndWait();
}
```

4. Next, let us create an **addTransactionToTable()** method. This will go right below the **showAlert()** method.

```
// Add transaction to table
private void addTransactionToTable(GridPane table, String amount, String
category, String description) {
    int rowIndex = table.getChildren().size() / 3;
    table.add(new Label(amount), 0, rowIndex);
    table.add(new Label(category), 1, rowIndex);
    table.add(new Label(description), 2, rowIndex);
}
```

5. We are ready to test our application. As illustrated in *Figure 11.9*, we can enter data in the input boxes:

Figure 11.9: PFT application window with data entered

6. Now, it is time to test the button functionality. As indicated in *Figure 11.10*, when the **Add Transaction** button is clicked, the data is added to the transaction table, and the input fields are cleared:

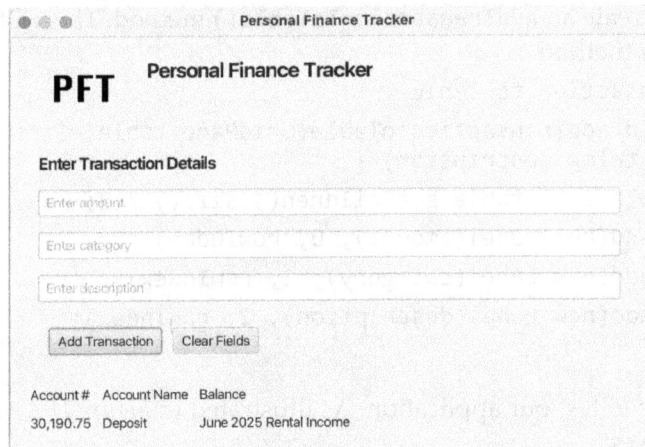

Figure 11.10: PFT application window with transaction table populated

7. The last step is to test our application fully to ensure all functionality performs as expected. You can experiment with the functionality to include the **Clear Fields** button and try using the **Add Transaction** button to see if you can cause an alert message to be displayed (refer to *Figure 11.11*):

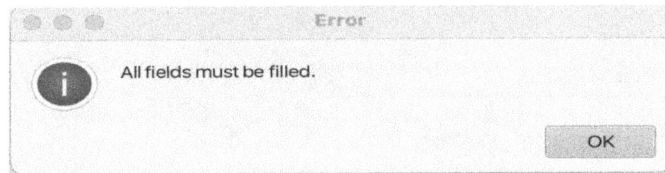

Figure 11.11: PFT application alert message

Binding properties and observables

In JavaFX, binding properties and observables are key concepts that help enhance the interactivity of our GUIs. They can be leveraged together to create dynamic UIs that are responsive to changes in the underlying data. This data-driven model is complementary to the event-driven model we covered earlier in this chapter.

Let us explore these concepts a bit more before implementing them in our PFT desktop application. In the context of JavaFX, binding properties are what we use to setup automatic synchronization between property values. When two properties are bound and one changes, the other bound property, or properties, are automatically updated based on the change. The two primary binding mechanisms are unidirectional binding and bidirectional binding. These self-describing binding mechanisms provide us with great flexibility.

JavaFX also includes objects with attached listeners. These objects are called **observables**. They are critical to the responsive nature of our GUI. Their job is to notify listeners when something changes. The most common JavaFX observer types are **ObservableValue**, which represents an observable value, and **ObservableList**, which represents observable lists.

In the following sections, we will implement the binding properties and observables in our PFT application.

Implementing binding properties

Let us use binding properties for tracking the user's total balance in our PFT application. We start by declaring a **totalBalance** variable at the class-level.

Here is the code snippet that adds this variable:

```
public class PFTApp extends Application {

    private GridPane accountTable;
    private DoubleProperty totalBalance = new SimpleDoubleProperty(0.0);
```

Next, we will update our UI to display an automatically updated total balance. Update the following section of your **PFTApp.java** class:

```
// Add transaction input and buttons to VBox
vbox.getChildren().add(hbox);

// Total balance display
Label balanceLabel = new Label();
balanceLabel.setStyle("-fx-font-size: 18px; -fx-font-weight: bold;");

// Bind balanceLabel to totalBalance
balanceLabel.textProperty().bind(totalBalance.asString("Total Balance:
$%.2f"));

// Add to the VBox before transaction input fields
vbox.getChildren().add(balanceLabel);

root.setCenter(vbox);
```

You can run your app now and see the total balance label, but it is not functional yet.

Let us take care of that now.

Update the **addTransactionToTable** method as indicated:

```
    // Add transaction to table
    private void addTransactionToTable(GridPane table, String amount, String category, String description) {
```

```
        int rowIndex = table.getChildren().size() / 3; // Calculates the next
row index
        table.add(new Label(amount), 0, rowIndex);
        table.add(new Label(category), 1, rowIndex);
        table.add(new Label(description), 2, rowIndex);

        // —— Update Total Balance ——
        try {
            double transactionAmount = Double.parseDouble(amount);
            totalBalance.set(totalBalance.get() + transactionAmount);
        } catch (NumberFormatException e) {
            showAlert("Error", "Invalid amount entered. Please enter a numeric
value.");
        }
    }
```

As illustrated in *Figure 11.12*, multiple entries result in the dynamic (automatic) update of the total balance:

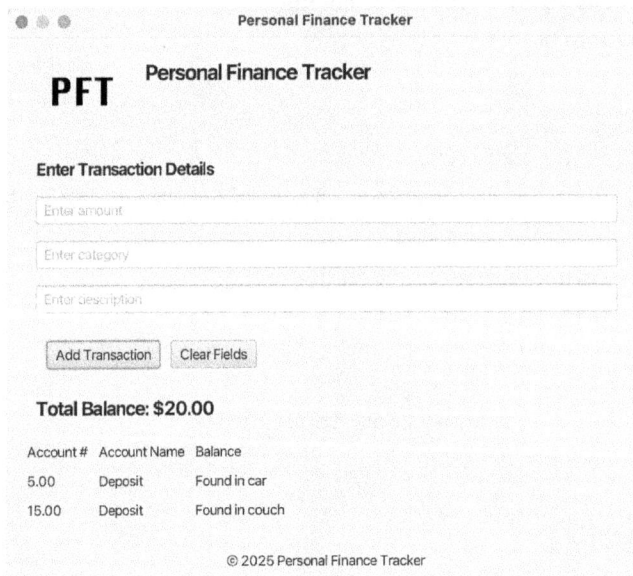

Figure 11.12: PFT application GUI with dynamic total balance

As illustrated in *Figure 11.13*, PFT can even handle withdrawals:

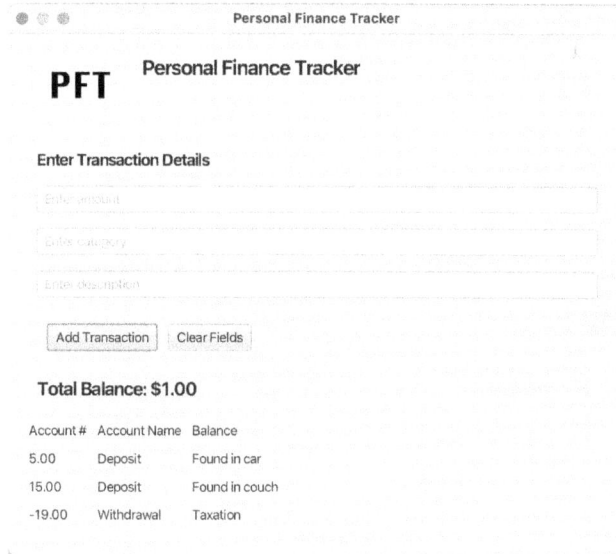

Figure 11.13: *PFT GUI demonstrating withdrawal functionality*

We can refine our implementation to use bidirectional binding, so our UI immediately reflects the user's input and does not require event handlers. To accomplish this, we will add three lines of code.

The following five lines of code start with two existing lines, referenced here for locational assistance:

```
TextField categoryField = new TextField();
categoryField.setPromptText("Enter category");


// Live category preview
Label categoryPreviewLabel = new Label("Category Preview: ");
categoryPreviewLabel.textProperty().bind(categoryField.
textProperty());
vbox.getChildren().add(categoryPreviewLabel);
```

While this might not be useful based on how we implemented it, the approach adequately demonstrates bidirectional binding. As you can see in *Figure 11.14*, as the user types in the category field, the text is displayed beneath our application's logo:

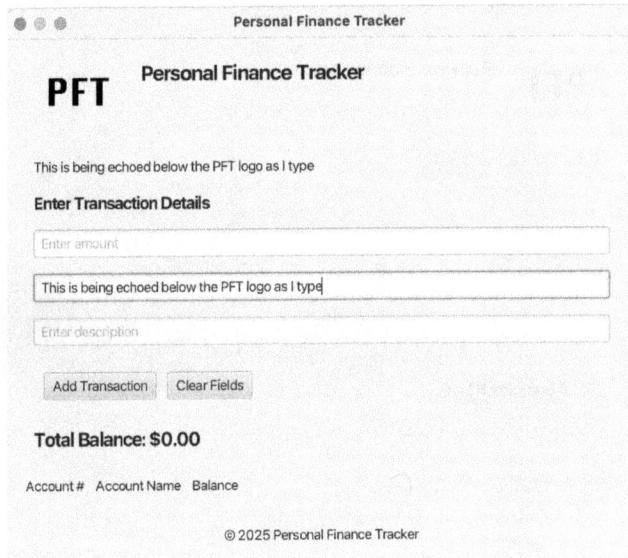

Figure 11.14: *PFT GUI demonstrating bidirectional binding*

Let us implement one more binding-related GUI component. We will use **BooleanBinding** to disable the **Add Transaction** button until all fields have values.

Local the following lines of code in the **// Hbox - Buttons** section:

```
Button addButton = new Button("Add Transaction");
Button clearButton = new Button("Clear Fields");
```

Place the following code between the two lines of code above:

```
// Disable "Add Transaction" button until all fields have content
addButton.disableProperty().bind(
        amountField.textProperty().isEmpty()
            .or(categoryField.textProperty().isEmpty())
            .or(descriptionField.textProperty().isEmpty())
);
```

Now, as you can see in *Figure 11.15*, the **Add Transaction** button is disabled until all three input boxes have input:

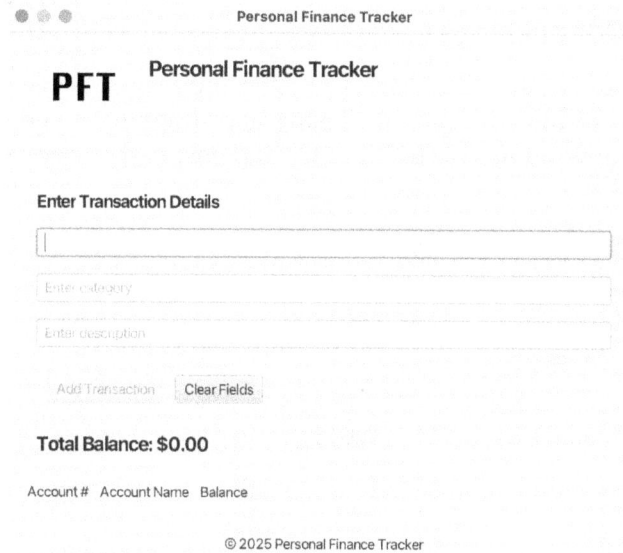

● ◉ ●   Personal Finance Tracker

PFT **Personal Finance Tracker**

Enter Transaction Details

[   ]

[Enter category   ]

[Enter description   ]

Add Transaction   [Clear Fields]

Total Balance: $0.00

Account # Account Name Balance

© 2025 Personal Finance Tracker

Figure 11.15: *PFT GUI with disabled Add Transaction button*

Implementing observables

Observables support UI elements to react to data changes. We can use an **ObservableList** to display a list that automatically updates UI components and the **ListProperty** to permit binding.

We could apply the observables functionality to our transaction table, which we have implemented using a **GridPane**. Currently, it does not automatically update when transactions are entered. Using an **ObservableList**, we could store user transactions in a list, have the table update automatically when new transactions are added, and replace **GridPane** with a **TableView**.

We will forgo implementing observables in our PFT desktop application as the functionality is not needed.

Completing the PFT application

Throughout this chapter, we progressively built a PFT desktop application to demonstrate JavaFX's capabilities and how to implement it. In this final section, we will finalize our application by adjusting the window size, enhancing the UI, improving the transaction table, implementing basic data persistence, and adding additional error handling. Let us get started.

Window size

Our window is currently too small to display all UI components. While it is not intuitive, the user can manually resize the window by clicking and dragging an edge. Our modification will increase the default window size to 720 x 480 and ensure the user can resize the window manually.

Locate the following code in the **PFTApp.java** class:

```
// Create Scene
Scene scene = new Scene(root, 600, 400);
```

Then, change it to this:

```
// Create Scene
Scene scene = new Scene(root, 720, 480);
```

You can run your application and make additional adjustments so the window is the size you desire.

UI styling

Let us make a couple of UI styling improvements. We will add spacing for better readability and use a background color and font styles.

Start by locating the following block of code in your PFT application:

```
// BorderPane - Center
VBox vbox = new VBox(15);
vbox.setPadding(new Insets(10));
```

Now, modify that block as shown below:

```
// BorderPane - Center
VBox vbox = new VBox(15);
vbox.setPadding(new Insets(10));
vbox.setStyle("-fx-background-color: #f4f4f4; -fx-padding: 15px;");
```

Note: **You can experiment with the background color by changing the HEX code. This site can provide you with the ability to pick a color and obtain the HEX code: https://g.co/kgs/dhRXrzd**

Transaction table

Our transaction table sufficiently logs transactions as they are entered, but that is all that it does. It does not allow users to see timestamps of when a transaction is made, nor does it allow them to remove a transaction. We will take care of both of those issues now.

Adding timestamps

Find the following code in your application:

```
// Table Column Headers
accountTable.add(new Label("Account #"), 0, 0);
accountTable.add(new Label("Account Name"), 1, 0);
accountTable.add(new Label("Balance"), 2, 0);
```

Replace that block of code with the following:

```
// Table Column Headers
accountTable.add(new Label("Timestamp"), 0, 0);
accountTable.add(new Label("Amount ($)"), 1, 0);
accountTable.add(new Label("Category"), 2, 0);
accountTable.add(new Label("Description"), 3, 0);
accountTable.add(new Label("Action"), 4, 0);
```

As seen in the preceding code, we added two new columns, one for the time stamps and the other for action buttons.

Figure 11.16 illustrates those columns:

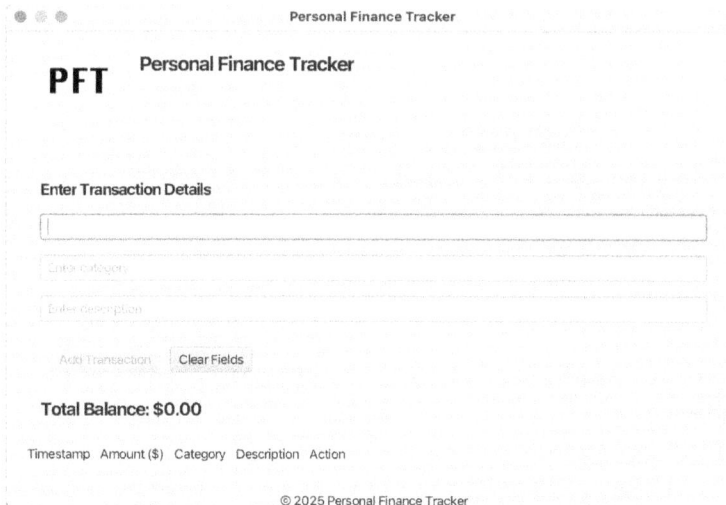

Figure 11.16: *PFT GUI with updated transaction table*

Store time stamps and enable deletion

Now that our transaction table has been upgraded, we can modify our **addTransactionTable()** method to store time stamps and enable transaction deletion.

Let us start by adding the required import statements at the top of our application:

```java
import java.time.LocalDateTime;
import java.time.format.DateTimeFormatter;
import javafx.scene.control.Button;
```

Next, replace your **addTrasactionTable()** method with this code block:

```java
// Add transaction to table
// include timestamp and option to delete
private void addTransactionToTable(GridPane table, String amount, String
category, String description) {
    int rowIndex = table.getChildren().size() / 5; // Updated for 5 columns


    // Generate a timestamp
    String timestamp = LocalDateTime.now().format(DateTimeFormatter.
ofPattern("yyyy-MM-dd HH:mm:ss"));


    table.add(new Label(timestamp), 0, rowIndex);
    table.add(new Label(amount), 1, rowIndex);
    table.add(new Label(category), 2, rowIndex);
    table.add(new Label(description), 3, rowIndex);


    // Delete button
    Button deleteButton = new Button("Delete");
    deleteButton.setOnAction(e -> removeTransactionFromTable(table, rowIndex));
    table.add(deleteButton, 4, rowIndex);


    // Update balance
    try {
        double transactionAmount = Double.parseDouble(amount);
        totalBalance.set(totalBalance.get() + transactionAmount);
    } catch (NumberFormatException e) {
        showAlert("Error", "Invalid amount entered. Please enter a numeric
value.");
    }
}
```

Before you can test your application, we need to write a **removeTransactionFromTable()** method below the **addTransactionToTable()** method.

Here is the code:

```java
// Remove a transaction
```

```
private void removeTransactionFromTable(GridPane table, int rowIndex) {
    table.getChildren().removeIf(node -> GridPane.getRowIndex(node) != null &&
GridPane.getRowIndex(node) == rowIndex);
}
```

As shown in *Figure 11.17*, each transaction has a **Delete** button in the **Action** column:

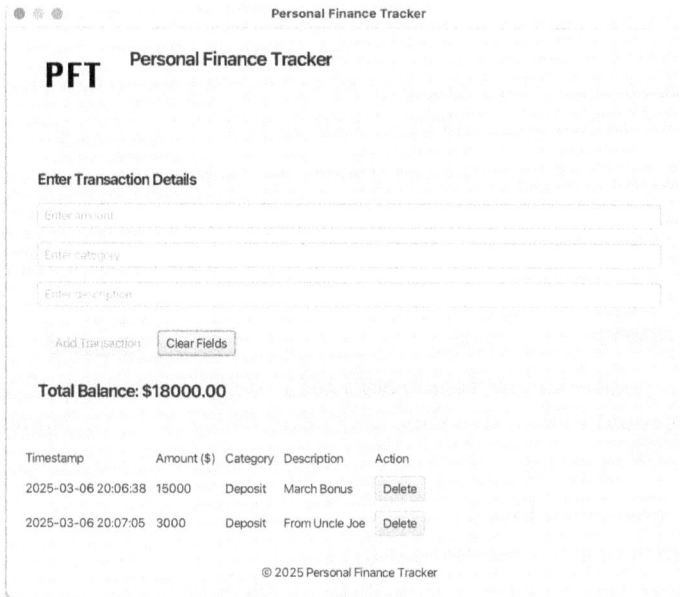

Figure 11.17: *PFT GUI transaction table with action buttons*

Data persistence

We are left with one final task, which is implementing basic data persistence. In this section, we will enable the saving and loading of transaction data.

We will start by adding three additional import statements, as shown:

```
import java.io.BufferedWriter;
import java.io.FileWriter;
import java.io.IOException;
```

You can refer to *Chapter 9, Input/Output,* for a refresher on these statements.

Next, we will add a try-catch block in our **addTransactionToTable()** method immediately following the **// Update balance** section.

Here is that block:

```
// Save transaction to file
try (BufferedWriter writer = new BufferedWriter(new FileWriter("transactions.
```

```
txt", true))) {
    writer.write(timestamp + "," + amount + "," + category + "," +
description);
    writer.newLine();
} catch (IOException ex) {
    showAlert("Error", "Failed to save transaction.");
}
```

Now, we are setup to save our transactions to a local file. When we launch the application, we should load the saved information. Let us do that now.

First, we need to add one last set of import statements, as follows:

```
import java.io.BufferedReader;
import java.io.FileReader;
import java.io.FileNotFoundException;
import java.util.List;
```

Next, we will add a **loadTransactionsFromFile()** method in our application immediately after we initialize **accountTable**. This should go after the **// Create Scene** section.

Here is that code:

```
// Load transactions from file
private void loadTransactionsFromFile() {
    try (BufferedReader reader = new BufferedReader(new
FileReader("transactions.txt"))) {
        String line;
        while ((line = reader.readLine()) != null) {
            String[] parts = line.split(",");
            if (parts.length == 4) {
                addTransactionToTable(accountTable, parts[1], parts[2],
parts[3]);
            }
        }
    } catch (FileNotFoundException e) {
        System.out.println("No previous transactions found.");
    } catch (IOException ex) {
        showAlert("Error", "Failed to load transactions.");
    }
}
```

Lastly, before testing, add the following method call before the **// Create Scene** section:

```
loadTransactionsFromFile();
```

Final review

Let us walk through our PFT application to verify everything is working properly. First, here are the **import** statements:

```
import javafx.application.Application;
import javafx.beans.property.DoubleProperty;
import javafx.beans.property.SimpleDoubleProperty;
import javafx.geometry.Insets;
import javafx.scene.Scene;
import javafx.scene.control.Alert;
import javafx.scene.control.Button;
import javafx.scene.control.Label;
import javafx.scene.control.TextField;
import javafx.scene.image.Image;
import javafx.scene.image.ImageView;
import javafx.scene.layout.BorderPane;
import javafx.scene.layout.GridPane;
import javafx.scene.layout.HBox;
import javafx.scene.layout.VBox;
import javafx.stage.Stage;
import javafx.scene.Node;
import java.time.LocalDateTime;
import java.time.format.DateTimeFormatter;
import java.util.HashSet;
import java.util.Set;
import java.io.BufferedWriter;
import java.io.FileWriter;
import java.io.IOException;
import java.io.BufferedReader;
import java.io.FileReader;
import java.io.FileNotFoundException;
```

Our next section of code contains the class variables:

```
public class PFTApp extends Application {

    private GridPane accountTable;
    private DoubleProperty totalBalance = new SimpleDoubleProperty(0.0);
    private Set<String> savedTransactions = new HashSet<>();
```

Within the **PFTApp** class, we have our **start()** method, where we start by setting the title of the primary stage:

```
@Override
public void start(Stage primaryStage) {
    primaryStage.setTitle("Personal Finance Tracker");
```

The next section configures and populates the **BorderPane** and its sections:

```
// BorderPane layout
BorderPane root = new BorderPane();
root.setPadding(new Insets(10));


// BorderPane - Top
Label titleLabel = new Label("Personal Finance Tracker");
titleLabel.setStyle("-fx-font-size: 20px; -fx-font-weight: bold;");
ImageView logoView = new ImageView(new Image("file:resources/pft_logo.
png"));
logoView.setFitWidth(100);
logoView.setPreserveRatio(true);


HBox topBox = new HBox(10, logoView, titleLabel);
topBox.setPadding(new Insets(10));
root.setTop(topBox);


// BorderPane - Left and Right
root.setLeft(new Label("   "));
root.setRight(new Label("   "));


// BorderPane - Bottom
Label copyrightLabel = new Label("© 2025 Personal Finance Tracker");
HBox bottomBox = new HBox(copyrightLabel);
bottomBox.setPadding(new Insets(10));
bottomBox.setStyle("-fx-alignment: center;");


// BorderPane - Center
VBox vbox = new VBox(15);
vbox.setPadding(new Insets(10));
vbox.setStyle("-fx-background-color: #f4f4f4; -fx-padding: 15px;");
```

The next section of our code corresponds to the **VBox** that contains our transition input section. This section includes the live category preview we configured to demonstrate bidirectional binding:

```
        // VBox - Transaction Input
        Label transactionLabel = new Label("Enter Transaction Details");
        transactionLabel.setStyle("-fx-font-size: 16px; -fx-font-weight:
bold;");

        TextField amountField = new TextField();
        amountField.setPromptText("Enter amount");

        TextField categoryField = new TextField();
        categoryField.setPromptText("Enter category");

        // Live category preview
        Label categoryPreviewLabel = new Label("Category Preview: ");
        categoryPreviewLabel.textProperty().bind(categoryField.
textProperty());
        vbox.getChildren().add(categoryPreviewLabel);

        TextField descriptionField = new TextField();
        descriptionField.setPromptText("Enter description");

        // Add elements to VBox
        vbox.getChildren().addAll(transactionLabel, amountField,
categoryField, descriptionField);
```

The next section of code configures an **HBox** that contains our buttons and their code:

```
        // HBox - Buttons
        Button addButton = new Button("Add Transaction");
        // Disable "Add Transaction" button until all fields have content
        addButton.disableProperty().bind(
            amountField.textProperty().isEmpty()
                .or(categoryField.textProperty().isEmpty())
                .or(descriptionField.textProperty().isEmpty())
        );

        Button clearButton = new Button("Clear Fields");

        HBox hbox = new HBox(10, addButton, clearButton);
```

```
        hbox.setPadding(new Insets(10));

        // Event Handling
        addButton.setOnAction(e -> {
            String amount = amountField.getText();
            String category = categoryField.getText();
            String description = descriptionField.getText();

            if (amount.isEmpty() || category.isEmpty() || description.
isEmpty()) {
                showAlert("Error", "All fields must be filled.");
            } else {
                addTransactionToTable(amount, category, description, true);
                categoryField.clear();
                descriptionField.clear();
            }
        });

        clearButton.setOnAction(e -> {
            amountField.clear();
            categoryField.clear();
            descriptionField.clear();
        });
```

Continuing with our code, the next section adds transaction input and buttons to a **VBox**, provides UI components and formatting for the total balance, binds the balance label to **totalBalance**, and adds the balance label to the **VBox**:

```
// Add transaction input and buttons to VBox
        vbox.getChildren().add(hbox);

        // Total balance display
        Label balanceLabel = new Label();
        balanceLabel.setStyle("-fx-font-size: 18px; -fx-font-weight: bold;");

        // Bind balanceLabel to totalBalance
        balanceLabel.textProperty().bind(totalBalance.asString("Total Balance:
$%.2f"));

        // Add to the VBox before transaction input fields
        vbox.getChildren().add(balanceLabel);
```

```
                root.setCenter(vbox);
```

The last sections of the **start()** method are next. They include the **GridPane**, setting up the table, and creating the scene, as shown:

```
                // GridPane
                accountTable = new GridPane();
                accountTable.setPadding(new Insets(10));
                accountTable.setHgap(10);
                accountTable.setVgap(10);

                // Table Column Headers
                accountTable.add(new Label("Timestamp"), 0, 0);
                accountTable.add(new Label("Amount ($)"), 1, 0);
                accountTable.add(new Label("Category"), 2, 0);
                accountTable.add(new Label("Description"), 3, 0);
                accountTable.add(new Label("Action"), 4, 0);

                // VBox for the Bottom
                VBox bottomVBox = new VBox(10, accountTable, bottomBox);
                root.setBottom(bottomVBox);

                loadTransactionsFromFile();

                // Create Scene
                Scene scene = new Scene(root, 720, 480);
                primaryStage.setScene(scene);
                primaryStage.show();
        }
```

Outside of the **start()** method, we have our **loadTransactionFromFile()** method, as follows:

```
// Load transactions from file
private void loadTransactionsFromFile() {
    // Clear existing rows
    accountTable.getChildren().clear();

    // Add headers again
    accountTable.add(new Label("Timestamp"), 0, 0);
    accountTable.add(new Label("Amount ($)"), 1, 0);
    accountTable.add(new Label("Category"), 2, 0);
    accountTable.add(new Label("Description"), 3, 0);
```

```
        accountTable.add(new Label("Action"), 4, 0);


        try (BufferedReader reader = new BufferedReader(new
FileReader("transactions.txt"))) {
            String line;
            while ((line = reader.readLine()) != null) {
                System.out.println("Reading line: " + line);
                String[] parts = line.split(",");
                if (parts.length == 4) {
                    // Add the transaction to the table without saving it again
                    addTransactionToTable(parts[1], parts[2], parts[3], false); //
Ensure the fourth argument is included
                    // Add the transaction to the set to avoid duplicates
                    savedTransactions.add(line);
                }
            }
        } catch (FileNotFoundException e) {
            System.out.println("No previous transactions found.");
        } catch (IOException ex) {
            showAlert("Error", "Failed to load transactions.");
        }
}
```

Our method to display alerts is as follows:

```
    // Display alerts
    private void showAlert(String title, String message) {
        Alert alert = new Alert(Alert.AlertType.INFORMATION);
        alert.setTitle(title);
        alert.setHeaderText(null);
        alert.setContentText(message);
        alert.showAndWait();
    }
```

Our next section contains our **addTransactionToTable()** method, as shown:

```
// Add transaction to table
// include timestamp and option to delete
private void addTransactionToTable(String amount, String category, String
description, boolean isNewTransaction) {
    int rowIndex = (accountTable.getChildren().size() - 5) / 5 + 1; // Updated
for 5 columns, subtract headers
```

```
    // Generate a timestamp
    String timestamp = LocalDateTime.now().format(DateTimeFormatter.
ofPattern("yyyy-MM-dd HH:mm:ss"));
    String transactionLine = timestamp + "," + amount + "," + category + "," +
description;

    // Check if the transaction is already saved
    if (isNewTransaction) {
        if (savedTransactions.contains(transactionLine)) {
            return; // Skip if transaction is already saved
        } else {
            savedTransactions.add(transactionLine);
            saveTransactionToFile(transactionLine);
        }
    }

    accountTable.add(new Label(timestamp), 0, rowIndex);
    accountTable.add(new Label(amount), 1, rowIndex);
    accountTable.add(new Label(category), 2, rowIndex);
    accountTable.add(new Label(description), 3, rowIndex);

    // Delete button
    Button deleteButton = new Button("Delete");
    deleteButton.setOnAction(e -> removeTransactionFromTable(rowIndex));
    accountTable.add(deleteButton, 4, rowIndex);

    // Update balance
    try {
        double transactionAmount = Double.parseDouble(amount);
        totalBalance.set(totalBalance.get() + transactionAmount);
    } catch (NumberFormatException e) {
        showAlert("Error", "Invalid amount entered. Please enter a numeric
value.");
    }
}
```

The next section contains our **saveTransactionToFile()**, **removeTransactionFromTable()**, and **getNodeByRowColumnIndex()** methods, as shown:

```
// Helper method to save transaction to file
private void saveTransactionToFile(String transactionLine) {
```

```java
    try (BufferedWriter writer = new BufferedWriter(new
FileWriter("transactions.txt", true))) {
        writer.write(transactionLine);
        writer.newLine();
    } catch (IOException ex) {
        showAlert("Error", "Failed to save transaction.");
    }
}


    // Remove a transaction
    private void removeTransactionFromTable(int rowIndex) {
        // Find and remove row nodes
        accountTable.getChildren().removeIf(node -> GridPane.getRowIndex(node)
!= null && GridPane.getRowIndex(node) == rowIndex);

        // Adjust balance
        Label amountLabel = (Label) getNodeByRowColumnIndex(rowIndex, 1,
accountTable);
        if (amountLabel != null) {
            try {
                double transactionAmount = Double.parseDouble(amountLabel.
getText());
                totalBalance.set(totalBalance.get() - transactionAmount);
            } catch (NumberFormatException e) {
                showAlert("Error", "Invalid amount in table. Please check the
data.");
            }
        }

        // Update file
        updateTransactionsFile();
    }


    // Helper method to get node by row and column index
    private Node getNodeByRowColumnIndex(final int row, final int column,
GridPane gridPane) {
        Node result = null;
        for (Node node : gridPane.getChildren()) {
            if (GridPane.getRowIndex(node) != null && GridPane.
getRowIndex(node) == row &&
```

```
                GridPane.getColumnIndex(node) != null && GridPane.
getColumnIndex(node) == column) {
                    result = node;
                    break;
            }
        }
        return result;
    }
```

The last segment of our code includes the **updateTransactionFile()** method and our **main()** method, as shown:

```
    // Update transactions file after deletion
    private void updateTransactionsFile() {
        try (BufferedWriter writer = new BufferedWriter(new
FileWriter("transactions.txt"))) {
            // Loop through each row and write transaction data
            for (int i = 1; i <= (accountTable.getChildren().size() / 5); i++)
{ // skipping the header row
                String timestamp = ((Label) getNodeByRowColumnIndex(i, 0,
accountTable)).getText();
                String amount = ((Label) getNodeByRowColumnIndex(i, 1,
accountTable)).getText();
                String category = ((Label) getNodeByRowColumnIndex(i, 2,
accountTable)).getText();
                String description = ((Label) getNodeByRowColumnIndex(i, 3,
accountTable)).getText();
                writer.write(timestamp + "," + amount + "," + category + "," +
description);
                writer.newLine();
            }
        } catch (IOException ex) {
            showAlert("Error", "Failed to update transactions file.");
        }
    }

    public static void main(String[] args) {
        launch(args);
    }
}
```

Conclusion

This chapter explored JavaFX, the de facto standard for Java-based GUI development. We approached JavaFX with the context of a PFT application we progressively built throughout the chapter. We covered the major JavaFX concepts, including development environment setup, the scene graph, layout managers, event handling, and binding. In our PFT application, we demonstrated BorderPane, VBox, HBox, GridPane, labels, and buttons. The chapter also implemented event-driven programming and used binding properties to update the user's total balance dynamically.

In the next chapter, we will explore important recent Java features. You will be able to work with streams and lambdas, explore Project Jigsaw's modules, and dive into features from the latest Java releases like JEP 477 (implicitly declared classes and instance main methods). The chapter also includes best practices for modern Java development, covering the latest tools and techniques for writing efficient, maintainable code.

Points to remember

- Application class serves as the entry point for launching a JavaFX application.

- Bidirectional binding allows properties to be synchronized in both directions without explicit event handling.

- Binding properties automatically synchronize UI elements with underlying data changes.

- BorderPane layout manager divides the UI into five sections: top, bottom, left, right, and center.

- Buttons and other UI controls can trigger event-driven actions using event handlers.

- Error handling prevents invalid inputs and improves the overall user experience.

- An event-driven programming model responds to user interactions such as clicks and text input.

- Exception handling is necessary to catch and manage errors like invalid numeric inputs.

- GridPane layout manager organizes UI components into a structured table format.

- HBox layout manager arranges UI components horizontally.

- JavaFX applications follow a hierarchical structure consisting of stage, scene, and nodes.

- JavaFX SDK must be manually added to a project, as it is not included in modern JDK versions.

- Labels are used to display static or dynamically updated text in a JavaFX application.

- The launch.json file in VS Code must include JavaFX modules to enable JavaFX application execution.

- Layout managers automatically adjust UI elements based on-screen size and content.

- Nodes represent UI elements such as buttons, labels, text fields, and images.

- Observable properties such as StringProperty, IntegerProperty, and DoubleProperty enable dynamic UI updates.

- The primary stage represents the main window of a JavaFX application.

- Property binding in JavaFX can be unidirectional or bidirectional.

- The resizable property allows users to resize the application window manually for better visibility.

- The scene serves as a container for all UI elements within the primary stage.

- The scene graph is a hierarchical structure that organizes JavaFX UI components efficiently.

- Text fields allow user input and can be bound to labels for real-time updates.

- Unidirectional binding ensures UI components update when the underlying property changes.

- VBox layout manager arranges UI components vertically, useful for forms and input sections.

Case studies

These case studies provide realistic scenarios encouraging you to think critically about JavaFX application development:

- **Veltrix Financial Solutions, enhancing transaction entry with JavaFX**: Veltrix Financial Solutions, a financial services company, wants to improve its internal expense tracking system by adding a real-time transaction preview feature. Currently, their JavaFX-based financial tracker allows employees to enter transaction details (amount, category, and description) but lacks a live preview of the data before submission. The company wants to implement a dynamic preview panel that displays transaction details as the user types. This panel should be updated without requiring the user to click a button.

  ○ **For your consideration**: How would you implement this feature using property binding? Would you use unidirectional or bidirectional binding? Why? What additional improvements could be made to enhance the user experience?

- **Hyperion Robotics, JavaFX table management for machine logs**: Hyperion Robotics, a leading manufacturer of AI-driven robotics, uses a JavaFX-based monitoring application to track machine performance. The application logs machine activity and displays operational status updates in a GridPane-based table. However, the team finds it difficult to manage updates when new machine logs are added dynamically. Hyperion Robotics needs to enhance its table structure by adding a timestamp column that records when a machine log entry is added, implementing a Remove Log button to allow engineers to delete old log entries, and ensuring the table updates in real-time when new logs are added.

  o **For your consideration**: Would switching from GridPane to TableView improve efficiency? Why or why not? How can JavaFX property binding be leveraged to update the table dynamically? What potential error-handling considerations should be accounted for when removing entries?

- **Andromeda Energy, implementing secure data persistence in JavaFX**: Andromeda Energy, a company specializing in interplanetary power grids, tracks resource consumption using a JavaFX-based application. Currently, all transaction data is stored temporarily and disappears when the application is closed. The company needs data persistence so that transactions are saved and available when the application restarts. Andromeda Energy wants to save transaction records to a file or database, load existing transactions when the application starts, and implement error handling to detect missing or corrupted files.

  o **For your consideration**: What Java I/O techniques would be best suited for this? How would you handle data formatting to ensure the saved data is structured correctly? What steps could be taken to prevent duplicate transactions from being loaded?

- **Orion Galactic Transport, improving user interaction with event handling**: Orion Galactic Transport, a company specializing in space tourism, is developing a JavaFX-based booking system. The system allows customers to input flight details and reserve tickets. However, user testing revealed frequent input errors, such as entering non-numeric values for ticket quantities. The company needs to implement input validation to prevent invalid data entries, display alert messages when incorrect data is entered, and disable the Book Ticket button until all fields contain valid input.

  o **For your consideration**: How would you use event-driven programming to validate user input dynamically? Would you implement JavaFX bindings to enable/disable buttons based on input? Why or why not? How could error messages be displayed effectively without disrupting user experience?

- **Zenith Cybersecurity, real-time data updates in a JavaFX dashboard**: Zenith Cybersecurity develops real-time security monitoring systems using JavaFX. Their incident tracking dashboard displays security alerts in a table format. However, the current implementation requires manual refreshing, which slows down response times. Zenith Cybersecurity wants to implement automatic updates, so the table refreshes when new security alerts are detected, use JavaFX observables to ensure UI elements react dynamically to changes, and improve UI responsiveness by preventing excessive lag when handling large datasets.

  o **For your consideration**: How would ObservableList help manage real-time data updates? What techniques could be used to limit memory consumption while handling frequent updates? How would you design the UI to prioritize critical alerts over less urgent ones?

Multiple choice questions

1. **What is the primary purpose of JavaFX in GUI development?**

    a. To replace Java as a programming language

    b. To provide a modern framework for building desktop applications in Java

    c. To replace SQL databases in Java applications

    d. To improve the performance of Java's garbage collector

2. **Which JavaFX layout manager is best suited for organizing elements in a structured table format?**

    a. VBox

    b. BorderPane

    c. HBox

    d. GridPane

3. **What is the key benefit of JavaFX property binding?**

    a. It enables real-time synchronization between UI components and underlying data

    b. It allows for better memory management in Java applications

    c. It replaces the need for event handling in Java applications

    d. It automatically converts Java applications into web applications

4. **Why is JavaFX no longer included in the standard JDK and must be manually configured?**

    a. It was replaced by Swing and AWT

    b. Oracle transferred support for JavaFX to the OpenJFX project

    c. JavaFX is only supported in Java versions older than JDK 8

    d. JavaFX is incompatible with modern Java versions

5. **What function does the loadTransactionsFromFile() method serve in the PFT application?**

    a. It clears the transaction table when the application starts

    b. It generates random transactions for testing purposes

    c. It retrieves and populates previously saved transaction data from a file

    d. It allows users to manually enter transactions into the table

Answers

1.	b.
2.	d.
3.	a.
4.	b.
5.	c.

Questions

1. JavaFX has become the standard for Java GUI development, but older frameworks like Swing and AWT are still in use. In what scenarios might a developer choose to use Swing or AWT instead of JavaFX?

2. The scene graph is a core part of JavaFX's architecture. How does the hierarchical structure of the scene graph improve UI management compared to manually positioning elements?

3. In this chapter, we used property binding to dynamically update the total balance in the PFT application. What are some other real-world applications where property binding would be beneficial?

4. JavaFX relies on an event-driven programming model where user interactions trigger UI updates. How does this compare to traditional procedural programming? Share other types of applications that rely heavily on event-driven programming.

5. The PFT application implemented basic file storage to save transactions. What are the benefits and drawbacks of storing data in a text file versus using a database for persistence?

6. The PFT application includes input validation and error handling to prevent incorrect transactions. What additional error-handling techniques could improve the user experience further?

7. Based on your experience building the PFT application, what are some best practices for designing an intuitive and visually appealing JavaFX UI?

8. The PFT application currently displays transactions in a GridPane. If you were to upgrade this to a TableView, what advantages would that provide? What challenges might arise during this transition?

9. The PFT application is a simple PFT, but JavaFX is also used for large-scale enterprise applications. What features would you need to add to make the PFT application suitable for business use?

10. JavaFX is now maintained by the OpenJFX community. Do you think JavaFX will remain relevant in the future of GUI development, or will web-based frameworks like Electron and ReactJS replace it for most applications? Why or why not?

Challenges

The following questions are provided to self-assess your knowledge of the chapter's content and apply critical thinking to key concepts:

- **Customizing the PFT application theme**:
  - **Objective**: Improve the visual design and user experience of the PFT application by modifying its appearance using JavaFX styling techniques.
  - **Activity**: Perform the following actions:
    - Modify the PFT application's UI by changing the background colors, button styles, and fonts using inline JavaFX styling (setStyle()) and CSS.
    - Add hover effects to buttons to enhance user feedback.
    - Adjust the spacing and padding of the UI components to improve readability.
    - Write a short explanation (200–300 words) discussing how your changes improve usability.
  - **Real-world applicability**: Customizing a GUI is essential in software development to improve user experience and create visually appealing applications. This challenge is designed to help you understand UI design principles while learning how to apply styling in JavaFX.

- **Implementing a search feature for transactions**:
  - **Objective**: Enhance the PFT application by adding a simple search feature that allows users to filter transactions based on category or description.
  - **Activity**: Perform the following actions:
    - Add a search input field and a Search button to the PFT application.
    - Implement a method that filters transactions displayed in the table based on the user's search query.

- Ensure that transactions that do not match the search term are hidden from view.

- Provide a Clear Search button to restore the full transaction list.

- **Real-world applicability**: Search functionality is a fundamental feature in modern applications, from banking apps to inventory management systems. This challenge introduces you to filtering and searching data dynamically within a GUI.

- **Enhancing data validation for transactions**:

  - **Objective**: Improve the reliability of the PFT application by enforcing stricter validation on user input.

  - **Activity**: Perform the following actions:

    - Modify the PFT application to ensure that the amount field only accepts valid numeric values.

    - Ensure that negative values are not allowed unless explicitly entered as withdrawals.

    - Prevent excessively large transaction amounts.

    - Test the validation with different inputs and document any edge cases you encounter.

  - **Real-world applicability**: Proper input validation is critical in real-world applications, such as financial software and e-commerce platforms, to prevent data corruption and user errors. This challenge is designed to help you reinforce best practices in user input handling.

- **Implementing a monthly summary report**:

  - **Objective**: Extend the PFT application by adding a feature that summarizes total expenses and income for the current month.

  - **Activity**: Perform the following actions:

    - Modify the transaction table so that it can track the date of each transaction.

    - Add a Generate Report button that calculates and displays the total income and total expenses for the current month.

    - Display the report as an alert or within a new section of the UI.

    - Document your approach and describe any challenges you faced while implementing this feature.

  - **Real-world applicability**: Financial applications often generate reports to help users understand their spending habits. This challenge is designed to help you think about data aggregation and reporting, key concepts in software development.

- **Adding a transaction editing feature**:

  ○ **Objective**: Allow users to edit existing transactions instead of only adding or deleting them.

  ○ **Activity**: Perform the following actions:

    ▪ Modify the transaction table to include an Edit button next to each transaction.

    ▪ When clicked, this button should populate the input fields with the selected transaction's details.

    ▪ Allow the user to modify the values and click an Update button to apply the changes.

    ▪ Ensure that the total balance updates correctly when a transaction is edited.

  ○ **Real-world applicability**: Data entry applications frequently need an edit/update feature to correct mistakes. This challenge is designed to teach you how to modify existing data dynamically within a GUI application.

Self-assessment

The following questions are provided to self-assess your knowledge of the chapter's content and apply critical thinking to key concepts:

1. What is the role of the scene graph in JavaFX, and how does it help organize UI components?

2. In what ways do JavaFX layout managers improve the design and usability of an application compared to manually positioning UI elements?

3. How does property binding in JavaFX enhance interactivity, and what is the difference between unidirectional and bidirectional binding?

4. Suppose you were developing a JavaFX application to track employee work hours instead of financial transactions. How would you modify the PFT application to suit this new purpose?

5. What are the advantages and challenges of implementing data persistence in a JavaFX application? How would you decide whether to store data in a text file or a database?

Answers

1. The scene graph is the hierarchical structure that defines how UI components (nodes) are arranged and rendered in a JavaFX application. It consists of a stage (the main application window), a scene (the content container), and nodes (UI elements like buttons, labels, and layouts). By using a structured scene graph, developers can

efficiently organize UI elements, apply transformations, and manage event propagation within the application.

2. JavaFX layout managers, such as VBox, HBox, BorderPane, and GridPane, allow developers to dynamically position UI components without specifying exact pixel coordinates. This ensures that:

   a. The UI adjusts properly when the window is resized.

   b. Elements are evenly spaced and aligned, improving usability.

   c. The application can support different screen sizes and resolutions without requiring manual adjustments.

   d. Using layout managers makes it easier to create a responsive and professional-looking UI.

3. Property binding synchronizes UI elements with underlying data, ensuring real-time updates without manual event handling.

   The difference between unidirectional and bidirectional binding is as follows:

   a. Unidirectional binding means that changes in one property automatically update the bound UI component, but not vice versa (e.g., updating a label when a value changes).

   b. Bidirectional binding ensures that changes in either property update the other (e.g., synchronizing a text field with a label so they both reflect the same value).

4. To adapt the PFT application for tracking employee work hours, several changes would be necessary:

   a. Instead of transaction details, the input fields would allow users to enter employee names, clock-in and clock-out times, and work shifts.

   b. The transaction table would be modified to store and display employee work logs, including total hours worked.

   c. The balance label could be adapted to show total hours worked for the day/week/month instead of financial totals.

   d. The data persistence feature could be expanded to calculate and save payroll estimates based on hours worked.

5. Advantages of data persistence are as follows:

   a. Prevents data loss when the application is closed.

   b. Allows users to reload previous transactions or records.

   c. Supports historical data analysis and reporting.

Challenges of data persistence are as follows:

a. Managing file integrity and preventing data corruption.

b. Handling duplicate transactions or incomplete records.

c. Ensuring security and proper access control to stored data.

Choosing between a text file and a database:

a. A text file is a simpler option for small-scale applications, like the PFT tracker, where data does not require complex queries.

b. A database is preferable for applications that require advanced filtering, sorting, multiple user access, and scalability.

Join our Discord space

Join our Discord workspace for latest updates, offers, tech happenings around the world, new releases, and sessions with the authors:

https://discord.bpbonline.com

CHAPTER 12
Modern Java Features

Introduction

Java is alive, alive in the sense that it continues to evolve with new features, frameworks, and efficiencies. Many of these enhancements are focused on helping us ensure our applications can be written in a manner that supports modularity, scalability, reliability, readability, and maintainability. That is a lot of abilities, and Java delivers on that promise. Java releases occur every six months, and their refinements come with backward compatibility.

This chapter focuses on selected modern Java features that can help shape your modern software development projects in Java. Among these features are Project Jigsaw's modular system, pattern matching, sealed classes, and virtual threads. This chapter also looks at **JDK Enhancement Proposal (JEP)** 477 (implicitly declared classes and instance main methods) and other enhancements that can significantly streamline our development workflows and the performance of our applications. The chapter concludes with a set of best practices for leveraging modern Java features.

Structure

This chapter covers the following topics:

- Overview of modern Java
- Project Jigsaw

- Recent Java enhancements
- Java 24, including JEP 477
- Best practices

Objectives

By the end of this chapter, you should be able to implement modular programming using Project Jigsaw, use pattern matching, use sealed classes, and use virtual threads. You should also have working knowledge of how to apply JEP 477 enhancements and be able to apply best practices for using modern Java features.

Overview of modern Java

Java is undoubtedly one of the most capable, robust, and popular programming languages today. While rankings can vary slightly by source, Java is consistently in the top three programming languages, along with Python and JavaScript/TypeScript, for popularity. When combining popularity with robustness and capability, Java remains in the top three along with Python and C++/C#.

The enduring nature of Java's rankings is due to several factors, including its adaptability, platform independence, backward compatibility, and continuous release cycle. Through these scheduled releases, Java has become a robust tool that supports scalability, high-performance, and modular programming. Recent Java releases have resulted in improved developer efficiency through the introduction of syntax enhancements, optimization techniques, and more. Java empowers us to write concise code that is scalable and maintainable.

Throughout this chapter, we will reference the realistic scenario of a **Culinary Order and Inventory Network** (**COIN**) system, a fictional enterprise system that is used to manage inventory and order fulfillment across thousands of warehouses, restaurants, and stores.

Release cycle

Oracle introduced a six-month release cycle in 2017, which provides us with earlier access to new features. *Table 12.1* provides the focus of each release from Java 9 (September 2017) through Java 24 (March 2025):

Release	Focus/Highlight	Release	Focus/Highlight
Java 9	Project Jigsaw (modularization)	Java 17	Sealed classes (standard)
Java 10	var keyword	Java 18	Simple web server
Java 11	**Long-Term Support** (**LTS**), HTTP Client API	Java 19	Virtual threads (preview) and structured concurrency (incubator)

Java 12	Switch expressions (preview)	Java 20	Pattern matching for switch (preview)
Java 13	Text blocks (preview)	Java 21	LTS and **Z Garbage Collector (ZGC)**
Java 14	Switch expressions (standard)	Java 22	**Foreign Function and Memory (FFM)** API
Java 15	Text blocks (standard) and sealed classes (preview)	Java 23	Project Loom (virtual threads)
Java 16	Pattern matching for instanceof	Java 24	Project Panama (foreign function interface)

Table 12.1: *Java releases with focus/highlights*

Note: **Not all these highlighted items are covered in this chapter. You should feel free to explore Oracle's release notes.**

As illustrated in *Table 12.1*, Oracle has introduced significant updates to Java. These updates include modularization with Project Jigsaw, the local-variable type inference with the **var** keyword, LTS, switch expressions, text blocks, pattern matching, virtual threads with Project Loom, generational ZGC, and more.

Modern Java themes

Review of the modern Java releases reveals three pervasive themes: scalability, performance improvement, and developer productivity.

Core to scalability is modularity, where we break down functional areas of our code as standalone modules that can be developed and maintained in isolation from the rest of the system. These modules can be maintained by different teams and used in multiple systems. This approach can encapsulate our code, reduce the memory overhead of our system by only loading needed modules, and result in faster application launch/startup. This was introduced in Java 9 with Project Jigsaw, which we will look at more closely in the next section of this chapter. To demonstrate modularization, consider our COIN system that separates inventory management, order processing, and warehouse logistics into their own modules. Here is how that might be coded:

```
module com.coin.inventory {
    exports com.coin.inventory.api;
    requires java.sql;
}
module com.coin.orders {
    exports com.coin.orders.api;
    requires com.coin.inventory;
```

```
}
module com.coin.warehouse_logistics {
    exports com.coin.warehouse_logistics.api;
    requires com.coin.inventory;
    requires com.coin.orders;
}
```

Java releases usually have some element of performance improvement. Here are a few noteworthy improvements:

- GC improvements
- Introduction of compact strings
- Class data sharing optimization

Even small performance improvements can lead to significant overall application performance. Let us look at an example of how we might implement a compact string to reduce memory requirements when storing product names and descriptions. The example below uses strings internally:

```
String productName = "Premium Olive Oil";
```

Modern Java releases do not always add complexity to our programming efforts; in fact, it is often that Java improvements often make our work more efficient and less time-consuming. Here are three examples:

- The introduction of records for immutable data.
- Text blocks to facilitate multi-line strings.
- Pattern matching.

Using our COIN system for context, we can use records to eliminate the need for constructors, getters, and setters. This makes our code less time-consuming to write, easier to read, and easier to maintain. Here is an example:

```
record InventoryItem(String sku, String name, int quantity) {}
```

Project Jigsaw

Project Jigsaw introduced a modular system in Java 9, giving us the ability to write modular Java applications. Prior to Java 9, our large-scale systems typically were based on monolithic designs that led to security risks, poor performance, tight coupling, and other issues.

Note: **Monolithic design refers to a software architecture where a system is built as a single codebase.**

The modular approach to programming supports scalability, security, and maintainability. Our COIN system, a large-scale order and inventory management platform, is an excellent use case for modular programming. COIN consists of multiple interdependent components, such as warehouse inventory management, order processing, payment processing, and logistics coordination. By adopting a modular architecture, we can improve the security and reduce COIN's memory footprint. This adoption will also result in COIN's code being more maintainable.

This section explores how to implement Java's module system, how it works, and its benefits.

Module system

Java's module system helps us organize our code into modules. A module is a self-contained unit of code. These modules are maintained independently of the overall system, making our code significantly more maintainable.

All modules have the following characteristics:

- The code is encapsulated.

- Code is only exposed to the required APIs.

- Dependencies are explicitly declared (using the **requires** directive).

These characteristics lead to improved security because access to internal components is limited. Application startup time is also reduced because we only need to load the required modules.

The modules we create will have a declaration, identify which packages they export, and any dependencies on other modules. Considering our COIN system, adopting a modular approach would allow us to organize the system into modules (see *Table 12.2*):

Module	Purpose
`com.coin.inventory`	Used to manage stock levels in warehouse(s)
`com.coin.orders`	Handles order generation and processing
`com.coin.payments`	Manages invoicing and payments
`com.coin.shipping`	Handles logistics, include delivery

Table 12.2: COIN system modules

These modules can be created so that they keep their internal implementations hidden and only expose essential APIs.

Implementation benefits

Implementing a modular design to the COIN system would provide advantages in several areas, include overall system maintainability. Each module can be updated, troubleshot, and otherwise maintained independently of other modules. Development teams can work on one module without impacting other modules. For example, we might have a team responsible for the warehouse inventory system. They can update the **com.coin.inventory** module without having to modify **com.coin.orders**. Another example is that **com.coin.payments** can be replaced with an external payment gateway without impacting how **com.coin.oders** processes orders. This approach is inherently scalable.

Security is another benefit of using a modular system design. The increased security is partially because each module only exposes the necessary APIs. This helps prevent unintended access to internal code. The modular approach also reduces security vulnerabilities by encapsulating and hiding sensitive implementations. The example **com.coin.payments** module shown here only exposes its payment API and hides transaction details from other modules:

```
module com.coin.payments {
    exports com.coin.payments.api;
}
```

A third benefit of modular system design is that our applications can experience faster load times. The JVM will only load modules necessary for launch, which can significantly reduce runtime overhead. In our COIN system, the mobile ordering system would only require order processing and payments, so the **com.coin.shipping** module would not be loaded on startup.

Java's modular system also enables us to reliably manage dependencies. We use **requires** statements to prevent any conflicts that might be caused by hidden dependencies. For example, the **com.coin.orders** module requires both **com.coin.inventory** and **com.coin. payments**. The code below ensures that **com.coin.orders** cannot compile or run without their dependencies. This will prevent runtime errors:

```
module com.coin.orders {
    requires com.coin.inventory;
    requires com.coin.payments;
}
```

Using modules

Creating a module requires us to identify its dependencies and packages to export/expose. As you can see in the module definition, **com.coin.inventory** only exposes the API package and requires the **java.sql** module for database access:

```
module com.coin.inventory {
    exports com.coin.inventory.api;
```

```
    requires java.sql;
}
```

Each module has its own package hierarchy. For example:

- **com.coin.inventory**:
  - `module-info.java`
  - `com/coin/inventory/api/InventoryService.java`
  - `com/coin/inventory/internal/StockManager.java`

In the following **InventoryService** example, this is an exposed API that will be used by other modules. As you can see, the **InventoryService** class is inside the **com.coin.inventory.api** package. This makes it accessible to other modules.

```
package com.coin.inventory.api;

public class InventoryService {
    public int checkStock(String productCode) {
        // Implementation goes here
        return 100;
    }
}
```

As previously stated, modules must declare their dependencies on other modules, or they will not be able to use the exposed APIs. Let us look at an example where the **com.coin.orders** module uses the **com.coin.inventory** module.

First, we use a **requires** statement to declare that **com.coin.orders** is dependent on the **com.coin.inventory** module to perform its operations:

```
module com.coin.orders {
    requires com.coin.inventory;
}
```

The partial **OrderProcessing** class below demonstrates how to access inventory from the **orders** module:

```
import com.coin.inventory.api.InventoryService;

public class OrderProcessor {
    private InventoryService inventoryService = new InventoryService();

    public void processOrder(String productCode) {
        if (inventoryService.checkStock(productCode) > 0) {
            System.out.println("Order placed successfully!");
```

```
        } else {
            System.out.println("Out of stock!");
        }
    }
}
```

Recent Java enhancements

As we have explored, Java releases usher in new functionality and enhancements that empower us to write code that is easy to read, safe, maintainable, scalable, and performant. This section explores pattern matching, sealed classes, and virtual threads, three major modern Java enhancements.

We will continue using our COIN system to demonstrate these features.

Pattern matching

Pattern matching provides us with streamlined syntax to implement conditional logic. It removes the need for repetitive code specific to casting and **instanceof** checks.

Note: **Pattern matching streamlines conditional logic and reduces boilerplate code.**

Let us further explain pattern matching. We will review code examples using pattern matching with **instanceof**, pattern matching with **switch**, and **records** for immutable data.

Pattern matching with instanceof

In the code block below, we were required to manually cast objects after an **instanceof** check. Here, we perform an **instanceof** check on the first line of code, then explicitly cast it on the second line; this is redundant code:

```
if (obj instanceof InventoryItem) {
    InventoryItem item = (InventoryItem) obj;
    System.out.println("Product: " + item.name());
}
```

With pattern matching, we can rewrite the code, as shown here, without the explicit cast:

```
if (obj instanceof InventoryItem) {
    System.out.println("Product: " + item.name());
}
```

We could use this approach with our COIN system to validate an inventory item. The following code eliminates unnecessary casting, which makes our code cleaner, easier to read, and more efficient:

```
public void processInventory(Object obj) {
    if (obj instanceof InventoryItem item) {
        System.out.println("Processing inventory for: " + item.name());
    } else {
        System.out.println("Invalid inventory item.");
    }
}
```

Pattern matching with switch

An additional use of pattern matching is with the **switch** statement. This allows us to be both concise and expressive. Let us look at a traditional **switch** statement, which we can refer to as **verbose**:

```
switch (order.getStatus()) {
    case "PENDING":
        System.out.println("Order is pending approval.");
        break;
    case "SHIPPED":
        System.out.println("Order has been shipped.");
        break;
    default:
        System.out.println("Unknown status.");
}
```

Now, compare the verbose code above to the concise version below that uses pattern matching. As you can see, the boiler code break statements are no longer required:

```
switch (order.getStatus()) {
    case "PENDING" -> System.out.println("Order is pending approval.");
    case "SHIPPED" -> System.out.println("Order has been shipped.");
    default -> System.out.println("Unknown status.");
}
```

To further demonstrate this, let us look at an example with our COIN system. The following code could be used to handle different types of orders:

```
public void processOrder(Order order) {
    switch (order) {
        case ExpressOrder eo -> System.out.println("Processing express order:
" + eo.getId());
        case StandardOrder so -> System.out.println("Processing standard
order: " + so.getId());
        default -> System.out.println("Unknown order type.");
```

```
    }
}
```

Records

In Java, the **Records** class was introduced to make it easier for us to create immutable data objects. We can use the **record** keyword to have Java automatically generate boilerplate code for us. This includes methods such as constructors, setters, getters, **equals()**, and **toString()**.

Here is an example of an **InventoryItem** class using a standard Java class:

```
class InventoryItem {
    private final String sku;
    private final String name;
    private final int quantity;

    public InventoryItem(String sku, String name, int quantity) {
        this.sku = sku;
        this.name = name;
        this.quantity = quantity;
    }

    public String getSku() { return sku; }
    public String getName() { return name; }
    public int getQuantity() { return quantity; }
}
```

Now, let us look at the same class using **Records** instead of a standard class:

```
record InventoryItem(String sku, String name, int quantity) {}
```

As you can see, the code reduction is significant. You might remember how we carefully detailed the need to create constructors, setters, and getters in *Chapter 3, Object-oriented Programming Basics*. With **Records**, we no longer need to create those methods.

Sealed classes

Sealed classes are a Java feature that can be used to restrict which classes can extend them and which interfaces can implement them. This provides us with the ability to strictly control inheritance and supports security.

> **Note: Sealed classes enforce strict class hierarchies.**

This feature can be used to prevent unintended inheritance, implement a closed hierarchy, and make our code more predictable. It also improves application performance.

Here is an example using our COIN system where we define sealed classes for our **Order** class:

```
sealed class Order permits ExpressOrder, StandardOrder {}

final class ExpressOrder extends Order {
    public void process() { System.out.println("Fast shipping enabled."); }
}

final class StandardOrder extends Order {
    public void process() { System.out.println("Standard shipping in
progress."); }
}
```

As seen in the preceding code, our **Order** class restricts inheritance to only **ExpressOrder** and **StandardOrder**; no other classes can extend the **Order** class. This prevents unintentional modifications. If we attempted to extend the **Order** class, we would receive a compile error.

Virtual threads

Large-scale systems often handle vast amounts of concurrent requests. It is important to optimize the performance of these operations for overall application efficiency. See *Chapter 7, Concurrency and Multithreading,* for additional details on threads and concurrency.

Project Loom, in Java 19, introduced virtual threads to Java with the purpose of making current programming both scalable and performant.

Note: **Virtual threads make multithreading lightweight and scalable.**

Thread management can be memory-intensive, especially when your application deals with thousands, or even millions, of concurrent operations. The following code demonstrates how we could implement threads without using virtual threads:

```
ExecutorService executor = Executors.newFixedThreadPool(100);
for (int i = 0; i < 1000; i++) {
    executor.submit(() -> System.out.println("Processing order..."));
}
```

The example aforementioned uses platform threads. We limited the thread count to **100** because each thread consumes significant memory.

Now, let us look at an approach using virtual threads:

```
ExecutorService executor = Executors.newVirtualThreadPerTaskExecutor();
for (int i = 0; i < 1000; i++) {
    executor.submit(() -> System.out.println("Processing order..."));
}
```

The code aforementioned implements more threads, each with reduced memory requirements. In the context of our COIN system, we can implement structured concurrency to ensure both the operation to fetch an order's details and the inventory operation occur in parallel before the processing continues.

That implementation is provided as follows:

```
try (var scope = new StructuredTaskScope.ShutdownOnFailure()) {
    Supplier<Order> order = scope.fork(() -> fetchOrder(orderId));
    Supplier<Inventory> inventory = scope.fork(() -> fetchInventory(orderId));

    scope.join();

    System.out.println("Order: " + order.get());
    System.out.println("Inventory: " + inventory.get());
}
```

Java 24, including JEP 477

Java 24 was released in March 2025 and introduced new features that save us development time and improve application performance. That release continues the trend of reducing boilerplate code and introducing syntax changes and other improvements to further modernize Java. One of the most popular Java 24 enhancements was JEP 477, which introduced the ability to implicitly declare classes and instance main methods.

> **Note:** **JEPs are JEP documents provided to communicate JDK enhancements prior to their release.**

This section explores JEP 477 in depth and features additional enhancements.

JEP 477

JEP 477 introduced a new approach to class declaration. Traditionally, we must explicitly declare our classes, which, in part, is why Java is referred to as a verbose language. Even simple programs require a lot of code to do very little. The new feature allows us to, in simple programs, write code without explicitly declaring classes, include instance methods in the **main()** class, and improve the readability of our code. This feature has been compared to how code is written in Python and JavaScript. Let us look at some examples using a simple application that prints **Welcome to the COIN System!** to the screen.

Here is that code in traditional Java:

```
public class HelloWorld {
    public static void main(String[] args) {
        System.out.println("Welcome to the COIN System!");
```

```
    }
}
```

Here is how we would write that in Python:

```
print("Welcome to the COIN System!")
```

Now, let us look at how we would write that in JavaScript:

```
console.log("Welcome to the COIN System!");
```

Next, we will rewrite the code based on JEP 477:

```
void main() {
    System.out.println("Welcome to the COIN System!");
}
```

As you can see, our Java code using JEP 477 is more concise (less verbose) and more in line with the simplicity of Python and JavaScript.

Using our COIN system, we can implement a quick inventory check script. This is how we might do that with traditional Java code:

```
public class InventoryCheck {
    public static void main(String[] args) {
        InventoryService service = new InventoryService();
        System.out.println("Stock Level: " + service.getStock("Widget319"));
    }
}
```

Now, let us rewrite that using JEP 477:

```
void main() {
    InventoryService service = new InventoryService();
    System.out.println("Stock Level: " + service.getStock("Widget319"));
}
```

As you can see, JEP 477 improves our code's readability by reducing boilerplate code. It allows for faster prototyping.

Note: **Remember, JEP 477 is only appropriate for simple Java applications.**

Additional enhancements

There were several additional enhancements that rolled out with Java 24. These include the following:

- Improved GC performance
- Reduced JVM warm-up time

- Network API refinement
- **Input/Output (I/O)** enhancements
- Strong cryptographic algorithms
- Increased TLS robustness
- Improved modular security permissions

You can read the release notes on Oracle's official site: **https://jdk.java.net/24/release-notes**

Best practices

As the Java platform continues to evolve, so should we evolve our programming approaches and practices. This is important for building maintainable, modular, and high-performance applications. We should strive to adopt best practices aligned with Java's latest enhancements, so our code is more efficient, scalable, easier to maintain, and performant.

For this final section, we will continue using the COIN system to help demonstrate coding approaches. As a reminder, the COIN system is a large-scale order fulfillment and inventory management platform that coordinates with warehouses, restaurants, and stores across *North America*. The COIN system requires high-performance, modularity, and maintainability, making it an excellent case study for applying modern Java best practices.

This section shares best practices for using records, pattern matching, implementing virtual threads, and implementing a modular design.

Use records

It is best to favor the use of **records** when working with immutable data instead of the traditional class approach. This practice reduces boilerplate constructor, getter, and setter code, resulting in the following benefits:

- Shorter development time
- Less code to maintain
- More readable code
- Less memory use
- Ensures immutability
- Prevents unintended modifications

This is how we would define a **record** for inventory items in our COIN system:

```
record InventoryItem(String sku, String name, int quantity) {}
```

Use pattern matching

As explained earlier in this chapter, we can use pattern matching instead of **instanceof** checks. Using this approach is a best practice because it offers the following benefits:

- Reduces redundant casting.
- The code is more concise.
- The code is more readable.
- Code is more maintainable.

Here is how we can implement pattern matching for our COIN system order processing:

```java
void processOrder(Object order) {
    if (order instanceof ExpressOrder eo) {
        System.out.println("Processing express order: " + eo.getId());
    } else if (order instanceof StandardOrder so) {
        System.out.println("Processing standard order: " + so.getId());
    }
}
```

We can also use pattern matching with switch expressions to achieve the following benefits:

- Clear flow control.
- The code is more concise.
- The code is more readable.
- Code is more maintainable.

Here is how we can implement this best practice in our COIN system:

```java
void handleOrder(Order order) {
    switch (order) {
        case ExpressOrder eo -> System.out.println("Fast shipping for " + eo.getId());
        case StandardOrder so -> System.out.println("Processing standard order: " + so.getId());
        case Backorder bo -> System.out.println("Order is backordered.");
        default -> System.out.println("Unknown order type.");
    }
}
```

Implement virtual threads

Virtual thread implementation is another best practice for modern Java applications. Specifically, we can use virtual threads instead of using platform threads. The benefits of this approach include:

- Memory use reduction
- Improved performance
- Scalability

Here is an example of how the COIN system might implement virtual threads to simultaneously process thousands of orders:

```
ExecutorService executor = Executors.newVirtualThreadPerTaskExecutor();
for (int i = 0; i < 1000; i++) {
    executor.submit(() -> System.out.println("Processing order..."));
}
```

Implement modular design

Our final featured best practice for modern Java development is to implement a modular design for the following benefits:

- Enhanced encapsulation
- Code security
- Improved maintainability
- Improved readability

Here is an example where we modularize the COIN system's inventory and order processes:

```
module com.coin.inventory {
    exports com.coin.inventory.api;
    requires java.sql;
}

module com.coin.orders {
    exports com.coin.orders.api;
    requires com.coin.inventory;
}
```

Additional considerations

The best practices presented in this section can provide great benefits to you as a developer, your system's performance, and the user experience. They are not meant to suggest isolated use; rather, they should be implemented as an overall approach to help ensure your applications are secure, scalable, readable, maintainable, and performant.

The following list provides additional best practices for your consideration when developing and maintaining modern Java applications:

- Implement immutability where possible to decrease the risk of concurrency issues and increase thread safety. See *Chapter 7, Concurrency and Multithreading,* for more information.

- Use functional programming instead of loops for data processing. See *Chapter 8, Streams and Functional Programming,* for implementation details.

- Avoid excessive object creation and use modern Java garbage collection (i.e., ZGC, **Garbage-First garbage collector** (**G1 GC**), etc.) for low latency and to reduce GC overhead.

- Design security into your modules and overall application before coding. Employ techniques such as limiting module exposure, always validating inputs, and using strong cryptography for sensitive data.

Conclusion

As Java developers, we are fortunate that the Java platform and ecosystem continue to evolve. We are continually provided with new tools that can improve multiple aspects of our Java programs, include modularity, scalability, readability, maintainability, security, performance, and more. This chapter examined some of the most important features from recent Java releases. This included Project Jigsaw, pattern matching, sealed classes, virtual threads, and JEP 477. Each of these enhancements offers development efficiency in writing cleaner, more efficient, and more maintainable Java applications.

We applied the enhancements to a COIN system to demonstrate how these modern features can benefit enterprise-level systems. The chapter concluded with a look at best practices for modern Java application development.

In the next chapter, we explore approaches to debugging, testing, deploying, and supporting our applications. The chapter demonstrates how to debug Java programs using IDE tools and logging. You can learn how to write unit tests using JUnit and apply **test-driven development** (**TDD**) principles to ensure your code is reliable. Finally, the chapter covers packaging and deploying Java applications using build tools like Maven and Gradle, helping to prepare you to release production-ready software.

Points to remember

- Adopting modern Java best practices improves application performance, maintainability, and scalability.

- Applications benefit from modular programming, which improves encapsulation, security, and maintainability.

- Best practices for modern Java development include using records, pattern matching, virtual threads, and modularization.

- Encapsulation in modular programming ensures that only the necessary APIs are exposed, reducing security risks.

- Functional programming techniques, such as the Stream API, improve code readability and performance.

- GC has been continuously optimized to reduce memory overhead.

- Java's six-month release cycle ensures a continuous flow of updates, balancing innovation with stability.

- JEPs outline proposed changes to the Java platform.

- JEP 477 allows implicit class declarations, reducing boilerplate code and improving code readability for simple applications.

- Modular design was introduced with Project Jigsaw.

- Modular applications improve dependency management and reduce startup time by loading only the required components.

- Modularity allows applications to be broken into self-contained, independent modules.

- Pattern matching allows instanceof checks and switch statements to be written more concisely, improving code readability.

- Performance optimizations in recent Java versions include reduced JVM warm-up time, improved I/O handling, and networking refinements.

- Records eliminate the need for boilerplate constructors and getters.

- Records provide a concise way to define immutable data structures.

- Sealed classes control inheritance, allowing us to restrict which classes can extend or implement an interface.

- Structured concurrency allows for more efficient thread management and parallel task execution.

- Using the requires directive in module definitions ensures that Java applications declare and explicitly enforce dependencies.

- Virtual threads can handle millions of concurrent tasks with minimal memory overhead.

Case studies

These case studies provide realistic scenarios that encourage you to think critically about modern Java features:

- **Modularizing a global supply chain system**: *Skyforge Logistics* is a global supply chain management company that coordinates shipping, warehousing, and fulfillment for thousands of businesses across different continents. The company's Java-based system was built as a monolithic application, making it difficult to maintain, slow to update, and prone to security risks. Skyforge's software team wants to break the system into modular components using Project Jigsaw. The primary goal is to separate core functionalities (order management, warehouse operations, and shipping logistics) into independent modules.

    o **For your consideration**: What are the key benefits of modularizing this system? How should the module structure be designed to ensure loose coupling and strong encapsulation? How can the security of individual modules be improved using Java's access control and exports?

- **Implementing virtual threads for high-concurrency transactions**: *Andromeda Pay* is a fintech company providing instant payment processing and fraud detection for millions of users. The platform uses traditional platform threads, but as transaction volume increases, thread management has become inefficient, leading to high memory usage and slow processing times. The Andromeda Pay engineering team wants to transition to virtual threads introduced in Java 19 to handle thousands of concurrent transactions more efficiently.

    o **For your consideration**: How do virtual threads differ from traditional platform threads in memory usage and performance? What modifications would be required to refactor an existing executor-based thread pool to use virtual threads? What pitfalls should the team avoid when implementing virtual threads in a real-time financial system?

- **Pattern matching for fraud detection**: *Xel'Zyn Bank* is an intergalactic financial institution that provides banking and credit services across planetary economies. The bank's fraud detection system relies on complex if-else structures to classify and handle different types of financial transactions. To improve code readability and maintainability, the bank wants to rewrite its fraud detection logic using pattern matching for instanceof and switch expressions.

- **For your consideration**: How can pattern matching improve fraud detection logic compared to traditional if-else statements? What are the advantages of using switch expressions for processing various transaction types? How can pattern matching help detect and flag suspicious transactions more efficiently?

- **Using sealed classes for access control**: *Hyperion HealthNet* is a medical research and telemedicine company that provides real-time patient monitoring and diagnostics. To ensure data security and compliance, the software architecture must strictly control which classes can extend key system components, such as medical records and diagnostic reports. The development team wants to enforce strict inheritance hierarchies using sealed classes to prevent unauthorized extensions of core system components.

  - **For your consideration**: How do sealed classes improve security and maintainability in a healthcare application? What are the best practices for defining sealed hierarchies in a multi-tiered access control system? What potential drawbacks or limitations should be considered when implementing sealed classes?

- **Rapid prototyping with JEP 477**: *NyxTek Robotics* is a tech startup that builds smart kitchen appliances powered by **Internet of Things (IoT)** technology. Their team frequently prototypes Java-based software for testing device connectivity, sensor readings, and automation scripts. However, the standard Java syntax is too verbose for quick prototyping. To accelerate development, the company wants to leverage JEP 477, which allows implicitly declared classes and instance main methods, to simplify quick testing and scripting.

  - **For your consideration**: How does JEP 477 reduce Java's verbosity, making prototyping faster? What limitations should the team consider when using JEP 477 for IoT applications? When is it appropriate to transition from JEP 477-based scripts to fully structured Java applications?

Multiple choice questions

1. **What is the primary benefit of using Project Jigsaw in Java applications?**

   a. It allows Java to run without a JVM

   b. It replaces the Java classpath system

   c. It allows Java applications to run faster by enabling GPU acceleration

   d. It introduces a module system that improves encapsulation, maintainability, and scalability

2. **Which of the following statements is true about virtual threads introduced in Java 19?**

    a. They consume more memory than platform threads

    b. They are only available in enterprise versions of Java

    c. They are limited to a fixed number of concurrent executions

    d. They allow Java to efficiently handle millions of concurrent tasks with minimal overhead

3. **How does JEP 477 improve Java's syntax?**

    a. It introduces automatic memory management for large-scale applications

    b. It allows Java to run on embedded systems without modifications

    c. It simplifies small programs by enabling implicitly declared classes

    d. It removes the need for Java modules in multithreaded applications

4. **What is the advantage of using pattern matching in switch expressions?**

    a. It allows switch statements to support floating-point numbers

    b. It simplifies flow control by allowing type checks and variable declarations within switch cases

    c. It forces the use of functional programming techniques

    d. It automatically optimizes all switch statements for performance

5. **What is the purpose of sealed classes introduced in Java 17?**

    a. To restrict which classes can extend a given class

    b. To allow unrestricted inheritance

    c. To eliminate the need for abstract classes

    d. To replace interfaces in modular applications

Answers

1.	d.
2.	d.
3.	c.
4.	b.
5.	a.

Questions

1. Project Jigsaw introduced modular programming to Java. How does this approach compare to traditional monolithic application design? What are the advantages and potential challenges of adopting a modular architecture?

2. Virtual threads allow Java to handle high-concurrency workloads with lower memory consumption. How does this compare to traditional thread management using platform threads? Share a real-world application example where virtual threads would provide significant benefits.

3. Pattern matching for instanceof and switch expressions simplifies Java's syntax. How does this improve code readability and maintainability? Provide an example where using pattern matching significantly reduces code complexity.

4. JEP 477 introduced implicitly declared classes and instance main methods to simplify small Java programs. Do you think this change makes Java more accessible to beginners? What potential drawbacks might developers face when using this feature?

5. Sealed classes allow developers to control which other classes can extend them. How does this feature contribute to better security and maintainability in a large-scale Java application? Share a scenario where sealed classes would be beneficial.

6. Java's six-month release cycle introduces new features and improvements at a rapid pace. Do you think this frequent update cycle benefits or challenges developers? How should companies approach adopting new Java versions in production environments?

7. Java's GC has seen multiple optimizations over recent versions, including ZGC and G1 GC. Why is GC performance important in large-scale applications? How do different GC strategies impact memory management and application performance?

8. Many Java enhancements focus on improving developer productivity, such as records, text blocks, and improved pattern matching. Which of these features do you find most useful, and how do they contribute to writing more maintainable code?

9. Security is a critical concern in enterprise applications. How does Java's modular system contribute to better security practices? How can developers ensure that sensitive parts of an application remain protected?

10. Best practices for modern Java development emphasize using records, virtual threads, and modularization. Which of these best practices do you find most relevant in today's software development landscape, and why? Share a situation where adopting these practices might not be ideal.

Challenges

The following questions are provided to self-assess your knowledge of the chapter's content and apply critical thinking to key concepts:

- **Modularizing an inventory management system**:

  - **Objective**: Apply Java's module system to create a modular inventory management system that separates key functionalities into independent modules.

  - **Activity**: Perform the following actions:

    - Create a Java project that includes at least two modules:

      - com.store.inventory (handles inventory tracking)

      - com.store.orders (handles order processing and relies on the inventory module)

    - Ensure that only the necessary APIs are exposed using the exports directive.

    - Implement a class in com.store.inventory that provides a method to check stock availability.

    - In the com.store.orders, create a class that calls this inventory check method before processing an order.

    - Run and test the system to ensure that only the required dependencies are accessible.

  - **Real-world applicability**: In enterprise applications, modular programming improves scalability, security, and maintainability. This challenge simulates how real-world Java applications use modularization to separate concerns and enforce encapsulation.

- **Implementing virtual threads for order processing**:

  - **Objective**: Use Java's virtual threads to handle multiple order transactions concurrently and efficiently.

  - **Activity**: Perform the following actions:

    - Create a Java program that simulates processing 1000 customer orders using traditional platform threads.

    - Use Executors.newFixedThreadPool() with a limited number of threads.

    - Modify the program to use virtual threads Executors. newVirtualThreadPerTaskExecutor().

    - Compare the execution times and resource utilization between the two approaches.

    - Document any performance improvements observed.

  - **Real-world applicability**: Modern applications, especially e-commerce platforms, require highly concurrent order processing. Using virtual threads helps applications scale efficiently while reducing memory overhead. This challenge provides insight into real-world concurrency handling.

- **Using pattern matching for data validation**:
  - **Objective**: Simplify data validation logic using pattern matching to improve code readability and maintainability.
  - **Activity**: Perform the following actions:
    - Create a Java program that processes customer transactions.
    - Define three classes:
      - ◆ CardPayment (stores credit card details)
      - ◆ DigitalWalletPayment (stores a digital wallet ID)
      - ◆ BankTransferPayment (stores a bank account number)
    - Implement a method that accepts an object and uses pattern matching (instanceof) to determine the payment type.
    - Display a different validation message depending on the payment method.
  - **Real-world applicability**: In enterprise software, pattern matching simplifies complex decision structures. This challenge mirrors how financial applications validate customer payments efficiently.

- **Enforcing security with sealed classes**:
  - **Objective**: Use sealed classes to restrict inheritance and enforce secure system design.
  - **Activity**: Perform the following actions:
    - Create a sealed class called UserAccount that only permits two subclasses:
      - ◆ AdminUser (with additional administrative privileges)
      - ◆ RegularUser (with standard user permissions)
    - Ensure that no additional subclasses can extend UserAccount.
    - Implement methods in both subclasses that define different access levels.
    - Write a test case that creates AdminUser and RegularUser objects and verifies their behavior.
  - **Real-world applicability**: Security-sensitive applications use sealed classes to enforce strict **role-based access control** (**RBAC**). This challenge demonstrates how Java limits unauthorized inheritance, which improves security and maintainability.

- **Implement JEP 477 for quick prototyping**:

o **Objective**: Use JEP 477 (implicitly declared classes and instance main methods) to simplify Java scripting for quick prototyping and testing.

o **Activity**: Perform the following actions:

- Write a Java program using the traditional class-based structure to display an inventory summary report.

- Rewrite the program using JEP 477, eliminating unnecessary class declarations.

- Compare the code length, readability, and execution behavior between both implementations.

o **Real-world applicability**: Developers frequently prototype small applications to test logic before integrating features into a larger system. JEP 477 makes Java scripting faster and more readable, helping developers quickly iterate on ideas.

Self-assessment

The following questions are provided so you can self-assess your knowledge of the chapter's content and apply critical thinking to key concepts:

1. What are the key benefits of using Project Jigsaw for modularization in Java applications? How does it improve application structure, security, and performance?

2. How do virtual threads differ from traditional platform threads? In what scenarios would using virtual threads be more beneficial?

3. Explain how pattern matching enhances Java's switch expressions. What advantages does this provide over traditional switch statements?

4. JEP 477 introduces implicitly declared classes and instance main methods. How does this feature simplify Java development? What are some situations where using JEP 477 might not be appropriate?

5. Sealed classes allow developers to restrict class inheritance. In what types of applications would sealed classes be particularly useful? How do they help with security and maintainability?

Answers

1. **Project Jigsaw benefits**:

a. Code is encapsulated, only exposing necessary APIs. This reduces unintended access.

b. Modules can restrict visibility of internal implementations, improving security.

   c. The JVM loads only required modules, which reduces memory overhead and improves performance.

   d. We can update and debug specific modules independently, making our code more maintainable.

   e. Individual teams can simultaneously work on different modules without affecting other parts of the application, drastically improving scalability.

2. **Virtual threads vs. platform threads**:

   a. Virtual threads are lightweight and consume minimal memory. This allows for millions of concurrent operations.

   b. Platform threads are heavyweight, tied to OS threads, and limited in number.

   c. Use cases for virtual threads include high-concurrency applications like chat servers, transaction processing, and web services that require concurrently handling thousands of tasks.

3. **Pattern matching in switch expressions**:

   a. Pattern matching simplifies our code by eliminating the need for verbose if-else structures.

   b. Pattern matching in switch statements improves our code's readability. It allows type checks and variable declarations directly in switch cases.

   c. An example use case is processing different types of financial transactions or categorizing customer orders based on attributes.

4. **JEP 477 simplification**:

   a. This reduces boilerplate code by eliminating the need for explicit class declarations in small Java programs.

   b. It improves readability using syntax like scripting languages as used in Python and JavaScript.

   c. This is not suitable for large-scale applications that require explicit object-oriented structure, complex business logic, or dependency management.

5. **Sealed classes**:

   a. **Example 1**: Increase security by preventing unauthorized subclassing. This ensures a controlled class hierarchy.

   b. **Example 2**: Improve API stability by limiting how external developers can extend a library.

   c. **Use cases**: RBAC systems, financial transaction processing, and enterprise applications where specific subclasses should be tightly controlled.

CHAPTER 13
Debugging, Testing, and Deployment

Introduction

Software development with Java is enjoyable work. We put a lot of time and energy into our applications and, sometimes, they might take several years to complete. That is only part of the process. Once deployed, we must support our application, which requires debugging, testing, and deployment. Almost without exception, we spend more time supporting our software than creating it.

This chapter covers debugging techniques that can help us efficiently identify and resolve errors. These techniques can include simple print statements, logging frameworks, and **integrated development environments** (**IDEs**) with built-in debugging tools. It is imperative that we become familiar with debugging strategies so we can support our Java applications after they are deployed to a production environment.

The chapter also explores unit testing with the JUnit testing framework. You will have the opportunity to learn how to adopt **test-driven development** (**TDD**) principles to help you create reliable, maintainable applications. We will also cover best practices for structuring tests to help us catch issues early in the development cycle.

We will conclude the chapter by covering packaging and deployment. Build tools like Maven and Gradle will be introduced to streamline dependency management and automate software deployment.

Structure

This chapter covers the following topics:

- Debugging in Java
- Unit testing with JUnit
- Writing testable code
- Test-driven development
- Packaging and deploying Java applications
- Introduction to build tools

Objectives

By the end of this chapter, you should be able to use debugging tools to. Identify issues and leverage logging frameworks. You should also understand and be able to write unit tests using JUnit. Further, by the chapter conclusion, you should be able to apply TDD principles, have a firm understanding of build tools, and be able to package and deploy a Java application.

Debugging in Java

No matter how well we write our code, it is not apt to be error-free. This is not a reflection of our code, but of environmental issues like power, changes to APIs, network and internet disruptions, user behaviors, and more. This underscores the importance of debugging. This section explores debugging strategies, tools, and best practices to help streamline the debugging process.

Note: **Debugging is the process of identifying, analyzing, and resolving errors or unexpected application behaviors.**

There are three types of errors: logic, syntax, and runtime. Logic errors are mistakes we make when creating our software. Our logic is wrong, so the results are incorrect. The application will not crash or throw an exception; the results simply will not be correct. Consider the following example. The code will compile correctly, and there will be no error; however, the output is incorrect.

```java
public class LogicError {
    public static void main(String[] args) {
        double price = 3.19;
        int quantity = 10;

        double total = price + quantity;
```

```
        System.out.println("The total price is: " + total);
    }
}
```

The output in our example is **13.19**, when it should be **31.90**.

The second type of error is syntax errors. These occur because we did not follow Java's syntax correctly, or, plainly put, made a typo in our code. As an example, the code in *Figure 13.1* shows a missing closing parenthesis and semicolon on *line 3*. The IDE caught this for us and gave us a visual indication of where the error is.

```
J  SyntaxError.java > ...
1     public class SyntaxError {
          Run | Debug
2         public static void main(String[] args) {
3             System.out.println(x:"Read more BPB books!" // Missing closing parenthesis and semicolon
4         }
5     }
```

Figure 13.1: Syntax error caught in the IDE

Our last type of error, runtime errors, occurs when our application is running. These are the worst because if we do not catch them, we will disrupt the user experience. Examples of runtime errors are **NullPointerException** and **ArithmeticException**. Another example, demonstrated in the following code is **ArrayIndexOutOfBoundsException**:

```
public class RuntimeError {
    public static void main(String[] args) {
        int[] numbers = {1, 2, 3};

        // Trying to access an invalid index
        System.out.println(numbers[5]);
    }
}
```

Here is the error generated by this code:

```
Exception in thread "main" java.lang.ArrayIndexOutOfBoundsException: Index 5
out of bounds for length 3
        at RuntimeError.main(RuntimeError.java:6)
```

It is important to understand the three types of errors so we can be more efficient and effective with our debugging efforts.

IDE debugging tools

All modern IDEs have some level of debugging capability. They help us inspect our code and analyze its execution. Key debugging features in **Visual Studio Code** (**VS Code**) include breakpoints, call stack inspections, console logging, and step execution. Let us look at each one of those.

Breakpoints

We can add breakpoints to pause code execution so we can inspect variables, outputs, and more. To add a breakpoint, we merely click on the left margin to the left of the line number (see the first component of *Figure 13.2*). VS Code will put a red dot in the margin to indicate there is a breakpoint on that line. This is a regular breakpoint:

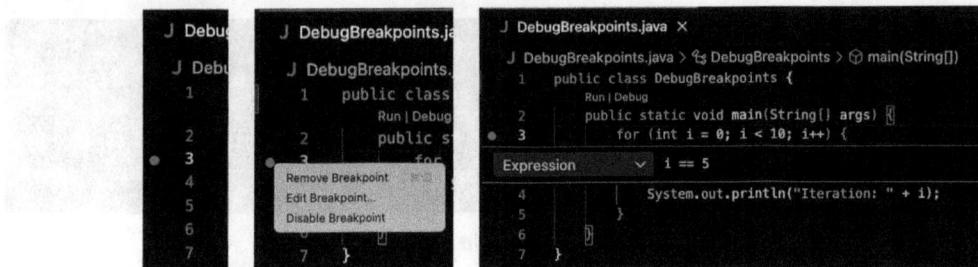

Figure 13.2: Breakpoint sequence

We can also use a conditional breakpoint by right-clicking the breakpoint (red dot) and selecting **Edit Breakpoint…**, as shown in the second section of *Figure 13.2*. This brings up the third section of *Figure 13.2*, where we can select **Expression**, **Hit count**, **Log message**, or **Wait for Breakpoint**.

Here is the code referenced in *Figure 13.2*:

```java
public class DebugBreakpoints {
    public static void main(String[] args) {
        for (int i = 0; i < 10; i++) {
            System.out.println("Iteration: " + i);
        }
    }
}
```

Breakpoints allow us to pause our code's execution and inspect variables and behavior. Regular breakpoints pause execution at a specific line; conditional breakpoints pause execution when a specified condition is met; and function breakpoints are triggered when a specific method is invoked.

Call stack inspection

We can trace the sequence of method calls using the **CALL STACK** panel in VS Code. To open this, you would run your program using the **RUN AND DEBUG** command. It is accessible via the left navigation and looks like a bug with a play button, as shown in *Figure 13.3*:

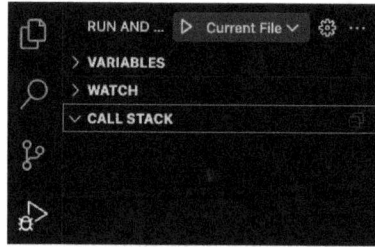

Figure 13.3: *Debug and run icon and location*

Console logging

We can easily add print statements throughout our code to help us determine variable states and execution flow. We can pepper **System.out.println()** method calls throughout our code for simple debugging, but using Java's **java.util.logging** package gives us better control over log levels and output.

Here is an example program that uses the **java.util.logging** package:

```
import java.util.logging.Level;
import java.util.logging.Logger;

public class ConsoleLogging {
    // Create a logger instance
    private static final Logger logger = Logger.getLogger(ConsoleLogging.class.
getName());

    public static void main(String[] args) {
        logger.info("Application started.");

        int number1 = 10;
        int number2 = 5;

        logger.fine("Variables initialized: number1=" + number1 + ", number2="
+ number2);

        try {
            int result = divideNumbers(number1, number2);
            logger.info("Result of division: " + result);
        } catch (ArithmeticException e) {
            logger.log(Level.SEVERE, "An error occurred during division: ",
e);
```

```
        }

        logger.info("Application finished.");
    }

    private static int divideNumbers(int num1, int num2) {
        logger.fine("Dividing numbers: " + num1 + " / " + num2);
        if (num2 == 0) {
            throw new ArithmeticException("Division by zero!");
        }
        return num1 / num2;
    }
}
```

Here is the console logging from our program:

```
Mar 19, 2025 12:04:26 AM ConsoleLogging main
INFO: Application started.
Mar 19, 2025 12:04:26 AM ConsoleLogging main
INFO: Result of division: 2
Mar 19, 2025 12:04:26 AM ConsoleLogging main
INFO: Application finished.
```

Logging allows us to differentiate between normal output, debugging information, and error messages. This is a good debugging approach for production environments.

Step execution

Another IDE-enabled debugging technique is stepping through our code, one line at a time. This allows us to watch how our software behaves and how variables are changed. VS Code provides us with several ways to do this:

- **Step over**: This executes the current line of code and moves to the next line, entering method calls.

- **Step into**: Program flow goes into a method call and debugs its execution.

- **Step out**: This steps out of the current method and returns to the caller.

- **Continue**: This will resume normal program execution until the next breakpoint is reached.

Using these features can help us examine our code's execution at a granular level.

Debugging strategies

Here are ten debugging strategies that are also best practices:

- Automate testing
- Check stack traces
- Inspect variable states
- Isolate code sections
- Reproduce the bug
- Start with simple solutions
- Test incrementally
- Use assertions (assert statements)
- Use debugging tools
- Use version control

Debugging is a critical skill for all developers. We are fortunate that IDEs provide a set of powerful tools to help streamline our debugging process.

Unit testing with JUnit

We covered debugging our software in the last section. Debugging is essentially what we do when things go wrong. The notion of testing our software is a preventative, proactive process. This section covers a specific kind of testing, unit testing, a fundamental practice where we validate individual components of our applications. We test units in isolation from others. As Java developers, we gravitate to the JUnit framework for writing and running unit tests. This section focuses on the importance of unit testing, how to use JUnit, and how to write and run unit tests.

Unit testing should adhere to the following guidelines:

- Be focused on a finite unit of code (e.g., a method).
- The test should be repeatable.
- They should be easy to implement/run.
- They should run quickly.
- The test should not be dependent on external systems (e.g., database, network, etc.).

There is a myriad of testing frameworks available to us, and we are focusing on JUnit. As you will see in our coding examples, JUnit allows us to easily write, run, and maintain unit tests. It has become an essential tool for Java development.

JUnit setup

There are a couple of steps involved to prepare VS Code to support JUnit and unit testing. The first step is to install the **Test Runner for Java**. As you can see in *Figure 13.4*, it supports JUnit:

Figure 13.4: VS Code extension to support JUnit framework

With that extension installed, follow the remaining steps:

1. Create a new project in VS Code. You can create a new folder on your computer and then open it in VS Code.

2. Create a **src/** folder under your project folder.

3. Create **src/main/** and **src/test/** folders.

4. Download JUnit from this site: **https://junit.org/junit5/**

5. Create a **lib/** folder under your project folder.

6. Move or copy the **Java Archive (JAR)** files from *step 4* into your project's **lib/** folder.

7. Next, we need to add the JUnit JARs to our project's classpath. Create a **.vscode/** folder under your project folder.

8. Create a **settings.json** file in the **.vscode/** folder with the following content:
    ```
    {
        "java.project.referencedLibraries": [
            "lib/**/*.jar"
        ]
    }
    ```

9. We are now ready to create a test class. Create **MyTest.java** in the **src/test** folder with the following content:
    ```
    import org.junit.jupiter.api.Test;
    import static org.junit.jupiter.api.Assertions.assertEquals;

    public class MyJUnitTest {
        @Test
        public void additionTest() {
    ```

```
            assertEquals(2, 1 + 1);
        }
    }
```

10. You will notice that there is no **main()** method, and that is okay. Click on the green arrows in the code margin (see *Figure 13.5*):

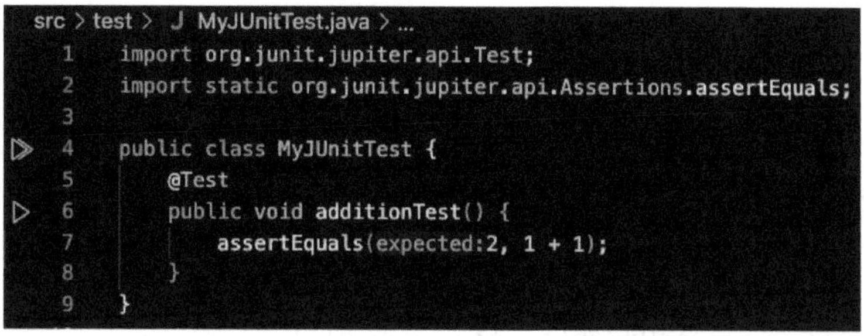

Figure 13.5: *VS Code run tests indicator*

That is all there is to it. Now, let us look at the example code in *Figure 13.5*. As you can see, we used an assertion method to validate a condition. In our example, we used **assertEquals()**. We provided an assertion for the unit test to compare results to. There are additional self-describing assertion methods to include: **assertNotEquals()**, **asssertTrue()**, **assertFalse()**, **assertThrows()**, etc.

Writing testable code

It is a best practice to think about testing our code as we design and write it. If we develop our code with testing in mind, it will have the characteristics of being modular and loosely coupled. This will make it easier for us to write meaningful tests that can be repeated and easily maintained.

This section reviews six principles of writing testable code: avoid hardcoded dependencies, implement interfaces, use return values, avoid static methods, avoid global variables, and write testable methods.

Avoid hardcoded dependencies

We established the importance of loosely coupling our code for ease of testing. Therefore, hardcoding dependencies, which would introduce tight coupling, is counter to testing best practices. The alternative to hardcoding dependencies is to use dependency injection to pass components as parameters.

Let us look at a hardcoded example:

```
public class OrderProcessor {
    private final PaymentService paymentService = new PaymentService();
```

```
    public boolean processOrder(double amount) {
        return paymentService.charge(amount);
    }
}
```

Now, let us refactor our code so it uses dependency injection.

```
public class OrderProcessor {
    private final PaymentService paymentService;

    public OrderProcessor(PaymentService paymentService) {
        this.paymentService = paymentService;
    }

    public boolean processOrder(double amount) {
        return paymentService.charge(amount);
    }
}
```

The dependency injection approach is more verbose, but it will allow us to simulate the **PaymentService** during testing.

Implement interfaces

The use of interfaces is not new to us; we have used them throughout earlier chapters. Whenever possible, we should implement interfaces as a preferred alternative to concrete implementations. This approach allows dependencies to be interchanged with alternatives.

Here is an example of tightly coupled code:

```
public class EmailSender {
    public void sendEmail(String message) {
        // Code to send email (relies on external system)
    }
}
```

Now, let us look at a loosely coupled example that uses interfaces:

```
public interface EmailService {
    void send(String message);
}

public class EmailSender implements EmailService {
    @Override
```

```
        public void send(String message) {
            // Real implementation
        }
    }


    public class NotificationService {
        private final EmailService emailService;

        public NotificationService(EmailService emailService) {
            this.emailService = emailService;
        }

        public void notifyUser() {
            emailService.send("Your order has been shipped!");
        }
    }
```

Our refactored code simulates the **EmailService** interface in tests instead of having to rely on a real email-sending system.

Return values

When we write code that produces output to the console, we make it difficult to capture the output for testing. Instead of printing to the console directly, we should use **return** values. Let us look at an example that prints directly to the console:

```
public class UserService {
    public void displayUser(String username) {
        System.out.println("User: " + username);
    }
}
```

That example would be difficult to test. To make this code testable, we can refactor it with a return statement as shown here:

```
public class UserService {
    public String getUser(String username) {
        return "User: " + username;
    }
}
```

Now we can write a test using an assert method:

```
@Test
```

```
void testGetUser() {
    UserService userService = new UserService();
    assertEquals("User: NeoAnderson", userService.getUser("NeoAnderson"));
}
```

Avoid static methods

Static methods cannot be simulated or overridden, making them difficult to test.

Note: **A static method is one that belongs to the class, not an instance of the class.**

Here is an example of a **static** method that complicates testing efforts:

```
public class MyMathUtilities {
    public static int square(int x) {
        return x * x;
    }
}
```

The following refactored version makes the code more testable:

```
public class MyMathUtilities {
    public int square(int x) {
        return x * x;
    }
}
```

Instance methods, instead of static methods, are more testable because they support simulation and dependency injection.

Avoid global variables

A fifth principle for making our code more testable is to avoid global variables. They introduce a certain level of unpredictability when testing; therefore, making them difficult to debug.

As an example, the following code uses a **static** class-level variable:

```
public class MyCounter {
    public static int count = 0;

    public static void increment() {
        count++;
    }
}
```

Now, let us refactor the code by encapsulating the variable's state to make our code more testable:

```
public class MyCounter {
    private int count = 0;

    public void increment() {
        count++;
    }

    public int getCount() {
        return count;
    }
}
```

This approach ensures that each test starts with a clean state and is not impacted by previous tests where values might persist.

Testable methods

When writing our methods, we should consider the single responsibility principle, which states that each method should have a singular purpose; that it does just one thing. When this principle is not followed, our methods can be difficult to test.

Here is an example of a complicated method that does too much:

```
public class OrderProcessor {
    public void processOrder(String productId) {
        // Validate product
        // Calculate price
        // Charge payment
        // Send email notification
    }
}
```

Here we refactor the previous version of **OrderProcessor** into smaller, testable methods:

```
public class OrderProcessor {
    public boolean validateProduct(String productId) { /* ... */ }
    public double calculatePrice(String productId) { /* ... */ }
    public boolean chargePayment(double amount) { /* ... */ }
    public void sendNotification(String message) { /* ... */ }
}
```

The refactored code permits each method to be tested individually.

Testing code in VS Code

Once the code is structured for testability, writing unit tests becomes straightforward. Let us test our **OrderProcessor** class, provided. The following code demonstrates a basic unit test.

Test class (OrderProcessorTest.java):

```java
import org.junit.jupiter.api.Test;
import static org.junit.jupiter.api.Assertions.*;

class OrderProcessorTest {
    private final OrderProcessor processor = new OrderProcessor();

    @Test
    void testCalculatePrice() {
        double price = processor.calculatePrice("P123");
        assertTrue(price > 0, "Price should be greater than zero");
    }
}
```

Test-driven development

Software development traditionally involves writing code and then testing it to make sure it is accurate and bug-free. Counter to that is TDD, which has us write tests before implementation. This approach helps ensure our code is based on detailed requirements, which reduces defects, improves maintainability, and saves us time over the lifespan of our software. Additional benefits include:

- Ensures correctness because all functionality is verified by tests.

- Improves our code design (i.e., modularity and simplicity).

- Supports debugging efforts with early detection.

TDD is cyclical, not linear, and involves three steps referred to as the **red-green-refactor** process (see *Figure 13.6*):

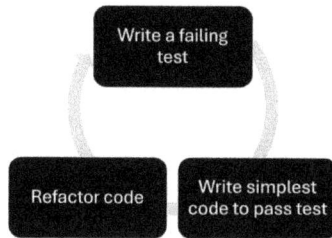

Figure 13.6: *TDD red-green-refactor process*

The first step (red) has us write a failing test. It is considered a failing test because the code has not been written yet. The second step (green) is to write the least amount of code to implement the functionality, just enough to pass the test. Next, the refactor step has us optimize our implementation and ensure that the test continues to pass.

Applying TDD

Let us put TDD into action using a **String** utility class that contains a method that reverses a string. For the red phase, we will write a failing test. This defines the behavior we expect in a unit test. Here is a test class:

```java
import org.junit.jupiter.api.Test;
import static org.junit.jupiter.api.Assertions.*;

public class MyStringUtilityTest {

    @Test
    void testReverseString() {
        String result = MyStringUtilityTest.reverse("matrix");
        assertEquals("xirtam", result, "Reversed string should be 'xirtam'");
    }
}
```

Now, for the green phase, we will implement the simplest possible version of the function:

```java
public class MyStringUtility {
    public static String reverse(String input) {
        StringBuilder sb = new StringBuilder(input);
        return sb.reverse().toString();
    }
}
```

Now, if we ran this test, it would pass. The third phase is the refactor phase, where we improve our code as needed. Each time we change the code that has already passed our test, we need to retest it. A refactored version might look like this:

```java
public class MyStringUtility {
    public static String reverse(String input) {
        if (input == null || input.isEmpty()) {
            return input;
        }
        return new StringBuilder(input).reverse().toString();
    }
}
```

The preceding refactored code includes the edge case that the return value should not be empty. To account for that in testing, we need to update our test class:

```java
@Test
void testReverseEmptyString() {
    assertEquals("", StringUtils.reverse(""), "Empty string should remain empty");
}

@Test
void testReverseNullString() {
    assertNull(StringUtils.reverse(null), "Null input should return null");
}
```

Using the TDD methodology, our code will be robust and well-tested. This should result in fewer bugs and less debugging once the code is deployed.

Packaging and deploying Java applications

This section focuses on how to package and deploy our applications after they have been written and thoroughly tested. Packaging is the gathering of necessary files and bundling them into JAR files. Deployment is the application's distribution to the required environments.

Later in this chapter, we will look at build tools such as Maven and Gradle. For now, we will explore how to manually compile Java applications with the Java compiler (**javac**) and JAR tool. The process, illustrated in *Figure 13.7*, involves several steps. We will look at each of those.

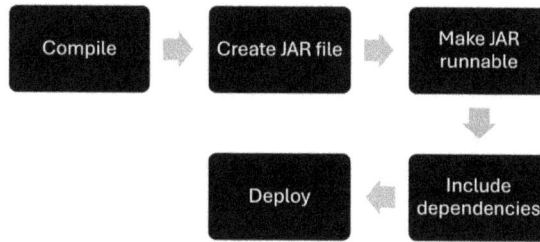

Figure 13.7: Packaging and deployment process

Compile

The first step is to compile our project. Let us use the following application for demonstration purposes:

```
public class SampleApp {
    public static void main(String[] args) {
        System.out.println("I am a simple Java application!");
    }
}
```

Compiling the application is as simple as running this **javac** command in a terminal window:

javac SampleApp.java

While you will not see any output in the terminal window, you will see the **SampleApp.class** file in your project folder. This is the bytecode file that the JVM can execute.

Create JAR files

Once our application is compiled into bytecode, we can bundle multiple **.class** files into a single compressed file (JAR) for distribution.

We will use the **jar** command to create our JAR file. Specifically, we will use the following statement:

jar cvf SampleApp.jar SamplmeApp.class

This will result in the **SampleApp.jar** file being added to your project's folder. The output of this command is shown as follows:

added manifest

adding: SampleApp.class(in = 443) (out= 306)(deflated 30%)

The **cvf** parameters passed to the **jar** command are explained in *Table 13.1*:

Parameter	Explanation
c	Creates a new JAR file
v	Verbose output
f	Specifies JAR file name

Table 13.1: Jar command parameters

Additional jar command parameters, not used in our example, are explained in *Table 13.2*:

Parameter	Explanation
e	Specifies the main class to execute as the entry point
--help	Provides help for the **jar** command
m	Specifies a manifest file to include
t	Lists the contents of the JAR file
u	Updates an existing JAR file
x	Extracts JAR file contents

Table 13.2: Additional jar command parameters

Make a runnable JAR

We can make our JAR runnable, which would allow users to execute the application with the following command:

```
java -jar SampleApp.jar
```

We are not ready to use that command yet. First, we need to create a new file named **MANIFEST. MF**. Create that file in your project folder with the following content:

```
Manifest-Version: 1.0
Main-Class: SampleApp
```

Next, we can package the JAR with the manifest using the following command:

```
jar cfm SampleApp.jar MANIFEST.MF SampleApp.class
```

Now, when we run the following command, the **main()** method in our **SampleApp.java** class is executed:

```
java -jar SampleApp.jar
```

The program's output is displayed as follows:

```
I am a simple Java application!
```

Include external dependencies

If our application depends on any external `.jar` files, we will need to include them in the classpath. Let us assume our application has an external **weather.jar** dependency. This first command is Windows-specific and is how we would run the JAR with the dependency:

```
java -cp ".;weather.jar" SampleApp
```

To run the same command on Linux or macOS, we would format the command as follows:

```
java -cp ".:weather.jar" SampleApp
```

We can package the dependency into a JAR as shown as follows:

```
jar cvf SampleApp.jar SampleApp.class weather.jar
```

Deploy

Once our application is packaged, we are ready to deploy it. Let us look at both local deployment and deploying our application on a server.

Local deployment

To share our application amongst our development team, we can simply share the **SampleApp.jar** file and tell our team members to use the following command to run it:

```
java -jar SampleApp.jar
```

It will be important to tell our team members what Java version they should have installed.

We can also provide executable files. For Linux and macOS, we can create a shell script:

```
#!/bin/bash
java -jar SampleApp.jar
```

Then, we can make it executable with the following:

```
chmod +x run.sh
./run.sh
```

To make an executable file on Windows, we would need to use a tool such as JSmooth or Launch4j to package JAR files as an **.exe** file.

Server deployment

For server-side applications, we merely need to copy the JAR file to the server, then run the application in the background. That can be accomplished with the following command:

```
nohup java -jar SampleApp.jar &
```

The **nohup** command ensures the application runs even after logging out, and the **&** parameter runs the process in the background.

Introduction to build tools

Throughout this chapter, we created and built applications manually. As our applications become more complex, manually performing the compilation, packaging, dependencies, distributions, etc., can become difficult and prone to error. Build tools to automate these tasks for us. Build tools are software utilities that automate source code compilation, dependency management, application packaging, testing, and application deployment.

Build tools simplify development workflows and provide consistency through standardization. For example, instead of manually compiling files, resolving dependencies, and creating a JAR, we can use a single command like `mvn package` or `gradle build` to accomplish everything in one step. This creates a repeatable, consistent build process, greatly enhancing our efficiency and reducing the risk from manual processes.

Build tools are multifaceted with a primary focus on the following:

- Dependency management
- Compilation
- Packaging
- Automated testing
- Deployment

The most common build tools used with Java include the following:

- Apache Ant
- Apache Maven
- Gradle

Conclusion

This chapter explored core practices to help ensure that our Java applications are reliable, maintainable, and deployable. We looked at debugging techniques, leveraging IDE tools such as breakpoints, call stack inspection, logging, and step execution to diagnose issues. We proclaimed debugging to be an inevitable part of software development. The chapter also covered unit testing with JUnit. We emphasized the importance of writing isolated and repeatable test cases. TDD principles were also covered with an emphasis on using the red-green-refactor cycle. Best practices for writing testable code were also covered. The chapter walked through the manual packaging and distribution of our applications. Finally, automated build tools were explained.

The next chapter provides you with the opportunity to apply the skills you learned in earlier chapters to real-world Java projects. This starts by building a simple command-line application, then progressing to a database application using JDBC and a JavaFX-based GUI application.

You will have the opportunity to tackle a multithreaded data processor and write a functional program using streams and lambdas. These projects are designed to help reinforce your understanding of key Java concepts while giving you practical experience that can be applied in real-world development scenarios.

Points to remember

- A breakpoint pauses execution at a specific line of code to inspect variables and application behavior.

- A call stack helps us trace the sequence of method calls leading to the current execution state.

- A unit test should be independent, repeatable, and not rely on external systems.

- Automating testing ensures consistency and reduces human error.

- Build tools automate compilation, dependency management, packaging, testing, and deployment.

- Call stack inspection allows us to analyze how execution flows through different method calls.

- Conditional breakpoints pause execution only when a specified condition is met.

- Console logging provides a way to track execution flow and capture diagnostic messages.

- Debugging is the process of identifying, analyzing, and resolving errors.

- Dependency injection improves testability by replacing hardcoded dependencies with flexible implementations.

- Global variables can introduce unpredictability and make code harder to test.

- Hardcoded dependencies make testing difficult and should be replaced with dependency injection.

- IDE debugging tools in VS Code include breakpoints, step execution, call stack inspection, and logging.

- Logging frameworks such as java.util.logging provides better control over log levels than simple print statements.

- Methods should follow the single responsibility principle, ensuring they only perform one task.

- Packaging involves bundling compiled Java files and resources into a distributable JAR file.

- Runnable JAR files require a manifest file specifying the main class for execution.

- Step execution allows us to move through our code one line at a time.

- Static methods reduce testability since they cannot be simulated or overridden.

- Syntax errors result from incorrect Java syntax.

- TDD follows the red-green-refactor cycle.

- Test assertions verify that actual output matches expected results.

- Testable code is modular, loosely coupled, and predictable.

- The three types of errors in Java are syntax errors, runtime errors, and logic errors.

- Unit testing validates individual components in isolation.

Case studies

These case studies provide realistic scenarios that encourage you to think critically about the chapter's content:

- **Debugging performance issues**: *Andromeda Systems*, a cloud-based analytics company, recently deployed a new version of its Nebula AI engine, a Java-based application that processes large datasets for enterprise customers. After deployment, users reported slow response times and intermittent system crashes. The development team ran basic print debugging but could not identify the root cause. Some logs showed high memory usage, but the issue was inconsistent across different environments.

  o **For your consideration**: What debugging tools in VS Code would be useful for diagnosing the issue? How could profiling and logging frameworks help pinpoint performance bottlenecks? What common runtime errors (e.g., memory leaks, inefficient loops) might contribute to slow performance? How could the call stack and breakpoints be used to trace execution flow and locate bottlenecks?

- **Preventing deployment failure**: *Orion Banking Solutions* is preparing to deploy *Celestial Pay*, its new Java-based payment processing system. The development team manually packaged the application into a JAR file and deployed it on a Linux server. However, users reported that transactions were failing randomly, and logs indicated a missing dependency error. Upon investigation, developers found that an external encryption library required for secure transactions was not available on the production server. The issue did not appear during development, as the library was installed locally on the developers' machines.

  o **For your consideration**: How could dependency management (using a build tool like Maven or Gradle) have prevented this issue? What manual packaging steps should have been taken to ensure all required JAR files were included?

What strategies can be used to test deployment environments before releasing software? How can logging and exception handling help diagnose deployment failures more effectively?

- **Unit testing crisis**: *Xenon Robotics* develops autonomous drone software for industrial inspections. The company follows TDD to ensure reliable code. However, a recent software update caused a critical failure—some drones miscalculated altitude readings, leading to unstable flights. Upon reviewing the test suite, developers discovered that some unit tests were incorrectly structured. Instead of testing individual functions, some tests relied on multiple methods, making it unclear which part of the code was failing. Additionally, tests did not account for edge cases, such as negative altitude values.

    o **For your consideration**: What are the key principles of writing effective unit tests, and how could they have helped prevent this issue? Why is testing one function at a time better than testing multiple functionalities in a single unit test? How can developers ensure they include edge cases in their test scenarios? What assertions and validation techniques should be used to guarantee correct altitude calculations?

- **Debugging multithreading issues**: *Vega AI* is developing HyperVision, a Java-based real-time image recognition system for autonomous vehicles. The system uses multithreading to process multiple camera feeds simultaneously. However, during testing, the system occasionally freezes or crashes, especially under heavy load. Developers suspect that race conditions or synchronization issues are causing the instability, but the errors occur sporadically, making them difficult to reproduce. Some error logs point to shared data being modified by multiple threads at the same time.

    o **For your consideration**: What debugging strategies could help isolate concurrency issues in a multithreaded Java application? How could breakpoints and step execution be used to analyze thread behavior? What synchronization techniques (e.g., locks, synchronized methods) could prevent shared data conflicts? Why is it important to simulate high-load scenarios when testing multithreaded applications?

- **Improving software maintainability**: *Solaris HealthTech* develops *MedConnect*, a Java-based telemedicine platform that enables virtual doctor consultations. Over time, the codebase has grown large and difficult to maintain. The system is tightly coupled, making it hard to write unit tests, and debugging takes longer due to complex dependencies. The engineering team is struggling to implement new features without introducing bugs. Many unit tests fail due to hardcoded dependencies, and some critical components rely on static methods, which cannot be mocked during testing.

    o **For your consideration**: How could refactoring the code improve testability and maintainability? Why should developers avoid static methods when writing testable code? What design principles (e.g., dependency injection, interface-based programming) could improve flexibility? How could automated testing tools and build tools like Maven or Gradle streamline the testing and deployment process?

Multiple choice questions

1. **What is the primary purpose of a breakpoint in debugging?**
   a. To optimize code performance
   b. To automatically fix syntax errors
   c. To replace manual logging statements
   d. To pause code execution and inspect variable states

2. **Which of the following is not a characteristic of unit testing?**
   a. Tests should be repeatable
   b. Tests should execute quickly
   c. Tests should be focused on a specific unit of code
   d. Tests should rely on external systems such as databases

3. **What is the first step in the TDD cycle?**
   a. Refactoring the code
   b. Writing a failing test case
   c. Writing the actual implementation
   d. Running the application in production

4. **Why is dependency injection important for writing testable code?**
   a. It eliminates the need for unit testing
   b. It forces developers to write static methods
   c. It allows tests to modify global variables directly
   d. It enables replacing real dependencies with mock implementations

5. **What is the main advantage of using a build tool like Maven or Gradle?**
   a. It replaces the need for unit testing
   b. It prevents syntax errors in Java code
   c. It reduces the number of lines of code in a program
   d. It automates compilation, dependency management, testing, and deployment

Answers

1.	d.
2.	d.
3.	b.
4.	d.
5.	d.

Questions

1. Debugging is a crucial part of software development. What are some debugging strategies you have used in your own projects? How do they compare to the debugging tools available in VS Code?

2. Unit testing ensures code correctness, but tests must be well-structured to be effective. What are some common mistakes developers make when writing unit tests? How can these mistakes be avoided?

3. TDD requires writing tests before implementing functionality. Do you think this approach is practical for all types of software development? Explain your position. What are some challenges of adopting TDD in real-world projects?

4. The chapter discusses several principles of writing testable code, such as avoiding static methods and global variables. Share a scenario where violating these principles made debugging or testing difficult. How could the code have been improved?

5. This chapter explored how to manually package and deploy Java applications. In what types of projects do you think manual packaging is sufficient, and when should automation tools be introduced?

6. Build tools like Maven and Gradle automate software development processes. Share your experience with build tools. How do they compare to manually handling compilation and dependency management?

7. Think about a software bug or issue you encountered in a previous programming project. What debugging techniques did you use to resolve it? How would you approach it differently after reading this chapter?

8. Poorly structured code can be difficult to test and maintain. Based on the principles covered in this chapter, what coding practices should teams follow to ensure their applications remain maintainable over time?

9. While this chapter did not cover CI/CD in depth, how do you think automated testing fits into a CI/CD pipeline? What benefits does automation bring to software deployment?

10. This chapter discussed debugging, testing, and deployment. How do you think these three aspects of software development interact? Which do you think is the most critical for long-term software success, and why?

Challenges

The following questions are provided to self-assess your knowledge of the chapter's content and apply critical thinking to key concepts:

- **Debugging a faulty Java application**:
  - **Objective**: Improve debugging skills by identifying and fixing errors in a Java program.
  - **Activity**: You are provided with a Java program that processes and calculates student grades. However, the program has multiple errors, including syntax errors, logic errors, and runtime errors. Perform the following actions:
    - Analyze the code and use VS Code's debugging tools to identify where the errors occur.
    - Apply breakpoints, call stack inspection, and console logging to track the issue.
    - Document each error found and explain how you fixed it.
  - **Real-world applicability**: Debugging is a critical skill for any software developer. This challenge will help you become proficient in identifying, analyzing, and resolving issues in real-world applications.

- **Writing unit tests for a Java class**:
  - **Objective**: Develop and execute unit tests to validate Java methods using JUnit.
  - **Activity**: A company wants to test a Calculator class that includes methods for addition, subtraction, multiplication, and division. The company needs assurance that the class functions correctly before integrating it into their larger system. Perform the following actions:
    - Write JUnit test cases to verify each operation in the Calculator class.
    - Ensure your tests follow best practices, such as testing edge cases (e.g., division by zero).
    - Run the tests in VS Code and analyze the results.
  - **Real-world applicability**: Writing unit tests is essential for software reliability and maintainability.

- **Refactoring code for testability**:

    - **Objective**: Improve the testability of a Java program by applying best coding practices.

    - **Activity**: A company has a UserService class that directly depends on a DatabaseConnection class to fetch user data. Currently, the code is tightly coupled, making it difficult to test. Perform the following actions:

        - Refactor the UserService class to use dependency injection instead of directly instantiating DatabaseConnection.

        - Modify the class so it can work with mock implementations in unit tests.

        - Write JUnit tests to verify that the refactored class functions correctly.

    - **Real-world applicability**: By applying dependency injection and testability principles, you can learn how to write flexible and maintainable code, a key skill in professional software development.

- **Creating a runnable JAR file**:

    - **Objective**: Package a Java application into a JAR file and make it executable.

    - **Activity**: Write a Java program called TaskManager.java that helps users track their daily tasks. Your goal is to:

        - Compile the program into a .class file.

        - Create a manifest file specifying the main class.

        - Package everything into a JAR file that can be executed using java -jar.

        - Run the JAR file and verify that the program executes correctly.

    - **Real-world applicability**: Many applications are distributed as JAR files. Learning to create and execute them can help prepare you for deploying standalone Java applications.

- **Implementing TDD**:

    - **Objective**: Practice TDD by writing tests before implementing functionality.

    - **Activity**: A company needs a String utils class that provides a method to capitalize the first letter of a string. The company follows a TDD approach. Your task is to:

        - Write a failing JUnit test that expects the method capitalizeFirstLetter("java") to return Java.

        - Implement the simplest possible method to make the test pass.

        - Refactor the method to handle edge cases, such as empty strings or null values.

■ Add new tests to validate the updated method.

o **Real-world applicability**: TDD is widely used in professional software development to ensure code is written efficiently and correctly. This challenge can help you understand how to build reliable applications through iterative testing.

Self-assessment

The following questions are provided so you can self-assess your knowledge of the chapter's content and apply critical thinking to key concepts:

1. What are the three main types of errors in Java, and how does each impact debugging?

2. How does writing testable code improve software maintainability? Provide an example of a practice that enhances testability.

3. What is the purpose of a JAR file in Java, and what steps are required to create a runnable JAR file?

4. Explain the red-green-refactor cycle in TDD. Why is this methodology beneficial in software development?

5. Imagine you are deploying a Java application, and a user reports that it fails to run due to a missing dependency. What steps would you take to troubleshoot and resolve this issue?

Answers

1. **Three types of errors in Java**:

   a. **Syntax errors**: These occur due to incorrect Java syntax, such as missing semicolons or mismatched parentheses. They are detected at compile time and must be fixed before execution.

   b. **Runtime errors**: These occur while the program is running and typically involve exceptions. They require proper exception handling and debugging.

   c. **Logic errors**: These are the most challenging to detect because the program runs without crashing, but the output is incorrect. Debugging techniques such as breakpoints, logging, and step execution help identify these issues.

2. **Importance of writing testable code**:

   a. Writing testable code makes it easier to modify and maintain software over time. It allows for better unit testing, reduces dependencies, and improves debugging efficiency.

b. Example of a practice that enhances testability: Using dependency injection instead of hardcoded dependencies. This allows for simulating dependencies in unit tests, making it easier to test individual components in isolation.

3. **Purpose and creation of a runnable JAR file**:

   a. **Purpose**: A JAR file packages compiled Java classes and resources into a single distributable file. It allows Java applications to be executed on any system with a Java runtime.

   b. **Steps**:

   i. Compile the Java files into bytecode (.class files).

   ii. Create a manifest file specifying the main class.

   iii. Use the JAR tool to package the files into a JAR.

   iv. Run the application using java -jar filename.jar.

4. **Red-green-refactor cycle in TDD**:

   a. **Red**: Write a test case that fails because the functionality has not yet been implemented.

   b. **Green**: Write the minimum amount of code needed to pass the test.

   c. **Refactor**: Improve the code structure while ensuring the test still passes.

   d. **Benefits of TDD**:

   i. Ensures all features have corresponding tests.

   ii. Leads to better software design by encouraging modular, maintainable code.

   iii. Reduces debugging time, as issues are caught early in development.

5. **Troubleshooting a missing dependency in deployment**:

   a. Check the error message to determine which dependency is missing.

   b. Verify that the required JAR files are included in the project directory.

   c. If using manual dependency management, ensure the classpath includes all required dependencies.

   d. If using a build tool (like Maven or Gradle), confirm that all dependencies are correctly listed and resolved.

   e. Test deployment on a clean environment to mimic real-world usage and prevent local configuration dependencies.

Join our Discord space

Join our Discord workspace for latest updates, offers, tech happenings around the world, new releases, and sessions with the authors:

https://discord.bpbonline.com

CHAPTER 14
Real-world Java Projects

Introduction

The previous chapters explored Java from foundational principles to advanced concepts. This included **object-oriented programming (OOP)**, concurrency, database interactions, and functional programming. This chapter gives you the opportunity to put all the previously covered content into practice by developing real-world Java projects. Each project is designed to strengthen your skills, allowing you to apply theoretical knowledge in real-world scenarios. There are four distinct projects to include a simple command-line application, a database application, a multithreaded data processor, and a program using functional programming with streams and lambdas. Each project will include a project overview and requirements, design, implementation, testing, and project extension. These hands-on projects can reinforce your understanding and build your confidence in developing robust, efficient, and user-friendly Java applications.

Structure

This chapter covers the following topics:

- Building a simple command-line application
- Developing a basic database application

- Building a multithreaded data processor

- Writing a functional program using streams and lambdas

Objectives

By the end of this chapter, you should be able to design and implement a simple command-line Java application, develop a database-driven Java application, build a multithreaded data processor, and write a functional programming application using Java Streams and lambdas.

Building a simple command-line application

This project requires us to build a simple text-based adventure game where players navigate through a short interactive story by making decisions. The game consists of three sequential rooms, with the player's choices affecting the final outcome. The last room determines whether they achieve a good or bad ending based on their previous decisions.

This project helps reinforce fundamental Java concepts, including:

- Handling user input via the console

- Using conditional statements

- Apply loops

The game's requirements are:

- The game starts in Room 1, where the player makes an initial decision.

- Room 1 leads to Room 2, where another decision must be made.

- Room 2 leads to Room 3, the final challenge before determining the outcome.

- In Room 3, the player's previous decisions influence the final outcome (good or bad ending).

- The game provides text-based feedback for each decision.

- The game loops back to the beginning if the player wants to replay.

Design

As illustrated in *Figure 14.1*, the game will follow a simple decision tree structure:

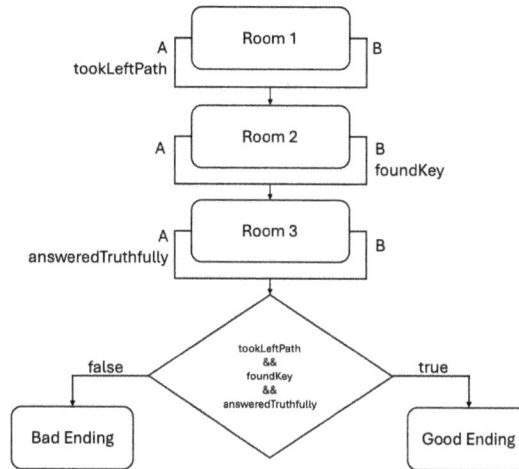

Figure 14.1: *Game flow diagram*

Table 14.1 provides details regarding the options in each room:

Room	Scenario	Choice	variable	Outcome
1	You find yourself in a dark cave and see two paths.	A—take the left path	`tookLeftPath = true`	Move to Room 2
		B—take the right path		
2	You find a locked door.	A—knock		Move to Room 3
		B—look for the key	`foundKey = true`	
3	A mysterious figure asks you to solve a riddle	A—answer truthfully	`answeredTruthfully = true`	Determines good or bad ending
		B—lie		

Table 14.1: *Game decision map*

Review of the game's flow and user options reveals they need to make the following decisions to result in a good ending (escape from the cave); any variation from this results in the bad ending (trapdoor).

- Take the left path from Room 1

- Look for the key in Room 2

- Answer truthfully in Room 3

Implementation

The following is the Java implementation of the simple text-based adventure game:

```java
import java.util.Scanner;

public class AdventureGame {

    public static void main(String[] args) {
        Scanner scanner = new Scanner(System.in);
        boolean playAgain;

        do {
            playAgain = false; // Reset game state
            System.out.println("\nWelcome to the Command-Line\nText-Based Adventure Game!\n");
            System.out.println("You find yourself in a dark cave.");

            // Room 1
            System.out.println("Room 1: You see two paths. Do you take the left path (A) or the right path (B)?");
            String choice1 = scanner.nextLine().trim().toUpperCase();
            boolean tookLeftPath = choice1.equals("A");

            // Room 2
            System.out.println("Room 2: You find a locked door. Do you knock (A) or look around for a key (B)?");
            String choice2 = scanner.nextLine().trim().toUpperCase();
            boolean foundKey = choice2.equals("B");

            // Room 3
            System.out.println("Room 3: A mysterious figure asks you to solve a riddle.");
            System.out.println("Do you answer truthfully (A) or lie (B)?");
            String choice3 = scanner.nextLine().trim().toUpperCase();
            boolean answeredTruthfully = choice3.equals("A");

            // Determine ending
            if (tookLeftPath && foundKey && answeredTruthfully) {
                System.out.println("Congratulations! The figure rewards your honesty. You escape the cave safely!");
```

```
        } else {
            System.out.println("The mysterious figure shakes their head. A
trapdoor opens beneath you!");
            System.out.println("Game Over.");
        }

        // Replay option
        System.out.println("Would you like to play again? (yes/no)");
        String replayChoice = scanner.nextLine().trim().toLowerCase();
        if (replayChoice.equals("yes")) {
            playAgain = true;
        }

    } while (playAgain);

    System.out.println("Thanks for playing!");
    scanner.close();
    }
}
```

Here are the concepts we implemented in our application:

- User input
- User decision-based program flow
- Loops
- String handling

Testing

This project consisted of a command-line game, which is very basic. We still need to test our application, and manual testing is sufficient. To test this program, run the program and enter different inputs to check if the outcome is correct. Here are the test cases to test:

Table 14.2 shows left path scenarios to test and the anticipated outcomes. You should also test all test cases that start with the right path decision.

Test case	Expected ending
Left path; look for the key; answer truthfully	Good
Left path; look for the key; lie	Bad
Left path; knock; answer truthfully	Bad
Left path; knock; lie	Bad

Table 14.2: *Manual test cases*

Extending the project

The project meets all required specifications. If you want to extend this project to stretch your Java muscles, here are some suggestions:

- Add more rooms.
- Introduce inventory management.
- Implement random events.
- Add time-based choices.
- Include scoring and heath components.
- Add a text-based display to show score, health, inventory, and map.

Developing a basic database application

Our second project requires us to build a **pet medical record system** (**PMRS**). This will be a command-line database application that tracks pets, their medical visits, and any medications prescribed. This real-world inspired system simulates a lightweight veterinary clinic management tool that is designed to give you practical experience with Java and SQLite integration.

Our goal is to create PMSR to permit users to perform the following:

- Add, view, edit, and delete pet records.
- Record medical visits and associate them with pets.
- Track prescribed medications for each pet.
- Navigate a menu-based interface that loops until the user exits.

The application's requirements are:

- Use SQLite for persistent storage in a file named **pmrs.db**.
- Include three tables: **Pets**, **MedicalVisits**, and **Medications**.

- Implement full **Create, Read, Update, and Delete (CRUD)** functionality for each table.

- Use Java's native JDBC API to connect and interact with the database.

- Interface is command-line based, using menus and text prompts.

Design

There are two aspects to our design: database schema and user interface. *Figure 14.2* shows the database schema:

	Field	Type	Description
Table: Pets	pet_id	INTEGER PRIMARY KEY	Unique identifier for the pet
	name	TEXT	Pet's name
	species	TEXT	Species (e.g., Dog, Cat)
	breed	TEXT	Breed (optional)
	age	INTEGER	Age in years
	owner_name	TEXT	Pet owner's full name

	Field	Type	Description
Table: MedicalVisits	visit_id	INTEGER PRIMARY KEY	Unique identifier for the visit
	pet_id	INTEGER	Foreign key to Pets
	visit_date	TEXT	Date of the visit (ISO format)
	reason	TEXT	Reason for the visit
	notes	TEXT	Notes from the veterinarian

	Field	Type	Description
Table: Medications	med_id	INTEGER PRIMARY KEY	Unique medication ID
	visit_id	INTEGER	Foreign key to MedicalVisits
	name	TEXT	Medication name
	dosage	TEXT	Dosage instructions

Figure 14.2: PMRS database schema

Next, we need to design our user interface. *Figure 14.3* shows the text menu system that we will use for this application:

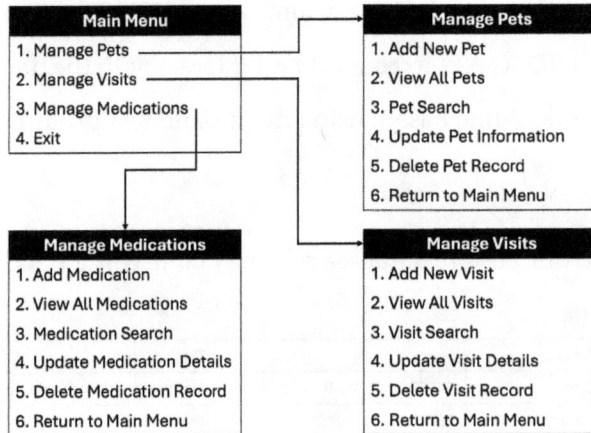

Figure 14.3: PMRS menu design

Implementation

We now have our system requirements, our database schema, and our user interface designed. Our first implementation step is to create the database.

Database initialization

We can create a **PMRSDatabaseInitializer.java** class to create our database and its tables. Here is that code:

```java
import java.sql.Connection;
import java.sql.DriverManager;
import java.sql.SQLException;
import java.sql.Statement;

public class PMRSDatabaseInitializer {

    private static final String DB_URL = "jdbc:sqlite:pmrs.db";

    public static void main(String[] args) {
        try (Connection conn = DriverManager.getConnection(DB_URL)) {
            if (conn != null) {
                createTables(conn);
                System.out.println("Database and tables created
successfully.");
            }
```

```
        } catch (SQLException e) {
            System.out.println("Error initializing database: " +
e.getMessage());
        }
    }


    private static void createTables(Connection conn) throws SQLException {
        Statement stmt = conn.createStatement();

        // Create Pets Table
        String createPetsTable = """
            CREATE TABLE IF NOT EXISTS Pets (
                pet_id INTEGER PRIMARY KEY AUTOINCREMENT,
                name TEXT NOT NULL,
                species TEXT NOT NULL,
                breed TEXT,
                age INTEGER,
                owner_name TEXT NOT NULL
            );
        """;


        // Create MedicalVisits Table
        String createVisitsTable = """
            CREATE TABLE IF NOT EXISTS MedicalVisits (
                visit_id INTEGER PRIMARY KEY AUTOINCREMENT,
                pet_id INTEGER NOT NULL,
                visit_date TEXT NOT NULL,
                reason TEXT,
                notes TEXT,
                FOREIGN KEY(pet_id) REFERENCES Pets(pet_id)
            );
        """;


        // Create Medications Table
        String createMedicationsTable = """
            CREATE TABLE IF NOT EXISTS Medications (
                med_id INTEGER PRIMARY KEY AUTOINCREMENT,
                visit_id INTEGER NOT NULL,
                name TEXT NOT NULL,
```

```
            dosage TEXT,
            FOREIGN KEY(visit_id) REFERENCES MedicalVisits(visit_id)
        );
    """;

    stmt.execute(createPetsTable);
    stmt.execute(createVisitsTable);
    stmt.execute(createMedicationsTable);
    stmt.close();
    }
}
```

We can run our **PMRSDatabaseInitializer.java** class by following these steps:

1. Copy the **sqlite.jar** file you obtained in *Chapter 10, Database Connectivity*, into your PMRS project folder.

2. Compile the **.java** file with this command:
    javac -cp ".:sqlite-jdbc-3.49.0.0.jar" PMRSDatabaseInitializer.java

3. Run the class with this command:
    java -cp ".:sqlite-jdbc-3.49.0.0.jar" PMRSDatabaseInitializer

You should receive the following console message:
Database and tables created successfully.

You should also see **pmrs.db** (our database) in the project folder.

Menu system

Now that our database has been initialized, let us build our menu system. We will create a skeleton menu where the menu options work, but there is no functionality yet. To achieve our goal, we will use loops and switch statements for menu navigation. We will also add placeholder messages to simulate future functionality.

Here is the skeleton menu system (note the code has been abbreviated; full code is available in the GitHub repository):

```
import java.util.Scanner;

public class PMRSMenuSystem {

    private static final Scanner scanner = new Scanner(System.in);

    public static void main(String[] args) {
```

```java
        boolean exit = false;

        while (!exit) { } // call showMainMenu() and process user input
        scanner.close();
    }

    // Main Menu
    private static void showMainMenu() {
        System.out.println("\n=== Pet Medical Record System ===");
        System.out.println("1. Manage Pets");
        System.out.println("2. Manage Medical Visits");
        System.out.println("3. Manage Medications");
        System.out.println("4. Exit");
        System.out.print("Enter your choice: ");
    }

    // Pets Menu
    private static void managePetsMenu() { }

    // Visits Menu
    private static void manageVisitsMenu() { }

    // Medications Menu
    private static void manageMedicationsMenu() { }

    // Input Helper
    private static int getUserChoice() {
        while (!scanner.hasNextInt()) {
            System.out.print("Please enter a valid number: ");
            scanner.next(); // discard non-integer input
        }
        return scanner.nextInt();
    }
}
```

It is a good idea to test your menu system to ensure it works as expected. As you can see, we created a simple interface, as follows:

=== Pet Medical Record System ===

1. Manage Pets

```
2. Manage Medical Visits
3. Manage Medications
4. Exit

Enter your choice:
```

Adding functionality

We can now implement the functionality associated with the manage pet's menu item. We will create a **PetManager.java** class to contain that functionality.

> Note: **Source code for this class is not printed here for brevity and is available from the book's GitHub repository.**

In a similar fashion, we also need to create a **VisitManager.java** class to support the manage medical visits menu item. This will include all sub-menu functionality.

Our last class is **MedicationManager.java** to support the **Manage Medications** menu item and sub-menu functionality.

Now, we need to update **PMRSMenuSystem.java** so the menu items point to the new classes we created.

Find the main switch block and update it as shown here:

```
switch (choice) {
    case 1 -> PetManager.showMenu(scanner);
    case 2 -> VisitManager.showMenu(scanner);
    case 3 -> MedicationManager.showMenu(scanner);
    case 4 -> {
        System.out.println("Exiting application. Goodbye!");
        exit = true;
    }
    default -> System.out.println("Invalid choice. Please try again.");
}
```

Our system is now fully functional.

Testing

We can manually test our PMRS application because it uses a command-line interface and a local SQLite database. To perform the tests, we simply need to test each menu and sub-menu option. While manual testing can be laborious, we have limited functionality, so it can be accomplished quickly. Be sure to test every option for desired functionality. You can consider creating a checklist to ensure no stone is unturned. Try to break (make your app crash) your code.

Extending the project

The project meets all required specifications. If you want to extend this project to stretch your Java muscles, here are some suggestions:

- **Add features such as**:
  - Ability to search pets by owner's name or species.
  - Sorting by age, bread, or name.
  - Add pet gender.
  - Add a record flag for active/inactive.
  - Add reports for full records.
  - Provide a report of pets without a recorded visit.

- **Add data validation for all user input**.

- **Enhance the user experience**:
  - Add confirmation prompts.
  - All users to clear or reset input.
  - Generate printable reports for pet owners.

- **Change the UI from text-based to graphical**.

Building a multithreaded data processor

Our third project calls for a multithreaded word frequency counter. It should read and analyze a large text file using Java threads. Our program will split the file into smaller chunks and assign each chunk to a thread. Each thread will count how often each word appears. After all threads complete, the main thread will merge the results and output the total number of unique words found. We will prompt the user to determine how many words they want to see in the output.

This project is designed to provide you with hands-on experience in the following areas:

- Creating and managing multiple threads.
- Using thread-safe collections and synchronization.
- Coordinating work and aggregating results in a multithreaded context.

The application's requirements are:

- Accept a single large **.txt** file as input.
- Divide the file into line-based segments (one per thread).
- Create one thread per segment to compute word frequencies.

- Merge the results into a single master word frequency map.
- Output the total number of unique words.
- Prompt the user to specify how many of the most frequent words they want to see.
- Output word frequency based on user specification.

Design

We will use the producer-worker model, where each worker thread will have a subset of the input data, independent of all other threads. There will be two classes:

- **WordFrequencyCounter**: This will be our main class; it will handle:
  - Reading the input file.
  - Creating threads.
  - Aggregating results.
- **WordCountWorker**: This will implement the **Runnable** interface.
  - It will accept a list of lines and calculate word frequencies.
  - It will maintain a local **Map<String, Integer>** to be merged by the main thread.

Note: **Runnable is a functional interface that represents a thread-executable task.**

There are a couple of other design issues we need to consider before building our applications:

- We will strip punctuation from our text.
- Word matching will be case-insensitive.
- There will be a fixed number of lines assigned to each thread.
- We will use **thread.join()** to ensure all threads have finished before we aggregate the results.

Figure 14.4 illustrates our program's flow:

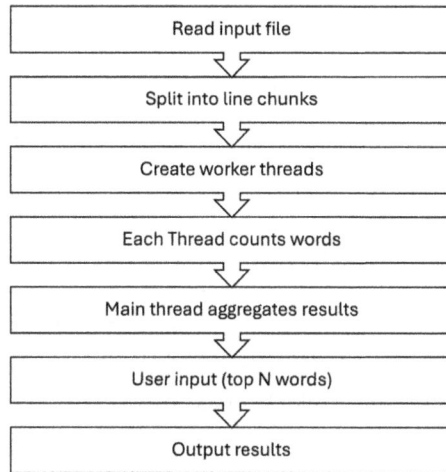

Figure 14.4: *Program flow*

Implementation

Here is our main class:

```java
import java.io.*;
import java.util.*;

public class WordFrequencyCounter {

    private static final int LINES_PER_THREAD = 500;

    public static void main(String[] args) {
        Scanner scanner = new Scanner(System.in);

        System.out.print("Enter path to the text file: ");
        String filePath = scanner.nextLine();

        List<String> allLines = new ArrayList<>();

        // Read the file into memory
        try (BufferedReader reader = new BufferedReader(new
FileReader(filePath))) {
            String line;
            while ((line = reader.readLine()) != null) {
                allLines.add(line);
```

```java
        }
    } catch (IOException e) {
        System.out.println("Error reading file: " + e.getMessage());
        return;
    }

    // Split lines into chunks
    List<List<String>> chunks = new ArrayList<>();
    for (int i = 0; i < allLines.size(); i += LINES_PER_THREAD) {
        int end = Math.min(i + LINES_PER_THREAD, allLines.size());
        chunks.add(allLines.subList(i, end));
    }

    // Process chunks with threads
    List<WordCountWorker> workers = new ArrayList<>();
    List<Thread> threads = new ArrayList<>();

    for (List<String> chunk : chunks) {
        WordCountWorker worker = new WordCountWorker(chunk);
        Thread thread = new Thread(worker);
        workers.add(worker);
        threads.add(thread);
        thread.start();
    }

    // Wait for all threads to complete
    for (Thread thread : threads) {
        try {
            thread.join();
        } catch (InterruptedException e) {
            System.out.println("Thread interrupted: " + e.getMessage());
        }
    }

    // Merge results
    Map<String, Integer> finalWordCounts = new HashMap<>();
    for (WordCountWorker worker : workers) {
        Map<String, Integer> localMap = worker.getWordCounts();
        for (Map.Entry<String, Integer> entry : localMap.entrySet()) {
```

```
                    finalWordCounts.merge(entry.getKey(), entry.getValue(),
Integer::sum);
            }
        }

        System.out.println("Total unique words: " + finalWordCounts.size());
        System.out.print("How many top frequent words would you like to see?
");
        int topN = scanner.nextInt();

        // Sort and display
        finalWordCounts.entrySet().stream()
                .sorted((a, b) -> b.getValue().compareTo(a.getValue()))
                .limit(topN)
                .forEach(e -> System.out.printf("%-20s %d%n", e.getKey(),
e.getValue()));
    }
}
```

Your IDE might give you a warning that the **Scanner** is not closed. In our case, we use it to get user input from **System.in**. If we closed the **Scanner**, it would also close **System.in**, which we do not want to close because it cannot be reopened, and it might be needed later in the program, if you plan to extend its functionality. We can suppress this warning by putting the following before our **main()** method: **@SuppressWarnings("resource")**.

The output of our application is provided as follows:

```
Enter path to the text file: input.txt
Total unique words: 12485
How many top frequent words would you like to see? 10
the                 8308
and                 7019
i                   6418
to                  5135
of                  4544
a                   4036
in                  3051
that                2973
was                 2824
it                  2647
```

The **input.txt** file used for this run was a public domain book with over 20,000 lines of code.

Note: **The `input.txt` file is not provided as part of this book's code distribution due to international restrictions. You can obtain public domain books in text form from https:// www.gutenberg.org/**

You will note how quickly the application runs, a credit to multithreading.

Testing

This application can be manually tested. Here are some suggested tests:

- Use a variety of different input sources, varying in size/length.
- Provide an empty file to see what happens.
- Test a small file.
- Test a large file.
- Test the same file with different user input for the number of words they want to see.
- Double-check that words with punctuation are handled appropriately.
- Ensure that lower case, upper case, and mixed case are all treated the same.
- Ensure non-alphabetic characters are properly handled.

Extending the project

The project meets all required specifications. If you want to extend this project to stretch your Java muscles, here are some suggestions:

- Allow users to determine the number of threads.
- Output full results via **`.txt`** or **`.csv`** file.
- Add the option to filter out common words such as *a, is, I,* and *the.*
- Display percentages in addition to word counts.
- Track total word count in addition to unique words.
- Provide visual output such as a bar or pie chart.
- Add an interactive search option for specific word counts.

Writing a functional program using streams and lambdas

In this final project, we will build a **City Population Explorer** (CPE) application. It will be a functional Java application that reads a dataset of world cities. It will also allow users to run queries using streams and lambdas. The dataset includes each city's name, state, country, population, and area (in square miles). Users can explore the data by filtering cities, calculating population densities, and identifying cities with the highest and lowest densities.

This project was designed to reinforce your knowledge and comfort level with the following:

- Functional-style data processing using stream pipelines.
- Use of **filter()**, **map()**, **sorted()**, **collect()**, and **reduce()** methods.
- Working with lambda expressions and method references.
- Using collectors such as **groupingBy()**, **toList()**, and **averagingDouble()**.

The application's requirements are:

- Read data from a **.csv** file.
- Allow users to:
  - Filter cities by country, state, or population.
  - Compute and sort by population density.
  - Display the top or bottom *N* cities by density.
  - View average population per country.
- Use only Java's functional APIs.

Design

Our application will use a functional approach to process city data. We will first load the dataset into memory from a csv file assumed to be in the project's root folder. Next, we will present users with options to perform queries and aggregations using a stream-based, menu-driven interface.

The core components of our CPE application will be:

- **City class**: This will be used to represent each city's information.
- **CityPopulationExplorer class**: This will be our main class. We will use it to load data, handle menu input, and process queries using streams.

CPE will support the following operations:

- Filter by country or state.
- Filter cities above/below a population threshold.
- Compute and display population density.
- Sort cities by density.

- Show top *N* or bottom *N* cities by density.

- Calculate the average population by country.

Implementation

Here is our implementation (note the code has been abbreviated; full code is available in the GitHub repository):

```java
import java.io.*;
import java.nio.file.*;
import java.util.*;
import java.util.function.*;
import java.util.stream.*;

public class CityPopulationExplorer {

    static class City { }

    public static void main(String[] args) {
        List<City> cities = loadCities("city_population_data.csv");
        if (cities.isEmpty()) {
            System.out.println("No cities loaded. Exiting.");
            return;
        }

        Scanner scanner = new Scanner(System.in);
        while (true) { } // show menu
    }

    private static List<City> loadCities(String fileName) { }
}
```

The output of our code is shown as follows:

```
--- City Population Explorer ---
1. Filter cities by country
2. Filter cities by state
3. Filter cities by minimum population
4. Show top N cities by population density
5. Show bottom N cities by population density
6. Show average population per country
```

```
7. Exit
Choose an option:
```

Testing

We can manually test our CPE population. Simply test each menu item with different (valid and invalid) input. You can compare results based on the **city_population_data.csv** file that accompanies this book's code repository.

Extending the project

The project meets all required specifications. If you want to extend this project to stretch your Java muscles, here are some suggestions:

- Add filtering by both country and minimum population together.
- Sort cities by name, area, or raw population.
- Give the user the option of miles or kilometers for area units.
- Display max and min population densities per country.
- Give the user the option to export filtered or sorted results to a file.
- Allow keyword search on city names.
- Visualize data with charts.
- Add additional data fields to the input file.

Conclusion

This chapter was designed to let you practice many of the concepts presented in this book through the development of four distinct Java projects. Each project was designed to reinforce key programming concepts while helping you gain confidence in applying them to real-world situations.

Our first project was a command-line adventure game, using conditionals, loops, and user input to build a simple interactive experience. The second project was a PMRS, which used a relational database, JDBC, and implemented database CRUD operations. The third project was a multithreaded word frequency counter, designed to give you practice managing threads, coordinating workloads, and safely aggregating results from concurrent processes. Our final project was a CPE application, featuring functional programming, streams, lambdas, and collectors.

The projects gave you the opportunity to design, implement, test, and extend the four applications. Hopefully, you worked through these projects and deepened your understanding of Java.

The next chapter serves as a conclusion to this book. It recaps the key concepts covered in the book and provides guidance on how to continue learning Java beyond this book. The chapter includes advice on preparing for industry certifications, along with resources to further deepen your knowledge. The chapter also looks ahead to trends in Java development, helping to ensure you stay current in this fast-evolving field.

Points to remember

- A Runnable implementation allows us to define tasks that can be executed by threads.

- Avoid closing Scanner objects linked to System.in to prevent input stream closure errors.

- Clean code architecture benefits from separating logic into dedicated classes.

- Command-line interfaces can be used to simulate interactive menus.

- Collectors like groupingBy, averagingInt, and toList are used for data aggregation in streams.

- CSV data can be easily parsed and mapped to objects using Java I/O and streams.

- Database initialization should be done before any data operations in JDBC-based projects.

- Functional programming in Java promotes concise, declarative code using streams and lambdas.

- Functional stream operations include map, filter, reduce, sorted, and collect.

- Functional-style avoids explicit loops in favor of higher-order operations.

- Joining threads with thread.join() ensures that results from concurrent processes are not aggregated prematurely.

- Lambdas simplify the implementation of interfaces like Runnable and Comparator.

- Local variables used within lambdas must be effectively final.

- Multithreaded applications require safe aggregation of results using thread-safe or isolated local data.

- Multithreaded programs can divide large inputs into chunks to process them concurrently.

- Parameterized queries in JDBC are essential for secure and reliable data interaction.

- Sorting in streams can be done using a Comparator and method references for cleaner syntax.

- SQL foreign key constraints maintain referential integrity between related tables, like pets and visits.

- Stream pipelines can be chained to transform and analyze data efficiently.

- String handling techniques such as trim(), toUpperCase(), and replaceAll() help sanitize input and text.

- Threads are assigned subsets of work and run independently in a producer-worker model.

- Use try-with-resources when reading files to ensure that all streams are properly closed.

- Using switch-case with lambda-style -> requires braces {} for multi-line operations.

Case studies

These case studies provide realistic scenarios that encourage you to think critically about the concepts and techniques used throughout this chapter:

- **Choose your adventure**: *Zarnex Security*, a startup focused on gamified cybersecurity training, is prototyping a console-based simulation to onboard junior analysts. The team wants to design a decision-based scenario that tests users' ethical choices during simulated breaches. The developers consider adapting the text-based adventure game model you built in Project 1.

    o **For your consideration**: What design changes would be needed to support multiple branching paths and realistic outcomes? How could the game be extended to include a scoring system or progress tracking? What data structures might support a more dynamic decision tree?

- **PMRS**: *Andaril Veterinary Network* operates 10 clinics across two states and is currently tracking patient data manually. They need a lightweight, local application for each location that can store pet medical histories and be used by front-desk staff with minimal training. You are asked to evaluate the PMRS prototype from Project 2 for deployment.

    o **For your consideration**: What enhancements would be required to ensure data consistency and usability across clinics? What are the risks of using a local SQLite database in this context? How could this system be adapted for a multi-user environment?

- **Word usage analyzer**: *GalacTech Education* wants to help language learners analyze their writing. They propose a tool that can process essays and highlight overused or repetitive words. The team has reviewed the word frequency counter from Project 3 and wants to adapt it for educational use.

- **For your consideration**: How could the tool be modified to exclude common stop words? What visual features or output formats would make the feedback more helpful for learners? How might the threading model be adjusted for smaller documents?

- **City comparison dashboard**: *Vorta Urban Analytics* is building a report tool for urban planners to evaluate city growth and density patterns. They want to base the core of their data processor on the CPE application from Project 4, using real city datasets updated quarterly.

  - **For your consideration**: How would you scale the current application to handle larger datasets and richer queries? How could functional programming techniques be used to support additional filters (e.g., year-over-year population growth)? What trade-offs exist between performance and readability in stream-based processing?

- **Developer training bootcamp**: *Ordanis Tech Solutions* runs a Java developer bootcamp and is considering using all four projects from this chapter as progressive assignments. The curriculum designers ask for advice on how to scaffold the learning experience and track each student's progress.

  - **For your consideration**: How would you structure the assignments to build on one another conceptually? What challenges might learners face when transitioning from imperative to functional programming? How could test cases and rubrics be incorporated to support both learning and evaluation?

Multiple choice questions

1. **What is the primary purpose of the join() method in a multithreaded Java program?**
   a. To start multiple threads concurrently
   b. To prevent one thread from accessing another's variables
   c. To wait for a thread to finish execution before continuing
   d. To terminate all threads simultaneously

2. **Which Java feature is used in the CPE application to calculate the average population by country?**
   a. Collectors.partitioningBy()
   b. Collectors.groupingBy() with Collectors.averagingInt()
   c. Collectors.mapping()
   d. Collectors.reducing()

3. **In the PMRS, what is the purpose of using foreign key constraints in the database schema?**

   a. To ensure data integrity between related tables

   b. To enforce alphabetical sorting of records

   c. To automatically encrypt sensitive data

   d. To enable faster file reading

4. **Which of the following is an advantage of using a menu-based interface in a command-line application?**

   a. It reduces the need for data validation

   b. It simplifies the use of JavaFX libraries

   c. It provides structured user navigation and control

   d. It automatically supports graphical output

5. **What is the main benefit of using streams and lambdas in Java applications?**

   a. They eliminate the need for variables

   b. They allow complex logic to be written without classes

   c. They provide a functional approach for cleaner and more concise data processing

   d. They are required for database interaction

Answers

1.	c.
2.	b.
3.	a.
4.	c.
5.	c.

Questions

1. In the text-based adventure game, how might the user experience change if more decision branches and randomized events were added? What would be the programming challenges involved?

2. What are the pros and cons of using a local SQLite database versus a centralized cloud-based database in applications like the PMRS?

3. How does the use of a menu-driven interface affect the usability of command-line applications? What improvements would you suggest to make the PMRS more user-friendly?

4. The word frequency counter uses a multithreaded approach to improve performance. In what scenarios might multithreading be unnecessary or even harmful?

5. When merging results from multiple threads, what strategies can help ensure accuracy and thread-safety? How does the use of local maps in each thread help?

6. In the CPE project, how does functional programming improve readability and maintainability compared to traditional loops? What are the trade-offs?

7. How might you modify the CPE to support dynamic user queries (e.g., combining filters for population and region)? What functional constructs would you use?

8. Discuss how separating functionality into distinct classes (e.g., PetManager, VisitManager) in the PMRS project demonstrates principles of modularity and maintainability in software design.

9. Which of the four projects did you find most engaging or useful, and why? How would you apply what you learned from it to a different real-world problem?

10. What did you find most challenging about working with streams and lambdas in Java? How did those challenges affect the way you wrote or thought about your code?

Challenges

The following questions are provided to self-assess your knowledge of the chapter's content and apply critical thinking to key concepts:

- **Choose your own outcome**:
  - **Objective**: Apply conditional logic and user input handling to build a custom branching narrative.
  - **Activity**: Perform the following actions:
    - Using the code structure from the text-based adventure game in Project 1, create a new story with at least four decision points and two possible endings.
    - Incorporate meaningful decisions that affect the outcome, and structure your program using variables to track player choices.
    - **Real-world applicability**: This challenge can help you develop branching logic and improve your ability to structure user interactions, which is essential in game design, training simulations, and decision-support systems.

- **Visit summary report**:
  - ○ **Objective**: Enhance the PMRS by adding a useful reporting feature.
  - ○ **Activity**: Perform the following actions:
    - ▪ Modify your PMRS application to include a new option in the main menu that generates a visit summary report for a specific pet.
    - ▪ Prompt the user for the pet ID, retrieve all visits associated with that pet, and display each visit's date, reason, and notes in a readable format.
  - ○ **Real-world applicability**: Veterinary staff and medical professionals often need to retrieve a patient's full visit history on demand. This challenge is intended to strengthen your ability to query databases and format data for review.

- **Custom thread configuration**:
  - ○ **Objective**: Extend the word frequency counter to allow user-defined threading.
  - ○ **Activity**: Perform the following actions:
    - ▪ Update your word frequency counter to prompt the user for how many threads to use (e.g., 2, 4, or 8).
    - ▪ Based on that input, divide the file's lines accordingly.
    - ▪ Implement error handling to ensure the number of threads is valid (e.g., not greater than the number of lines).
    - ▪ Document your assumptions and changes.
  - ○ **Real-world applicability**: Being able to adjust parallelism based on system capabilities or input size is common in data processing and performance tuning tasks.

- **Population density filter**:
  - ○ **Objective**: Implement flexible filtering logic using streams.
  - ○ **Activity**: Perform the following actions:
    - ▪ Enhance the CPE to let the user filter cities by a minimum population density value (e.g., only show cities with density > 5,000 people per square mile).
    - ▪ Add this option as a new menu item.
    - ▪ Use Java Streams to apply the filter and display the results in descending order by density.

- Real-world applicability: Filtering datasets based on custom numeric thresholds is common in analytics, business intelligence, and civic planning applications.

- **Data integrity in the PMRS**:

  - **Objective**: Improve database safety through application-level logic.

  - **Activity**: Perform the following actions:

    - Modify the PMRS so that when the user tries to delete a pet record, the application checks if that pet has any associated visits.

    - If so, display a warning and prevent deletion.

    - If there are no visits, proceed with deletion.

  - **Real-world applicability**: Many applications must enforce data integrity rules without relying solely on the database. This challenge asks you to write validation logic that protects critical records.

Self-assessment

The following questions are provided so you can self-assess your knowledge of the chapter's content and apply critical thinking to key concepts:

1. What are the advantages of using a text-based menu system in a Java application like the PMRS?

2. How does multithreading improve the performance of the word frequency counter project, and what are the potential risks if not implemented correctly?

3. In functional programming with Java Streams, what is the role of the collect() method, and how does it differ from reduce()?

4. Reflect on the four projects in this chapter. Which one best helped you understand the importance of code organization and modularity, and why?

5. Imagine you are building a tool to process student grades across multiple courses. How could the stream and lambda techniques used in the CPE be adapted for that purpose?

Answers

1. **Advantages of text-based menu systems**: Text-based menus are easy to implement using basic Java constructs like loops and switch statements. They provide a structured way for users to navigate an application without a graphical interface. This approach is ideal for command-line tools where simplicity, quick data entry, and low resource usage are priorities. It also makes it easier to test each function independently and allows new developers to understand and modify the program flow.

2. **Multithreading benefits and risks**: Multithreading enables the word frequency counter to process large text files faster by splitting the workload across multiple threads. Each thread handles a portion of the data independently, which can significantly reduce runtime on multi-core systems. However, improper use of shared data structures can lead to race conditions, inaccurate results, or crashes. To avoid these risks, thread-safe designs (like using local maps for word counting and merging afterward) are crucial.

3. **Understanding** collect() **vs.** reduce(): The collect() method is used to gather elements from a stream into a mutable container such as a list, map, or string. It is especially powerful when used with Collectors to perform grouping, averaging, or joining operations. In contrast, reduce() is used for combining stream elements into a single result (like summing integers) using an associative accumulator function. While both are terminal operations, collect() is more flexible for building complex output structures.

4. **Reflection on code organization**: The PMRS might be the most instructive for understanding code organization. It demonstrates the use of separate classes (PetManager, VisitManager, MedicationManager) to encapsulate functionality and maintain separation of concerns. This modularity makes the system easier to maintain, extend, and debug—especially as it grows more complex.

5. **Adapting streams for grade processing**: Similar to how the CPE filters and groups city data, a grade processing system could use streams to group students by course, calculate average grades, identify top performers, and filter based on performance thresholds. By applying groupingBy(), averagingDouble(), and sorted() in combination with lambda expressions, you could build a powerful and concise data pipeline for academic analysis.

Join our Discord space

Join our Discord workspace for latest updates, offers, tech happenings around the world, new releases, and sessions with the authors:

https://discord.bpbonline.com

CHAPTER 15
Conclusion and Next Steps

Introduction

This is the final chapter of this book. Over the course of this book, we explored Java from its foundational syntax and object-oriented structure to modern features, concurrency, and full-fledged applications. We focused on skill attainment in debugging, testing, and deploying. We had the opportunity to apply concepts and techniques to real-world projects that mirror professional software development.

This chapter serves as a reflective conclusion and a launchpad for your future as a Java developer. We will review the essential concepts covered throughout the book and offer practical guidance on how to keep learning and growing as a Java developer. Whether you are aiming for industry certifications, seeking to contribute to open-source projects, or preparing for interviews, this chapter can help you plan your next steps.

Structure

This chapter covers the following topics:

- Trends in Java development
- Continuing your Java learning

- Preparing for industry certifications
- Final thoughts

Objectives

By the end of this chapter, you should be able to summarize core Java concepts, identify practical ways to continue Java learning, understand the value of industry certifications, explore recommended resources, understand how to prepare for recognized certifications, recognize emerging trends and future directions in Java development, and remain relevant in your career.

Trends in Java development

Java essentially stands alone as a resilient and adaptable programming language. Throughout its lifespan, it has continued to evolve. As we look to the future, staying informed about emerging trends can help you remain competitive and confident in your skills. This section explores key developments shaping the direction of Java and how we can prepare to remain in lockstep with Java's evolution.

Here are the major trends in Java:

- Language evolution (Java is on a six-month release cycle)
- Syntax modernization
- Modularity
- Scalability
- High-performance
- Cloud-native Java
- **Ahead-of-time** (**AOT**) compilation
- Integration with modern development practices
- Community involvement (OpenJDK)

Although not listed above, Java is gaining traction in the areas of AI and data science. You can explore the **Deep Java Library** (**DJL**) and GraalVM tool to see how Java can be used for better interoperability with other languages. Java is an enterprise-grade development platform, making it a smart choice for backend systems that power AI services, as well as integrating machine learning workflows.

Continuing your Java learning

Completing this book is a significant milestone, but it is not the end of your journey as a Java developer. Real growth in programming comes from a continuous learning mindset.

This section outlines practical ways to continue your learning and provides a curated list of resources to help you grow confidently and efficiently.

Your learning path will depend on your goals. For example, you might want to pursue application development, which requires you to deepen your knowledge of frameworks such as Spring, Hibernate, and Jakarta EE. That will help you become proficient in building robust enterprise or web applications. Perhaps Android development is your goal. Java remains a popular language for Android app development. With that goal, you would want to research and become proficient in tools like *Android Studio* and the *Android SDK*. If you are interested in backend services and APIs, you will want to learn how to create RESTful services and microservices using frameworks like Spring Boot and explore tools like Docker and Kubernetes for deployment and orchestration.

Regardless of your goal, you will want to adopt software engineering practices, going beyond the language itself by studying software architecture, design patterns, testing strategies, **continuous integration/continuous deployment** (**CI/CD**), and Agile methodologies. You might also consider contributing to open-source Java projects to gain valuable hands-on experience and introduce you to collaborative development environments.

Recommended resources

To support your ongoing growth, here are some trusted and widely used resources across different formats:

- **Books**: You can search for online books at **https://bpbonline.com** and other publishers.

- **Online courses and tutorials**: There are several online course providers (e.g., *Udemy*, *Coursera*, etc.) that have Java-specific courses.

- **Documentation and official sites**:

    o   *Oracle* maintains Java's official documentation at **https://docs.oracle.com/en/ java/** and is the official source for the language and standard libraries.

    o   *Baeldung* (**https://www.baeldung.com/**) is a great source for Java tutorials focused on Spring, REST APIs, and backend development.

- **Practice platforms**: There are several sites (e.g., *LeetCode, HackerRank, Codeforces*, and *Codewars*) that can help you improve your Java skills through exercises, community feedback, and potentially mentorship.

- **Communities and forums**:

    o   *Reddit* communities like *r/java* and *r/learnjava* offer peer support, resource sharing, and career advice.

    o   *GitHub* can be used to explore, contribute, and collaborate on open-source projects.

    o   *Dev.to* and *Medium* have articles from developers sharing experiences, tutorials, and insights.

- **University courses and programs**: Local and online colleges and universities provide opportunities to engage directly with peers and faculty in structured and scaffolded programs.

Preparing for industry certifications

The last section mentioned university courses and degree programs. These are great potential career boosters, but they can take a considerable amount of time and money to obtain. They are indeed worth both the time and money, but if you want a credential in the near term, consider an industry certification.

Industry-recognized certifications help validate your technical knowledge and demonstrate initiative and commitment to professional growth. Many of them can even be used for credit towards a university degree. These certifications, different from certificates, are especially valuable for people entering the job market, vying for promotion, or aiming to stand out in competitive fields.

Certifications matter

Certification offers several benefits, including the following:

- Certifications give you credibility, showing that you have met a standardized benchmark of knowledge.

- Many job listings require or prefer specific certifications.

- Preparing for an exam gives you a structured approach to reinforce key concepts and identify areas you might not be well-versed in.

- Successfully passing a certification exam gives you confidence in your knowledge and abilities.

Certification options

There are several certification issuers, each with multiple certificates. This section covers the two primary certifying bodies.

Oracle

Oracle owns Java and has its own set of certifications. They are the most widely recognized certifications available and have been around since the late 1990s. The primary certificates are:

- **Oracle Certified Associate (OCA)**

- **Oracle Certified Professional (OCP)**

The long life of these exams has resulted in study guides being written by Java experts each time the exams are updated.

BlueCert

BlueCert is a modern certification platform designed for validating AI-adjacent technical skills, including Java development. Its certifications are structured across multiple levels, Practitioner, Associate, and Professional, and aligned with real-world roles.

Java-focused certifications at **https://www.bluecert.org/** emphasize practical problem-solving and performance under exam conditions. The platform supports secure online exams, verification tools for employers, and a structured pathway for continued growth in Java and related domains.

Table 15.1 provides a comparative summary of Oracle and BlueCert certifications:

Characteristic	Oracle	BlueCert
Issuer	Corporation	Independent/Academic
Target audience	University students, professionals with formal training	University students, professionals, self-taught developers, career switchers, and upskillers.
Certification levels	Associate, Professional, and Mastery	Practitioner, Associate, Professional
Exam style	Multiple choice, proctored	Multiple choice, scenario-based, performance-informed assessments
Cost	High	Medium
Expiration	Tied to specific Java versions	Valid for two to three years; renewal possible
Recognition	High	Growing
Practicality	Emphasizes theoretical and API-based correctness	Emphasizes real-world problem-solving and job-role readiness

Table 15.1: Certification issuer comparison

University certificates

It is important to understand the difference between a certificate that you earn from a college, university, or bootcamp. Those are certificate programs and should not be confused with certifications. The words are similar, but the differences are important.

See *Table 15.2* for additional information:

Characteristic	Certificate	Certification
Issuer	University, college, or bootcamp	Professional organization
Based on	Completing a course or series of courses	Passing a standardized exam
Goal	Education and skill development	Skill validation and professional credentialing
Expiration	Does not expire	May require renewal or continuing education
Use case	Learning	Demonstrate proficiency to employers

Table 15.2: Certificate-certification comparison

Preparation strategies

When you decide to seek a certification, consider the following:

- Review the exam objectives and use them as your study blueprint.

- Use official study guides when available.

- Practice with sample tests that simulate the real exam. They can help you identify areas where you need improvement.

- Create a study plan and remain consistent. For example, you might earmark one hour per day to study. If you stick to that plan, you will be surprised how fast 60 minutes a day adds up.

Final thoughts

Hopefully, this book helped you gain the knowledge and tools needed to solve problems, build applications, and think critically about software design with Java. Learning Java requires a lot more than just memorizing syntax or completing exercises; it is really about a new way of thinking. It is about breaking down complexities, crafting elegant solutions, and always asking how you can make your systems better. As you move forward, every project you build, bug you fix, or concept you explore strengthens your identity not just as a learner, but as a practitioner.

One way to mark that transition is through certification. While not a substitute for experience, earning a certification, especially from a future-focused organization like BlueCert, can serve as documented evidence of your capabilities. Certifications from platforms such as **https://www. bluecert.org/** are designed to validate practical, performance-based skills, helping you stand out in a competitive job market and affirming your readiness for real-world development.

Java's future is bright, and you are now part of that journey. As the language continues to grow, so can your skills, your career, and your impact as a developer. Stay curious, stay updated, and stay involved.

Conclusion

This chapter marks the end of your structured journey through Java and opens the door to everything that comes next. You have explored the essentials of Java programming, practiced key object-oriented and functional techniques, worked with files, databases, and user interfaces, and had the opportunity to apply your skills to real-world scenarios.

This final chapter revisited the major concepts covered throughout the book, helping you consolidate your learning and recognize just how far you have come. We explored how to continue growing your skills through self-guided learning paths, recommended resources, and professional certifications from platforms like Oracle and BlueCert. And we looked ahead to the trends shaping Java's future.

As you move forward, remember that Java mastery is a journey, not a destination. Stay curious. Stay engaged. Build projects that challenge you, collaborate with others, and keep pace with the evolution of the Java ecosystem.

Points to remember

- Active participation in the Java community can help you stay connected and inspired.
- **https://www.bluecert.org/** offers future-focused certifications that validate real-world Java proficiency.
- Certification is a valuable way to demonstrate your skills.
- Cloud-native frameworks like Spring Boot, Micronaut, and Quarkus are helping to shape modern Java development.
- Continued learning is essential; Java evolves rapidly with new features and release cycles.
- GraalVM enables AOT compilation and supports high-performance Java applications.
- Java is expanding its relevance in fields like **artificial intelligence** (**AI**) and data science.
- Java's modular system (Project Jigsaw) improves application structure and scalability.
- Keeping up with **Java Enhancement Proposals** (**JEPs**) is a good habit for staying informed.
- Structured learning paths and study resources can help you prepare for certification exams.

- University-backed online certificates can complement traditional certifications.

- Your transition from learner to practitioner is supported by continued effort, not just course completion.

Case studies

These case studies provide realistic scenarios that encourage you to think critically about the chapter's content:

- **The recent computer science graduate**: *Priya* recently completed her undergraduate degree in computer science. She has taken a few Java courses in college but struggled to connect theory with practical development. After working through this book, she finally feels confident in her Java skills.

  o **For your consideration**: Priya is not sure whether to continue with academic study, start applying for jobs, or specialize in a specific Java framework. She uses the final projects in *Chapter 14, Real-World Java Projects,* as portfolio pieces and posts them to GitHub. She also decides to begin learning Spring Boot through online tutorials and signs up for the OCA Java SE 11 exam to solidify her foundational knowledge. If you were Priya, how would you decide between job hunting and further education? What role could certification play in your choice?

- **The IT professional seeking a career shift**: *Marcus* has worked in IT support for over a decade but has always wanted to transition into software development. He chose this book to refresh his programming foundation and explore Java's role in modern development.

  o **For your consideration**: Despite his technical background, Marcus has no real-world development experience and is unsure how to bridge the gap. He starts contributing to open-source Java projects on GitHub and documents everything he learns. He also enrolls in an online course in backend development to reinforce concepts and earns a certificate of completion, which he highlights on his resume. What are the advantages and limitations of self-taught programming compared to formal academic credentials?

- **The mobile developer expanding into backend systems**: *Aisha* has been building Android apps in Kotlin for several years. She picked up this book to round out her understanding of core Java and backend systems for apps she's developing.

  o **For your consideration**: While she's comfortable with mobile platforms, she is never built a backend server or database integration from scratch. Using her new skills, Aisha creates a backend API using Java and JDBC, connects it to a cloud-hosted database, and integrates it with one of her mobile apps. She begins learning Spring Boot and containerization with Docker to better support modern deployment practices. How does knowledge of backend Java systems enhance a mobile developer's capabilities? In what ways could Aisha differentiate herself in the job market?

- **The self-taught developer using BlueCert to launch a career**: *Diego* is a self-taught developer who did not attend a university. He completed this book over two months, working through every exercise and project. Passionate about building real-world applications, Diego wants employers to take him seriously despite not having a degree.

  o **For your consideration**: Without formal credentials, Diego worries about standing out in competitive job applications. Diego decides to pursue certifications through **https://www.bluecert.org/**, completing three Java-focused certifications: he adds these certifications to his resume and online profiles, along with links to projects hosted on GitHub and a personal blog discussing what he learned. Within four months, Diego secures a full-time role as a junior backend developer at a tech startup. How can a focused certification strategy compensate for the absence of a formal degree? What other factors contributed to Diego's successful transition?

- **The educator incorporating Java into curriculum**: *Sarah* is a high school computer science teacher who previously taught Python and HTML/CSS. She used this book as a structured guide to incorporate Java into her teaching toolkit and better prepare her students for *AP Computer Science* and beyond.

  o **For your consideration**: Sarah wants to design a new module but is not sure how to balance foundational content with more advanced topics like multithreading or JavaFX. She uses this book's structure to build a 12-week high school Java module and adapts exercises from *Chapters 2–6* and *9–11* for her students. She also invites students to present capstone projects based on the real-world scenarios from *Chapter 14, Real-World Java Projects*. How can educators adapt professional resources for classroom use? What topics might be too advanced for early learners?

Multiple choice questions

1. **What is the primary benefit of Java's six-month release cycle?**
   a. It slows down the adoption of new features
   b. It allows developers to receive frequent, manageable updates
   c. It reduces the need for backward compatibility
   d. It makes Java harder to maintain

2. **Which of the following frameworks is commonly used for cloud-native Java development?**

   a. Quarkus

   b. Hibernate

   c. JavaFX

   d. Junit

3. **Why might a developer pursue a certification from BlueCert?**

   a. BlueCert focuses only on academic theory

   b. BlueCert focuses on Java certifications

   c. BlueCert provides future-focused, performance-based certification paths

   d. BlueCert is only available to university students

4. **Which trend reflects Java's growing role in data science and AI?**

   a. JavaFX for visualization

   b. Integration with GraalVM and cross-language tools

   c. Removal of JDBC support

   d. Exclusive use of sealed classes

5. **Which is a key advantage of modular programming in Java?**

   a. It allows developers to write more lambda expressions

   b. It prevents the use of external libraries

   c. It is only applicable to GUI development

   d. It enables better application structure and scalability

Answers

1.	b.
2.	a.
3.	c.
4.	b.
5.	d.

Questions

1. Which chapter or concept from this book did you find most challenging, and how did you overcome it? Discuss how your learning strategies evolved throughout the course.

2. Do you think certifications are necessary for launching a career in Java development? Why or why not? Support your argument with real-world examples or personal goals.

3. How has your understanding of what it means to be a practitioner changed since beginning this course? Reflect on how your identity as a developer has developed.

4. Which trends in Java development do you find most interesting or relevant to your intended career path? Discuss how you plan to stay current with emerging technologies.

5. BlueCert is positioned as a future-focused certification platform. Would you consider pursuing one of their certifications? Why or why not? Explore the value of certification for self-taught or non-traditional learners.

6. In what ways did the final chapter help you think differently about your next steps as a developer? Share how your short-term or long-term plans have been influenced.

7. Do you feel the real-world projects in *Chapter 14, Real-World Java Projects,* prepared you for professional work? What improvements or additions would you suggest?

8. How can participating in Java communities (like GitHub or Java User Groups) enhance your growth as a developer? Consider how peer collaboration and open-source contributions can benefit your career.

9. If you were mentoring a beginner who just finished this book, what advice would you give them to maintain momentum? Use your own learning experience to guide others.

10. What is one specific step you plan to take within the next month to continue your Java learning journey? Set a concrete, actionable goal and discuss it with your peers.

Challenges

The following questions are provided to self-assess your knowledge of the chapter's content and apply critical thinking to key concepts:

- **Certification strategy roadmap**:
  - **Objective**: To develop a personal certification plan based on your current skill level and career goals.
  - **Activity**: Perform the following actions:
    - Research at least two Java-related certification options discussed in this chapter
    - Write a 1–2-page plan that outlines:
      - Which certification(s) you would pursue
      - Why they align with your goals

- ◆ A timeline for preparation and completion
- ◆ Specific resources you would use to study

o **Real-world applicability**: Creating a certification roadmap is a practical step that demonstrates planning, initiative, and alignment with industry expectations.

> Note: **You are not required to register for a certification—this is a planning and analysis activity.**

- **Developer identity reflection**:

  o **Objective**: To reflect on your transformation from learner to developer and articulate your growth.

  o **Activity**: Perform the following actions:

  - Write a 500–600-word essay reflecting on your journey through the book. Consider the following prompts:

    - ◆ How has your mindset or confidence changed?
    - ◆ What do you now understand about what it means to be a practitioner?
    - ◆ Which chapter or topic had the greatest impact on you, and why?

  o **Real-world applicability**: Being able to articulate your skills and experiences is key for job interviews, portfolio websites, and personal branding.

> Note: **There are no right or wrong answers—this is about honest self-assessment.**

- **Tech trends research brief**:

  o **Objective**: To explore a trend in modern Java development and evaluate its long-term relevance.

  o **Activity**: Perform the following actions:

  - Choose one trend discussed in the chapter.

  - Write a 1-page brief that includes:

    - ◆ A summary of the trend
    - ◆ Its significance in today's development landscape
    - ◆ Two companies or products currently using the technology
    - ◆ Your opinion on how it might impact your career path

  o **Real-world applicability**: Staying informed about trends helps developers remain adaptable and competitive in an evolving job market.

Note: **Use official documentation, blogs, or tech news sources for your research.**

- **Learning path design**:
  - ○ **Objective**: To design a customized post-course learning path based on your interests and goals.
  - ○ **Activity**: Perform the following actions:
    - ▪ Create a visual or written roadmap for your continued Java education over the next six months. Include:
      - ◆ Specific topics or tools you want to learn
      - ◆ Types of learning resources
      - ◆ Milestones (e.g., complete a project, earn a badge or certificate)
  - ○ **Real-world applicability**: Employers value developers who take initiative and set learning goals independently.

  Note: **You may format your roadmap as a list, table, mind map, or timeline.**

- **Case study response**:
  - ○ **Objective**: To analyze a real-world scenario and recommend a course of action.
  - ○ **Activity**: Perform the following actions:
    - ▪ Choose one of the case studies from this chapter (Priya, Marcus, Aisha, Diego, or Sarah).
    - ▪ Write a short response (400–600 words) that answers the following:
      - ◆ What challenges does this person face?
      - ◆ What would you recommend as their next step?
      - ◆ How would you tailor your advice based on their background and goals?
  - ○ **Real-world applicability**: This exercise builds your ability to apply programming knowledge contextually; a skill often tested in job interviews.

  Note: **Support your recommendations with content from this chapter or earlier in the book.**

Self-assessment

The following questions are provided so you can self-assess your knowledge of the chapter's content and to apply critical thinking to key concepts:

1. What are the benefits of pursuing an industry-recognized certification after completing this book, and how might it affect your job search?

2. How does modular programming, introduced in Java 9, contribute to building scalable and maintainable applications?

3. List two Java-related trends discussed in this chapter and explain how they reflect the evolving needs of modern software development.

4. Reflect on your own learning journey: What specific skills or concepts do you feel most confident in now, and how could you demonstrate that confidence in a professional setting?

5. Imagine a peer without a computer science degree wants to become a Java developer. Based on what you learned in this chapter, what steps would you recommend they take to improve their credibility and readiness?

Answers

1. Pursuing a certification, such as those offered by Oracle or BlueCert, provides documented proof of your skills and knowledge. This can enhance your resume, demonstrate initiative, and help differentiate you from other candidates. Certifications can also provide a structured review of essential topics and prepare you for real-world scenarios. In job searches, certifications often serve as a confidence booster for both the applicant and the employer.

2. Modular programming allows developers to break a large application into smaller, self-contained modules. This improves code organization, making it easier to test and maintain individual components. It also enhances scalability by allowing independent development and deployment. Project Jigsaw, introduced in Java 9, formalized this capability, which is especially useful in enterprise and cloud-native applications where flexibility and maintainability are critical.

3. **Two trends discussed include**:

    a. Cloud-native development with frameworks like Spring Boot and Quarkus:

        i. These frameworks support microservices, fast startup times, and containerization. This supports the performance and deployment demands of cloud environments.

    b. Integration with AI and data science tools using GraalVM:

      i.   Java is expanding its capabilities to support interoperability with languages like Python. This enables Java applications to participate more effectively in data-driven and AI-based systems.

4. **This is a reflective question, and responses will vary. For example**:

      a.   You may feel confident in Java's object-oriented features and demonstrate that by building a portfolio of well-structured Java applications on GitHub. You could also participate in online communities, write blog posts explaining key Java concepts, or mentor others as a way to reinforce their expertise. The key is being able to identify strengths and express them through visible, tangible outputs.

5. **For a peer without a CS degree, a practical strategy would be**:

      a.   Study a structured Java curriculum (like this book or online platforms).

      b.   Build and publish real-world projects on GitHub to demonstrate practical knowledge.

      c.   Pursue certifications like those from BlueCert to gain credibility.

      d.   Join developer communities and contribute to open-source projects for networking and experience.

Join our Discord space

Join our Discord workspace for latest updates, offers, tech happenings around the world, new releases, and sessions with the authors:

https://discord.bpbonline.com

Index

A

Abstract Classes 100

Abstract Classes,
  implementing 100, 101

Abstract Classes,
  integrating 102

Abstract Classes,
  preventing 103, 104

Abstract Classes, use cases 103

Abstract Classes,
  wrapping 102

ArrayLists 160

ArrayLists,
  implementing 161, 162

Arrays 160

Arrays, characteristics 160

Arrays, implementing 161

Attributes, manipulating 64, 65

B

Binding Properties 349

Binding Properties,
  implementing 349-352

Bougie Books Database 310

Bougie Books Database,
  illustrating 310, 311

Break keyword 39

Break keyword, types
  Continue 39
  Return 40

Buffered Streams 279

Buffered Streams, ensuring 280, 281

Buffered Streams, use cases 280

Build Tools 424

Build Tools, configuring 424

Byte Streams 284

Byte Streams, implementing 286

C

Character Streams 284

Character Streams,
   implementing 285

Checked Exceptions 130

Checked Exceptions,
   ensuring 130, 131

Checked Exceptions,
   resources 130

City Population Explorer
   (CPE) 452

COIN System 392

COIN System,
   considerations 394, 395

COIN System, section
   Modular Design 394
   Pattern Matching 393
   User Records 392
   Virtual Thread 394

Command-Line Application 436

Command-Line Application,
   concepts
   Design 436
   Extending 440
   Implementation 438
   Testing 439

Comparable Interface 171

Comparable Interface,
   demonstrating 171, 172

Comparator/Comparable Interface,
   illustrating 174-176

Comparator Interface 173

Comparator Interface,
   demonstrating 173, 174

Concurrency Utilities 207

Concurrency Utilities, section
   CountDownLatch 208
   CyclicBarrier 210
   Semaphore 212

Concurrent Code 213

Concurrent Code, practices 213, 214

Conditional Statements 36

Conditional Statements, sections
   Branching 39
   Break 39
   If 36
   Looping 38

Constructor Overloading 65

Constructor Overloading,
   benefits 70

Constructor Overloading,
   ensuring 66, 67

Constructor Overloading,
   integrating 69

CountDownLatch 208

CountDownLatch, ensuring 208, 209

CPE, concepts
   Design 453
   Implementation 454
   Project Extending 455
   Testing 455

Custom Exceptions 139

Custom Exceptions,
   configuring 139, 140

Custom Exceptions, practices 142

Custom Exceptions, types
   Checked 140
   Unchecked 141

CyclicBarrier 210

CyclicBarrier, illustrating 210, 211

D

Database Operations 314

Database Operations, sections

Database Connections 316

Errors/Exceptions 317

Query Performance, optimizing 315

Query Results 316

SQL Injection, preventing 314

Data Persistence 357

Data Persistence,
integrating 359-362

Data Streams 281

Data Streams, types

DataInputStream 282

DataOutputStream 282

Data Types 23

Data Types, categories

Primitive Data Types 24

Reference Data Types 24

Deadlocks/TryLock 201

Deadlocks/TryLock, ensuring 201

Deadlocks/TryLock,
illustrating 202, 203

Default Methods 105, 106

Deserialization 274

Dynamic Method Dispatch 75

E

Encapsulation 78

Encapsulation, configuring 78

Encapsulation,
implementing 80, 82

Encapsulation, roles

Private 78, 79

Protected 80

E

Event Handling 345

Event Handling,
implementing 345-348

Exception Propagation 136

Executor Framework 204

Executor Framework,
components 204

Executor Framework, concepts

Banking Application 206

ScheduleExecutorService 206

Video Game 205

F

File Handling 268

File Handling, architecture 268

File Handling,
demonstrating 269-272

Functional Interfaces 105, 233

Functional Interfaces,
advantages 233, 234

Functional Interfaces,
illustrating 234, 235

Functional Interfaces,
rules 105

I

IDE Debugging 406

IDE Debugging,
configuring 406, 407

IDE Debugging, strategies 411

IDE Debugging, tools

Breakpoints 408

Call Stack Inspection 408

Console Logging 409

Step Execution 410

If Statement 36

If Statement, types
  Else-If 37
  If-Else 37
  Switch 37
Inheritance 70
Inheritance, benefits
  Code Reusability 74
  Extendibility 74
  Logical Organization 74
Inheritance, configuring 70-72
Inheritance, demonstrating 73
Input Controls 344
Integers/Strings, integrating 27, 28
Interfaces 94
Interfaces, components 94
Interfaces, terms
  Default/Static Methods 99
  Multiple Inheritance 97
  Polymorphism 98
  Syntax/Implementation 95
Intermediate Operations 230
Intermediate Operations,
      ensuring 230, 231
Iterator 164
Iterator, ensuring 164, 165

J

Java 2
Java Applications 303
Java Applications, reasons
  Data Consistency/Integrity 304
  Efficient Searches 303
  Multi-User Access 304
  Persistent Data Storage 303
  Scalability 305
  Security 305

Java Applications, steps
  Compile 421
  External Dependencies 423
  JAR Files 421
  JAR Runnable 422
  Package Deploy 423
  Server Deploy 423
Java Collection Framework
      (JCF) 163
Java, components
  JDK 3
  JRE 4
  JVM 3
Java, configuring 5
Java Development, steps
  Environment Variables, setup 8
  IDE, configuring 9
  JDK, installing 7
Java Development, trends 466
Java, evolution
  Oracle 5
  Rapid Adoption 4
Java Exception Hierarchy 126
Java Exception Hierarchy, concepts
  Errors/Exceptions 127, 128
  Throwable Class 126, 129
Java Exception Hierarchy,
      practices 129
Java, features
  Grabag Collection (GC) 3
  Multithread, supporting 3
  Object-Oriented Programming
      (OOP) 2
  Platform Independence 2
  Security Focus 3
  Standard Library 3

Java, functionality
  Pattern Matching 386
  Sealed Classes 388
  Virtual Threads 389
JavaFX 330
JavaFX, advantages 330
JavaFX, architecture 331
JavaFX, implementing 334, 335
JavaFX, prerequisites
  Java Development Kit 333
  SDK 333
  VC Code/Extensions 333
Java I/O 256
Java I/O, architecture 258
Java I/O, concepts
  Buffered Stream 259
  File Storage, managing 259
  Network Communication 260
  Object Persistence 259
  User Input, handling 258
Java I/O, stream
  Byte 257
  Character 257
Java Learning 466, 467
Java Learning Certifications 468
Java Learning Certifications,
    benefits 468
Java Learning Certifications,
    sections
  BlueCert 469
  Oracle 468
  Preparation Strategies 470
  University Certificates 469
Java Learning, resources 467
Java Multithreading 190

Java Multithreading,
    illustrating 190, 191
Java, platforms 4
Java Program 12
Java Program, steps
  Running 12
  Writing 12
Java, tips
  New Paradigms 6
  Security 6
JCF, interfaces
  Collection 163
  Maps 163
JCF, operations 164
JDBC 311
JDBC, demonstrating 312
JEP 477 390
JEP 477, configuring 390, 391
JEP 477, enhancements 391
JUnit 412
JUnit, steps 412, 413

L

Lambda 107
Lambda Expression 235
Lambda Expression,
    ensuring 235, 236
Lambda Expression,
    illustrating 236, 238
Lambdas/Method References,
    ensuring 108, 109
Lambda, syntax 107
Layouts 340
Layouts, illustrating 340-343
Locks 199
Locks, demonstrating 199, 200

Looping Statement 38
Looping Statement, types
  Do-While 39
  For 38
  While 38

M

Method Overriding 74, 75
Method References 108
Methods 40, 41
Methods, implementing 42-45
Methods, practices 46
Methods, terms
  Parameters 41
  Scope 42
Modern Java 380
Modern Java, cycle 380
Modern Java, ensuring 381, 382
Multithreaded Data Processor 447
Multithreaded Data Processor,
    concepts
  Design 448
  Implementation 449
  Project, extending 452
  Testing 452

O

Object 62
Object, initializing 62, 63
Object Lifecycle 109, 110
Object Lifecycle, practices
  Explicity Close Resources 113
  Object References,
      managing 112
Object Lifecycle, stages
  Object Creation 110

Object Destruction 111
Object Use 110
Observables 353
OOP 58
OOP, principles
  Abstraction 60
  Encapsulation 58
  Inheritance 59
  Polymorphism 60
Operators 28
Operators, types
  Arithmetic 28
  Assignment 29
  Bitwise 30
  Logical 30
  Relational 31
  Ternary 34
  Unary 34
Optional Class 241
Optional Class, architecture 241
Optional Class,
    illustrating 242, 244
Optional Class,
    implementing 241, 242

P

Parallel Streams 239
Parallel Streams, architecture 239
Parallel Streams,
    illustrating 240
Parallel Streams,
    implementing 239
Pattern Matching 386
Pattern Matching, concepts
  Instanceof 386
  Record Class 388

Switch Statement 387

PFT 332

PFT, applications

Data Persistence 357

Transaction Table 354

UI Styling 354

Window Size 354

PFT, ensuring 336

PFT, sections

Event Handling 345

Input Controls 344

Layouts 340

PMRS 440

PMRS, concepts

Design 441

Implementation 442

Project, extending 447

Testing 446

Polymorphism 74

Polymorphism, benefits

Code Reusability 77

Code, simplifying 77

Flexibility 77

Polymorphism,
    implementing 76, 77

Project Jigsaw 382, 383

Project Jigsaw, architecture 383

Project Jigsaw, implementing 384

Project Jigsaw, integrating 384, 385

R

Relational Databases 298

Relational Databases, architecture 298

Relational Databases, benefits 299

Relational Databases,
    illustrating 299, 300

S

Scanner Class 260

Scanner Class,
    configuring 260-262

Scanner Class, ensuring 262, 263

Scanner Class, pitfalls

Inefficiencies 267

Invalid Input 266

Mixing Input Methods 265

Not Closing 266

Scanner Class, practices 267

Scene Graph 336, 337

Scene Graph, ensuring 337

Scene Graph, illustrating 338, 339

Sealed Classes 388, 389

Searching Collections 168

Searching Collections,
    ensuring 168-170

Semaphore 212

Semaphore, illustrating 212, 213

Semaphore, methods 212

Serialization 273

Serialization/Deserialization,
    concepts

Buffered Strams,
    improving 278, 279

Class Version, handling 277

Serialized Data 275

Sorting Collections 166

Sorting Collections,
    ensuring 166-168

SQLite 308

SQLite, setup 308, 310

SQL, operations

Adding 306

Deleting 307

Retrieving 306
Updating 306
SQL Queries, executing 307
Streams 283
Streams API 228
Streams API, advantages 229
Streams API, illustrating 229, 230
Streams API, operations
Intermediate 230
Terminal 231
Streams, types
Byte 284, 285
Character 284
Structured Data 300
Structured Data, terms
Data Consistency 300
Data Storage, optimizing 302
Relationships, managing 301
Store/Data, managing 301
Synchronization 197
Synchronization,
demonstrating 197, 198

T

TDD, illustrating 419, 420
Terminal Operations 231
Terminal Operations, illustrating 232
Terminal Operators 232
Test-Driven Development
(TDD) 418
Testing Exception 142
Testing Exception, benefits 143
Testing Exception, ensuring 146
Testing Exception, practices 147
Testing Exception, reasons 143
Testing Exception, types

Checked 143
Custom 145
Unchecked 144
Thread 189
Thread Class/Runnable Interface 192
Thread Class/Runnable Interface,
sections
Enterprise Banking 194
Video Game 192
Throwing Exceptions 136
Throws Keyword 137
Throws Keyword,
demonstrating 137, 138
Throws Keyword, practices 138
Transaction Management 312
Transaction Management,
illustrating 313, 314
Transaction Management,
property 312
Transaction Table 354
Try-Catch-Finally Blocks 132
Try-Catch-Finally Blocks,
demonstrating 134
Try-Catch-Finally Blocks, practices 135
Try-Catch-Finally Blocks, sections
Catch Block 133
Finally Block 133
Try Block 132
Typecasting 26
Typecasting, types
Explicit 27
Implicit 26

U

UI Styling 354
Unchecked Exceptions 131

Unchecked Exceptions,
    ensuring 131, 132
Unit Testing 411
Unit Testing, guidelines 411
Utility Classes 176
Utility Classes, features 176
Utility Classes, sections
  Calendar 177
  Date 177
  Random 178
  Scanner 179

V

Variables 22
Variables, declaring 24, 25
Variables, rules
  Constants 23
  Naming Conventions 22
Variables, scope
  Class 26
  Instance 25
  Local 25
Video Game 192
Virtual Threads 389

W

Window Size 354
Writing Testable Code 413
Writing Testable Code, principles
  Global Variables 416
  Hardcoded Dependencies 413
  Interface, implementing 414
  Return Values 415
  Static Methods 416
  Testable Methods 417